MONEY AND SCHOOLS

Third Edition

David C. Thompson
Kansas State University

R. Craig Wood
University of Florida

EYE ON EDUCATION
6 DEPOT WAY WEST, SUITE 106
LARCHMONT, NY 10538
(914) 833–0551
(914) 833–0761 fax
www.eyeoneducation.com

Library of Congress Cataloging-in-Publication Data

Thompson, David C.
    Money and schools / by David C. Thompson, R. Craig Wood — 3rd ed.
        p.   cm.
    Includes bibliographical references and index.
    ISBN 1-59667-003-7
    1. School budgets—United States—Handbooks, manuals, etc. 2. Schools
—United States—Accounting—Handbooks, manuals, etc. 3. Education—
United States—Finance—Handbooks, manuals, etc. I. Wood, R. Craig. II.
Title.

    LB2830.2 .T56 2005
    371.2'06'0973—dc21

                                                                        2005000926

    10 9 8 7 6 5 4 3 2 1

Editorial and production services provided by
Freelance Editorial Services
52 Oakwood Blvd., Poughkeepsie, NY 12603-4112
(845-471-3566)

ABOUT THE AUTHORS

Professor David C. Thompson's professional career has spanned classroom teacher, elementary principal, high school principal, superintendent of schools, and the professoriate. A specialist in school finance litigation, his publication record is prolific and encompasses numerous book chapters, monographs, and refereed journal articles. A frequently invited author in respected circles, he has published chapters in four consecutive *American Education Finance Association Yearbooks* and has been widely published in the *Journal of Education Finance*, the National Organization on Legal Problems of Education's *NOLPE Handbook of School Law*, West's *Education Law Reporter*, books by the Association of School Business Officials International (ASBO), and many others. He has served on boards including the Authors' Committee of West's *Education Law Reporter*, is legislative editor for the *Journal of Education Finance*, has written an invited review of finance litigation for West's *Education Law Reporter*, and is chair of the board of editors of the scholarly journal *Educational Considerations*. His textbooks include *Fiscal Leadership for Schools: Concepts and Practices* (Longman), *Principles of School Business Management, Third Edition* (ASBO), and *Education Finance Law: Constitutional Challenges to State Aid Plans, Third Edition* (Education Law Association). He also served as author, editor, and consultant to the Core Finance Data Task Force's 2004 rewrite of the U.S. Department of Education's authoritative handbook, *Financial Accounting for Local and State School Systems*, which significantly changed how school districts must report financial data to superior units of government. His consulting work has included advisement or expert analysis for state departments of education, state legislatures, attorneys general, and litigants in school finance. His research has been presented to numerous major organizations including the American Education Finance Association, Education Law Association, National Center for Education Statistics, National Education Association, National Conference of State Legislatures, and other keynote addresses to large audiences. Dr. Thompson is Professor in the Graduate School, Department of Educational Leadership chair, and codirector of the University Council for Educational Administration's (UCEA) Center for Education Finance at Kansas State University.

Professor R. Craig Wood's professional career has spanned classroom teacher, grant administrator, business manager, and assistant superintendent of schools for school districts in Wisconsin and Connecticut. He currently is Professor at the University of Florida. Dr. Wood's publication record exceeds more than 125 book chapters, monographs, and refereed journal articles. He has published in several *American Education Finance Association Yearbooks*, the *Journal of Education Finance, ELA Handbook of School Law*, West's *Education Law Reporter*, books by ASBO, and others. His texts include *Fiscal Lead-*

ership for Schools: Concepts and Practices (Longman), *Principles of School Business Management, Thirrd Edition* (ASBO), and *Education Finance Law: Constitutional Challenges to State Aid Plans, Third Edition* (ELA). His consulting work has included advisement or expert analysis for state departments, legislatures, attorneys general, and attorneys and litigants in school finance. Dr. Wood is codirector of the UCEA Center for Education Finance. He is a past president of the American Education Finance Association.

ACKNOWLEDGMENTS

No book is ever written without the valuable assistance of others. This includes manuscript reviewers and resource people trusted for their ability to discern and clarify a variety of issues that may escape authors during the writing stage.

The authors wish to thank the following people who contributed in important ways to this current edition and to earlier editions of *Money and Schools*. In particular, the authors are grateful to reviewers of the previous two editions, whose advice continues to strongly influence this latest iteration: Eric Bartleson, Mankato State University; Michael Boone, Southwest Texas State University; William E. Camp, University of North Texas; Leonard Etlinger, Chicago State University; John Freeman, University of Alabama; Catherine Glascock, Ohio University; Seth Hirshorn, University of Michigan; Larry K. Kelly, Arizona School Administrators Association; Dennis Lauro, Assistant Superintendent, Pelham, NY; T. C. Mattocks, Idaho State University; Joseph Natale, Superintendent, Warwick Valley, NY; Doug Nelson, Washington State University; Ross Rubenstein, Georgia State University; William Salwaechter, Oklahoma State University; Catherine Sielke, University of Georgia; David Steele, Seattle Pacific University; Ed Stehno, Fort Hays State University; Gary C. Wenzel, State University of West Georgia; and Richard Wiggall, Illinois State University.

Gratitude is especially expressed to reviewers and commentators of portions of the third edition: Dennis Brennan, University of the Pacific; Frank Gallant, University of Idaho; William Owings, Old Dominion University; Ray Proulx, University of Vermont; Augustana Reyes, University of Houston; Donald Tetreault, University of South Carolina; and Bill Thornton, University of Nevada, Reno.

The authors are further grateful for thoughtful book reviews and other extended commentary from Faith Crampton, former Senior Professional Research Associate at the National Education Association, Washington, DC, and now Associate Professor at the University of Wisconsin-Milwaukee; and Richard A. King, Professor at the University of Northern Colorado. We are, of course, humbly grateful for the acceptance of our work by the field, whose opinions we value most of all.

TABLE OF CONTENTS

PART II: OPERATIONALIZING SCHOOL MONEY

PART III: A VIEW OF THE FUTURE

FOREWORD TO THE THIRD EDITION

OVERVIEW

Welcome to the third edition of this book! To our contemporaries who used the first and second editions, we welcome you back as old friends and trusted colleagues. To new users, we offer a special welcome to this new edition and hope you will be able to satisfy your quest for knowledge about school finance through this book. As was true with each previous edition, we have again attempted to shed new light on the critical needs of the field in a way that is clear, precise, and engaging. Our reasoning for this approach is simple: We believe that how schools are funded is of critical importance in today's world of high stakes accountability, and we believe that skilled leaders in schools must be knowledgeable about the relationship between money and the aims of education *and* highly sensitive to public perceptions about how fiscal resources are used. In our view, the topic is vibrant and the need for clarity and preciseness cannot be overstated.

WHO WE ARE

Our approach in this book is due in large part to who we are as authors. Our own personal histories as practitioners and university professors permeate the entire book by reflecting on how we believe new generations of school leaders should be trained. Who we are, therefore, says a great deal about what readers should expect from this third edition of *Money and Schools*. Plainly put, we are very experienced scholars and public school practitioners, and we believe the impact of both identities is important to readers' willingness to accept what we say in this book. We are scholars because we now work in major research universities, carrying out scholarly agendas and teaching courses in educational leadership, specifically in school finance-related issues. Equally important, though, is that we have deep and timeworn practitioner roots. Collectively, we have served as superintendents, assistant superintendents, school business managers, grant managers, principals, and classroom teachers in public school systems across the United States. We have also provided extensive consulting work on behalf of school districts, and for more than a decade we've been deeply involved in legal battles in more than a dozen states as expert witnesses on behalf of plaintiffs or defendants seeking adequate and equitable funding for schools. The especially important aspect of our professional histories is that we have not written this book solely from a theory base, nor have we used the book as a bully pulpit to advance any political views about how national, state, or local units of government fund schools. Instead, who we are relates to this book at the most basic level by virtue of the fact that we are practitioners who have done the things readers are most interested in—we've built budgets, cut budgets, raised taxes, faced angry constituents, hired and fired staff, experienced the accountability and student achievement wars, and so on. As a result, we believe readers' experience with this book will be enhanced by knowing us for who we are—for the most part, we are school people like most of our readers.

THE NEW CONTEXT

As we go to press with this third edition, the context of schooling has changed greatly in only a few years. The new federal No Child Left Behind (NCLB) law has brought great change to the American education landscape. State legislatures have had to respond to NCLB, and many states themselves have separately demanded increased fiscal efficiency and student performance accountability in exchange for continued school funding. Not surprisingly, school leaders have been subjected to enormous pressures in this regard, and the profession itself has brought pressure to bear on its own ranks through other reforms aimed at testing the competencies of licensed school leaders. Although our profession has always believed that education is a high stakes enterprise in which children deserve the best education regardless of individual circumstance, the result of these many changes to the context of schooling has been to engage leaders at a higher level of understanding about just how critical leadership is to guaranteeing the universally coveted (and mandated) student performance outcomes.

As a consequence, the die is already cast only a few years into the new millennium. The new context of schools demands that school leaders must be highly skilled, and a critically important component is understanding the relationship between not only opportunity and money but also outcomes and money. The new Interstate School Leaders Licensure Consortium's (ISLLC) standards for school leadership preparation, promulgated by the Council of Chief State School Officers, goes to exactly this issue when it declares that all leaders should be competent in six standards, wherein fiscal resources can make or break schools' ability to produce acceptable student outcomes:

♦ **Standard 1:** A school administrator is an educational leader who promotes the success of all students by facilitating the development, articulation, implementation, and stewardship of a vision of learning that is shared and supported by the school community.

♦ **Standard 2:** A school administrator is an educational leader who promotes the success of all students by advocating, nurturing, and sustaining a school culture and instructional program conducive to student learning and staff professional growth.

- ◆ **Standard 3:** A school administrator is an educational leader who promotes the success of all students by ensuring management of the organization, operations, and resources for a safe, efficient, and effective learning environment.
- ◆ **Standard 4:** A school administrator is an educational leader who promotes the success of all students by collaborating with families and community members, responding to diverse community interests and needs, and mobilizing community resources.
- ◆ **Standard 5:** A school administrator is an educational leader who promotes the success of all students by acting with integrity, fairness, and in an ethical manner.
- ◆ **Standard 6:** A school administrator is an educational leader who promotes the success of all students by understanding, responding to, and influencing the larger political, social, economic, legal, and cultural context.

Although perhaps some measure of these standards can be accomplished by simply working harder, there is strong sentiment that neither the spirit nor the detail of modern school reform can be met without adequate resources in significantly greater supply than exists in public schools today. To meet NCLB's demands at the level of required academic performance means to bring all children literally to the same outcome, and school leaders are regarded as key to meeting such accountability. The ISLLC standards on which school leaders' training is to be judged clearly supports the same end, and in equally clear fashion the standards call for school leaders to understand the economic context of schools *and* its causal relationship to the outcomes of teaching and learning. As a result, the context of this third edition of *Money and Schools* is that federal law now demands equality of educational outcomes for all children; that school performance accountability expectations at other levels of government has increased simultaneously; and that the education profession itself has embraced heightened performance accountability and has targeted school leadership in its sights by demanding a new generation of school leaders who understand the complex nature of schooling and the relationship of money to educational opportunity and outcome.

WHO SHOULD READ THIS BOOK

From its title, it is evident that this book is meant for both broad and specialized audiences. Choosing this book indicates that readers have a connection to schools that causes them to demonstrate a high level of interest in education's costs. Specifically, this book reaches out to school administrators, classroom teachers, boards of education, and laypersons from the broader public. Although that sounds like everyone, each of these audiences has a different use for the book. Administrators will find that the material confirms their existing knowledge, reminds them of things not thought of recently, and extends their knowledge by considering the context of recent federal and state reform movements. We've also long advocated that the first group of people who should know more about school funding is classroom teachers. Teachers often complain about school budgets and understand that new requirements are stretching inadequate dollars even thinner, but they typically have little knowledge of how school budgets work—for example, sources of revenue and permissible expenditures. We also believe school board members will benefit from this book—whereas it is popular to bash boards as insensitive to the financial shortcomings of schools, it is altogether too easy to forget that board members are asked to make difficult and highly unpopular decisions, usually without being professionally trained in recognizing education's needs—and now in the context of tight fiscal resources overlaid by stringent federal and state accountability requirements. Finally, lay people can benefit from this book, in that all are taxpayers and would be better citizens if they were more knowledgeable about how schools are funded. So, in the end, this book is for nearly everyone, subject only to the limitations on what the book does and does not try to do.

WHAT YOU SHOULD EXPECT FROM THIS BOOK

The book is organized around three broad parts: an overview of *funding* concepts, an overview of *daily funding operations*, and an attempt to look into the *future*. Moving through these parts is like an inverted pyramid, starting with the broad social context of schools and continuing into specialized examinations in each individual chapter of various elements of school budgeting.

At the broadest level, it is important for everyone to understand that money and student achievement are related (Chapter 1). It is also critical to know that education's current condition is a product of a long history that involves the interplay of complex aspects of our cultural and governmental heritage (Chapter 2). The next logical step is to review sources of revenue and expenditure (Chapter 3), in that people's frustrations and misunderstanding of school budgets often can be traced back to these complex issues. After this broad overview, the book launches into a detailed view of daily funding operations. The focus is on our audience, however, seeking readability without the clutter of academic language or heavy research citation. We begin with the view that accountability, regulation, and ethics are the watchwords for the future, so that understanding the flow of money into schools and its proper handling is the basis for all good decision-making (Chapter 4). School budget planning (Chapter 5) is next addressed from the perspective of how budgets are built, with subsequent chapters looking in greater detail at the major elements of budget construction. Specifically, issues of budgeting for personnel (Chapter 6), budgeting for instruction (Chapter 7), and budgeting for student activities (Chapter 8) are elements that cut across wise budgeting behaviors at both district and school levels. The same can be said about budgeting for school infrastructure (Chapter 9), budgeting for transportation and food services (Chapter 10), and the need to budget for liability and risk management (Chapter 11). Clearly issues of site-based leadership under new performance accountability standards have strong budget implications (Chapter 12), with activities that occur at all levels in a school system. Finally, a look to the future is essential (Chapter 13) because schools continue to face radical changes.

WHAT THIS BOOK DOESN'T DO

We also want to be clear about what this book does not do. Specifically, it does not cover each topic to its greatest depth—given the limitations of space and purpose this is not within the scope of the book. It also does not intend to create a skilled practitioner. Again, space and purpose do not lend themselves to teaching specific skills at the level of practice. It also does not intend to represent the range of all necessary elements of good budgeting in schools. Although the premise of this book is that budgeting can be made less murky, it remains a highly complex activity when anyone attempts to actually carry it out. As a result, *knowledge rather than skills* is the goal of this book—knowledge needed by everyone because everyone pays taxes, sends children to school, or benefits from an educated citizenry.

HOW SHOULD YOU READ THIS BOOK?

The best method is to read the chapters sequentially because there is a logical progression. However, experienced administrators to whom the concepts are already familiar will have no difficulty picking and choosing chapters in any order. School board members, teachers, and laypersons may also read in any order, though they might find it necessary to dip back into earlier chapters if some point seems unclear.

HOW CAN YOU LEARN MORE?

If you find your interest piqued by issues in this book, there are many ways to learn more about school budgeting. The obvious ways are reading other books on the topic and taking classes relating to school funding. Several excellent textbooks are available that go more deeply into the issues introduced in this book—we've authored several such books. Courses at a reputable university can be helpful in refreshing your knowledge or extending your grasp of these difficult issues. Depending on your current professional employment and career goals, internships with practicing administrators can provide a critical learning tool, since no one has ever really experienced budgeting until it has become a "do-or-die" activity. Other ways to learn more include attending state department of education budget workshops, as well as seminars conducted by state professional groups such as administrator organizations, school board associations, and so on. Valuable resource people also exist right at home, such as your school district's business manager or school principal—each of these persons is required to carry out budgeting as a daily activity. Finally, you can contact us.

Part I

OVERVIEW OF BROAD CONCEPTS

1

SCHOOLS, VALUES, AND MONEY

THE CONTEXT OF PUBLIC EDUCATION

It is hardly astounding to say that the context of public education is undergoing a dramatic change at the start of a new millennium. Education—indeed all of global society—is being massively restructured on a scale equal to many events from our past that history books now record as cataclysmic and that reshaped the fate of entire nations. A brief consideration of such change is essential as we begin our study of money and schools, because the nature of schools continues to change so rapidly and dramatically that broad-based support for education seems to be in constant danger.

The assertion that tenuousness exists for schools takes root in issues that have been raised at all levels of society over the past few decades. Although the past is often subject to a convenient romanticism that fails to objectively ask whether the world was ever as rational as we seem inclined to believe, the past few decades have engendered a new tendency toward hostile confrontation over a wide range of real and imaginary injustices—an eagerness that has led to a national character that no longer seems to care much about modeling civility or working collaboratively for a common good. Recent national elections provide excellent examples of how critics from the political right harshly ridicule what they regard as abandonment of traditional American values, claiming government spawns laziness, ingratitude, and immorality while simultaneously punishing law-abiding, industrious, and upright citizens—a view that seeks to criminalize any opposing view. In response, critics from the political left approach a near frenzy in making their platform known by shouting down anyone they regard as intolerant, while demonstrating a remarkable level of intolerance themselves for views other than their own. The breakdown of civility is evident in election results so closely drawn as to divide the nation along stark lines, so that it has become normal to challenge the outcome of elections through the courts. At its most fundamental level, the rift is based in vastly different views of the role of government in individuals' lives, and as people have come to see confrontation as a socially acceptable means for presenting their beliefs. The rift has come to dominate the news and to suggest that the issues are too deep to be resolved. In many cases, the rift has economic roots—a dangerous mix when fundamental values and huge amounts of money are cast into an arena where aggression is a significant element in play.

The implications of social turmoil for schools are great. Schools are an integral part of society, transmitting culture and winning approval (or scorn) for their success in preparing future generations for meaningful living in an increasingly national and transnational world. But because the forces in society are increasingly irreconcilable, schools today are caught more than ever among competing demands that see the mission of schools from starkly opposite ends of the political and social continuum. The questions arising from such a fragmented context are profound. For example, what are schools becoming? For that matter, where did schools come from, and what does that say about what schools are today? Of profound importance are the following questions: What *should* schools be doing? What are schools capable of doing? Difficult enough to answer objectively, these questions are dramatically heightened in impact by the fervent political agendas from the left and right that adopt them as causes, raising new questions that get at what advocates for each side would do if they could gain unlimited political power. The struggle is grandly illustrated by the recent No Child Left Behind Act,[1] which presumes to know the answers to earth-shaking questions that include: What is the impact of money on schools? What actually happens when schools get more money? It effectively raises the even more difficult question of whether schools really need more money. Together these questions, in a social and political context that seems eager to fight and never seek commonality, raise the ultimate specter of where public education may be eventually headed.

These are critical issues as we face a volatile future—issues that school leaders must be prepared to address head-on for reasons of national prosperity and survival. As a result, the remainder of this chapter, together with Chapter 13, sets the stage for the critical importance of schools and money in a new and politically unstable era. But as we launch into that discussion, we admit at the outset to a bias: That is, we strongly favor adequate and equitable support of every kind for public schools. Some of our bias comes from being insiders to the education establishment, as we have spent more than 60 years collectively in this massive industry. We know the criticisms we face as a result of our insider views, and we ourselves have often perceptively referred to education as a growth industry that tries to ensure its own future by creating an unending demand cycle—both by continuously raising standards and by the ever constant need for remediating our professional failures. But at the same time, our many years as school leaders at various levels of responsibility have caused us to truly believe that schools are America's last and finest hope, if for no other reason than the individual and collective well-being (including our own personal retirement prospects) of the nation and world depend on adequately preparing each new generation to pick up the economic and social reins of leadership. As a result, throughout this book is an honest and sometimes brutal view of schools and money, uncluttered by other bias or political

---

1.   P.L. 107–110, No Child Left Behind Act of 2001. Billed by Congress as an act to close the achievement gap with accountability, flexibility, and choice, so that no child is left behind.

posturing—a journey that begins within the context of public education because that is the context in which school budgets must function.

WHAT ARE SCHOOLS BECOMING?

A burning question on the minds of many people on both sides of the political aisle is: What is the emerging nature of schools? Although the question is too complex to answer exhaustively in this book, it is useful to at least raise the issue of change because speculating about the answer is fundamental to understanding schools and money as far into the future as we can see.

Where Did Schools Come From?

The battle for control of education is by no means new, although it has shown recent signs of intense escalation as the stakes for winners and losers have shifted over time in an increasingly knowledge-based economy. But it is important to recognize at the outset that part of the current struggle over schools stems from our past, in that people as a rule are resistant to change, particularly when it is perceived as threatening to their way of life. It is an important principle to know that nothing, including resistance to change, exists without roots, and the past gives many insights into a vast array of otherwise loosely connected realities.[2]

The unique history of the United States contributed much to current struggles over schools, in that the structure of education today is the product of an arduous evolutionary process. Most of us know the brief history of American education, beginning with establishment of schools in the original colonies. The first law formally requiring schools came into existence in 1642 with adoption of a law in Massachusetts requiring the town fathers to determine if children were being given adequate religious and occupational training. Similar action followed quickly in several other colonies, so that by 1720, laws mandating some amount of schooling were on the books in Connecticut, Maine, New Hampshire, and Vermont. These laws were destined to be broadened as the idea of enlightened self-government was added to the useful reasons for requiring public education, giving birth to the now familiar democratic principles as propounded by Thomas Jefferson, William Penn, and others who wielded great influence on the emerging nature of schooling in the new nation.

In addition to the practical reasons for encouraging public education, the intense isolation of the colonies and the later westward expansion were powerful contributors to the evolving structure of public schools. Colonies were jealously independent, even to the point of deciding separately whether they each would give financial support to the American Revolution. In the post-Revolution era, the early Congress struggled with its inability to pay its

---

2. For a more detailed discussion, see Chapter 2 in David C. Thompson, R. Craig Wood, and David Honeyman, *Fiscal Leadership for Schools: Concepts and Practices* (New York: Longman, 1994) 76–87.

war debts, much of which stemmed from fierce resistance to any central government, and it was a harbinger of a politically watchful future that the early nation witnessed a bitter war of contrasting ideologies such as those of Hamilton and Jefferson regarding a strong federal government. Westward expansion, with its geographic isolation, only exacerbated the independent streak of the new breed of Americans, leading to intensely local views on how education should be organized. Yet at the same time the nation's face was shifting dramatically in other ways, with soaring immigration, the establishment of great cities, and a growing sentiment against child-labor abuse. Through a series of complex events, the Common Schools Movement arose under advocates like Horace Mann, so that public schools resembling the structure of those today began to emerge by 1840 despite the stubborn independence that characterized the American landscape.

Probably the most striking features of emerging public schools in the growing nation were the frequency with which they were established and the parochialism in which they were based. The empty vastness of the nation led to the need for countless thousands of tiny schools. Although no one knows how many schools existed across the nation before a trend toward consolidation began, the number had to be at least equal to the number of towns in the states and territories at any given time. The only meaningful way to understand the staggering proliferation of schools is to look to the first formal attempts to tally public schools with U.S. Department of Education data showing that as recently as 1929, there were 238,306 elementary schools; 149,282 one-teacher schools; and 23,930 secondary schools—a total of 411,518 schools—all within slightly more than 119,000 school districts! The parochialism stemming from such proliferation and isolation goes far in explaining the fiercely local nature of schools, and it speaks clearly to why we still today find schools only two or three blocks apart with low enrollments in many cities. After all, if there were more than 100,000 school districts in the country, it stands to reason that there must have been an equal number of different preferences for how schooling should be carried out, especially because states did not attempt to regulate schools until only recently.

The evolution of public schools in the United States is, of course, much more complex than is presented here. But historic roots explain much about present realities. Just as children predictably take on some of the same values that were taught to them during their own upbringing, the customs and culture of local communities are deeply held values that affect the nature of schools, and the stubborn pride of Americans in creating and preserving local norms for schools is legendary. The sentiment of local control is well-captured by the fear of many rural school districts today, as citizens hasten to charge, "As the school goes, so goes the town." Indeed, we've served as senior administrators in communities where countless school district patrons repeatedly told us with great anxiety, "If the school goes, the post office and the churches will follow close behind"—in other words, schools make up the heart of the community in many people's minds, so much so that the strongest pillar of a community is lost when schools close. A long sense of local tradition produces a fierce willingness to fight at any cost to save the schools, and the entirety of the struggle over education—be it human sexuality, racial integration, local taxes, or school budgets—is rooted in the uniquely American tradition of local control and resentment toward outside interference. It is, in fact, markedly American to struggle fiercely for deeply held beliefs—an ingrained trait manifested in the cries of reformers and naysayers on both sides of the political aisle.

What Should Schools Be Doing?

Where schools have come from is part of the answer to what schools are becoming, at least in the sense of understanding how hard it is to agree on anything about schools. But part of the question about what schools are becoming is wrapped up in the subquestion: What should schools be doing?

Although we have come a long way from the political and social isolationism of the past, the persistently parochial nature of schools in the United States continues to stand as a reminder of the great difficulty of trying to reach consensus on what schools should be about. Almost any media report today chronicles some new dispute about schools, ranging from withdrawal of fiscal support to calls for more reforms because of some newly perceived breakdown in schools' effectiveness. Almost daily, administrators lose their jobs because of arguments over what schools should be doing. Teacher unions and professional negotiations become deeply mired in either restricting educational activities or in promoting programs of special interest. School board candidates often run on platforms of educational reform, and legislators are subjected to tremendous pressures from groups specifically organized to force (or prevent) changes in what schools are doing. No one is immune to such pressure, in large part because people intuitively understand that schools are a key player in the nation's future—so much so that control of schools is tantamount to control of the future.

Historic opinions on what schools should do have centered mostly on issues relating to morality, democracy, and equality. The intense interest among the early colonies in preparing children for a morally upright life was noted in our earlier discussion. Ideas from Jefferson, Mann, and others weighed in, extending the scope and arguing that an enlightened citizenry is the most effective curb against tyranny—as Benjamin Franklin said, "Government is not reason; it is not eloquence; it is force. Like fire, it is a dangerous servant and a fearful master." Franklin's statement captures the historical attitude of many Americans toward government control and paints a vivid portrait of a main purpose of schooling in earlier times in the nation's history. More recent times have evoked a concern for equality. The earthshaking effect of the *Brown v. Board of Education*[3] decision in 1954, which overturned the race-based doctrine of "separate but equal" as an acceptable social order, is clear evidence of increased concern about equality in education and all other

---

3. 374 U.S. 483 (1954).

aspects of the human condition. The Civil Rights Act of 1964 and the expansive civil rights laws that followed have had enormous educational implications, giving rise to a huge body of federal and state case law and statutes controlling expansive and far-reaching concepts, including gender equity, rights of students in special education, rights of citizens under equal access provisions, and so forth. As time has marched on, the volume and tenor of special interest legislation has intensified, accompanied by increases in aggressive advocacy for controversial positions.

Ever-increasing likelihood for conflict is an accurate assessment of current views on what schools should be doing, especially regarding the nature of education for equality. Little disagreement likely exists about education for basic economic productivity, although effectuating such education provides fertile ground for disagreement as it relates to equal access. Critics in this area charge that students have highly unequal access to skills such as technology or exclusion from higher education, which ensures the perpetuation of disadvantaged populations into the future, whereas their philosophical and political counterparts forcefully invoke local choice to exceed a minimum educational program. Some greater disagreement exists today about education for morality, particularly when issues infringe on parental prerogatives as with mandated sex education, creationism, or other issues seeking to limit parental control. Hysteria often rules, with dissenters threatening to leave public schools and proponents of compulsory uniform education angrily shouting back. But it is the broader issue of attempts to force uniformity on schools in social and academic equality that produces the greatest conflict on what schools should be about. Is it the role of schools to provide a *minimum* educational opportunity? Is it education's role to provide *exactly* equal educational opportunities? Is it the role of education to provide equal educational *outcomes*? Reformers have tended to argue at least for exactly equal opportunity, whereas the precedent of American history promotes some minimum opportunity with the freedom to exceed by local choice. Reformers emotionally argue that such freedom guarantees racially and economically segregated schools, an outcome in direct conflict with the U.S. Constitution's guarantees of equal protection.[4]

 Defenders of local choice hotly reply that communism is dead and that its rebirth in the United States would be an obscene irony. The debate is carried out at all levels: Courts struggle with lawsuits over school funding, legislatures experience intense pressure from political advocates of all stripes, and taxpayers engage in passive or overt revolt, whereas school boards, teachers, administrators, and children are caught in a tug-of-war that results in diminished resources because of expensive litigation and lack of cooperation. In the end, there is no one voice speaking for what education *should be doing* because the many voices seek different and fundamentally incompatible ends.

---

4.   U.S. Constitution, Amendment XIV.

What Are Schools Capable of Doing?

At least a piece of the current debate that is being overlooked is recognizing what schools are actually capable of doing. Partisan sides confidently act as if schools are capable of fully achieving each side's goals. Social reformers point to the gains of the twentieth century and argue that a combination of legal and social reforms has created a better, although imperfect, society. Advocates for reestablishing a more traditional society are just as convinced that restoring basic education and traditional values to schools would solve the social ills now afflicting the nation. With all the noise, it is difficult to know who is right, but the overriding conclusion is that each side fervently believes schools are the major vehicle to some desirable goal. Yet the question must be asked as to what schools are actually *capable* of doing—whether schools can achieve the goals of either side, and at what price. This generates subquestions, to which data offer some insight. For example: What is the effect of money on schools? What happens when schools get more money? Do schools really need more money? What will happen if schools receive less money? These questions envelop the larger question of what schools should be doing by making the stakes higher as factions seek to increase or decrease spending on schools. Although the questions are relatively clear, the answers are incomplete, especially relating to what schools are capable of doing.

What Is the Effect of Money on Schools?

An increasingly explosive issue is the impact of money on schools. Many questions form around this kernel, primarily inquiring at the most basic level whether money has any appreciable effect on student achievement. Obviously, people asking the question have many reasons for seeking the right answer. Educators generally believe the right answer would allow many things to be done that are not now possible given current funding because they assume the answer would inevitably spur new money. It is also reasonable to predict that an increase in funding would personally benefit educators at the same time. Legislators asking the same question are driven by complex goals, paramount among which is that limited public resources must be shared with other essential needs such as social services, public safety, roads, and so forth—all in a context of limited tax revenues gathered from increasingly surly taxpayers. School boards often share many of the same goals as educators, but with the added burden of making policy decisions in the context of local politics. At its root, however, the question about the impact of money on schools always asks: Does money make a difference in student achievement? The stakes are high, as advocates for higher funding levels may suffer a devastating setback if no clear effect is readily available, whereas education's critics will have gained a powerful reason to reduce funding for schools, or at least allow funding to stagnate at current levels.

Unfortunately, the answer to the question is very incomplete and unsatisfying. Much research has been done on the relationship between money and student achievement, but with limited—although significant—results. A sizable source of limitation springs from relative inexperience in researching such complex issues, in that formal interest is scarcely more than 30 years old—a fact that has led to accusations about inadequate methodologies used in assessing the complex relationships between money and achievement. Additionally, at times bias has affected the answers obtained by research, in that some investigators may have approached the question in search of a preferred answer. Although we cannot provide an unassailable answer to the effect of money on schools in this book, much can be learned by considering what is regarded with reasonable respect at this point.

A significant body of research on the relationship between student achievement and money is known as *production-function* research, and efforts to extend this line of inquiry and to find new avenues of exploration are constantly pursued. Various sources have chronicled the development of this line of research. Production-function studies began with the Coleman Report,[5] which was funded by the federal government as part of the Civil Rights Act of 1964. The study focused on questions about racial inequality, indicators of quality such as curriculum, teacher qualifications, and student learning as measured by standardized tests, all within the context of socioeconomic status. The Coleman Report's findings were very pessimistic about both the impact of resources and the school's ability to overcome the effects of genetics and the home environment.

Response to the Coleman Report was swift and dramatic. Educators were incensed at the notion that education had limited impact, particularly for disadvantaged children, and reformers chose to view the study with skepticism because it did not promise much educational benefit for disadvantaged children. A spate of counter-studies sprang up after the Coleman Report, typified by the Summers and Wolfe[6] study, which examined 627 sixth-grade students in the Philadelphia schools, finding that certain variables such as better teacher preparation, presence of high achievers, smaller class size, and so forth did have a positive effect on achievement for all children. The Effective Schools Movement, initiated soon after the Coleman Report, similarly was based in protest, seeking to identify traits of effective schools that could be emulated to increase student achievement. Although all such studies yielded useful insights into improving student achievement through resource allocation, all were based at least in part in a desire to counter the Coleman Report—an observation that weakened the objectivity of any new findings because researchers were seeking to refute data they found objectionable.

Although the dust has never settled, researchers have continued to pursue production-function research, giving rise to an ongoing bitter dispute focusing on attacking research methodologies and conducting more individ-

---

5. James Coleman, Ernst Campbell, Carol Hobson, James McPartland, Alexander Mood, Frederic Weinfeld, and Robert York, *Equality of Educational Opportunity* (Washington, DC: U.S. Government Printing Office, 1966).

6. Anita Summers and Barbara Wolfe, "Do Schools Make a Difference?" *American Economic Review 67*, no. 4 (1977): 639–52.

ual studies and meta-analyses of existing research. There is little to be gained by considering individual studies; more can be learned by looking at criticisms and the generalizations sought by meta research, including new developments since the last edition of this text.

Criticism of production-function research is captured by examining the attacks on the Coleman Report. Although considered at the time to be a good study, the Coleman Report has been subjected to intense criticism for methodological flaws. Chief among its criticisms have been *nonresponse* and *stratification* of variables resulting in noncomparable data, *errors* in data entry, and *misinterpretation* of interaction effects. Simply put, nonresponse refers to the misleading impression of a very large data set when in fact the number of respondents was much smaller than intended, raising questions of generalizability. Stratification refers to data being examined in separate sets, perhaps wrongly constructed, so that effects of variables such as race, religion, and so forth might have been exaggerated or misleading. Errors in data entry plague all large data sets and make the results suspect. Finally, misinterpretation of interaction effects refers to a lack of sophistication in research design, in which causal relationships are inferred that were not really verified in the data. These criticisms have been helpful in limiting misapplication of the Coleman Report, although some would argue that subsequent research has not improved greatly and has suffered equally scathing criticism.

A second useful tool for examining the effect of money on student achievement is meta-analysis. At some point, the body of literature on any topic becomes so large that it obscures the question because each study appears to have yielded the final answer. In production-function research, this tendency has been accentuated by large numbers of studies yielding seemingly opposite results, with thousands of studies in the available database. Meta-analysis seeks to find commonality of results among studies, so that the weight and direction of evidence can be evaluated. Representative studies from opposite views provide a summary of the debate.

The case against appreciable impact of money generally has been associated with Eric Hanushek's work. Through a series of studies with provocative titles such as *Throwing Money at Schools*[7] and *The Case for Equalized Mediocrity* . . . ,[8] Hanushek historically made a case that some readers have interpreted to fully support the Coleman Report. On separate occasions, Hanushek published meta-analyses of existing studies finding in sum that the relationship between school resources and student achievement is not directional, or is at least not strong and consistent given current funding practices. The essence of his argument against assumptions about correla-

---

7. Eric A. Hanushek, "Throwing Money at Schools," *Journal of Policy Analysis and Management* 1 (1981): 19–41.

8. Eric A. Hanushek, "The Quest for Equalized Mediocrity: School Finance Reform without Consideration of School Performance," in *Where Does The Money Go? 16th Annual Yearbook of the American Education Finance Association,* ed. Lawrence Picus and James Wattenbarger, 20–43 (Thousand Oaks, CA: Corwin Press, 1996).

tions between money and achievement is that the ways in which education's costs have increased should not have been expected to yield achievement gains. The assertion takes two forms. First, Hanushek argued that expenditures apart from direct instructional costs have increased far more sharply than costs for direct instruction. He concurrently argued that such costs should not be expected to produce gains, even when held to be valid instructional expenditures such as for improved teacher retirement plans. Second, he argued that attempts to spend more for direct instruction have been ill advised. For example, schools have rushed to spend more to reduce class sizes, to hire better educated teachers, and to improve teacher salaries—all in the face of weak evidence that massaging such variables leads to true achievement gains. On the other side, several studies have found favorable impact of *selected* resources on student achievement.[9] One of the more comprehensive meta-analyses finding for positive impact was conducted by Laine, Greenwald, and Hedges[10] in which they reviewed a set of carefully selected studies. They concluded that resources *are* related to achievement, so that variables such as per-pupil expenditure, smaller classes, smaller school size, teacher ability, teacher education, and teacher experience have positive measurable impacts. The debate has recently taken on new direction, as researchers have increasingly called for disaggregation of data at the student level (in contrast to traditional interdistrict comparisons) and greater discernment and analysis in evaluating research results in hopes of finding better answers to these perplexing questions.[11] Raymond and Hanushek,[12] for example, recently held that biased search for evidence relating to student

9. See, e.g., Bettye MacPhail-Wilcox and Richard King, "Production Functions Revisited in the Context of Educational Reform," *Journal of Education Finance* 12, no. 2 (1986); see also Bettye MacPhail-Wilcox and Richard King, "Resource Allocation Studies: Implications for School Improvement and School Finance Research," *Journal of Education Finance* 11, no. 4 (1986).

10. Richard Laine, Rob Greenwald, and Larry Hedges, "Money Does Matter: A Research Synthesis of a New Universe of Education Production Function Studies," in *Where Does The Money Go? 16th Annual Yearbook of the American Education Finance Association*, ed. Lawrence Picus and James Wattenbarger, 44–70 (Thousand Oaks, CA: Corwin Press, 1996).

11. See, e.g., Allan Odden and Carolyn Busch, eds. "Special Issue: Collection of School-Level Finance Data," *Journal of Education Finance* 22, no. 3 (1997) entire issue; Margaret Goertz and Leanna Stiefel, eds. "Special Issue: Collection of School-Level Finance Data," *Journal of Education Finance* 23, no. 4 (1998) entire issue; Lawrence O. Picus and Ed Robillard, "The Collection and Use of Student Level Data: Implications for School Finance Research," *Educational Considerations* 28, no. 1 (Fall 2000); William E. Camp, David C. Thompson, and John Crain, "Within-District Equity: Issues of Desegregation and Microeconomic Analysis," in *Microlevel School Finance. 1989 American Education Finance Association Yearbook*. (Cambridge: M. Ballinger, 1989).

12. Margaret Raymond and Eric Hanushek, "Shopping for Evidence against School Accountability," in *Developments in School Finance: 2003*. Fiscal Proceedings from the Annual State Data Conference of July 2003, 117–129 (Washington, DC: National Center for Education Statistics, 2004).

outcomes still persists and that the emerging data in fact tend to support the idea that reform (as expressed by states having strong achievement account-ability systems) is more consistently correlated with improved student achievement than is true in states where accountability systems are less rigor-ous. Similarly, Grissmer[13] recently argued that the confusion over results in the literature likely relates to poor research methodology. His own reanalysis of experimental, nonexperimental, and historical data holds that the evidence increasingly leans toward the view that targeted expenditures can raise achievement scores, especially for disadvantaged students.

Under these general conditions, the answer to questions about the effect of money on schools is still incomplete, contradictory, and even confusing. History reveals some inexpert attempts at disentanglement, although such studies may have been the best possible efforts at the time. To make matters worse, different answers may be viable and can depend on one's political beliefs. For example, educators are justified in thinking more could be done with extra money. Legislators are justified in knowing that they must divide a finite pie among many competing audiences. Taxpayers are correct in ask-ing why they should pay more, especially in the context of years of national reports bemoaning declining student achievement. Boards and administra-tors are faced with the hard task of making painful resource decisions, know-ing that some aspects of schooling will be deemphasized as a result of spend-ing in other areas, while feeling pressured to support all groups and perhaps knowing that increased spending might only result in higher taxes. For all constituencies, asking if money makes a difference in student achievement yields no clear answers. Yet the question reverberates with deafening pro-portion: If there is no effect, then more will make no palpable difference—a question that inevitably raises the logical speculation that less might have no bad effect either. Conversely, if there is an effect, then more money will be presumed to produce a linear relationship that causes achievement to rise in unison—a relationship now unsupported by the literature.[14]

13. David Grissmer, "Research Directions for Understanding the Relationship of Educa-tional Resources to Educational Outcomes," in *Education Finance in the New Millen-nium. Yearbook of the American Education Finance Association*, 139–55 (New York: Eye on Education, 2001).

14. Yet the debate goes on. See, for example, Michael Rebell and Joseph Wardenski, *Of Course Money Matters: Why the Arguments to the Contrary Never Added Up* (New York: Campaign for Fiscal Equity, January 2004).

What Happens When Schools Get More (or Less) Money?

Production-function research indicates three plausible answers to the question of how more money would affect schools. One answer comes from the longstanding perspective that it is difficult to know the limits on the impact of money. Childs and Shakeshaft[15] made this point long ago in an earlier meta-analysis (not discussed here) when they wryly noted that there have never been any public schools with enough money to be able to see what might happen when schools have enough to spend. Although some would argue that a small number of public schools are very wealthy, it remains that no systematic studies of this specific question have been conducted. Such a study would maximally benefit from manipulation of fiscal inputs for the express purpose of determining the impact of money on student achievement—a feature difficult to carry out in schools because of the ethics of a scientific method that would require intentionally withholding resources from one group compared to another group.

A second possible answer relates to the absence of data on experimental control. As we just noted, by virtue of ethical prohibitions we are largely left to speculate as to the impact of more money. Experience and intuition tempt us to predict that one immediate effect of a sudden infusion of new resources would be the most logically possible response by schools—that is, the purchase of more (or at least more expensive) human resources, in that most school budgets are largely consumed by personnel costs. In other words, increased funding for schools typically buys more staff or results in higher salaries for existing staff. Although such a scenario is not without merit, the argument for more funding is difficult to make because no corresponding achievement gain can be promised, whereas higher salaries can almost surely be predicted.

A third possible answer also relates to what can be intuitively known. Even granted that new money would go toward higher salaries, it is reasonable to believe that some new funds would be used to redress nonpersonnel costs. Schools have many unmet needs, possibly because they have tried to resolve their human resource shortfalls first. Among the unmet needs are a decaying school infrastructure, antiquated buildings unable to support new technologies, unsafe buses and other transportation needs, and outdated curriculum materials and teaching aids. Even assuming no direct causal link between how money is currently being spent and increased achievement, no sensible person could argue against using money for reducing class sizes, providing safe school buildings, providing new instructional materials and textbooks, and so forth. Although nothing can excuse lax or wasteful spending, neither can it be presumed that money spent is wasted simply because it cannot be shown to have effectuated a change in the bottom line of schools.

---

15. Stephen Childs and Charol Shakeshaft. "A Meta-Analysis of Research on the Relationship Between Educational Expenditures and Student Achievement," *Journal of Education Finance* 12, no. 2 (1986): 249–63.

We find two nearly criminal behaviors in these arguments—that is, it is preposterous to gut the nonpersonnel side of instruction in favor of a mad race to inflate salary costs, and it is equally absurd to believe that the servant metaphor of schools should result in near-slavery for school staffs merely because education is held in low esteem by segments of the American public.

An equally interesting question is raised by asking what would happen if schools were to receive less money. Here again, voices on either side of this debate hypothesize very different outcomes. In all fairness, few (if any) inside education would advocate for reduced spending merely because desired linkages between expenditures and student achievement are not well established. Such a call is more likely the response of taxpayers who believe that, because money is wasted through the lack of a profitable bottom achievement line, the proper punishment is to withhold revenue from schools. In contrast, most scholars argue for increased scrutiny of *how* money is spent, although Monk captured the dark abyss of such behavior when he noted that this might demand more psychoanalytic expertise than the discipline possesses to understand the extremes of such microanalysis.[16] Notwithstanding, some elements of sophisticated micro-level inquiry have begun to develop, partly in response to the fact that relative expenditure levels have indeed dropped in some states over the last several years[17] and as scholarly interest in analyzing school level data has taken on new strength.

Unfortunately, like the effects of more money, the answer to what happens if significantly less money were available is largely speculative. However, intuition and observation of some current realities again have to play an important part in estimating the effect of revenue losses. Intuition tells us that many districts already are skating near the edge of disaster, as state support for education has stagnated or has not kept up with rising costs in many locations. Costs have soared as liability has increased, as teacher unions have been successful in raising pay and benefits, and as nonpersonnel operating costs have increased. Schools are not immune to market forces, including costs for products *and* patrons who vote at the polls on local option school taxes and vote with their feet in other ways that cause enrollments and revenues to shift, sometimes downward. Intuition says that many districts cannot survive much more pressure, already having been forced into equipment and maintenance deferral, program and staff reductions, closure of attendance centers, consolidation of school districts, and even bankruptcies. Experience tells us that districts in some states actually have been faced with such scenarios, including academic or fiscal receivership under new and aggressive state accountability laws. On the other hand, the lack of impending crisis in any given district should not make school leaders feel that they do not need to critically examine spending patterns and long-term fiscal health. In this era of

16. David H. Monk, *Educational Finance: An Economic Approach*, 345 (New York: McGraw-Hill, 1990).

17. See, e.g., David C. Thompson and Faith E. Crampton, "The Impact of School Finance Litigation," *Educational Considerations* 28, no. 1 (Fall 2000): 1–12.

social and economic unrest, education is obligated to examine itself carefully, which may include admitting that it is too easy to spend tax dollars without asking truly hard questions about efficiency and effectiveness in school operations. All school districts would do well to recognize the danger of the flip side of the "more money is better" argument; that is, if there are no data to support a linear increase in achievement for each additional dollar invested, neither are there clear data to support a view that fewer dollars would spark a drop in achievement—an argument that says to many people, "less money might be better, too." In other words, less money is a reasonable option for many people in society, especially those who strongly champion alternatives to public education.

On balance, however, most schools are not faced with either extreme anytime soon. Most schools are not faced with financial ruin, although money certainly has become far more difficult to secure and its distribution increasingly more contentious. Most schools have not yet faced an enraged public threatening dire outcomes if student achievement does not turn around immediately. But on the other hand, it is a stark reality that educational accountability, both achievement-based and fiscal efficiency-driven, has become a powerful weapon in the hands of state legislatures, as states have demanded sweeping reforms and as courts have ruled on a staggering array of issues under the banner of equal education. All these events underscore fierce competition for scarce fiscal resources and an increasingly fragmented society that is in no mood to pour vast sums of new money into schools in return for more of the lofty and imprecise educational jargon of the past.[18]

WHERE PUBLIC SCHOOLS MAY BE HEADED

At the outset of this chapter, we called attention to several important concepts. First, we admitted to having certain strong biases, arguing that no one could expect us to offer a compelling defense for why public school funding should be scaled back. We also revealed our personal attitudes for a moment, admitting we deeply believe that public schools are America's last and finest hope, although our view quickly proved utilitarian in that we see universal

---

18. See, e.g., Allan Odden and Sarah Archibald, *Reallocating Resources: How to Boost Student Achievement Without Asking for More* (Thousand Oaks, CA: Corwin Press, 2001). Odden and Archibald argue rather persuasively that significant new resources will not be forthcoming, as there is a formidable sentiment at policy-making levels that all the necessary resources are now in place—it is a matter of better and more responsible utilization. To secure the seriousness of this claim, they argue that policy makers expect student proficiency to reach high standards as defined by the National Assessment of Educational Progress (NAEP), where current proficiency is pegged at only 25%. Odden and Archibald believe that policy makers expect proficiency to reach as high as 90%—a staggering task when realizing that an increase to only 50% would require doubling educational productivity from today's performance standard. As the authors put it, these are ambitious goals—all in a context that expects this outcome with no great influx of new resources.

education as the single key to preserving American economic and social prosperity, including our own personal prospects. We also said we would be straightforward, presenting a view of money and schools that refuses to accept the shrillness of either political left or right, although we have focused heavily on presenting the sometimes unsavory arguments propounded from various political angles. In fact, that is an appropriate point to make now: Our view of schools and money was well expressed by Saul Alinsky when he said, "It is a world not of angels, but of angles."[19] Although we strongly support a benevolent world in which everyone genuinely cares for everyone else, we are realists who know well that schools, money, and politics are indivisible.

These realities affect what we see as we look to the future and wonder where public schools may be headed. We will return to this theme in the final chapter in some greater detail, and we continue with this line of thinking in Chapter 2 as we next consider the broad historical trends that have led to how we currently fund education in the 50 states. But as we prepare to look more specifically at the operational elements of schools and money in upcoming chapters, we are convinced that schools must do a much better job of communicating their strategic operational plans, including clear budget goals and processes, to an increasingly critical and vocal public. Patrons have the power to cause many changes in schools—whereas they've always had that power, it is a weapon that has only recently been used with real sophistication. And it should not be forgotten that today's clients are tomorrow's taxpayers. In other words, schools must begin to promote their virtues, take the lead in performance accountability, and engage their constituents where they are—a thread that runs throughout this book. If public schools fail, then it is quite clear where education is headed: into a world that includes ever-expanding alternatives to public education, with loss in support for public schools of every kind. Preventing that outcome involves all of education's stakeholders: administrators, boards, teachers, policy makers, and laypersons.

SUGGESTED FOLLOW-UP PROJECTS

♦ Write a position paper in which you identify your personal beliefs about what schools are capable of doing. Present your paper as a class project, seeking reactions to your views.

♦ Interview several persons in your community on attitudes about money and schools. Draw these persons from various walks in life: for example, a school board member, a teacher, an administrator, a businessperson, a retired person, a student, and so on.

♦ Talk to the person(s) in your school district who are responsible for assessing school performance. This might include central

19. Saul Alinsky, *Rules for Radicals* (New York: Random House, 1971).

office and school site personnel such as directors of assessment or curriculum, principals, counselors, and so forth. Ask about district or school performance profiles and trends and determine how the district and individual schools go about raising student achievement levels. Ask if any formal attempt is made to link money and achievement.

♦ Develop a list of the 25 most influential persons in your community. Profile these influencers, identifying why you included them on your list. Try to predict their attitudes toward money and schools and state the basis for your thinking. Bring your list to class and reach consensus on your community's power structure.

♦ Research newspapers in your community for the last year, tracing the general attitude toward schools. Especially look for reporting on school performance data. Try to identify the general attitude of the press, the issues deemed newsworthy, and any community opinions you can glean. Use your findings to estimate your community's support level.

2

FUNDING SCHOOLS: A POLICY PERSPECTIVE

A MORE EXPANSIVE VIEW

We ended the previous chapter with a warning that there is a growing conviction in the United States that public education's performance is at least lackluster, if not suffering a serious crisis of confidence. Certainly, data on linkages between student achievement and funding levels do not inspire "investor" enthusiasm, but there is more to the issue than just economics. At the same time, it is never as simple as mere economics, because the whole discussion revolves around fiscal considerations in tandem with other important social principles that cannot be ignored if we hope to sustain a civil democracy.

We need to expand our discussion to include other issues that both aggravate and explain how school leaders should act (and react) in today's intensely sociopolitical environment. It is never as simple as looking only at growth in revenue and spending for schools, so we must spend time looking at the broader scope of funding schools from a policy perspective. The issue of investment in education, versus an attitude of expenditure control, is important as well because spending for schools should take into account the value of education to the economy and to society itself. Certainly, a key part of spending on children's educational needs is affected by whether federal, state, and local governments are appropriately sharing in the duty to support schools. And of course, issues of adequate and equitable funding have become real thorns in the side of educators, politicians, and taxpayers alike. In essence, the debate about money for schools is larger than just thinking about good test scores; it also includes considering the ethics of social responsibility, at least as long as we truly believe we want opportunity, equality, and liberty for every child.

WHAT IS THE SCOPE OF EDUCATION FINANCE IN AMERICA?

Nearly every text on funding schools in the last 50 years has remarked that education is big business. Although we are used to hearing about huge costs attached to almost every part of society, the enormity of the demands of modern living on human and fiscal resources is still staggering. Most of us know our nation is deeply in debt, but the sum of $7.4 trillion that we owed at the end of 2004 (up from $5.5 trillion in the last edition of this book) seems unfathomable. This abstract number takes on personal meaning when it is understood that in late 2004, each citizen's share of the national debt exceeded $25,200, while at the same time, the national debt was growing by more than $1.6 billion per day! During the same period, Americans were raising vast sums for public schools—an estimated $400 billion in 2004. In contrast to ever-increasing national debt, however, funding for schools is usually paid on a current basis, meaning that revenues must match expenditures. Inasmuch as most government spending goes toward domestic and international programs, including support for schools, the level of public sacrifice in the United States is sizable. Under these conditions, it is not surprising that Chapter 1 was entitled "Schools, Values, and Money."

Revenue Growth for Schools

Growth in school revenue has been phenomenal in historical perspective, even in earlier times when education's needs were simpler. Notwithstanding, school revenues have moved regularly upward even in times of economic downturn. Although good records were not kept until very recently, revenues from 1920–2000 have reflected the increasing importance of education to our nation (see Figure 2.1). In 1920, total revenues for K–12 schools were $970 million. By 1930, revenue had increased to $2.09 billion (+215%). A useful observation is that despite the huge costs of World War I, school revenue had risen steadily, due partly to the need for training a fighting force and partly to postwar prosperity.

Growth in school revenue has experienced only brief lags over the years. Although the first 30 years of the last century saw rapid increases, only the Great Depression caused visible slackening in revenue growth. Funding grew from 1930 to 1940, despite the severe economic depression after the stock market crash in 1929. From 1930–1940, revenue grew only slightly from $2.09 to $2.26 billion (+8%), yet the increase was remarkable in light of the economic horrors experienced in the nation, leaving the conclusion that school revenues have been steady, if not elastic, even in times of great national distress.

The rapid rise in money for schools resumed with the recovery spurred by World War II. From 1940–1950, revenue rose to $5.4 billion (+241%). A similar pattern continued from 1950–1960, aided by the space race, which was triggered by the launch of the Soviet satellite Sputnik, giving rise to a national education agenda under the National Defense Education Act (NDEA) in 1958. NDEA led to unprecedented growth in school funding, as Congress reacted to fears of a Soviet menace, with massive federal funds aimed at math and science education and fueling an era in which information would become recognized as the replacement for a fading industrial economy.

Figure 2.1. Summary of K–12 Revenues 1920–2001

[in thousands of dollars]

School Year	Total	School Year	Total
1919–20	$970,121	1977–78	$81,443,160
1929–30	2,088,557	1978–79	87,994,143
1939–40	2,260,527	1979–80	96,881,165
1941–42	2,416,580	1980–81	105,949,087
1943–44	2,604,322	1981–82	110,191,257
1945–46	3,059,845	1982–83	117,497,502
1947–48	4,311,534	1983–84	126,055,419
1949–50	5,437,044	1984–85	137,294,678
1951–52	6,423,816	1985–86	149,127,779
1953–54	7,866,852	1986–87	158,523,693
1955–56	9,686,677	1987–88	169,561,974
1957–58	12,181,513	1988–89	192,016,374
1959–60	14,746,618	1989–90	208,547,573
1961–62	17,527,707	1990–91	223,340,537
1963–64	20,544,182	1991–92	234,581,384
1965–66	25,356,858	1992–93	247,626,168
1967–68	31,903,064	1993–94	260,159,468
1969–70	40,266,923	1994–95	273,149,449
1970–71	44,511,292	1995–96	287,702,844
1971–72	50,003,645	1996–97	305,065,192
1972–73	52,117,930	1997–98	325,925,708
1973–74	58,230,892	1998–99	347,377,993
1974–75	64,445,239	1999–2000	372,864,603
1975–76	71,206,073	2000–2001	400,919,024
1976–77	75,332,532		

SOURCE: United States Department of Education, NCES, *Digest of Education Statistics 2002* (Washington, DC: United States Department of Education, 2003).

Global awareness because of Sputnik was accompanied by rapid changes in the social structure of the nation, especially from 1950 to 1970. As the nation moved out of rural America to become an economic and political world power toughened by economic depression and war, social problems were reshaping the nation and its schools. Two events forever changed education and its fiscal patterns. The first was *Brown v. Board of Education*,[1] when the U.S. Supreme Court ruled that racial segregation as "separate but equal" was not allowed under the federal Constitution. The second event was the social revolution of the 1960s, typified by the War on Poverty under President Lyndon Johnson. Although *Brown* reshaped the fundamental nature of public schools by requiring desegregation, with massive costs to taxpayers, the War on Poverty marked the beginning of a vast list of federal entitlements in schools. Although the federal government had long tried to aid schools, these events sparked a revolution that altered the face of public education in America. Although these events did not account for all growth in school funding during this time, the era 1950–1970 is unmatched as revenues grew to $14.7 billion (+271%) by 1960 and to $44.5 billion by 1970 (+819% more than 1950). Although inflation was a factor, revenue grew at an historic pace during these years of social progress and economic prosperity.

The Great Depression proved that school funding is responsive to economic conditions. Yet short of world wars or total economic ruin, school monies have shown great resilience up to the present day. The era from 1970 to 1980 was marked by more social reform and high inflation, as many states had their systems for funding schools ruled unconstitutional and costs soared because of inflation. By 1980, revenues nearly hit $106 billion (+238%). Although public education's share of Gross National Product (GNP) began wavering in 1980, revenue growth was still real because massive redistribution of wealth and funding increases followed the dramatic restructuring of school finance systems required by the courts. The resiliency of school revenues was also evident during the economic downturn of the 1980s, more than doubling to $223 billion in 1990, and continuing throughout the roaring economy of the 1990s to nearly $401 billion in 2001.

Although these data suggest that education has little to complain about, another view is worth consideration. Although revenue has risen, there are at least three factors that may have limited schools' ability to sustain or increase services to children. First, the data speak only to national totals. Each state faces different social and economic situations tied to their fiscal abilities and voter preferences. Second, some data suggest that schools' ability to serve children may have diminished despite fiscal growth, particularly in the economic downturn of the new millennium and inasmuch as student achievement has declined despite greater fiscal resources. Third, educators argue that any funding increases may wrongly portray reality because schools are undergoing enormous demographic changes—an expensive population is

---

1.   374 U.S. 483 at 493 (1954).

now in school that must be adequately served if the nation is to sustain its prosperity and world preeminence. An embarrassment of riches from spiraling revenues thus seems open to acrimonious debate.

Based on reams of data, both sides have held views that make genuine solutions difficult. Two points emerge, however, that are critical to a comprehensive view of the social and economic context of money and schools. First, Americans have long seen education as a key to economic prosperity and social mobility, in that they have fought hard for good schools under strong local control. Second, Americans have historically provided vast resources to schools, a fact that underscores how much they value education because people resist paying for what does not matter to them. But as critics have noted, the United States now believes it is in a crisis of increasing costs and declining educational productivity. So it is reasonable to ask whether the public will continue to provide funding to a school system that appears to be losing ground. As a result, we should consider views that see schools as an investment, rather than as a failing business that throws good money after bad when other educational choices are readily available.

HOW ARE EDUCATION AND ECONOMICS RELATED?

Debate over the quantifiable value of education has not been limited to recent fears about student achievement. For many years, economists have believed that education makes a positive contribution to national economic and social wellbeing, and there have been attempts to quantify the value of education. The work of economists is helpful to anyone who faces criticism when trying to make a case for adequate and equitable school funding.

Economics Defined

Although it is hard to reduce a complex field such as economics to a brief discussion, it is helpful to think of economics as the study of the production, allocation, and consumption of goods and services for the satisfaction of human needs and wants. Most importantly, economics is interested in goods and services in relation to supply and demand. Rogers and Ruchlin captured it well when they stated, "Economics is concerned with two primary phenomena, desires and resources. The confrontation is brought into being . . . because desires are infinite, whereas resources are finite."[2] Economics in a society where commodities must be purchased, then, means that some goods and services will be scarce or unequally available, whereas others are plentiful and less valued.

This definition is a problem for a capitalist democracy like the United States. Capitalism needs markets, whereas democracy expects equality in the essential commodities that nurture freedom and promote economic productivity and social mobility. The problem arises because education in a capital-

---

2.   Daniel C. Rogers and Hirsch S. Ruchlin, *Economics and Education*, 5 (New York: The Free Press, 1971).

ist democracy must be purchased, raising questions about how to fairly fund and equally distribute educational opportunities to all people in all different circumstances.

Education as an Economic and Social Good

Because economics deals with goods and services and the supply of those commodities to individuals and society, it has a direct relationship to education, which has as its goal the supply of valuable knowledge to the public. Among the most important are that education produces human capital, contributes to economic health, and helps decide the economic and social welfare of nations. These benefits accrue at individual and societal levels. As such, they are essential to knowing whether education is an investment or an expense.

Education and Human Capital

The series of national reports starting in the 1980s on the condition of education served as a reminder of enduring beliefs that education produces human capital. Economists have explored the link between economic prosperity and education, concluding that whereas linkages are not yet fully explained, education and economics are codependent. Leading economists including John Kenneth Galbraith, Milton Friedman, and Theodore Schultz have all found a positive relationship, arguing that historic elements of land, capital, and labor must be expanded to include human capital. Schultz captured this well when he said, "Human capital has the fundamental attributes of the basic economic concept of capital; namely, it is a source of future satisfactions, or of future earnings, or both of them. What makes it human capital is the fact that it becomes an integral part of the person."[3]

Using this view, education clearly takes on real worth. Whereas ownership of land, growth in capital assets, and costs of unskilled labor were the old bases of economics, the addition of human capital sees the costs of unskilled labor as a true cost, whereas the expense of creating skilled workers becomes an investment. Because capital is used to create new wealth, human capital is an important step in knowing whether education is an expense or an investment because creating smarter workers is viewed as a key to economic growth.

Education and National Economic Health

The justification for a capitalist society is the freedom to acquire private wealth by competition in a free market. The justification for a democratic society is based in part on the abuses that occur in a survival-of-the-fittest economy when wealth is allowed to grow unchecked. Thus a capitalist mar-

---

3.   Theodore Schultz, "The Human Capital Approach to Education," in *Economic Factors Affecting the Financing of Education*, ed. Roe L. Johns et al., 31, (Gainesville, FL: National Educational Finance Project, 1970).

ket in a democratic society demands controls to prevent extreme imbalances in wealth. Applied to education, schooling in a free market would favor only those able to buy it. The ultimate test of the idea of education as human capital has occurred in the United States, where one of the most powerful controls has been to distribute education widely so that more people can create a greater store of private wealth (education), and in turn, sell their skills in an open market at a higher price. This restraint on freedom reflects a belief that education results in wide benefits. Rather than the negative effects of competition and high labor costs hurting production, wide distribution of education at public expense has been assumed to yield a stronger economy and better social conditions.

Belief in a link between economics and education has been strong throughout our nation's history, especially in the last century. In 1918, the Commission on Reorganization of Secondary Education declared the need to prepare students for work as one of its *Seven Cardinal Principles.* In 1938, the Educational Policies Commission included economic efficiency among its aims for schools. In 1951, the *Ten Imperative Needs of Youth,* issued by the National Association of Secondary School Principals, gave new emphasis to job training. In 1955, the White House Conference on Education promoted various goals for schools, among which good work habits were prominent. Also in 1955, the U.S. Chamber of Commerce said, "People who have a good education produce more goods, earn more money, buy and consume more goods, read more magazines and newspapers, are more active in civic and national affairs, enjoy a higher standard of living, and in general, contribute more to the economy… ." More recently, the many national reports on education confirmed an ongoing belief in the direct link between economic and social productivity and schooling.

Whether there is proof of a link between education and national economic health seems less arguable when comparing developed and under-developed nations. Few would argue that education, widely dispersed, does not aid economic and social progress. As the World Bank noted, "The emphasis in low income countries is on the development of low-cost basic education. . . . In middle-income countries, where first-level education is already widely available, educational quality is emphasized and with it the expansion of facilities to meet the needs of an increasingly sophisticated economy. . . . As absorptive capacity . . . grows, the priority shifts toward providing higher level technical skills, as well as developing skills in science, technology, information processing, and research."[4] No defense of this claim is needed, as Americans have long recognized that education feeds itself as an industry by creating jobs and feeds the total job market by providing the technology to create more and better products and the consumerism to acquire those products and services. If human capital was a first step in see-

---

4.   Habte Aklilu, *Education and Development: Views from the World Bank* (Washington, DC: World Bank, 1983), 8.

ing the investment represented by education, linking schools and national economic health was a second step because the economy would stumble without the demand education creates for itself.

Education and Individual Benefits

Yet another way of knowing whether education is an investment or an expense rests in examining the individual benefits of education. Individuals are the prime beneficiaries of schooling because others are excluded from direct and equal use of each person's unique skills. Individuals benefit because they enjoy greater social mobility, better pay and higher status, and more cultural opportunities. Benefits spill over to society as well, because salaries are returned to the economy as affluence leads to more active consumerism and higher lifestyles. This leads to other benefits, as better-educated people are healthier, have less unemployment, are more open to change, and work more efficiently.

Individual benefits are dramatic when looking at data on salaries tied to educational level. Figure 2.2 shows that a person with more years of school can expect more and better employment, whereas a person with less education can expect a lifetime of lower returns. The gap is large, as four or more years of college leads to unemployment of only 2.3%, whereas dropping out of high school results in 7.3% unemployment. Although total earnings do not have the same linear relationship because of career choice, Figure 2.2 strikingly shows how education has a powerful impact on employment options and lifetime earnings for individuals.

Social and Economic Efficiencies of Education

Our discussion of "spillover" effects shows that it is illogical to claim that educational opportunity does not benefit all of society. People who claim that education is a commodity that should be free of social controls are claiming that education does not deserve equality of distribution because they see it as solely individual in value. These people would likely agree that a minimum level of schooling for everyone is essential, but they miss a fourth step in knowing if education is an investment or an expense by not seeing that society and the economy would suffer greater costs if it were not for certain efficiencies inherent to public education.

The exclusion principle is the basis for arguing against broad social services and in favor of the view that high spending for schools is inefficient. As with everything, there is a grain of truth here, and it rests in whether social spending (including schools) yields a positive return or whether it merely drains off money to pay for the low achievement scores we saw earlier. This view ignores the facts that social services are meant to prevent even greater social decay and that spending for public aims is actually more efficient because it would fall to charity to pay these costs absent tax support, but that it is inefficient (even impossible) to provide many such services on a charitable basis. A couple of illustrations make this clear. The exclusion principle sees one person as the sole beneficiary of an expenditure or good or service.

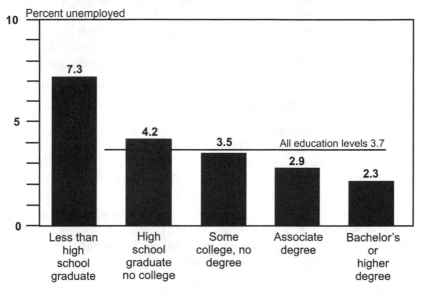

Figure 2.2. Unemployment Rates of Persons 25 Years Old and Older by Highest Level of Education: 2001

SOURCE: U.S. Department of Labor, Bureau of Labor Statistics, Office of Employment and Unemployment Statistics, Current Population Survey, 2001.

Implicit is the idea that exclusion is at least neutral in its impact on others and, importantly, economically efficient for the recipient. In other words, for exclusion to work, depriving others of a benefit cannot result in great harm, and the cost should be attractive to the beneficiary. Highway taxes are a good example of the impracticality arising from a strict application of the exclusion principle. It might be argued that failure to provide public roads does not cause unconscionable harm to others. But even if we accept that doubtful premise, applying the exclusion principle to roads leads to economic *inefficiency* because most people could not provide their own roads because of the prohibitive cost. Analogously, depending on charity to pay the costs of many social services sets up inefficiencies and introduces the unconscionable risk that society would fail to support these services if the force of taxation suddenly were removed. In other words, many services are more efficiently produced in the public sector at a relatively small individual cost, so that small sacrifices by many make up a collective benefit that otherwise would be very difficult to provide and would be enormously missed.

Like many government services, education's efficiencies compete with other ideas in a capitalist democracy. Arguments to privatize schools to improve performance and enhance individual freedoms weigh against proof that education does not neatly fit the exclusion principle. Critics stumble when they claim that students are the sole beneficiaries of schooling because spillover in social mobility, higher pay, socioeconomic status, more employment, cultural opportunities, and other by-products suggest that spending on schools improves wellbeing for everyone. Likewise, a democracy anticipates an informed citizenry; most people could not privately pay for education so that equality among individuals would vary greatly. For many reasons, the benefit of investing in public schools cannot be efficiently gained by any exclusionary mechanism.

Returns on Educational Investment

In Chapter 1, we examined the negative side of spending for education, presenting data showing that critics have had much to complain about when attacking productivity of schools. We admitted that the data are unimpressive: Achievement is lackluster, and it is sensible for taxpayers to ask if pouring more money into schools is wise when alternatives exist.

In this chapter we've taken a different approach, suggesting that whereas school revenues and expenditures are huge, there is a return on investment that achievement data overlook. Our discussion so far has focused on broad concepts, and we should now consider other kinds of studies that have taken a harder look at the cost benefit debate. The field of economics has provided studies of returns on educational investment that can be grouped into at least two kinds. The first group looks at the relationship between education and economic growth, whereas the second examines returns on investment to individuals and society. It is useful to think of the latter as rate-of-return studies.

Education and Economic Growth

We said earlier that Americans have long believed in education's effect on economic prosperity. Although the student achievement literature has been unable to show the level of return that critics desire, a few classic studies have assessed the contribution of school expenditures to economic growth. These studies have generally examined changes in GNP to estimate the impact of education (i.e., the added value of human capital).

Questioning the return on investment in a society that provided about $401 billion in 2001 for public K–12 schools is reasonable. Answering questions of quality with concrete numerical analysis, however, is more difficult. Although economists like to work with discrete variables, they are sometimes forced to settle for less finite estimates. Because no way exists by which to measure exact output of educational investment relative to dollar inputs, economists have estimated residual effects in the economy.

A *residual* effect can be likened to the analogy of a sum and its parts, where a series of values are added to conclude that the whole is greater than the sum of its parts. Although the analogy to economics is not precisely correct, it helps explain the approach taken by some economists in assessing the dynamic contribution of education to the economy. Economics has usually considered economic growth to be a function of changes in land, labor, and volume of physical capital. If a variable changes, production changes as a for-mula response. This means that changes in GNP depend on changes in land, capital, and labor. Where the equation fails is in relation to changes in the "educational stock" of employees (human capital) because labor has not tra-ditionally included a value for worker qualifications. Failure to account for human capital has resulted in an unexplained *residual* effect. In other words, solving the equation results in the analogy of the sum and its parts, as land, labor, and capital sum to *less* than 100% of dynamic increase in GNP, with the residual being human capital.

Studies have supported the idea of residual effects on economic produc-tivity. Schultz argued that people acquire a stock of knowledge and skills that is useless until put to work. As worker knowledge grows, productivity increases. Schultz examined data on the labor force, looking at distribution of education by years of schooling and the cost at each level after adjusting for increases in length of the school year over the last century.[5] He found that the "stock of education" as measured by the cost of producing that same educa-tion had increased from $180 billion (adjusted to 1956 prices) in 1929 to $535 billion in 1957. He also found that only $69 billion in costs could be tied to the 38% growth in size of the labor force. From this, he imputed that the remain-ing $286 billion represented a net increase in the stock of education. At the same time, labor income grew $71 billion beyond where he estimated it would be if earnings had stayed constant at 1929 levels. The $71 billion was termed residual. After annualizing returns to individuals, Schultz held that the increase in education per person from 1929 to 1957 explained 36–70% of residual economic growth. In essence, Schultz argued that the economy was 36–70% better off because of investing in schools.

A second approach is seen in Denison's oft-cited work.[6] He studied the impact of 20 variables in the United States from 1909 to 1957, including changes in worker age, sex, hours, and so on. He calculated increases in labor productivity, holding wages constant, and found a residual of 0.93%, with 0.67% of this amount attributed to education. The net effect found 23% of increased productivity because of schooling. In a later study, Denison showed that increases in education explained one-third of growth in GNP from 1973 to 1981. A third Denison study was even more supportive, in which he examined the economies of nine Western nations, concluding that the value of education is highest for the United States.

5. Theodore Schultz, "Education and Economic Growth," in *Social Forces Influencing American Education. 16th Yearbook of the National Society of Education*, ed. N. B. Henry, 63 (Chicago: University of Chicago Press, 1961).

6. Edward Denison, *The Sources of Economic Growth in the United States and the Alterna-tives Before Us* (New York: Committee for Economic Development, 1962).

Rate-of-Return Studies

The impact of education can also be seen at smaller levels by considering the relative value of schooling at elementary, secondary, and postsecondary levels. These studies have followed two models: calculating the present discounted value of education and individual rates of return for added schooling. Both methods imply that consumer decisions about how much education to buy have an effect on personal income.

The present-discounted-value (PDV) method takes actual present value of schooling and multiplies by a discount rate to estimate future value. The PDV is like a price deflator to hold dollars constant for purchasing power over time. For example, the average teacher salary in 1970 in current dollars was $8,626. By 2003, the figure had risen to $45,822. Although factors like seniority and educational achievement account for some of the increase over time, a large part of the change is because of inflation. Holding prices constant and deflating salaries to the same year permits comparison of true gains or losses. The analogy helps in understanding the PDV method of assessing the worth of education to an individual at some future time.

The individual rate-of-return (IRR) method also has been used. Its advantage rests in not having to predict an accurate discount rate by using a zero interest rate; in other words, what is education worth in *today's* market? The IRR looks at the cost of each level of education compared to benefits at each level. The principle is that the higher the expected income and the lower the cost, the higher the rate of return will be. Figure 2.3 shows data on annual earnings based on dropping out, completing high school, and several levels of college. It shows that for a male, a bachelor's degree results in about 67% more income than for a high school graduate, and about 2.5 times the annual salary of a high school dropout. By these data, the rate of return is persuasive.

Of course, the cost varies for different levels of education. Elementary schooling costs less, if for no other reason than facility costs are lower than for vocational needs in high schools. But there are other costs associated with different levels of education that affect profitability of extra units of schooling. For example, in more advanced nations, child labor is nonexistent. Yet as children grow, the cost of education includes loss of earnings from being in school instead of in the workforce. Similarly, at postsecondary levels, costs are increased by tuition, room and board expenses, and so on. Additionally, more units (years) of education do not yield uncapped earnings because career choice has an effect on income. For example, a teacher with a doctorate degree will not approach the income of a physician, even though the value to society may be equal. In other words, elementary, secondary, and postsecondary education have intrinsic traits affecting the ultimate rate of return.

Only a few studies have tested returns on elementary education. In advanced nations, the logic has been that there is a moral duty here regardless of cost and that some minimum skills are needed for employment. Existing studies have calculated high returns on elementary schooling, mostly be-

Figure 2.3. Median Annual Income of Persons 25 Years Old and Older by Highest Degree Attained and Gender: 2000

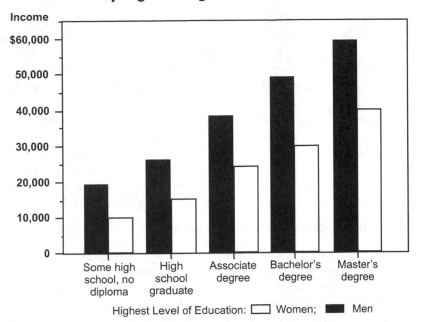

SOURCE: U.S. Department of Commerce, Bureau of the Census, Current Population Reports, Series P-60, "Money Income in the United States: 2000."

cause opportunity costs (foregone earnings) and actual costs (set off against a person gainfully employed) are nearly zero. Hansen found infinite returns,[7] and Hanoch argued for a 100% return.[8] Other studies vary widely; Schultz, rejecting the high return in most studies, held that return on elementary schooling was 35%.[9] Although lower than other studies, Schultz argued that return on elementary schooling is still high because the return on education exceeded returns for investment in physical capital.

More studies have examined returns on secondary schooling. Returns have been lower than for elementary education, mostly because of opportunity costs. Becker studied returns in the twentieth century, finding an IRR for high school graduates of 16% in 1939, 20% in 1949, and 28% in 1958.[10] His estimates were close to Schultz's, who estimated the return on high school at

7. Lee Hansen, "Total and Private Rates of Return to Investment in Schooling," *Journal of Political Economy* 71 (1963): 128–40.

8. Giora Hanoch, "An Economic Analysis of Earnings and Schooling," *Journal of Human Resources* 3 (1967): 310–29.

9. Schultz, "The Human Capital Approach to Education."

10. Gary Becker, *Human Capital: A Theoretical and Empirical Analysis, with Special Reference to Education* (New York: National Bureau of Economic Research, 1964).

25%. Other studies have agreed, with the added note that human capital has grown at the same time that the share of income because of property has fallen.

Returns on postsecondary education are murkier. Career choice has a bearing on earnings, and the point of diminishing returns affects higher levels of education by reaching a point where more school does not lead to more income. There is also an argument that the United States is over-invested in higher education, creating a glut of overqualified persons because the nation's progress toward a professional economy cannot keep up with the supply of college graduates. Postsecondary studies show returns on undergraduate degrees varying by career field, with graduate degrees even more dependent on the chosen field. Yet despite variation, returns on educational investment are sizable because when the options are weighed, history has shown that poorly educated people are left behind in a nation that has steadily escalated its social and economic standards for more than a century.

Education and Socioeconomic Investment

Arguments that many services are best served by public investment are well founded, especially from an efficiency perspective. But other benefits are important too, including freedom, lower crime, less need for other public aid, and enabling socioeconomic mobility. These benefits have led scholars to claim that society supports many such costs as a way to stem an adverse tide, whereas the cost of schools actually helps reverse the tide and pays long-term dividends.

At the most basic level, the greatest return is survival of democracy itself. Democracy may be described as government by consent, with the freedom to decide to be led and to decide for oneself the leaders to be followed. These decisions are not made lightly because they require defenses against abuse: namely, a level of independent thinking and literacy to prevent class-based greed and to foster wise voter behavior. This view has been held by liberals and conservatives alike. Long ago, Adam Smith noted in *The Wealth of Nations* that education is necessary to prevent people from becoming incapable of self-enlightenment and devoid of all charity.[11]

Thomas Jefferson, a great champion of public schools, argued eloquently that the most basic needs of a free people include the ability to discern corruption and make wise choices in leadership, a concept he wrote into the Declaration of Independence:

> That to secure these rights, Governments are instituted among Men, deriving their just powers from the consent of the governed ...whenever any form of government becomes destructive to these ends, it is the right of the people to alter or abolish it....

---

11. Adam Smith, *An Inquiry into the Nature and Causes of the Wealth of Nations* (New York: Modern Library, 1937), 734–35.

The relationship between education and democracy cannot be overestimated, and from these roots flow other benefits as people are empowered to lead productive lives. Much data, for example, point to reduced crime because of education. If the cost of schools is high, the cost of crime is higher because that money could be put to better use. Prison data are alarming—according to the Koch Commission on Crime,[12] in the eight years between 1990 and 1998 the rate of incarceration in the United States grew by 1,708 new inmates per week, although the report claimed that such staggering numbers actually represented a decline because of a get-tough-on-crime posture by states. More recent reports, however, indicate no reprieve, resulting in such data as 4 million ex-convicts currently denied the right to vote and with a staggering 7.7 million persons expected either to be in jail or to have served jail time by the year 2010, with many such convictions being drug-related.[13] Large numbers of offenders are prime candidates for education, as many of those jailed are juveniles. When the cost of education is compared to the price of locking up a child, the loss to society through failure to educate is tragic.

In addition, less need for other aid follows educational investment. Low income is linked to lack of education, and we know that low income is closely associated with welfare, unemployment, and other social programs. In 2003, the federal government spent $21.4 billion (up from $19 billion in the last edition of this text) for food stamps, whereas combined federal and state spending for basic assistance alone exceeded $10 billion during that same year. Even the harshest critics would agree that money is better invested in schools and job training because mopping up schools' failures has been far more costly than spending up front for good schools. Perhaps the greatest accolade to investing in education was stated by Marshall, as he said:

> We may then conclude that the wisdom of expending public and private funds on education is not to be measured by its direct fruits alone....[O]ne new idea, such as Bessemer's chief invention, adds as much to England's productive power as the labour of a hundred thousand men....All this spent during many years in opening the means of...education to the masses would be well paid for if it called out one more Newton or Darwin, Shakespeare or Beethoven.[14]

Recent Economic Thought

The views of classical economics have held unquestioned for many years. In fact, the influence of theorists such as Schultz, Denison, and Becker drove

---

12. *The Falling Crime Rate. White Paper Report* (Koch Crime Institute, April 1998).
13. "U.S. Notches World's Highest Incarceration Rate," *The Christian Science Monitor*, August 18, 2003.
14. Alfred Marshall, "Education and Invention," in *Perspectives on the Economics of Education*, ed. C. S. Benson (1963), 83.

development of many governmental policies by justifying investment in schools at very high levels of government. Although classical economics never prevented criticism of schools from flourishing in America, it was a force that spurred spending on education, including reforms such as President Lyndon Johnson's Great Society during the 1960s.

The Coleman Report in 1966, however, damaged the optimism that had long driven investment in schools. Infamous for its doubts on the ability to overcome the effects of social and economic conditions, the Coleman study gave rise to a mindset that questioned the very foundations of the economics of education. In fact, the Coleman study was the impetus for the harsh criticism of schools that arose over the next decades, as an avalanche of calls for reform followed after the *Nation at Risk* report released in 1983 by the National Commission on Excellence in Education. Timing for reform was ripe, as the era of production function studies in the 1970s had yielded little data in support of classical economics, at least in the way that critics wanted data showing continual achievement gains, and the result was an angry cry for schools to justify their costs.

In large part, the result led to today's clamor for parental choice in schooling, for state-supported standards-based education reform, and the most recent iteration of alarmist rhetoric in the form of No Child Left Behind Act of 2001 (NCLB)—elements of a market ideology that expects an efficient return on investment in schools and that calls on the economic benefit of education to defend its platform. Sometimes called the New Institutional Economics, much reform in the nation today is based not only in outrage that schools are not better producers for achievement's own sake, but also in a view that changes can be made in schools by paying attention to market-based strategies that seek to maximize a cost-benefit equation. The notion states that schools have had a long time to prove their worth and that although society is ahead of where it would be had it not invested in education, schools are highly inefficient and can be improved by heeding the same consumer preferences that drive markets in the economy. The issue is both an all-out attack on school spending and an all-out argument that calculated investment can weed out unprofitable parts of the current educational model by forcing survival or death by accountability for fiscal and academic performance—in sum, a view that the entrenched school system must be torn down and rebuilt.

The New Economics applied to schools takes root in the larger culture of government scrutiny over the last century. Galvin[15] traced the issues involved in the New Economics as he described the history of regulatory reform in markets and in education, making a parallel that what has happened in the larger context of government is now being applied to schools as

---

15. Patrick Galvin, "Organizational Boundaries, Authority, and School District Organization," in *Balancing Local Control and State Responsibility for K–12 Education. 2000 Yearbook of the American Education Finance Association*, eds. Neil Theobald and Betty Malen (New York: Eye on Education, 2000).

well. The history of economic reform has ebbed and flowed, beginning with the Interstate Commerce Commission in the late 1880s, which was established to prevent monopolies and price fixing in a free market. Galvin traces this record of fitful federal control, noting the differing tides of opinion. The Depression in the 1930s introduced the idea that economies of scale should favor some monopolies (e.g., government services) to maximize public efficiency. A backlash followed, though, in the 1970s as antigovernment views gained popularity as the controls of big government were thought to hinder market efficiencies, especially during the severe economic recession in the last quarter of the twentieth century. It is well known that bad times cause tight purse strings, and the outrage of *Nation at Risk* was timed to the flow of economic thought that had begun to call for less government.

In the larger context, the New Economics was no less than a call to review the balance of power in government, with sympathy for market efficiencies and with implications for spending on education. Much of the point of the new economics is to evaluate who is best able to provide services, a question asserting that efficiency is met when consumers are happy. This view argues that the role of government may be only to set standards and protect consumers against abuse, allowing consumers to drive the rest of what happens, and implying that government is not the only or best way to deliver some services, including education. It has been in this context that demands for school choice and criticism of academic achievement have flourished.

The New Economics has become pervasive in today's government, although not entirely consistent with all governmental goals and behaviors. In a longstanding devolution spanning more than two decades beginning with former president Ronald Reagan, politicians have raced to see who will be known as the leader in dismantling big government. Logically, education has been affected. Although it is unlikely that schools will ever lose all public funds, and whereas claims are made that schools have recently received an infusion of new federal money in support of NCLB reforms, an economic model that pays slavish homage to consumer preferences (and a federal act that includes school choice in its title[16]) has huge implications for how investment in schools is seen and is responsible for much of the skepticism about spending for schools that is now evident in some sectors. In a bold new economic era, the federal government and the individual states have seized control of educational decision-making,[17] whereas providing only modestly greater funds as spending in constant dollars has not kept full pace with earlier decades. Local control of schools, by some accounts, has diminished as government has filled the void of educational accountability, demanding

---

16. Public Law 107–110 107th Congress. An Act to close the achievement gap with accountability, flexibility, and choice, so that no child is left behind (January 8, 2002).

17. See generally the *2000 Yearbook of the American Education Finance Association*, arguing that the politics of reform have eclipsed reform itself, with states largely gaining control of education in the absence of a strong federal presence and wresting control away from local communities.

sweeping reforms in exchange for continued funding, both from local tax-payers and to qualify for federal funds under the reforms demanded by NCLB—a new definition of devolution in government that wrests control of schools away from locals while simultaneously forcing the costs of compliance downward.

The view of economics and education has changed as we have moved away from blind faith in returns on investment in schools. Society today demands alternatives, and citizens are more aggressive in articulating their views and in questioning defenses for school spending. A comprehensive view of funding schools in a new millennium demands an appreciation for how far we have come in terms of revenue and expenditure growth, but it also demands awareness that criticism is increasing and will only soften when schools can compete in a new market ideology where clients demand a better bottom line. The market has changed, raising the question of how schools have historically been financed and where it may all be headed.

WHAT IS THE STRUCTURE OF SCHOOL GOVERNANCE IN AMERICA?

Americans who have grown up with the vast educational programs of the twentieth century may be surprised to learn that formal mandated public education is a recent event. Yet even ancient civilizations often had well planned education systems for their day. For instance, the Greeks saw education as the cornerstone of democracy, arguing that the mark of a free man was the ability to read, write, think, and speak. Americans today would likely argue that the Declaration of Independence provided an entitlement to education when it declared that the right to life, liberty, and pursuit of happiness are secure only in a nation governed by consent of an intelligent people. Surely, today's American would say, the nation's most precious document has since the founding of the nation promised everyone the educational wherewithal for self-governance.

Whether that guarantee was ever intended is not clear, but it is true that education resembling how we know schools today did *not* exist prior to the nineteenth century. This is not to say there were no schools, but the current nature of education is in vivid contrast to the historic reality of schooling in the United States.

Brief Historical Roots of American Education

Only a cursory knowledge of American history is needed to picture the struggles of settlers in a vast and hostile environment. Simply surviving the harsh climate and conquering a new way of life was hard enough without coping with the problems of setting up extensive government services. In the earliest days of the nation, little in the way of education occurred because settlers were too busy feeding themselves and ensuring their safety. And there was little motivation for schools, as the skills needed to survive had little to do with books.

Whenever schooling did occur in early America, it was the exclusive province of the home or church. But a concern for education was evident early on, as the first school law was passed by the Massachusetts Legislature in 1642, requiring towns to see if children were being taught to read and understand religion and to learn a vocation. Concern was sustained in 1647 when the Ye Old Deluder Satan Act was passed in that same state to strengthen the teaching of morality to children by reading the Bible. As the colonies grew, the idea of required education for morality gained popularity as Connecticut, Maine, New Hampshire, and Vermont all passed similar laws by 1720.

As civilizations move beyond survival, they seek higher order goals such as creating formal education systems. Toward the end of the eighteenth century, interest in formal schools had taken shape in most colonies. The War of Independence in 1776 had been hard-fought, and the reasons for the war brought about new concern in a young nation that had chafed under British rule. Although education for morality had been the aim of early school laws, new concern emerged based on a call for enlightened government to preserve the freedoms that had first led to war. Thomas Jefferson, the champion of liberty, was among the loudest voices calling for an end to ignorance through education for the common people. In a radical shift from centuries of elitist political control, Jefferson argued that ordinary citizens must be able to elect good leaders and keep a close guard on their government. These skills, he said, could only be developed by education for the commoner—a new idea in a world inexperienced in self-determination.

Despite a need to foster morality and self-rule, government-based education made slow progress for many years after the Revolutionary War. Caught up in westward expansion, there was no time for the luxury of schooling. Nor was there much sentiment, as liberal education had left a bad taste in the mouths of colonists whose experiences had associated education with aristocracy. For the majority, moral and economic education could be taught at home. In the mind of the colonist, morally literate and politically wise voters were a luxury that had to wait because liberal education was both useless and undesirable.

Survivalism and expansionism, however, did not last forever. Not everyone wanted to move west, and some were too poor to go. With droves of immigrants landing in America, great cities sprang up in the early 1800s. These groups were both the origin and result of industrialization of the new nation because they provided the labor on which to build great industries. As cities grew, more industry was attracted, fueling a need for more labor, which caused cities to grow again. As the cycle fed itself, industry began to recognize that not all growth was good because skills were lacking in the vast throngs of people seeking work. The response was to call for a new role for education by demanding training for vocational skills. Although industrialists argued about whether education solved a need or whether it increased labor costs, the effect was to add economics to the growing role played by education.

Rapid growth, especially in great cities, had the effect of accelerating demand for schools. Although the nation had opened its doors believing that rapid growth would aid settlement and expansion, the dizzying speed was unexpected. Around 1840, immigration skyrocketed out of control. From 1820–1840, the nation grew by only 751,000, while from 1840–1850 more than 1.7 million people entered the country. Immigration continued to soar, as from 1840–1900 more than 16 million new people came to the United States. The nation was ill equipped to deal with the influx, and problems were acute as immigrants clustered in cities and were often unskilled. Problems worsened as rural Americans migrated to industrial centers, too, either because they had tired of frontier life or were starved or driven from the land. From 1820–1900, the population grew from about 9.6 million to 76 million. As a result, cities were beset with problems of poverty and illiteracy.

Solutions had to be found. Educating for morality and self-government had to be upheld, argued leaders such as Horace Mann and Henry Barnard, but educating everyone for economic productivity was needed too. Under the leadership of Mann and Barnard, the beginnings of a uniform public school system emerged in the Common School Movement. Spurred by population growth, the Common School Movement reached its peak between 1840 and 1880, driven by education for economic productivity. But the movement held a fourth thread that would imbed itself in the national psychology of America. Because it had its roots in people who had fled horrific conditions in search of the American dream, the movement embraced a commitment not only to morality, self-determination, and economics, but also the seeds of loyalty to justice and equality.

The Common Schools Movement was nothing short of miraculous and laid a basis for refinements that would shape the nature and scope of American education. One refinement forever altered the face of schools. Although much of the nation's prosperity was brought about by a favorable climate for commerce, an unsavory aspect of industrialization before 1900 was the use of child labor. The United States had followed the European practice of scandalous profiteering by exploiting children, but with industrialization came labor unions, which in the last half of the nineteenth century worked to improve wages of adults with the side effect of promoting child labor laws. The Common Schools Movement was jointly aided because child labor laws had the effect of removing children from the workforce, making schools a ready caretaker.

By the dawn of the twentieth century, public schools only dimly resembled colonial education. But although resemblance was small, the roots were deep. Education for morality had moved from religion to humanism based on the views of social reformers, but the expectation that schools would build character remained. Likewise, as the nation won its freedom, education for self-governance held strong to help preserve democracy. As industry and commerce grew, education for economics was hastened by crises of immigration, setting the stage for the alarms and calls for reform that critics would issue in the twentieth century. By the dawn of the new century, schools had been given a key role in a nation that had become vast and diverse—a role reformers struggle with today as the wars over morality, democracy, economics, and equality still rage.

Development of School Organization in America

Not surprisingly, the history of the educational system in the United States has had a strong influence on school governance structure. Within the generalities of growth we just noted were other distinct trends over the last 200 years. For instance, the tendency to cluster on the basis of religious, political, or ethnic heritage led to strong views about education and how it should be governed. In New England, early attitudes led to a religious state with strong state regulation and taxation for schools. The middle colonies, including New Jersey, Pennsylvania, and Maryland, saw settlement by many religious groups that allowed for little sectarian control. Still another model arose as other middle colonies and the South were sympathetic to a view that public schools were for paupers, a view rejecting state control or tax support. Such attitudes were deeply rooted and are evident today, as geographic regions of the nation are notable for the prevalence or absence of private schools and where state school funding schemes may show sympathy for those same views.

It is not surprising that the diversity making up settlement and westward expansion led to fragmented educational designs. But given an ardent history in America where religious and political freedoms demand a lack of central control, it is not surprising that school systems could develop without a common organizational scheme. But above all, resistance to government control was especially fierce, leaving scholars to decry the problems of tracing educational history. Katz captured the tension well when he noted:

> The conflicts between the democratic localists and the bureaucrats often assumed the atmosphere of an undeclared guerrilla war of sabotage and resistance, as local school districts refused to comply with state regulation and parents refused to comply with the state's representative, the teacher. Insofar as most of the resistance came from inarticulate people, it is the hardest and most maddening aspect of nineteenth century educational history to document. That it existed is, however, beyond doubt, as the frustrated testimony of local and state reformers testifies in almost every document they wrote.[18]

Although reformers tried to impose a standard educational system, many years passed before their work yielded the design we see today. As the population center of the nation moved westward, political preferences

---

18. M. Katz, "From Voluntarism to Bureaucracy in American Education," in *Power and Ideology in Education*, eds. Jeremy Karabel and A.H. Halsey, 394 (New York: Oxford University Press, 1977).

formed as people settled in, formed communities, and built schools. Intolerant attitudes pushed dissidents to move on when local traditions did not satisfy their desires. Aided by long distances to school because of sparsely settled land, the result was often the creation of countless thousands of tiny schools serving equally tiny populations. Although there is no record of the exact number of schools in early America, scholars have complained that the disunity of modern school systems is likely a result of fierce isolationism during the nation's growth era. The sentiment was captured by Henry Morrison, a school finance scholar in the early twentieth century, as he referred to modern educational organization as "late New England colonial...a little republic at every crossroads."

Although the greatest number of school districts in the nation at any one time is not known, records give a sense of the size. Figure 2.4 (pp. 41–42) shows the number of schools and school districts from 1869–2002, making several points. First, most citizens can see schools in their communities today that seem unreasonably close to each other, but hark back to a time when travel was hard, making neighborhood schools a necessity. Second, in almost every earlier time each small town had its own school, a truly vast number given all the towns that have lived and died. Third, the number of school districts has been far greater than any other unit of government because school district boundaries in many states are not contiguous with other governments such as counties. Fourth, whereas no one knows how many school districts existed before the turn of the twentieth century, the number must have been enormous because it likely exceeded the 119,001 districts existing in 1938. Finally, the relationship between growing state control and the number of districts is clear, as the more than 119,000 districts in 1938 fell to only 14,559 in 2001—a number that includes the loss of 300 school districts since the last edition of this text!

Although education has changed by closing thousands of school districts over the years, change has not always resulted in standardization. The U.S. Constitution has allowed for wide variation by leaving control of schools to the individual states. States have responded by creating systems differing greatly in structure, operation, control, and support. The effect has been to create an image of local control, although our earlier discussion showed new evidence that local control is losing out as states have seized a reform agenda over the last several decades. Education is state-specific in many ways, and vast differences between and within states are found in Figure 2.5 (p. 43), which shows the large number of districts within the 50 states as late as 2001. Although geography in larger states may account for higher numbers of districts, the logic is weak because physically smaller states sometimes have some of the higher numbers of school districts. Of those states with more than 500 districts, Michigan, Missouri, New Jersey, Ohio, Oklahoma, and Pennsylvania are not physically large compared to California and Texas. Although

(Text continues on page 43.)

Figure 2.4. Number of Public School Districts 1870–2002

School Year	Public School Districts	Total: All Schools	Schools with Elementary Grades		Schools with Secondary Grades
			Total	One-Teacher	
1869–70	—	116,312	—	—	—
1879–80	—	178,122	—	—	—
1889–90	—	224,526	—	—	—
1899–1900	—	248,279	—	—	—
1909–10	—	265,474	—	212,448	—
1919–20	—	271,319	—	187,948	—
1929–30	—	248,117	238,306	148,712	23,930
1931–32	—	245,941	—	143,445	—
1933–34	—	242,929	236,236	138,542	24,714
1935–36	—	237,816	—	130,708	—
1937–38	119,001	229,394	221,660	121,178	25,467
1939–40	117,108	226,762	—	113,600	—
1941–42	—	222,660	—	107,692	—
1945–46	101,382	—	160,227	86,563	24,314
1947–48	94,926	—	146,760	75,096	25,484
1949–50	83,718	—	128,225	59,652	24,542
1951–52	71,094	—	123,763	50,742	23,746
1953–54	63,057	—	110,875	42,865	25,637
1955–56	54,859	—	104,427	34,964	26,046
1957–58	47,594	—	95,446	25,341	25,507
1959–60	40,520	—	91,853	20,213	25,784
1961–62	35,676	—	81,910	13,333	25,350
1963–64	31,705	—	77,584	9,895	26,431
1965–66	26,983	—	73,216	6,491	26,597
1967–68	22,010	—	70,879	4,146	27,011
1970–71	17,995	—	65,800	1,815	25,352
1973–74	16,730	—	65,070	1,365	25,906
1975–76	16,376	88,597	63,242	1,166	25,330

School Year	Public School Districts	Total: All Schools	Schools with Elementary Grades		Schools with Secondary Grades
			Total	One-Teacher	
1976–77	16,271	—	62,644	1,111	25,378
1978–79	16,014	—	61,982	1,056	24,504
1979–80	15,929	87,004	—	—	—
1980–81	15,912	85,982	61,069	921	24,362
1982–83	15,824	84,740	59,656	798	23,988
1983–84	15,747	84,178	59,082	838	23,947
1984–85	—	84,007	58,827	825	23,916
1985–86	—	—	—	—	—
1986–87	15,713	83,455	60,784	763	23,389
1987–88	15,577	83,248	59,754	729	23,841
1988–89	15,376	83,165	60,176	583	23,638
1989–90	15,367	83,425	60,699	630	23,461
1990–91	15,358	84,538	61,340	617	23,460
1991–92	15,173	84,578	61,739	569	23,248
1992–93	15,025	84,497	62,225	430	23,220
1993–94	14,881	85,393	62,726	442	23,379
1994–95	14,772	86,221	63,572	458	23,668
1995–96	14,766	87,125	63,961	474	23,793
1996–97	14,841	88,223	64,785	487	24,287
1997–98	14,805	89,508	65,859	476	24,802
1998–99	14,891	90,874	67,183	463	25,797
1999–2000	14,928	92,012	68,173	423	26,407
2000–01	14,859	93,273	69,697	411	27,090
2001–02	14,559	94,112	70,516	408	27,468

SOURCE: U.S. Department of Education, NCES. Digest of Education Statistics 2002. Washington, DC: 2003.

Figure 2.5. Number of School Districts by State, 2001–2002

State	Districts	State	Districts	State	Districts
United States	14,559	Kentucky	176	Ohio	662
Alabama	128	Louisiana	66	Oklahoma	543
Alaska	53	Maine	282	Oregon	198
Arizona	323	Maryland	24	Pennsylvania	501
Arkansas	312	Massachusetts	350	Rhode Island	36
California	986	Michigan	554	South Carolina	89
Colorado	178	Minnesota	380	South Dakota	176
Connecticut	166	Mississippi	152	Tennesee	138
Delaware	19	Missouri	524	Texas	1,040
District of Columbia	1	Montana	452	Utah	40
Florida	67	Nebraska	555	Vermont	292
Georgia	180	Nevada	17	Virginia	137
Hawaii	1	New Hampshire	178	Washington	296
Idaho	114	New Jersey	603	West Virginia	55
Illinois	893	New Mexico	89	Wisconsin	433
Indiana	294	New York	703	Wyoming	48
Iowa	371	North Carolina	121		
Kansas	304	North Dakota	222		

SOURCE: U.S. Department of Education, National Center for Education Statistics, The Common Core of Data, "Local Education Agency Universe Survey," 2000–01 and 2001–02 (April 2003).

transportation also might account for some small districts, the logic again is not strong as most states have many small attendance centers in close proximity.

The "little republic at every crossroads" has disappeared from American life, but the struggle over the purpose of schools has endured—a struggle not only over the aims of education and about who is in control, but also about who is responsible for education's costs, and at what level it should be funded.

FROM WHERE DO SCHOOLS
DERIVE FISCAL SUPPORT?

Although we have looked only briefly at the link between economics and schools and the development of school organization, it is easy to see that our history has a connection to how education is funded. Fiscal support for schools has followed a hard path marked by uncertainty about who should bear the costs. Although education has long interested federal, state, and local governments, the types and amounts of support from each have varied. In fact, how education is funded today is a function of how federal, state, and local governments have accepted (or denied) responsibility for schools.

Federal Support for Schools

If we were to ask anyone on the street about the extent of federal involvement in funding education, we would likely get an unsure response. But most people would say that even if the amount of federal support is questionable, the federal government has had a pervasive impact on schools. These answers would correctly reflect the federal government's role in education, as it indeed has exercised great influence in various ways.

Beginning with the Northwest Ordinance of 1787 making a survey of lands and granting the sixteenth section of every township for education, the federal government embarked on a three-fold mission of aiding schools in the name of national interest. One thrust was to enhance national defense. A second thrust was to assist higher education. A third thrust related to economic and social justice through educational programs. An additional, but indirect, thrust has been by way of appointments to federal judgeships, which have resulted in rulings on lawsuits affecting schools. These thrusts have often overlapped, so that the federal role has been greater than otherwise would have been true.

Although scholars often advocate a stronger federal hand in education, they agree on why the federal role has been limited. Many founding fathers opposed a national government, and even Alexander Hamilton, virtually the lone sympathizer of federalism at the Constitutional Convention in 1787, did not argue for a strong federal education role. Resistance to central government was so high that only two years after the Constitution was ratified, Congress passed a set of amendments, known as the Bill of Rights, with profound impact on education. The Tenth Amendment was the most important to education because its curbs on federalism spoke clearly to the framers' intent by saying, "The powers not delegated to the United States by the Constitution, nor prohibited by it to the States, are reserved to the States respectively, or to the people." With these words, the doctrine of sovereign limits was formed, so that the federal government was *forbidden* from a direct role in education because the Constitution is silent on education—that is, education is, by default, a state responsibility.

Although the die was cast making education a state function, Congress has managed a long history of influence on schools through other authority and indirect persuasion. Other authority has been derived in two ways. The first has been through the Powers of Congress in Article 1 of the Constitution, which requires Congress to provide a strong national defense—a duty that Congress has used to direct large sums of money to education. The second way has been by virtue of creative interpretation of Article 1, Section 8, wherein rests the General Welfare Clause, which reads that Congress shall have power "...to lay and collect taxes, duties, imposts and excises, [and] to pay the debts and provide for the common defense and general welfare of the United States." National defense has been an easy way for Congress to become involved in education, but more importantly, the General Welfare Clause has been construed by Congress and the courts to allow broad federal interest in schools, particularly in the social and economic justice arena. Aiding that path has been Congress's indirect influence, as it has used persuasive ways such as withholding federal funds from programs unrelated to schools unless states embrace federal education goals.

Federalism and Defense Education

Education for defense has a long history, with formal beginnings generally marked by establishment of the U.S. Military Academy in 1802. Designed to train military leaders, the academy gave rise to other defense colleges, with the Naval Academy in 1845, the Coast Guard Academy in 1876, and the Air Force Academy in 1954. The Reserve Officer Training Corps (ROTC) also was created at major universities so that future leaders could link civilian education with military training. Other aid followed, some of which was meant to enhance defense and other to help veterans reenter civilian life.

Although a full list of federal interests in defense education is unneeded, a sample gives the flavor and breadth. In 1918, the Vocational Rehabilitation Act provided disabled veterans with job training, and similar aid to World War II veterans was given in 1943 in the form of Public Law 78–16. In 1944, Congress created the Serviceman's Readjustment Act, known as the G.I. Bill (PL 78–346), providing educational benefits to millions of servicemen. In 1941, a change to the Lanham Act gave federal aid to construct and operate schools in areas impacted by federal facilities. In 1950, Congress passed PL 81–815 and PL 81–874, which enhanced this aid, a program that still sends millions of dollars to local school districts that have lost tax base to military installations. Immediately after World War II, the military established American schools overseas for the children of soldiers in foreign lands. These schools continue to operate as Department of Defense Schools (DODS).

Some of the largest outlays for defense education were sparked by cold wars and the technology race. In 1950, Congress created the National Science Foundation, which served defense by training math and science teachers. In 1958, the National Defense Education Act (NDEA) under PL 85–865 was enacted to further improve education in math, science, and foreign language in response to the launch of the Soviet satellite Sputnik. The NDEA also provided higher education loans and job training for defense occupations. More recently, PL 95–525 extended the G.I. bill to persons entering the service after 1985. Many other programs are typified by such laws as the Education for Economic Security Act of 1984 (PL 98–377), reflecting new thinking on defense in the modern world—an interest that continues still as typified by The National Defense Authorization Act passed in 2000 under PL 106–398.

Federalism and Higher Education

Aiding higher education has been a close corollary of federal defense. Generally, there is an attempt to separate federal interest in general higher education, with the debut of the federal government in nonmilitary higher education marked by the Morrill Act in 1862, establishing agricultural and mechanical colleges. The Morrill Act made land grants or direct payments to all states. A second Morrill Act followed in 1890, and in some instances these schools became the land grant universities of their respective states, with missions of research, teaching, and service in a practical tradition.

Federal interest in higher education did not end with the Morrill Acts. A few key acts underscore extensive federal activity. The 1935 Bankhead Jones Act (PL 74–320) made grants to states for agricultural experiment stations, a program that spilled over into K–12 schools as the Agricultural Adjustment Act (PL 74–320) of 1935 authorizing commodity supports, which later developed into school milk and lunch programs. The 1950 Housing Act (PL 81–475) authorized loans for construction of college housing. Likewise, the Higher Education Facilities Act of 1963 (PL 88–204) authorized aid for classrooms, libraries, laboratories, and other facilities.

With the vast social reforms of the 1960s, the federal government threw itself headlong into various aids and entitlements under the Civil Rights Act of 1964 (PL 88–352), some of which targeted higher education. The Civil Rights Act granted aid for in-service training in higher education, especially dealing with desegregation. Other grants such as the Health Professional Educational Assistance Amendments (PL 89–290) authorized scholarships to needy students; similarly, the Higher Education Act of 1965 (PL 89–329) gave grants for community service programs and teacher training, and created the National Teacher Corps and many graduate fellowships. Such programs were often aimed at disadvantaged populations. By 2002, federal investment in higher education was large, as Congress was providing nearly $23 billion to higher education exclusive of research support. Although K–12 education has been left to the states, the federal government has been able to support higher education aggressively.

Federalist Justice and Education

Federal interest in economic and social justice has not been perfectly separable from other federal interests, but it has been the most pervasive and sustained of all federal goals for education. Because of the Tenth Amendment's silence on education, the overlap between thrusts also has been most apparent here, as Congress has had to be creative to exert influence on schools. The legal basis for federal intervention rests in the General Welfare

Clause, which has been held to grant broad powers up to the point of free Congressional will unless overturned by a court. In *United States v. Butler*,[19] the Supreme Court ruled that the General Welfare Clause could be broadly construed unless Congress acts arbitrarily—a difficult judgment that must be made on a case-by-case basis. A further test came in *Helvering v. Davis*,[20] as the Court held that the General Welfare Clause need not be confined to constitutional framers' intent, but could shift with needs of the nation.

Social justice has long been at the core of federal education goals. *Brown v. Board of Education* (1954) changed the fundamental nature of schools by finding that segregated schools deny equal opportunity. But it was not until the Civil Rights Act of 1964 that serious federal entry into education began. The events that followed would have a lasting effect by sparking a massive influx of federal aid to a variety of programs aimed at fairness in the nation's schools.

Although again the list of federal interests is vast, a few are highlighted here. The Civil Rights Act of 1964 channeled significant aid to public schools. Smaller programs followed, including the 1965 Disaster Relief Act (PL 89–313), the 1968 Handicapped Children's Early Education Assistance Act (PL 90–538), and the 1970 Elementary and Secondary Education Assistance Programs extension (PL 91–230). However, two Congressional acts especially accounted for altering the federal relationship to schools in the form of the Elementary and Secondary Education Act (ESEA) of 1965 (PL 89–910), and the Education of the Handicapped Act in 1976 (PL 94–142).

One of Congress's greatest plunges into social activism through schools came with the ESEA. Much of the ESEA was aimed toward disadvantaged children because it was an outgrowth of the Civil Rights Act. ESEA made grants to elementary and secondary school programs for low-income children and provided library resource funds, textbooks, and money for other materials. ESEA also aided educational centers, strengthened state education agencies, and provided funds for research and training. The original ESEA had more than 40 entitlements under five titles, each addressing specific interests of Congress.

In fiscal outlays, the most far-reaching provisions of ESEA were found in Title I and were designed to provide supplementary services to low income and culturally disadvantaged children. Children could qualify if they met certain criteria, such as the $2,000 family income. Entire schools could qualify for Title I status if the school met threshold numbers of qualifying children in a single school. Schools qualified on three criteria: number of low-income families, number of children with Aid to Families with Dependent Children (AFDC), and a formula taking into account the statewide expenditure per pupil. Title I grew rapidly from $746.9 million in 1965 to its peak of $3.005 billion in 1980. In 1981, Congress repealed the ESEA in response to President Reagan's efforts to streamline the bureaucracy and to reverse erosion of state

---

19. 56 S. Ct. 312 (1936).
20. 57 S. Ct. 904 (1937).

control that had occurred under an activist Congress. In 1982, Congress passed the Education Consolidation and Improvement Act (ECIA), which continued ESEA but with a different effect. ECIA restructured federal involvement: For example, Title I continued as Chapter 1, but many other programs were collapsed. Chapter 1 changed, too, as more local discretion was given in a block grant system. More than 40 other programs were collapsed into Chapter 2, whereas new provisions relating to administration were made under Chapter 3, which reduced the role of the federal government and returned many powers to the states. ECIA did allow several other programs to remain freestanding, including Vocational Education, Education of the Handicapped, National School Lunch, Higher Education, Impact Aid, Title VII Bilingual Education, and Title IX Women's Educational Equity.

Congress also plunged deeper into justice by enacting PL 94–142, Education of the Handicapped Act (EHA) in 1976. EHA was the result of intensive litigation to ensure the rights of handicapped children to free and appropriate programs. The challenge that drove PL 94–142 was the 1972 lawsuit in PARC.[21] Although many states provided some special services, provisions were minimal, permissive, or nonexistent. PARC was a good test of the issue because the state of Pennsylvania provided services to *some* children but excluded "uneducable and untrainable" children. PARC was decided for plaintiffs, unleashing a series of lawsuits aimed at forcing states to provide special services to all children.

Partially in response to PARC, Congress enacted the EHA. States failing to provide services were denied federal aid to schools. In the year of EHA's passage, Congress granted $300 million to help defray special education costs and authorized legislation allowing Congress to provide up to 40% of all special education costs. Although federal support has never come close to the 40% goal, federal aid and pressure by courts have discouraged states from refusing to provide services. Special education laws have undergone periodic revision,[22] including changes to the Individuals with Disabilities

---

21. *Pennsylvania Association of Retarded Children v. Pennsylvania (PARC)*, 343 F. Supp. 279 (1972).

22. Although federal aid to special education has increased, it has been accompanied by more costs and new mandates. Due to EHA, the number of children served has increased greatly. Special education has become marked by powerful lobbies pushing for new services. Congress itself has raised the bar; e.g., the 1986 EHA amendments, Early Intervention Programs for Infants and Toddlers (PL 99–457), extended rights to 3- to 5-year-olds and made new provisions for early intervention for handicapped children age 0–2. Congress also passed PL 101–476, Individuals with Disabilities Education Act (IDEA), in 1990, as well as other laws with implications for special education such as the 1990 Americans with Disabilities Act (PL 101–336) requiring access for handicapped persons to public buildings, employment, and telecommunications.

Act (PL 105–17) in 1997 that have been termed the most significant since its inception.[23] By 2002, federal aid had reached $11.7 billion.

Federal interest in schools has continued to the present day (Figure 2.6, p. 50). Recent laws have included the Civil Rights Act of 1991 (PL 102–166), the 1994 passage of Goals 2000: Educate America Act (PL 103–227), the School- To-Work Opportunities Act of 1994 (PL 103–239), the Safe Schools Act of 1994 (part of PL 103–227), and the Improving America's Schools Act (PL 103–382), which revised the ESEA, and more. Topping the list of most recent laws having significant impact, of course, is the No Child Left Behind Act (PL 107–110) in 2001, which reauthorized the ESEA of 1965 and incorporated federal mandates in the areas of testing, accountability, early reading, and parental choice. These efforts show that whereas the federal government has no direct duty to education, it has taken great interest and at times has even commanded a central role. The only reasonable conclusion is that if the services supported in part by the federal government were funded entirely by local or state units of government, the impact would be significant.

State Support for Schools

Although people may be largely unaware of the federal role in education's support, they are far more certain that the state is heavily involved in funding schools. Much of that view is accurate and stems from the highly visible role played by states in the overall school funding scheme. In the absence of a federal duty to education, states have had to create aid plans to support the services demanded by citizens or else tell local communities that they must rely on local taxation to pay for schools. The inequalities of local ability to pay have been so great, however, that most states have assumed a central responsibility for education over the last century.

Education as the State's Responsibility

Our earlier discussion of the Tenth Amendment to the U.S. Constitution laid out reasons why states have had to accept responsibility for education's costs. Although this has become an accepted fact in recent times, it has been a hard battle that has caused a huge and still unsettled shift in the balance of power and expenditure ratio between local and state governments. The interdependency of federal, state, and local governments is a striking feature of Figure 2.7, where it is seen that, on a national average, states have moved from funding only about 16.5% of costs in 1920 to nearly 50% in 2001.

---

23. Deborah Verstegen, "Finance Provisions under the Individuals with Disabilities Education Act 1997 Amendments," *Educational Considerations* 28, no.1 (2000): 32–38.

Figure 2.6. Federal On-Budget Funds for
Education by Agency: Fiscal Year 2002

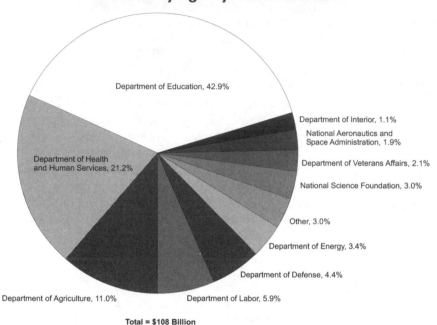

Department of Education, 42.9%

Department of Interior, 1.1%

National Aeronautics and
Space Administration, 1.9%

Department of Veterans Affairs, 2.1%

National Science Foundation, 3.0%

Department of Health
and Human Services, 21.2%

Other, 3.0%

Department of Energy, 3.4%

Department of Defense, 4.4%

Department of Agriculture, 11.0%   Department of Labor, 5.9%

Total = $108 Billion

SOURCE: U.S. Office of Management and Budget, Budget of the U.S. Government,
Fiscal Year 2003; and National Science Foundation, Federal Funds for Research and
Development, Fiscal Years 2000, 2001, and 2002.

In many ways, Figure 2.7 (pp. 51–52) is a terse summary of constitutional
duty to schools that draws three distinct lines of historical change. First, as
there are only three levels of government able to share school costs, it follows
that all costs fall in some ratio to this triad. Second, as a direct federal role is
forbidden, the federal branch cannot assume the lion's share. Third, because
local ability to pay varies greatly, and because the Constitution grants plenary powers to states, a major portion of school costs has fallen to the states.
Although slow to accept this, states have increasingly assumed greater proportions of these costs out of necessity and also because the courts have
found a legal duty to fund education arising out of individual state constitutional provisions.

The changing nature of federal, state, and local partnership is laid out in
Figure 2.7. Three observations are clear. First, although the federal share has
always been the smallest and although the percentage paid by the federal
government has wavered over time, it has still provided meaningful revenue
to schools, increasing from a low 0.3% to today's average of 7.3% in an
81-year period. Second, the local share dropped sharply at the same time,
down from 83% in 1920 to 43% in 2001. Although percentages may not reflect

Figure 2.7. Historical Summary of School Revenues: 1920–2001

School Year	In Thousands			Percentage Distribution			
	Total	Federal	State	Local	Total	Federal	State	Local
1919–20	$970,121	$2,475	$160,085	$807,561	100.0	0.3	16.5	83.2
1929–30	2,088,557	7,334	353,670	1,727,553	100.0	0.4	16.9	82.7
1939–40	2,260,527	39,810	684,354	1,536,363	100.0	1.8	30.3	68.0
1941–42	2,416,580	34,305	759,993	1,622,281	100.0	1.4	31.4	67.1
1943–44	2,604,322	35,886	859,183	1,709,253	100.0	1.4	33.0	65.6
1945–46	3,059,845	41,378	1,062,057	1,956,409	100.0	1.4	34.7	63.9
1947–48	4,311,534	120,270	1,676,362	2,514,902	100.0	2.8	38.9	58.3
1949–50	5,437,044	155,848	2,165,689	3,115,507	100.0	2.9	39.8	57.3
1951–52	6,423,816	227,711	2,478,596	3,717,507	100.0	3.5	38.6	57.9
1953–54	7,866,852	355,237	2,944,103	4,567,512	100.0	4.5	37.4	58.1
1955–56	9,686,677	441,442	3,828,886	5,416,350	100.0	4.6	39.5	55.9
1957–58	12,181,513	486,484	4,800,368	6,894,661	100.0	4.0	39.4	56.6
1959–60	14,746,618	651,639	5,768,047	8,326,932	100.0	4.4	39.1	56.5
1961–62	17,527,707	760,975	6,789,190	9,977,542	100.0	4.3	38.7	56.9
1963–64	20,544,182	896,956	8,078,014	11,569,213	100.0	4.4	39.3	56.3
1965–66	25,356,858	1,996,954	9,920,219	13,439,686	100.0	7.9	39.1	53.0
1967–68	31,903,064	2,806,469	12,275,536	16,821,063	100.0	8.8	38.5	52.7
1969–70	40,266,923	3,219,557	16,062,776	20,984,589	100.0	8.0	39.9	52.1
1970–71	44,511,292	3,753,461	17,409,086	23,348,745	100.0	8.4	39.1	52.5
1971–72	50,003,645	4,467,969	19,133,256	26,402,420	100.0	8.9	38.3	52.8
1972–73	52,117,930	4,525,000	20,699,752	26,893,180	100.0	8.7	39.7	51.6
1973–74	58,230,892	4,930,351	24,113,409	29,187,132	100.0	8.5	41.4	50.1
1974–75	64,445,239	5,811,595	27,060,563	31,573,079	100.0	9.0	42.0	49.0
1975–76	71,206,073	6,318,345	31,602,885	33,284,840	100.0	8.9	44.4	46.7
1976–77	75,332,532	6,629,498	32,526,018	36,177,019	100.0	8.8	43.2	48.0
1977–78	81,443,160	7,694,194	35,013,266	38,735,700	100.0	9.4	43.0	47.6
1978–79	87,994,143	8,600,116	40,132,136	39,261,891	100.0	9.8	45.6	44.6
1979–80	96,881,165	9,503,537	45,348,814	42,028,813	100.0	9.8	46.8	43.4
1980–81	105,949,087	9,768,262	50,182,659	45,998,166	100.0	9.2	47.4	43.4
1981–82	110,191,257	8,186,466	52,436,435	49,568,356	100.0	7.4	47.6	45.0
1982–83	117,497,502	8,339,990	56,282,157	52,875,354	100.0	7.1	47.9	45.0
1983–84	126,055,419	8,576,547	60,232,981	57,245,892	100.0	6.8	47.8	45.4
1984–85	137,294,678	9,105,569	67,168,684	61,020,425	100.0	6.6	48.9	44.4
1985–86	149,127,779	9,975,622	73,619,575	65,532,582	100.0	6.7	49.4	43.9
1986–87	158,523,693	10,146,013	78,830,437	69,547,243	100.0	6.4	49.7	43.9
1987–88	169,561,974	10,716,687	84,004,415	74,840,873	100.0	6.3	49.5	44.1
1988–89	192,016,374	11,902,001	91,768,911	88,345,462	100.0	6.2	47.8	46.0
1989–90	208,547,573	12,700,784	98,238,633	97,608,157	100.0	6.1	47.1	46.8
1990–91	223,340,537	13,776,066	105,324,533	104,239,939	100.0	6.2	47.2	46.7
1991–92	234,581,384	15,493,330	108,783,449	110,304,605	100.0	6.6	46.4	47.0

School Year	In Thousands				Percentage Distribution			
	Total	Federal	State	Local	Total	Federal	State	Local
1992–93	247,626,168	17,261,252	113,403,436	116,961,481	100.0	7.0	45.8	47.2
1993–94	260,159,468	18,341,483	117,474,209	124,343,776	100.0	7.1	45.2	47.8
1994–95	273,149,449	18,582,157	127,729,576	126,837,717	100.0	6.8	46.8	46.4
1995–96	287,702,844	19,104,019	136,670,754	131,928,071	100.0	6.6	47.5	45.9
1996–97	305,065,192	20,081,287	146,435,584	138,548,321	100.0	6.6	48.0	45.4
1997–98	325,925,708	22,201,965	157,645,372	146,078,370	100.0	6.8	48.4	44.8
1998–99	347,377,993	24,521,817	169,298,232	153,557,944	100.0	7.1	48.7	44.2
1999–00	372,943,802	27,097,866	184,613,352	161,232,584	100.0	7.3	49.5	43.2
2000–01	400,919,024	29,086,413	199,146,586	172,686,024	100.0	7.3	49.7	43.1

SOURCE: U.S. Department of Education, National Center for Education Statistics, Statistics of State School Systems; Revenues and Expenditures for Public Elementary and Secondary Education; and The NCES Common Core of Data (CCD), "National Public Education Financial Survey," 1987–88 through 2000–01 (August 2003).

true local tax burdens because states often allow local voter options to tax and spend more for schools, the change in local shares is still real due entirely to the fact that states have assumed a greater share of costs. As a result, the third observation is that the state is the only unit of government that has greatly increased its responsibility for school costs, increasing from only 16.5% in 1920 to nearly 50% in 2001—making the state the major contributor to school revenues.

Although courts have held education to be the state's duty, individual states have accepted that role with varying degrees of enthusiasm. State costs rose to an approximate average 50% by 2001, although actual experience in individual states reinforces that state willingness to aggressively fund schools has been widely disparate. It is relatively easy to describe how one federal government has aided education, but there are 50 different states so that a nearly equal number of ways to fund schools has emerged. Although some innovation has been observed, the results have not been equally good in every instance.

Notwithstanding, each state has chosen to provide aid for schools to some extent. The effect has depended on several factors. The first factor has usually relied on the wealth of each local school district and, in most instances, states have tried to equalize school spending by granting more aid to poorer districts. Politically, however, this has been difficult and in many states, has required legal action to force higher aid levels. A second factor has relied to some extent on the amount of federal aid flowing to a given state. A good example is federal impact aid. In some states, the amount of land exempt from local taxes because of federal installations is high. In those cases, state aid has been important, but the availability of impact aid may have moderated state aid requirements. A third factor has been the operation of political philosophies that have driven the design of state aid formulas. For example, some states have preferred equalization formulas inversely linking local wealth and state aid. Other states have chosen minimum foundation plans to help districts reach a base expenditure level before leaving the balance of costs to local voters. Only a few states have even proposed full state funding. A fourth factor of increasing importance has been the force of law in school funding lawsuits. The bottom line is that the choice of a state aid plan is a function of political, legal, and economic realities. The other bottom line, however, is that the level of state support for schools has developed very unevenly in the nation, resulting in wide mixes of federal, state, and local revenues (Figure 2.8, pp. 54–55), so that state aid to local districts varies from a low of 28.6% in Nevada to a high of 89.8% in Hawaii.

The fragmentation brought about by state sovereignty over many years, restrained only by state courts, along with fitful surges in federal aid, has left a patchwork effect in terms of how each of the 50 states has decided to fund public schools. Of course, the political process is strong at all levels—federal, state, and local—and the result has been that state aid to schools most often mirrors the economic and political realities of each state. It is unfortunate in some ways that such disparity has been able to develop because, to whatever extent money buys quality, the value of education itself may be unequal across states because the range of expenditure and programs is great. Not all states have given high priority to funding schools, whereas other states have given it great emphasis and have declared education to be a fundamental legal right. Beliefs about the value of education have had a powerful impact on the amount of money invested in state aid plans, and it is often accurate to say that states with low educational priorities are among the low spending states. Although it can be argued that needs and costs differ among states, it is difficult to show that widely differing expenditures per pupil are a result of careful analysis of educational needs. More often, expenditure levels are simply a statement of educational values. Although it is possible that such parochialism was acceptable in simpler times, the transportability of poor educational investment by states in a highly mobile society raises hard questions about the wisdom of 50 different educational systems at the beginning of a new millennium.

Figure 2.8. Revenues by Federal, State, and Local Source 2001

State or Jurisdiction	Total, in Thousands	Federal Amount, in Thousands	% of Total	State Amount, in Thousands	% of Total	Local and Intermediate Amount, in Thousands	% of Total
United States	$400,919,024	$29,086,413	7.3	$199,146,586	49.7	$163,479,177	40.8
Alabama	4,812,302	453,817	9.4	2,881,224	59.9	1,227,512	25.5
Alaska	1,370,271	215,921	15.8	782,348	57.1	333,592	24.3
Arizona	5,797,151	616,976	10.6	2,525,390	43.6	2,506,856	43.2
Arkansas	2,812,169	260,705	9.3	1,676,138	59.6	820,201	29.2
California	51,007,510	4,159,513	8.2	31,392,549	61.5	14,929,920	29.3
Colorado	5,349,899	299,576	5.6	2,222,083	41.5	2,576,924	48.2
Connecticut	6,460,491	276,427	4.3	2,553,180	39.5	3,527,302	54.6
Delaware	1,112,519	87,904	7.9	732,599	65.9	277,769	25.0
District of Columbia	1,042,711	115,527	11.1	†	†	918,793	88.1
Florida	17,866,868	1,599,259	9.0	8,695,213	48.7	6,917,556	38.7
Georgia	12,191,113	783,487	6.4	5,963,337	48.9	5,249,268	43.1
Hawaii	1,682,330	140,951	8.4	1,511,317	89.8	9,105	0.5
Idaho	1,593,966	128,646	8.1	977,438	61.3	461,605	29.0
Illinois	18,217,079	1,421,519	7.8	6,124,183	33.6	10,301,826	56.6
Indiana	9,033,180	464,489	5.1	4,833,954	53.5	3,477,771	38.5
Iowa	3,954,178	248,689	6.3	1,943,708	49.2	1,556,878	39.4
Kansas	3,597,726	231,473	6.4	2,198,216	61.1	1,074,216	29.9
Kentucky	4,509,893	448,073	9.9	2,702,932	59.9	1,258,841	27.9
Louisiana	5,060,133	580,356	11.5	2,497,875	49.4	1,921,174	38.0
Maine	1,934,178	153,100	7.9	863,295	44.6	880,399	45.5
Maryland	7,846,891	477,463	6.1	2,928,715	37.3	4,178,103	53.2
Massachusetts	10,148,498	511,198	5.0	4,420,622	43.6	5,052,863	49.8
Michigan	16,358,532	1,116,374	6.8	10,603,606	64.8	4,276,902	26.1
Minnesota	7,873,549	370,648	4.7	4,765,802	60.5	2,497,149	31.7
Mississippi	2,903,534	400,804	13.8	1,607,126	55.4	804,183	27.7
Missouri	7,102,501	491,233	6.9	2,661,904	37.5	3,680,122	51.8
Montana	1,140,168	131,299	11.5	542,692	47.6	418,700	36.7
Nebraska	2,307,804	168,036	7.3	805,419	34.9	1,210,412	52.4
Nevada	2,393,494	122,360	5.1	683,605	28.6	1,497,331	62.6
New Hampshire	1,714,147	77,365	4.5	884,875	51.6	712,119	41.5
New Jersey	15,967,075	628,834	3.9	6,669,858	41.8	8,351,731	52.3
New Mexico	2,426,705	338,213	13.9	1,725,551	71.1	316,268	13.0
New York	34,266,171	1,961,653	5.7	15,818,051	46.2	16,187,387	47.2
North Carolina	9,262,181	670,380	7.2	6,144,449	66.3	2,216,699	23.9
North Dakota	767,798	102,697	13.4	299,089	39.0	324,794	42.3
Ohio	16,649,361	1,007,370	6.1	7,187,325	43.2	7,840,209	47.1
Oklahoma	4,034,825	410,681	10.2	2,386,216	59.1	1,035,597	25.7
Oregon	4,564,408	336,992	7.4	2,566,099	56.2	1,528,766	33.5

State or Jurisdiction	Total, in Thousands	Federal Amount, in Thousands	% of Total	State Amount, in Thousands	% of Total	Local and Intermediate Amount, in Thousands	% of Total
Pennsylvania	17,053,891	1,107,854	6.5	6,443,673	37.8	9,176,463	53.8
Rhode Island	1,545,675	90,634	5.9	652,723	42.2	781,753	50.6
South Carolina	5,459,399	446,838	8.2	2,941,097	53.9	1,873,403	34.3
South Dakota	885,229	107,532	12.1	312,880	35.3	438,651	49.6
Tennessee	5,711,950	524,351	9.2	2,532,336	44.3	2,493,439	43.7
Texas	30,469,570	2,656,951	8.7	12,855,241	42.2	14,246,504	46.8
Utah	2,745,656	204,939	7.5	1,608,249	58.6	867,784	31.6
Vermont	1,035,679	60,523	5.8	732,563	70.7	226,175	21.8
Virginia	9,313,330	520,773	5.6	3,939,548	42.3	4,649,755	49.9
Washington	8,058,875	625,231	7.8	5,072,388	62.9	2,101,004	26.1
West Virginia	2,375,788	243,131	10.2	1,450,453	61.1	654,155	27.5
Wisconsin	8,327,255	418,472	5.0	4,424,429	53.1	3,295,254	39.6
Wyoming	803,414	69,176	8.6	403,020	50.2	317,995	39.6

SOURCE: U.S. Department of Education, National Center for Education Statistics, The NCES Common Core of Data (CCD), "National Public Education Financial Survey," 2000–01 (July 2003).

It is hard to accept the disparity in local school systems that exists today. It is also hard to explain to voters why their school taxes are going up in a milieu that increasingly calls for private alternatives to public education. For school leaders, it is especially difficult to explain the data in Figure 2.9 (p. 56) showing sustained spending increases for schools when the public is convinced that pupil achievement is not doing well. It is even harder to explain these realities when expenditure levels differ greatly not only across states, but across districts within single states as well. But regardless, past data show an ever-increasing state role in funding schools, and it is likely that recent attempts by states to take greater control of education will result in more cost shifting to the states.

Local Support for Schools

If citizens are generally aware of state aid to schools, they are firm in their belief that education is a locally funded enterprise. Their opinions arise from a variety of views, all of which relate to the fact that schools are highly visible in every community and have been regarded as locally owned from the earliest days of the nation. It is difficult to live and work today without being aware of the turmoil that surrounds local school boards, the high profile of local school leaders and student activities, and the tensions affecting local school taxes. Although we have made a case in this book that states have taken on a larger role in educational issues, especially by mandating reforms, we have also made a case that states have not equally assumed responsibility for school costs so that wide variance in method and amount of fiscal support continues to affect education. As a result, we should examine local cost-share issues to gain a comprehensive view of funding schools.

Figure 2.9. Constant Expenditures: 1960–2002

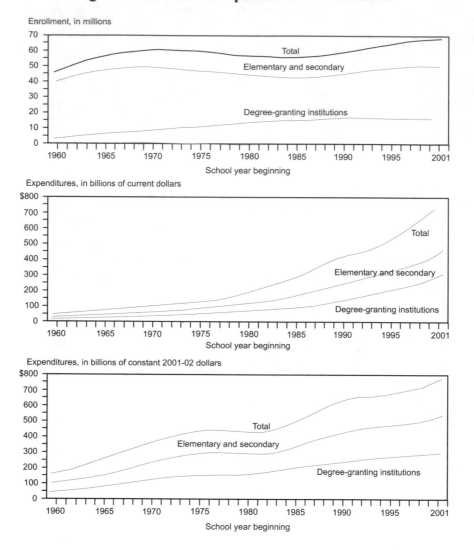

Enrollment, in millions

Expenditures, in billions of current dollars

Expenditures, in billions of constant 2001-02 dollars

SOURCE: U.S. Department of Education, NCES. Digest of Education Statistics 2002. Washington DC: 2002.

Features of Local Support

Although old records report only total revenues from all sources, it can be assumed that prior to 1919, school costs were mostly local. Beginning in 1919 with the first reported divisions of costs, 83% of the total $970 million in available funding fell to local districts. The first big shift came in 1940, as the local share of the $2.26 billion fell to 68%. By 1970, the local share of the $40.27 billion available to schools had fallen to 52%. By 1990, the local share made up 47% of the $209 billion cost for public K–12 education. By 2001, the local share remained mostly fixed at about 43% of the $401 billion (see Figure 2.7, pp. 51–52).

Although the ratio of spending for schools by local government regularly declined over the last century, the picture is not very stable. For example, it is true that local support for schools in the nation's early days was high as a percentage of total costs compared to today. But by some accounts, local dollars may not have declined, either in total or in aggregate burden. Locally, gross dollars demanded of taxpayers have increased because of inflation and as a result of increased costs tied to other factors such as expanded programs that have formed either by local choice or in response to federal and state mandates. Likewise, aggregate tax burden has not declined much overall and may have increased, as the additional dollars needed in complex school organizations have soared and as other governmental units have also increased taxes. Although the term "municipal overburden" was coined to depict demand on urban taxpayers from multiple taxing units such as cities, counties, police and fire departments, central water and sewage systems, schools, and other services, tax overburden in rural and urban settings alike has resulted in little easing of total taxpayer loads.

A second feature of local responsibility lies in recognizing the different realities of school funding in the various states. As we said earlier, states have been left free to develop funding systems except for the pressure of politics that can force some similarities between states and because of the demand by courts for funding reform that has occurred over the years. But despite these events, experience in individual states has not led to equal shifts in local districts' share of school costs. Although average local shares dropped from about 56% in 1960 to about 41% in 2001 (see Figure 2.8, pp. 54–55), actual local shares in 2001 ranged from 56.6% in Illinois (excluding the unique District of Columbia) to a low 0.5% in Hawaii. If Hawaii's unique school system were excluded, the range would still be great, as New Mexico requires only 13% local share by individual school districts. It is obvious that tax burdens are different among states, and that national averages do not speak to the differences among states.

A third feature of local responsibility rests in the basic nature of how local shares are decided. School districts usually derive revenue from a local tax base. Although some states tax more than one type of object to raise school revenues, most states rely on real property to define a district's tax base. This means that real estate is often the main source of tax revenue at the local level. No two districts contain exactly the same property values, so that highly unequal tax capacity is evident from one school district to the next. A simple illustration makes this point clear. Urban properties are often quite valuable, with businesses, homes, vacant lots, and other land commanding high prices. Rural land is often less costly because it is farther from commerce centers and less attractive for development. Unless rural land has other uses such as natural resources that make it valuable, urban centers will have much higher property wealth. That wealth, or assessed valuation, is generally the basis for deriving school revenue by assessing taxes against each property. For example, an urban acre of land might sell for $1 million or more depending on location. In a rural area, a one-acre home site might sell for $3,000—far less if it is remote pasture. A tax rate of 10 mills[24] on the urban acre would yield $10,000 in school tax revenue, whereas the rural home site would yield only $30—a vast difference with implications for the ability of a local district to provide schools.

Even the implications are complex. Although the data we just saw might suggest rural disadvantage and high urban wealth, the opposite can be true. For example, it is clear that one feature of an urban area is population density. Thus, high property wealth spread over a large population may actually yield low per capita wealth. The urban condition may bring high costs because of disadvantaged populations and tax base competition (i.e., municipal overburden). Many urban property owners are absentees, having no community loyalty and interested only in taking profits without reinvestment. Rural conditions are equally complex. Although property may be less costly, ownership rests in fewer hands, increasing individual tax loads for influential citizens. The lack of urban problems in rural areas does not always result in lower school costs, as smaller populations result in higher per pupil costs because of diseconomies of scale. Likewise, the reality of vastly unequal tax bases is a vexing problem that creates disparities in districts' ability to raise school taxes.

A fourth feature of local responsibility is actually a complication of how local districts determine their cost shares and, to some extent, their total spending levels. This wrinkle takes several forms and is made more complex by how districts' budgets are determined and the interdependency of tax bases and intergovernmental competition. The idea of municipal overburden was raised earlier, and the broader concept of tax overburden applies in some way to almost all schools, including rural areas. A by-product of overburden has been the hostility encountered by almost all local districts when seeking to increase funding. In a number of states, patrons must vote on school budgets. In other states, budgets rest with individual school boards, but any politically alert person knows that a board's desire to approve budget increases depends on local taxpayer attitudes. Additionally, many states allow for local option leeway, that is, giving local districts the option of additional local tax effort for schools. As state aid plans limiting voter leeway have come into existence, and as overall tax burdens have grown, voter approval to increase local spending has become harder to obtain. All these considerations are finally aggravated by the issue of fiscal dependence on other governmental units. In some states, local school budgets are submitted

---

24. A mill is 1/1000 of a dollar, so that 1 mill is $1 tax revenue per $1,000 assessed value. The formula calculates as: AV * mills = tax yield, so that $1,000,000 * 0.01 = $10,000. Likewise, $3,000 * 0.01 = $30. This does not consider fractional assessment, a practice in many states that takes only a portion of the market value of a piece of property.

to a higher authority in tandem with budgets of other taxing units such as cities and counties. Fiscal dependency creates problems because local schools may have trouble securing adequate revenue when competition for a finite tax pool is raised to a level of direct conflict.

The issues driving local responsibility and ability to pay for schools are endless, but our discussion shows that it is hard to tell simply from raw percentages whether the local share has declined as much as it appears because there are other issues such as local ability to pay that muddy the waters. What is clear is that districts differ in ability to pay and that experience in individual states varies. It is also clear that if local districts depended entirely on local tax bases, unconscionable disparities would exist. And it is finally clear that the federal, state, and local partnership has been both tenuous and necessary—tenuous because there is a natural tension among these three levels of government in our fiercely independent nation, and necessary because none of these units should be allowed to assume full control of schools. Education has long been a partnership in America: The real issue is the refinement of that partnership in ways that enhance fiscal adequacy and equity for every child.

WHAT CONSTITUTES ADEQUATE AND EQUITABLE FUNDING FOR SCHOOLS?

The importance of adequate and equitable funding is heightened by the vast scope and costs of education, changing demographics, and the link between education and economic and social progress. Even though research cannot support blind faith in the link between student achievement and money, there has been a belief that unless negative proof exists, we must guard against under-investing in schools to avoid engaging in destructive economic and social policy. In this uncertain context, policymakers have been challenged to fund education at an appropriate level.

The result has been a great and unending struggle over money and schools. Although some struggles have dealt with what schools mean to different segments of society, perhaps the greatest war has been over how school money is distributed. Part of the struggle has arisen because there has never been enough money for schools, so that distribution becomes even more critical. By all accounts, the war has escalated because of greater willingness to pursue confrontational solutions, such as legal challenges to state school aid formulas.

Unhappy reformers have been quick to embrace the view that more money makes better schools. They have argued that schools distribute economic and social opportunities, and that equal opportunity depends on the quality of schools children attend. They further contend that despite lack of a clear link between money and learner outcomes, school quality is powerfully affected by purchased resources such as teachers. Reformers secure their view by concluding that people who argue for the irrelevance of money still prefer more money for their own children. Under these conditions, litigants have aggressively chased fair and adequate funding, believing that how states fund schools has a direct effect on social and economic justice.

Origins of School Funding Challenges

For more than 100 years, school finance has been a deep concern for courts and policy makers.[25] Although school finance as a discipline only emerged during the twentieth century, issues of taxation have been a flashpoint since the early days of the nation. Likewise, schools have long been subjected to intense argument regarding equality of educational opportunity as it relates to discrimination, and it is easy to link discrimination to differences in amounts of funding available to schools.

The history of school finance litigation has played out in both federal and state courts. At the federal level, litigation has focused on the U.S. Constitution in the context of interpreting federal responsibility and in hopes of reading a guaranteed right to education into the Constitution. At the state level, litigation has focused on both the constitutional and statutory demands of each state. Pursuit of justice has been nerve-wracking, as constitutional interpretation is swayed by the times and attitudes of courts, particularly when there is wide variance among states in their constitutional and statutory provisions for school funding. In both federal and state cases, litigants have sought rulings to determine the meaning of equal opportunity and to test the strength of constitutional and statutory language. Traditionally, attacks have followed three claims: education as a *fundamental right,* the *equal protection* of law, and the *education articles* of state constitutions. Each of these can be traced from their federal and state origins into modern school finance litigation strategy.

Federal Origins

Although school finance litigation is largely regarded as state-specific, the federal case actually predates all other strategies. Plaintiffs first sought equality in funding by seeking a favorable U.S. Supreme Court ruling as the supreme law of the land. The logic was that if a favorable ruling were won, states would have to conform to federal demands.

Bringing a federal lawsuit was a sensible act. Equality had been an important issue since the days when the colonial charters sought freedom from British rule. Equality was a key part of the Bill of Rights, and the Fourteenth Amendment to the Constitution guaranteed equality under federal law. The

---

25. This section draws from many earlier original writings. See R. Craig Wood, David C. Thompson, Lawrence O. Picus, and Donald I. Tharpe, *Principles of School Business Management,* 2nd ed. (Reston, VA: ASBO International, 1995). See also David C. Thompson, R. Craig Wood, and David Honeyman, *Fiscal Leadership for Schools: Concepts and Practices* (New York: Longman, 1994). See also R. Craig Wood and David C. Thompson, *Education Finance Law: Constitutional Challenges to State Aid Plans,* 2nd ed. (Topeka, KS: Education Law Association, 1996), with updates to many of these writings in 2005.

Fourteenth Amendment was critically important because its provisions applied to the individual states, as it held:

> No State shall make or enforce any law which shall abridge the privileges or immunities of citizens of the United States; nor shall any State deprive any person of life, liberty, or property, without due process of law; nor deny to any person within its jurisdiction the equal protection of the laws.

A case for fiscal fairness was laid in a series of suits testing the limits of equality under the Constitution. Earlier cases had laid a broad groundwork, including overturning of racial separatism where the practical implications included the costs and organization of schools. The next step was to ask whether unequal money in schools is a kind of impermissible inequality under law.

This strategy was actually an extension of judicial sympathy that already existed in other fundamental rights. In addition to named rights in the Constitution, the Supreme Court had ruled on other rights that it found to be so basic that these rights could not be denied except by due process. The importance of fundamental rights could not be overstated, in that equality was so strong that these rights must be protected at all costs—a guarantee reformers hoped would link school funding and equal rights under Fourteenth Amendment equal protection. This line of thinking produced two litigation thrusts. One thrust came from defining unequal treatment of suspect classes: School funding litigation might win, plaintiffs thought, if they could show that money was tied to race or social class in schools. The second thrust came from seeking ways in which some fundamental right might be violated. Again, plaintiffs believed success might follow if they could show that education was so essential to freedom that denial violated the Constitution. The strategy was risky. If neither a fundamental right to education nor a suspect class of poor could be shown, claims would have to turn to individual states. On the other hand, victory would force school funding laws nationwide to be rewritten.

The Early Federal Case

Although federal racial equality litigation actually spanned many decades, it was in the *Brown* case in 1954 when equality of educational opportunity found its day as the U.S. Supreme Court overturned "separate but equal" provisions, which had allowed racially segregated schools. Overruling the entire social and economic history of the United States, the Court held that separate but equal is inherently unequal, and that education is important to the health and wellbeing of the nation. The Court stated:

> ...[E]ducation is perhaps the most important function of state and local governments....It is the very foundation of good citizenship....In these days, it is doubtful that any child may reasonably be expected to succeed in life if he is denied the opportunity of an

education. Such an opportunity, where the state has undertaken to provide it, is a right that must be made available to all on equal terms.[26]

Emboldened by *Brown*, reformers turned to fiscal inequality, believing the same analysis could apply to school funding because it was easily shown that money and educational opportunity vary greatly based on residence in school districts of unequal wealth. Of great value to this theory was a line of argument that unequal school district wealth made a case for wealth discrimination, so that residence could be interpreted as a wealth-based suspect class. By this logic, wealth-disadvantaged children were a perfect case in point.

The first federal suit took shape as *Burruss*[27] in Virginia in 1969. Plaintiffs based their claims on the Fourteenth Amendment, arguing that state aid was not given to school districts on the basis of educational need. The U.S. District Court, however, held that whereas "deficiencies and differences are forcefully put by plaintiffs' counsel...we do not believe they are creatures of discrimination by the State....We can only see to it that the outlays on one group are not invidiously greater or less than that of another." The court added that, "the courts have neither the knowledge, nor means, nor the power to tailor the public monies to fit the varying needs of these students throughout the state."

The tone of *Burruss* foretold much of the continued failure of a federal case. Over the coming years, plaintiffs heard the same logic, often as federal courts drew on the words of sister courts to express their own limitations. The nearly lone exception came in 1972 in *Van Dusartz*,[28] as a Minnesota federal court held that wealthy districts not only had greater revenue per child but also paid lower tax rates, conditions that depended on the child's residence. *Van Dusartz* was hardly the rule, however, as other federal courts complained that their hands were tied by a lack of judicially manageable standards. Equality in federal court was stated negatively, in that absence of money was not the same as discrimination.

The *Rodriguez* Case

Reformers realized, however, that a Supreme Court ruling was not yet in place, and a test case was carefully chosen. A case styled as *Rodriguez*[29] was selected, in which a U.S. District Court had upheld plaintiffs' view that the state must be neutral in aiding schools. The district court ruling had encouraged reformers, as it also held that education is a fundamental interest to the state. The case was appealed to the U.S. Supreme Court where plaintiffs argued that the Texas funding system violated federal equal protection by

26. Brown *v. Board of Education*, 347 U.S. at 492–493.
27. *Burruss v. Wilkerson*, 310 F. Supp. 572 (1969).
28. *Van Dusartz v. Hatfield*, 334 F. Supp. 870 (Minn. 1971).
29. *San Antonio Independent School District v. Rodriguez*, 411 U.S. 1 (1973).

discriminating against a suspect class of poor, and that students making up that class were denied the right to education. The Court rejected suspect class arguments, however, as it saw only students living in poor school districts, rather than being poor themselves. The Court noted that individual income did not correlate exactly with district wealth, and that even if the link had been strong, the Court's application of wealth suspectness is limited to absolute deprivation. Because no student was completely deprived of an education, fiscal inequalities were of only relative difference.

The Court also rejected education as a fundamental right. Plaintiffs had argued that education was so prerequisite to other rights that it created a nexus to other established rights. The Court disagreed, seeing no link between education and other rights. Although the Court criticized the disparities among Texas school districts, only a rational basis for the funding formula was required to defend the state aid plan absent invidious discrimination. A rational basis could be found in Texas's goal of promoting local control of schools, and the Court refused to intervene in such a complex and political arena.

Subsequent Federal Litigation

Although *Rodriguez* had a chilling effect on new federal lawsuits, other cases were brought to keep the question alive, particularly in light of the fact that the Supreme Court did not completely close the door. Three cases illustrate the importance of the federal courts to defining a future federal role in education.

Thirteen years after *Rodriguez*, plaintiffs in Mississippi sued for equal protection in revenue disparity based on Section Sixteen lands lost during the Civil War. Although the state provided aid to offset losses in affected school districts, by 1981 state funds were only $0.63 per pupil compared to $75.34 per pupil in districts where land had not been taken. Dismissed in federal district court, on appeal the Fifth Circuit Court held in *Papasan*[30] that whereas the Eleventh Amendment to the U.S. Constitution did not bar claims for equal protection, *Rodriguez* was the standard regarding fiscal disparity. The U.S. Supreme Court affirmed the immunity decision, but reversed the equal protection claim and sent the case back for further development. *Papasan* was notable for two reasons. First, the complaint was narrowly taken, never drawing the issue of fundamentality into the discussion. Second, a small window of federal interest in school funding was opened by remanding to the lower court, as the Supreme Court noted that unreasonable governmental action would attract the Court's interest.

A second important case arose in Texas a few years later, as the Supreme Court ruled in *Plyler*[31] that refusal by a state to educate illegal aliens could

---

30. *Papasan v. Allain*, 478 U.S. 265 (1986); *Papasan v. United States*, 756 F.2d 1087 (5th Cir. 1985).
31. *Plyler v. Doe*, 457 U.S. 202 (1982).

invoke federal equal protection. Although the Court stopped short of declaring education a fundamental right, it did approve a higher level of scrutiny in cases of absolute educational deprivation. The Court pointed to its hesitancy to slam the federal door completely, as it stated:

> Education provides the basic tools by which individuals might lead economically productive lives to the benefit of us all. In sum, education has a fundamental role in maintaining the fabric of our society. We cannot ignore the significant social costs borne by our Nation when select groups are denied the means to absorb the values and skills on which our social order rests.[32]

The third important federal case came in *Kadrmas*,[33] as plaintiffs in North Dakota argued that fees for bus service denied equal protection because the plaintiff child could not afford to pay for transportation. The Supreme Court held for the state, but its 5–4 vote was a bare majority and indicated the unsettled nature of federal education claims. The Court warned that *Rodriguez* was not the last word, in that there are nuances that interest the Court. The minority opinion expressed this well:

> The Court...does not address the question whether a state constitutionally could deny a child access to a minimally adequate education. In prior cases this court explicitly has left open the question whether such a deprivation of access would violate a fundamental constitutional right. That question remains open today.

Although *Rodriguez* has been said to close off hope for a federal claim, the record disagrees. Federal courts are sympathetic to judicially unmanageable standards, and they are inclined to defer to legislative prerogative. Likewise, the nation's highest court is reluctant to see education as a fundamental right. But it is also clear the Court takes interest in education as over time it revisits and qualifies earlier rulings. But in the end, it is finally clear that the case for fiscal reform in schools has had to turn nearly in sum to state courts to experience meaningful and systematic success.

State Origins

Development of the state case for equalizing resources in schools parallels the federal case in many ways. In particular, there has been significant overlap of both time and claims. In fact, lawsuits were often brought simultaneously in state and federal courts in the early days of reform. For example, *Burruss* and *Rodriguez* were both filed in federal court in the 1960s, but the California case of *Serrano*[34] ended at the state supreme court level in 1971 before the U.S. Supreme Court ruled in *Rodriguez* in 1973. Claims also over-

---

32. 457 U.S. 202 at 221 (1982).
33. *Kadrmas v. Dickinson Public Schools,* 487 U.S. 450 (1988).
34. *Serrano v. Priest,* 487 P.2d 1241 (1971).

lapped as state cases like *Serrano* made both federal and state constitutional claims. But whereas success on the federal front was scarce, state litigation occurred far more frequently and with significantly better results.

Early State Cases

The first state fiscal equalization case to gain attention was *Serrano*, as the California Supreme Court ruled in what would become a model for state school finance litigation. Plaintiffs sought a ruling on issues of a fundamental right to education, wealth as a suspect class, and federal and state equal protections. Plaintiffs charged that the state aid plan created disparity and that these differences impacted the quality of education. Plaintiffs also charged that some taxpayers paid higher tax rates and received poorer education. The net sum was to make quality of education dependent on differences in local wealth.

In a sweeping victory for plaintiffs, the state supreme court overturned the method of funding schools in California, holding that it violated both the Fourteenth Amendment and the state constitution's equal protection clause because the aid plan made the quality of education dependent on local property wealth. This ruling ran counter to every trend up to that point. The state's high court was harsh in its view of unequal opportunity, declaring:

> We have determined that this funding scheme invidiously discriminates against the poor because it makes the quality of a child's education a function of the wealth of his parents and neighbors. Recognizing as we must, that the right to an education in our public schools is a fundamental interest that cannot be conditional on wealth, we can discern no compelling state purpose necessitating the present method of financing.

The fact that the federal claim was later overturned in *Rodriguez* did not detract from the impact of *Serrano* at the state level. The lesson of *Serrano* was to prove that state courts would not always adopt the same posture as federal courts. *Serrano* provided a model for state litigation by its success on fundamentality and equal protection, and it showed that state constitutions might be vulnerable in ways that were denied at the federal level. The impact of *Serrano* was to provide a catalyst for copycat litigation, and many state legislatures saw *Serrano* as a sign of the future. As a result, an explosion of litigation followed in other states.

Subsequent State Litigation

Bolstered by *Serrano*, dozens of state funding lawsuits followed, a fact of life that still rages. But whereas reformers' hopes were raised by early victory, results have been uneven. In fact, the outcome can be divided into successes and failures at the state level.

Failures

The case for reform did not experience sudden or even sustained success. Although a full accounting of the history of litigation is beyond this book, a few early cases illustrate that the record included significant failures.

Shortly after *Serrano*, the Michigan Supreme Court handed down its decision in *Milliken*,[35] a ruling that flip-flopped in a dizzyingly short time. The original ruling was for plaintiffs and was modeled after *Serrano*, but the victory was short-lived because the state supreme court experienced a change of judges, ending in reversal of the decision. The new court vacated the prior decision on the basis that the evidence did not prove that equal protection of children in low-wealth districts was violated. Of particular importance to the court was the question of linkage between fiscal inputs and achievement, so that additional fiscal inputs could not be said to provide greater and more equal outcomes.

The logic in *Milliken* would prove to haunt reformers. The case for reform again went badly as, shortly after *Rodriguez*, the Arizona Supreme Court held for the state in *Shofstall*.[36] The court had been asked to decide if that state's school funding law violated the state equal protection clause and its "general and uniform" provision in the state's constitution. The court interpreted general and uniform to mean that the state would provide a minimum school year, certify personnel, and set course requirements and standards. Although the court found a fundamental right to education, it saw legislative redress as the right solution to political problems.

Still a third defeat came as the Illinois Supreme Court ruled in *Blase*,[37] denying a narrow reading of the state constitution. Plaintiffs had based their claim on the constitution's strong wording, which said, "the State shall provide for an efficient system of high quality public educational institutions and services [and that] the State has the primary responsibility for financing the system of public education." Plaintiffs wanted the state to provide no less than 50% aid, along with other strict equality provisions. The state supreme court rejected this view, ruling that the language only expressed a goal rather than a specific command.

One final defeat shows how plaintiffs may fail, even when the state constitution seems to strongly support equality. Plaintiffs failed in the state of Washington in *Northshore*[38] despite the fact that all the elements of victory seemed in place. Plaintiffs' claims included the charge that the state had disobeyed a provision of the constitution, which read, "...it is the paramount duty of the state to make ample provision for the education of all children" and that the state had failed to provide a general and uniform system of pub-

---

35. *Milliken v. Green*, vacated, 212 N.W.2d 711 (Mich. 1973); *Milliken v. Green*, 203 N.W.2d 457 (Mich. 1972).
36. *Shofstall v. Hollins*, 515 P.2d 590 (Ariz. 1973).
37. *Blase v. Illinois*, 55 Ill. 2d 94, 302 N.E.2d 46 (Ill. 1973).
38. *Northshore v. Kinnear*, 530 P.2d 178 (Wash. 1974).

lic schools. Regarded as one of the states having the most forceful constitutional requirements, the Washington Supreme Court nonetheless denied these claims, noting that even if the state were one giant school district, spending per child would still depend on geography, climate, terrain, social and economic conditions, transportation, special services, and local choices in curricula. The strength of language regarding ample provision for education was regarded unfavorably, as the court noted that, "constitutionally speaking, the duty or function is the same as any other major duty or function of state government."

Although we have yet to discuss the history of successes in school finance litigation, it is important to illustrate the unsettled nature of states' constitutional obligation by indicating that challengers still have not found a sure trigger to invoke adequate and equitable support for schools. Although we will say later that litigation has moved fair and adequate school funding ahead of where it would be today had the force of law not been applied, it is still true that plaintiffs risk significant defeat when raising what seems to them to be issues of basic justice in equal education. For example, in the last few years state supreme courts in the states of Alabama,[39] Alaska,[40] South Carolina,[41] and Wisconsin[42] have all upheld their school finance schemes, and there is a real possibility that plaintiffs in other states currently involved in litigation may fail as well. Although there is a need to accentuate the very real gains made in school funding over many decades of struggle, a realistic view recognizes that failure is an imminent possibility when contesting state school aid plans.

Successes

Although plaintiffs lost many times at the state level, a number of lawsuits were won that have dramatically affected how schools are funded. A few important state cases after *Serrano* help to understand the volatile context of school funding—a volatility that finds winners and losers even today.

The lessons of reform were aided by a victory following soon after *Serrano*, as the supreme court in New Jersey ruled in *Robinson*.[43] The court reviewed a lower court's holding for plaintiffs, wherein it was charged that the aid plan violated federal and state equal protection and denied students' fundamental right to education because tax revenue varied with district wealth and was not adequately equalized. To reformers' dismay, the court denied fundamentality and wealth suspectness, stating that such rulings would have the effect of changing our fundamental political structure. But

---

39. *Ex parte James,* 836 S0.2d 813 (2002).
40. *Matanuska-Susitna Borough School District v. State,* 931 P.2d 391 (1997).
41. *Abbeville County School District v. State,* 515 S.E.2d 535 (1999).
42. *Vincent v. Voight,* 614 N.W.2d 388 (2000).
43. *Robinson v. Cahill,* 287 A.2d 187 (N.J. Super. 1972), *aff'd as mod.,* 303 A.2d 273 (N.J. 1973).

the court still overturned the funding system by invoking the education article of the state constitution, which demanded a *thorough and efficient* system—a requirement that was not met because of lack of equalization in revenues that violated the state's equal protection clause.

Other decisions for plaintiffs emerged over the next several years. One of
the more expansive state supreme court rulings came in the Wyoming case of
Washakie,[44] in 1980, as the court found that poor districts showed a pattern of
less revenue because of low assessed valuation. The court accepted plaintiff
arguments that the quality of education is related to money. The court cut to
the core, stating, "until equality of financing is achieved, there is no practica-
ble method of achieving equality of quality." The Wyoming court reached its
decision based on the fact that certain provisions of the state constitution
were more demanding than federal equal protection and because education
was of such compelling value in that state that it was among the fundamental
rights. Unlike most courts, the Wyoming court embraced wealth as a suspect
class, saying, "the state has the burden of demonstrating a compelling
interest…served by the challenged legislation and which cannot be satisfied
by any other convenient legal structure."

The unsettled nature of state struggles is illustrated in the battle over
school funding that began in Texas with *Rodriguez* in federal court and later
moved to the state level. Failing in *Rodriguez*, plaintiffs turned to the Texas
Supreme Court, which ruled in *Kirby*[45] in 1988. The court held education as a
fundamental right in Texas and ordered the legislature to create a satisfactory
remedy within a specific time period—a requirement that the legislature has
had difficulty meeting, causing the case to return repeatedly for judicial
review of progress.

The case for reform is secured by two other important cases in Kentucky
and New Jersey, both of which have provided national focus on the nature
and extent of education reform. One of the more touted reform cases was the
Kentucky Supreme Court's ruling in *Rose*[46] in 1989. In a ruling that shook the
nation and spurred reform at the highest levels in many states, the Kentucky
court held that the system of common schools was not efficient. Holding for a
fundamental right to education, the court found that this right was denied
when the state's schools were under-funded and inadequate in educational
programs. Inequalities across districts caused the court to order a complete
overhaul of the system, with massive new funds and total redesign of the
education system. Similarly, the New Jersey case of *Abbott*,[47] in 1990 (a multi-
decade continuation of the original *Robinson* case from 1973), stirred high

---

44. *Washakie County School District v. Herschler*, 606 P.2d 310 (1980).
45. *Edgewood v. Kirby*, 761 S.W.2d 859 (Tex. 1988).
46. *Rose v. Council for Better Education*, 790 S.W.2d 186 (Ky. 1989).
47. *Abbott v. Burke*, 575 A.2d 359 (N.J. 1990); but in *Abbott v. Burke* 153 N.J. 480, 710 A.2d
     450 (1998) the state court finally ruled that the state legislature had largely met its
     obligation to poor urban schools. For fuller discussion, see Margaret E. Goertz and

national consternation as that state's finance system was again declared invalid because the state aid formula did not meet the needs of poor urban districts and because the formula still violated the thorough and efficient clause. The court stated, "[f]rom this record we find that certain poorer urban districts do not provide a thorough and efficient education to their students....We find the constitutional failure clear, severe, and of long duration." Although the court later found the level of resources to finally meet adequacy standards, New Jersey's experience has stood as a monument to the war over fair and adequate funding—a struggle spanning nearly 30 years in search of solutions.

Although school finance reformers still experience defeat today, other plaintiff cases continue to be recorded in the "win" column. In the very recent past, plaintiffs have won at the highest levels in the states of Arkansas,[48] New Hampshire,[49] Ohio,[50] Tennessee,[51] New York,[52] and Vermont.[53] Other cases have been won at trial court levels and are presently on appeal to the supreme courts of the respective states.[54] The message is clear: To fully appreciate the nature of school finance litigation requires both a willingness to risk failure and an acceptance that litigation is a campaign rather than a battle or even a war. In other words, a long view is the only way to evaluate the impact of school finance litigation on adequate and equitable levels of funding for schools.

Malek Edwards, "In Search of Excellence for All: The Courts and New Jersey School Finance Reform," *Journal of Education Finance* 25, no. 1 (1999).

48. *Lake View School District No. 25 of Phillips County v. Huckabee*, 91 S.W.3d (2002). Earlier, *Tucker v. Lake View School District No. 25*, S.W.2d 530 (1996). And later dismissing *Lake View School District No. 25 of Phillips County, Arkansas, et al., Appellants, vs Governor Mike Huckabee, et al.* 2004 Ark. LEXIS 425.

49. *Claremont School District v. Governor*, 703 A.2d 1353 (1997), reh'g den 725 A.2d 648 (1998).

50. *DeRolph v. State*, 677 N.E.2d 733 (1997). Later, *State v. Lewis*, 786 N.E.2d 60 (2003).

51. *Tennessee Small School Systems v. McWherter*, 91 S.W.3d 232 (2002).

52. *Campaign for Fiscal Equity v. State of New York*, 801 N.E.2d 326 (2003).

53. *Brigham v. State*, 92 A.2d 384 (1997).

54. For example, according to ACCESS, a Project of the Campaign for Fiscal Equity Inc., a nonprofit organization tracking school finance litigation, in late 2004, cases were anticipated, filed, or on appeal in the states of Georgia, Iowa, Kansas, Kentucky, North Dakota, Missouri, Louisiana, Nebraska, and Texas, among others. See http://www.schoolfunding.info/

The Long View[55]

The strategy first laid down in *Rodriguez, Serrano,* and *Robinson* has created a legacy of fierce struggle in most of the 50 states, with many state aid plans overturned at the state supreme court level. These rulings spurred the hopes of reformers, as each case helped refine the chance for success. The generalizability of plaintiff strategy has not been strong, however, as courts have reached different results when interpreting the unique demands of each state's constitution and statutes. Although there has been winning litigation in many states, aid formulas have also been upheld in other states where courts refused to read constitutional requirements narrowly. The issue has even been unsettled in states where litigation has previously been decided, as several states have had multiple rulings, often with opposite outcomes.

Lack of a consistently winning strategy has been discouraging. The aims of reform have been elusive, and there is even doubt about whether winning produces lasting results. More than three decades of struggle have been based mostly on a belief that lawsuits make a difference, even though the record of success has been rocky. To assume that litigation is an effective way to increase funding is risky because lawsuits are expensive in terms of money and time drained off during the litigation process. The risk is even greater because, although much research has been done on school finance litigation, the generalizable impact of suits has not been clear.

Research on litigation effects has fallen into four groups. The first group, the general literature, speaks hopefully but imprecisely about litigation, and the tone regarding the impact of lawsuits is at best cautious. Opinion is divided on whether seeking a legislative or judicial remedy is more useful. A scan of these writings concludes that the only clear impact of suing has been to increase legislative sensitivity to school funding. The real value of the general literature is in cautioning plaintiffs against naively looking for quick solutions.

A second set of studies examines litigation in single states, yielding two conclusions regarding lawsuits as a reform tool. First, most studies do not show a trend of greater equity, regardless of whether a suit was won, lost, or even filed. Second, most studies suggest that nearly as much change comes from voluntary legislative reform as from court-ordered reform. These stud-

---

55. See David C. Thompson, School *Finance Litigation: Does It Make a Difference? A Review of Literature and Analysis of Selected Data in Four States.* This research was funded by The National Education Association, Washington, DC (1998). More recently, see R. Craig Wood and David C. Thompson, "Politics of Plaintiffs and Defendants," in *Politics of Education Law: Effects on Education Finance. 2004 American Education Finance Association Yearbook* (New York: Eye on Education, 2004), 37–45. Relatedly, see Faith E. Crampton and David C. Thompson, "When the Legislative Process Fails: The Politics of Litigation in School Infrastructure Funding Equity," in *Politics of Education Law: Effects on Education Finance. 2004 American Education Finance Association Yearbook* (Larchmont, NY: Eye on Education, 2004), 69–88.

ies suggest mostly that funding has received new scrutiny that might not have occurred had litigation not been pursued.

The third group considers multi-state comparisons. Relatively few studies exist because it is difficult to compare data across states. The issue is where the money goes and how evenly it is distributed from a regional or national perspective. Again, studies do not show a clear improvement over time, with the majority suggesting that high levels of school funding variability persist after litigation in both reform and nonreform states.

The final group of studies has tried to measure the direct effects of bringing a lawsuit over school funding. Only a few studies have tried to quantitatively assess the impact, and again the results are not promising. Even in studies showing new money for plaintiffs, it is unclear whether gains in state funding were offset by lower local tax effort and particularly whether gains were dramatic enough to assist with true equalization. And equally questionable is whether even those courts that have issued strong rulings will continue to legislate reform: For example, the court in Kentucky, which many reformers cite as issuing the strongest mandate for fairness and widely heralded for appointing a special master to monitor progress, recently sent reform back to the legislature releasing jurisdiction over the legislature's response and thereby triggering another round of compliance litigation.[56] And in the end, alienation of exactly the same wealthy citizens whose taxes pay for reform may prove to haunt a winning case, thwarting long-term reform as political retribution and social withdrawal take their course. Sadly, equality of school resources cannot be reached without substantial decreases in average level of per-pupil spending—a condition that almost never occurs long-term because strong equalization plans generally reduce local taxpayer commitments of every kind,[57] whereas substantial increases in per-pupil spending are either unreachable or unsustainable over time.

CAN SCHOOLS SERVE ECONOMICS, EQUALITY, PRODUCTIVITY, AND LIBERTY?

Our discussion in this chapter has pointed up the difficult situation that education faces when trying to satisfy all its clients. Some parts of society pursue schooling for economic reasons, whereas others see schools as a forum to promote justice. Still other groups view schools as a place where the principles of liberty can operate, although there is disagreement about whether liberty means freedom to achieve differentially based on ability or whether freedom is only real when schools first enable society's less fortunate at the expense of the privileged. In all instances, however, a common

---

56. *Council for Better Education v. Willliams.* CV-03-CI-1152. Filed in circuit court, September 2003.

57. C. M. Hoxby, *All School Finance Equalizations Are Not Created Equal: Marginal Tax Rates Matter.* Unpublished working paper (Cambridge, MA: Harvard University, March 1996).

thread is the demand for educational productivity variously defined, a demand that is becoming ever more strident.

Maintaining—or even determining—adequate and equitable fiscal support for schools has grown increasingly difficult. As costs have risen steadily, taxpayer burden has risen at the same time that other social service needs have skyrocketed. Attitudes about adequate revenues for schools are a deep morass of desires, resentments, mandates, and frustrations. On one hand, the numbers are so enormous it is hard to imagine that revenues are not enough and that to ask for more must stretch the limits of reason, particularly because education is only one of many government functions. On the other hand, the depth of needs reflects increasing demands on schools from all quarters. At the same time, old assumptions about public education are being questioned. The struggle comes not so much from whether or not people want the benefits of schooling, but rather from how to distribute education in ways that respect our heritage and our debt to society without losing our individual freedom to accept or reject educational benefits or to obtain them from nonpublic sources.

The condition of schools is a mirror to the soul of a nation. As civilizations mature, education becomes more important to economic and social patterns—so much so that the nation becomes dependent on producing a continually better educational product. When a break enters the cycle, the security and prosperity of the nation and its people are at risk. Few would deny that productivity in the American education system has slipped and that part of the slippage is because of problems in the larger society. Our problems have created tension among the forces of economics, equality, productivity, liberty, and capitalist democracy—problems defying solution because they may be irreconcilable in our form of government. This is because equality and productivity are always at odds—as are equality and liberty. Yet solutions must be found because failure to support schools is a failure to support democracy—a form of self-destiny, which calls for diverse opinions and is itself a tension between liberty and equality. It is in this context that school finance policy is made.

SUGGESTED FOLLOW-UP PROJECTS

◆ Obtain documents on the history of education in your state. Identify important issues such as the history of school district reorganization, extent of legislative interest in schools, and the relative autonomy (degree of centralization or decentralization) of educational decision making in your state.

◆ Identify the major organizations in your state that have direct or indirect influence on educational policy making at state and local levels. State the nature of their influence and reflect on why they are successful.

◆ Identify the organizational chart in your school district, tracing the formal authority and power structure.

- ◆ Obtain a copy of your school district's budget and identify the relative contribution of federal, state, intermediate, and local units of government. Visit with your district's chief fiscal officer to learn his/her opinions regarding the state aid formula. Discuss how the district obtains its money and identify the general strengths and weaknesses of district funding.

3

BASIC FUNDING STRUCTURES

THE CONTEXT OF FUNDING SCHOOLS

In Chapter 2, we made a strong case that the context of funding schools is very complex, in large part because of the tense political environment in which education operates. Most organizations today are complex, but people in business or industry may have less chance of misunderstanding how their organization's funding happens. For most people, it's as simple as recognizing that a product or service is offered for which consumers are willing to pay a high enough price for the owner to make enough profit to want to stay in business. These same people know that the business will die if the product is no longer popular or is overpriced. The retail electronics industry is a good illustration of this point. It is common for retailers to hire analysts to track competitors' prices in the belief that a product selling for a few dollars less leads to thousands—even millions—of dollars in lost profits. To people in education, it seems puzzling that a slight difference could create such dire results until two facts are known. First, it is the effect of a slightly lower price creating a sale or no-sale and the subsequent loss of all mark-up that really counts. After all, everyone expects a retailer to make a sizable profit on each sale. Let's say a television has a $150 mark-up. If a store lost a sale because of a $10 advertised price difference, it lost far more than just $10. Multiply that times hundreds or thousands of lost sales, and the effect is huge. Second, retailers know that people do odd things—like spending time and money driving across town to save a very small amount. Hiring analysts to track prices thus might create an edge that helps businesses survive in a cutthroat world.

We are not suggesting that schools should engage in price wars to survive in an educational market-driven economy. Some useful ideas about educational entrepreneurship could follow, but our point is that education could profit greatly by recognizing that market forces really do drive school budgets. Like it or not, education competes for scarce tax resources, and people simply do not like to pay taxes at all. With that statement, we come to the crux of the current chapter. People in business clearly understand their sources of revenue in the form of product sales or services. Education's stakeholders, however, have a much fuzzier concept of revenue sources and in many cases never go beyond the general idea that taxes somehow fund schools.

Although the topic of education's funding sources is complex, we can obtain a working grasp of the issues by once again asking some common-sense questions to help frame this chapter. For example, what kinds of revenue are used to support schools? Because education is only one responsibility of government, what other governmental units compete with schools for funding? Because school districts are the basic educational unit, how are districts funded and how is fairness satisfied? Extending our earlier discussion from Chapter 2, what more can we learn about how the federal government figures into support for education? Similarly, what more can we learn about how much of the responsibility for the cost of schools falls to states? Likewise, is there more that needs to be said about whether the cost to local communities is increasing or decreasing? Importantly, how is money distributed to individual districts? Are there any funding innovations on the horizon? These and other questions serve to move our discussion to the next level: That is, now that we have a beginning grasp on the politics of schools, values, and money, it is time to extend our knowledge to include revenue sources and school funding plans.

REVENUE FOR SCHOOLS

A constant theme throughout this book is that revenue for schools is a source of growing contention in all states. The root of this struggle fundamentally derives from disputes over what schools should do and the unavoidable fact that school revenues are mostly derived from taxes. Although other revenue sources exist, it is unrealistic to think that taxes are less than the lion's share or that taxes will be replaced by some heretofore undiscovered pool of money.

WHAT IS THE OVERARCHING TAX SYSTEM?

The history of taxation is extensively covered in many locations, including our own books.[1]

Everyone realizes that taxes are necessary, and everyone enjoys the many benefits paid for by tax revenues. A strong national defense, highways, social security benefits, and revenue sharing are among the services funded by federal taxation. City streets, police and fire protection, and safety codes are among the local tax benefits enjoyed by citizens. Roads, clean water, and community development often emanate from taxes paid to intermediate units of government such as counties. Local taxes especially provide many highly visible services, including schools.

The overarching tax system therefore has three principal players in the form of federal, state, and local governments. Each has a very different role,

---

1. For a relatively brief history of taxation for public education illustrating contentiousness, see Chapter 3 in David C. Thompson, R. Craig Wood, and David Honeyman, *Fiscal Leadership for Schools: Concepts and Practices* (New York: Longman, 1994), 131–72.

although overlap is significant. Each level of government also has a relationship to schools in some varying proportion.

What Is the Federal Tax System?

The federal tax system that exists today is far removed from the early awkward attempts to create a federal tax structure. In a nation marked by suspicion of all central government, the federal tax system today has become a massive organization best perceived for overspending and uncontrolled growth in debt. The drama of overspending is reflected in the debate about a balanced budget amendment, a debate that ebbs and flows over time depending on the mood of Congress. That deficit reduction is important is nearly unchallenged, as we saw earlier that federal spending has resulted in a deficit that amounted in late 2004 to an unpaid liability of $25,200 against every man, woman, and child—a debt that continues to increase daily by staggering proportions.

The debate over federal spending takes root in efforts to limit the role of central government. Historically a nation of tax protesters, Americans have fought heavy federal taxation until only recently. Numerous attempts at taxation dating from the 1600s were bitterly opposed by the colonists and actually led to the Revolutionary War in 1776. Even the war itself was the target of tax protest, creating the first instance of a deficit as the new nation struggled with debt repayment. Early presidents and congressional leaders were themselves mostly antitax zealots, leading to a weak federal tax system that depended almost entirely on tariffs and customs taxes for the first 125 years of nationhood. Repeated attempts to enact a federal income tax failed or were rescinded shortly after enactment, including a case in which the U.S. Supreme Court declared an 1894 income tax law invalid on the grounds that the federal Constitution did not expressly authorize Congress to collect such a tax.

The growing needs of the nation, however, caused an impoverished Congress to propose the structure that eventually permitted the tax system that exists today. In 1909, Congress proposed a Sixteenth Amendment to the Constitution, which would grant Congress the power to "lay and collect taxes on incomes, from whatever source derived, without apportionment among the States, and without regard to any census or enumeration." The amendment was ratified in 1913, whereon Congress enacted a tax of 1% on incomes, quickly leading to the familiar progressive tax concept based on higher rates for higher incomes—a concept that has evolved into a massive arm of the federal government in the form of the Internal Revenue Service and yielding revenues that most people find staggering. By 2003, estimated individual income taxes exceeded $858 billion, corporate income tax $143 billion, social insurance $726 billion, excise taxes $68 billion, and so on almost endlessly.

These realities yielded more than $1.8 trillion in revenue, although massive federal debt continued to be a reality for every living American.[2]

Although the federal tax system and its revenues have grown by leaps and bounds, the path has not been smooth. At the same time that Congress has been under pressure to reduce both debt and taxes, people have continued to expect national defense, unemployment benefits, disability insurance, good retirement and highways, and so forth. Congress has always managed to spend more than it receives, and education has been one of its beneficiaries, although as we now know, the federal role has been indirect because the Tenth Amendment leaves education to the states. Nonetheless, federal revenues have been widely infused into schools. Ever since the Northwest Ordinance in 1787 first granted land to states for educational purposes, the federal government has tried to assist states in areas of federal interest. As we saw in the last chapter, the list of programs aided by Congress is long and includes special education, desegregation and other civil rights legislation, school lunch programs, vocational education, and many others. Although the role has been indirect, the dollars have not been trivial. Estimated federal support in 2003 for K–12 education totaled $32.8 billion, averaging about 7% of all public school revenues.[3]

These data, however, do not include other federal programs indirectly benefiting schools such as income security payments, social services grants, human development services, training and employment assistance, health services, and a wide scope of other federal aid to states. Similarly, higher education aid is not reflected in these amounts.

These programs are very familiar to people associated with public schools today. Although there is a common perception of relatively minor involvement by the federal government in education, the data on federal regulations, requirements for services, and even the amounts of federal school aid meaningfully dispute the notion of a weak federal role.

What Is the State Tax System?

An important aspect of taxation in the United States has been parallel development of tax systems. As everyone knows, states have played an important role in the nation's history, so much so that even today we hear issues of states' rights debated vigorously in widely respected forums. People feel strongly about the relationship of government to its constituents, and the authority and power of states has been jealously guarded.

The pervasive nature ascribed to the federal government is equally true of state tax systems. The dissimilarity, of course, is the possible number of

2. U.S. Bureau of the Census, *Statistical Abstracts of the United States 2003* (Washington, DC: U.S. Government Printing Office, 2003), 325. Data taken from Table 481, Federal Receipts by Source 1980–2003.

3. U.S. Bureau of the Census, *Statistical Abstracts of the United States 2003* (Washington, DC: U.S. Government Printing Office, 2003), 324. Data on outlays taken from Table 479, Federal Outlays by Detailed Function: 1980–2003.

variations on tax themes, as there are 50 states but only one federal government. As a result, each state's tax system has been affected by unique economic and political factors within the state and further affected by the relationship of states to the federal government.

As we saw earlier, colonial tax systems predated federal attempts to levy taxes. In fact, the system of representative government arising from elected representatives in Congress guaranteed that states would closely guard their autonomy, a fact borne out in the U.S. Constitution, which grants to the states all powers not exclusively reserved to Congress itself. Differences in geography, climate, economy, and preferences further ensured that states would approach taxation differently, as each region of the nation has been driven by unique needs. Many of the earliest government structures in the colonies were directly aimed at countering a strong federal seat of power, beginning with the Virginia legislature's defiance in 1619 against the Virginia Company's attempts to revoke certain freedoms. By 1700, all colonies had charters guaranteeing liberties borne of conflict between the Crown and independent-minded colonialists.

Not surprisingly, colonial (and later state) systems of taxation were tightly linked to local politics and economics. As the need for revenue expanded with growth in population, the New England colonies tended to tax personal property, land, and houses in the belief that every person's tax-paying ability was different and that everyone should be made to pay. Concentrated wealth in the South meant only a few persons would pay big taxes, so a revenue system based on exports and imports was developed to shift taxes away from the wealthy few. Other taxes such as poll and faculty taxes were used as proxies for ability to pay. The middle colonies picked up this system and made refinements to these taxes. Colonies also ran lotteries or invented other special revenue sources.

As the nation developed, strong state curbs on federal power were deliberate from the outset. The Constitution gave the federal government only limited power to lay taxes for the purpose of paying off debts and for the general welfare of the nation. States, however, were granted full powers, including control of local government, chartering of towns, building of roads and bridges, protection of civil liberty and, of course, care of the federal government by election to Congress. Such responsibility has not been without cost to states, however. By the end of the Civil War, colonial-style tax systems were no longer adequate given a growing population, and the answer seemed to be state authority to tax all property. Widespread tax evasion was the rule, however, in that houses and cattle were visible whereas property such as bonds, notes, and other negotiable instruments were easily hidden. The effect was to make states look bad, as the entire tax burden inadvertently fell to real property owners who could not hide their wealth.

Beginning in about 1880, study commissions began to explore new ways to improve state tax systems, especially administration of the property tax. This resulted in creation of tax equalization boards, efforts to improve property assessment, uncovering tax evasion, and refining tax requirements on various types of property. Efforts still met with only limited success, as equalization proved politically unfeasible and as evasion and resistance to taxes were impossible to eliminate. The numerous woes of property tax administration ultimately led to many recommendations that states should abandon the property tax in favor of other tax bases. Faced with property tax administration problems, states began to rely less on property, and by 1920 several states had adopted both individual and corporate income taxes. Although the property tax at the state level has never been eliminated, states have enacted many other taxes on commercial transactions such as sales and excise taxes. Income taxes have also been enacted in many states.

Growth in state taxation from 1902 until the present time has been phenomenal.[4] In 1902, states were levying only small property taxes and other miscellaneous taxes, whereas states now regularly charge taxes against real estate and motor vehicles and reap huge sales and gross receipts taxes and tax on personal income. Additionally, states long ago began withholding taxes for retirement and unemployment and many other programs. Federal revenue sharing entered the picture as well, so that by 2000, states were collecting more than $274 billion in federal aid, up from only $192 million in 1902. The greatest growth has been in the individual income tax, which in 2000 produced nearly $195 billion and in sales tax, which yielded another $252 billion to states. Although states depend on many sources for revenue, it is clearly sales and income that make up the lion's share.

Although state revenues have grown, states have also found ways to spend most of their resources. The biggest state costs have been education, welfare, highways, health, and natural resources. In 2000, state education expenditures exceeded $346 billion. Welfare costs reached nearly $239 billion in the same year, whereas highways received more than $74 billion. States generally have not engaged in deficit spending like the federal government, oftentimes because of individual states' cash basis laws that require balanced budgets. States also have found taxpayers more willing to support initiatives within state borders than has been true at the federal level, making state coffers relatively more flush. But that is not to say that state resources have been ample, as the same Constitution that prevents the federal government from assuming a direct educational role has assigned it to states. As a result, states have had to assume a massive part of education's costs, resulting in the complex state aid formulas discussed later in this chapter.

What Is the Local Tax System?

From our discussion so far, it is clear that tax systems in the United States are interrelated and independent at the same time. The federal tax system is limited to only those powers granted to Congress, and it has monopolized the individual income tax—a reality that effectively limits how much lesser

---

4.   U.S. Bureau of the Census, *Statistical Abstracts of the United States 2003* (Washington, DC: U.S. Government Printing Office, 2003), 296. Data taken from Table 454, State Governments—Summary of Finances: 1990–2000.

units of governments can go to the same source without angering taxpayers. The state tax system is expected to pick up where federal responsibility leaves off, but with broad state powers implied. States have opted to tax income too, although they have turned heavily to sales tax as well, with some additional reliance on the property tax. Yet states have often chosen to shift obligations downward to local government, in the belief that people prefer government at the lowest common denominator. Schools have been affected greatly by shifts in power among levels of governments, with implications for tax revenues and sources.

Although federal and state governments have tended to be centrally vested, local government has been highly fragmented to include counties, cities, schools, and other even smaller units such as townships. Despite overlapping small units, local tax systems have been limited mostly to the property tax to care for the many needs assigned to local government. Federal and state governments have dealt with broad issues, whereas local units of government have dealt with issues viewed as mostly local in scope. In many states, this has meant local responsibility for education, some kinds of welfare, local health, roads, police and fire protection, corrections, sanitation, and issues of economic development. In addition, local government is the most visible, so that patrons are able and more willing to invest time in being heard, including registering complaints and actively shaping the outcome of controversial issues.

Because federal and state governments have first claim on tax sources, local units have been left to tax the remainder. This has meant that local government has come to depend on three main sources for funding. Local units have turned to revenue sharing from the federal government, yielding more than $32 billion in 2000. A second source has been state revenue sharing, yielding about $317 billion in the same year. The third source has been local taxation, yielding nearly $333 billion, a burden mostly borne by the local property tax, which made up nearly 72% of the total local tax bill in the year 2000. But like higher levels, local government has found ways to spend most of what it collects, as local units (primarily cities and counties) spent about $996 billion of the more than $1.04 trillion it collected in 2000.[5]

But although schools are local units, they have not had the luxury of over-spending, as most states keep education on a strict cash basis. In addition, revenue sharing has meant little to schools, as federal and state grants-in-aid to education do not participate directly in revenue sharing. Although states have used their various revenue sources to fund their share of education's costs, local districts have been limited almost entirely to property taxes for support of schools.

---

5.   U.S. Bureau of the Census, *Statistical Abstracts of the United States 2003* (Washington, DC: U.S. Government Printing Office, 2003), 302. Data taken from Table 457, Local Governments—Revenue by State: 2000; also Table 458, Local Governments—Expenditures and Debt by State 2000, 304.

Tax System Summary

For schools, the effect of multiple and overlapping tax systems has been complex. First, federal aid to education has been sizable but limited in scope, with little expectation for change given federal Constitutional constraints. Second, state aid has become increasingly important as states have responded to education reform and to aggressive litigation testing state constitutional duties to schools. Third, local school districts have been heavily property tax-dependent, so that the mix of revenues to a typical district in the United States was 7.3% federal, 49.7% state, and 40.8% local in 2001.[6] Fourth, the revenue mix has been highly varied on a state-by-state basis, with local support ranging from a low 0.5% in Hawaii to a high 62.6% in Nevada in the same year. Fifth, schools usually have been prevented from tapping tax bases other than property, as most states do not allow schools to tax income or other kinds of wealth. The net sum is that schools are primarily supported by state and local taxes, with limited but meaningful federal assistance.

Answers to some questions we raised earlier are now possible. We see that the overarching tax system is made up of federal, state, and local tax structures. The federal system mostly relies on individual income taxes, and its relationship to schools is tertiary, although powerful. State systems are based mostly on individual income and retail sales taxes, with relationships to schools dependent on state preferences—a relationship that is consequently either primary or secondary. Local tax systems are based mostly on property taxes—a reality that has caused the property tax to be seen as a school tax, because schools seldom have any other taxing authority. Under these conditions, the local relationship to schools is very strong. From this flows the observation, then, that the kinds of revenue available to support schools are fundamentally sales and income taxes at the state level and property taxes at the local level. Likewise, our discussion showed that the answer to what other entities compete with schools for tax revenue is the whole gamut, taking in all of the many agencies sponsored and controlled by federal, state, and local governments.

FUNDING FOR SCHOOLS

With a basic grasp of tax systems behind us, we now turn to an overview of how school districts are funded. This is an issue that goes deeper than just overarching tax systems, as it raises questions of distributional fairness. If we believe, as we said in the first chapter, that the amount of money available to students is important to the success or failure of schools, then it follows that how money flows to school districts is a critical question of fundamental fairness, that is, an equity question.

In this last part of the chapter, we turn to exactly those issues. Again, we ask several important questions such as, how do states deal with aid distribu-

---

6.   See Figure 2.8, pp. 54–55.

tion? What is a fair formula for granting money to individual districts? Are there innovations or promises on the horizon? We tackle these questions because all the chapters in this book fit together like a house of cards: Even though the chapters can be read in any order, if one support mechanism is shaky, the house of cards collapses. It is our view that the whole educational system risks disaster if revenues are inequitably distributed. In sum, good tax systems must provide adequate revenue that is distributed to schools using equitable aid formulas, and schools in turn must build budgets that offer educational benefits to everyone—a serious challenge in today's social and economic climate.

WHAT ARE STATE AID FORMULAS?

Almost everyone realizes that money for schools comes primarily from taxes. In most states, the property tax is a major source of local revenue for schools. At the same time, however, almost everyone realizes that virtually no school district in the U.S. is completely at the mercy of local tax bases for the support of education. Local tax base is simply too uneven to permit the revenue variability that would arise from district wealth alone, a fact recognized by even the most recalcitrant state that believes the fairness debate has gone too far. Instead, most states have tried to develop state school aid schemes that speak to some basic elements of equity. Aid formulas thus attract a great deal of attention at federal, state and local levels, although states and local units of government have been the primary players in actually creating and implementing formula equity—both by choice and by force of litigation.

Under these conditions, state aid formulas are legislative tools used to intervene into the disparities in educational opportunity that would be present if schools were entirely dependent on local tax base. It is not hard to imagine the size of such disparity absent intervention, as most states have extremes of community wealth. A fairly common case, for example, is a public utility power plant in a small school district that creates vast wealth per pupil in the form of taxable property. Another district in the same state may be of similar geographic and population size, but may have only marginal farmland as its tax base. Disparities in wealth per pupil in such cases can easily be 100:1 or greater, meaning that the wealthy district can raise $100 for every $1 raised in the poorer district—all at the same tax rate! The example in Figure 3.1 is actually very common, with the wealthiest district able to raise $25 million locally, five times more than the poorest district—all at a uniform tax rate of 100 mills—ignoring the fact that a poor district likely cannot afford to tax itself at such a strenuous rate. The effect is vastly different tax rates to produce the same revenue per pupil, or vastly different expenditures per pupil if local patrons do not rally in support of the higher tax rate scenario. Any number of variations on this example can be created to fit any state's circumstances—states with huge cities, for example, face vast disparities in tax base because of suburban flight. In sum, a state school aid formula seeks to reduce tax base differences by actively offsetting the effects of wealth disparity on educational opportunity.

Figure 3.1. Tax Capacity at 100 Mills Uniform Effort

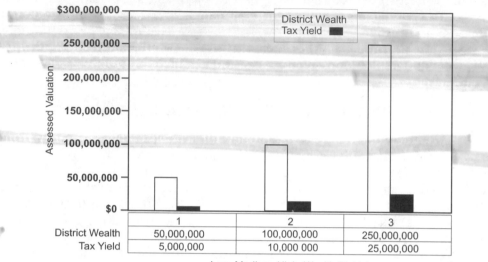

	1	2	3
District Wealth	50,000,000	100,000,000	250,000,000
Tax Yield	5,000,000	10,000 000	25,000,000

Low, Medium, High, Wealth Districts

WHERE DID AID FORMULAS COME FROM?

Americans have not been very enthusiastic about paying taxes at any time in the nation's history. A big part of the reluctance to pay taxes was cultural, but real problems have existed in tax administration, aggravating a bad situation. For example, tax evasion has plagued all levels of government, both as people simply have refused to pay taxes and as they have found ways to avoid taxes, both legally and illegally. The many tax problems faced by government led to study of tax fairness and administration, so that knowledge about good tax systems, with implications for schools, grew rapidly during the first half of the last century.

Growth of schools in the nation, accompanied by growth in state responsibility for education, also resulted in state interest in providing some fiscal aid to local school districts. Although we are skipping much historical development here, it is the case that by 1890 states were providing nearly $34 million in aid to schools or approximately 24% of revenues. A goodly portion of such aid was stimulated by the fledgling concept of educational equity that followed on the heels of the first studies within states that revealed vast disparities arising from local tax base dependence. Although state aid predates the work of Elwood Cubberley, he is credited with initiating the dramatic rise in interest in state aid, and in 1906 he published a monograph that set the tone for the future.[7] Cubberley's point was simple, as he argued that all the children of the state are equal and entitled to equal advantages. In studying several states, he concluded that few, if any, had met this demand because educational quality varied greatly and generally rose or fell in tandem with local wealth.

Cubberley's work sparked a entire growth industry, as other scholars began similar studies. Harlan Updegraff's work[8] in 1922 extended thinking another step. Studying rural schools in New York State, Updegraff argued that state aid should vary by local wealth and according to local tax effort. Where Cubberley had validated the need for aid and created the concept of equality, Updegraff introduced the ideas of equalization and reward for tax effort—that is, districts could receive more state aid by taxing themselves harder. The next major advance came in 1923 with the work of George Strayer and Robert Haig.[9] Accepting all that had already been done, Strayer and Haig took a giant step forward by advocating that concepts of equality and equalization should also result in a degree of minimum educational program opportunity. Their view essentially bound the state to go beyond just money to include some measure of program equality. They additionally argued that such a program should be available under uniform tax effort. The result was a foundation program, whereby the state would guarantee a foundation on which local districts could then build.

Another significant step was taken in the work of Paul Mort in 1924.[10] Mort extended the minimum program concept by defining the weighted pupil, that is, arguing that educational programs will have different costs to be equal. For example, small schools cost more because of inefficiencies. His contribution was to critically press how states determined aid to districts, arguing that aid should vary along multiple criteria based in trying to estimate true educational costs, rather than just granting aid in a blindly neutral fashion.

The ideas of these researchers were widely accepted when creating state aid programs, as states tried to conceptualize how they should aid schools. One last major breakthrough was less enthusiastically received, however. Henry Morrison, writing in 1930, was so disgusted by the extremes in the quality of educational programs that he argued vehemently for abolition of all school districts, while favoring a complete state takeover.[11] This was not radical in his view because he believed that states had the ultimate duty to

---

7. Elwood P. Cubberley, *School Funds and Their Apportionment* (New York: Columbia Teachers College, 1906).
8. Harlan Updegraff, *Rural School Survey of New York State: Financial Support* (Ithaca, NY: Author, 1992).
9. George D. Strayer and Robert M. Haig, *The Financing of Education in the State of New York*, vol. 1 (New York: Macmillan, 1923).
10. Paul Mort, *The Measurement of Educational Need* (New York: Columbia Teachers College, 1924).
11. Henry C. Morrison, *School Revenue* (Chicago: University of Chicago Press, 1930).

control education, so that fiscal inequality would never be resolved until tax base and educational program control were statewide affairs. Obviously, such thinking ran counter to local control and was not warmly embraced by legislatures—a sentiment that remains today.

What Is a Fair Formula?

Development of state aid plans clearly had fairness in mind, at least in terms of what theorists intended, by suggesting ways to make educational opportunities more equal through the use of money. A state aid formula, according to their thinking, should fit the unique needs and features of school districts within each state, and the plan should apply universally within the state's borders. States developed aid plans along these lines, with each plan reflecting certain educational and political philosophies and realities. For example, states taking an aggressive view of state responsibility for education developed school aid plans that made the state a fuller partner in funding schemes. Conversely, states taking a more local control perspective tended to devise aid plans that left considerable local freedom to exceed a set of educational minimums. These facts were the basis for a genre of state aid plans that fall into several general types, based on what states believed to be fair. Over the years, grant-in-aid plans have become known as flat grants, equalization grants, multi-tier grants, and full state funding grants.

Flat Grants

The earliest form of state aid, a flat grant is a flat sum of money paid to districts without concern for a local share or local capacity to pay. This plan was justified by its advocates as neutrally distributed. Critics, however, argued that wealth disparity remained unchanged and that aid amounts were too low to make a real difference. Flat grants were popular, however; at the turn of the century, 38 states were using them to aid public schools. Popularity fell only as school finance litigation began to escalate in the 1970s. No state now relies solely on flat grants as the principal finance scheme, although they are still used for other purposes or in multi-tier combinations.

The operation and effect of a flat grant is illustrated in Figure 3.2. The graph shows that while a $1,000 flat grant per pupil undoubtedly would be welcomed in low-, medium-, and high-wealth districts alike, its impact is completely unrelated to local ability to pay for education. It is likely most desperately needed in the low-wealth district, and it certainly represents a larger proportion of total expenditure per pupil in the poorer district. However, the introduction of a flat grant has absolutely no impact on equalization: that is, wealth-based inequalities are preserved while expenditures simply go up by exactly $1,000 in all districts (or alternatively, the local unit of government might choose to reduce local tax effort by an equivalent amount so that students are no better off after the introduction of state aid). The net sum in poor districts is no change in equalization, and the net sum in wealthy districts is enrichment unrelated to need. Flat grants thus represented a significant step forward in terms of state participation in education's costs, but it represented no gain at all in assuaging the inequalities related to unequal tax base.

Figure 3.2. Effect of a $1,000 Flat Grant

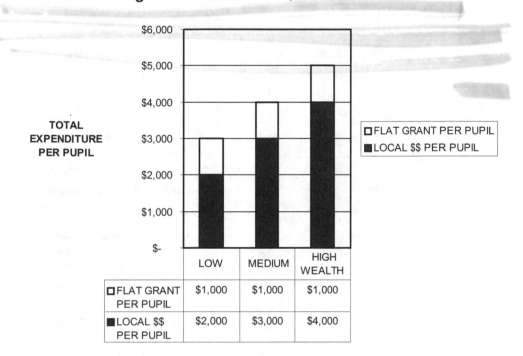

	LOW	MEDIUM	HIGH WEALTH
☐ FLAT GRANT PER PUPIL	$1,000	$1,000	$1,000
■ LOCAL $$ PER PUPIL	$2,000	$3,000	$4,000

Equalization Grants

Equalization plans include a wide variety of state aid formulas seeking to grant aid inversely to local ability to pay for schools. Largely in response to the nonequalizing effect of earlier aid plans, equalization grants were designed to bring expenditure levels in rich and poor districts closer together, or at least to better equalize poorer districts' opportunity to spend at the same level as wealthier districts. Although many kinds of equalization grants exist, all such plans are based on the idea of increasing state aid to those local districts with the least fiscal capacity. Differing political philosophies have driven the actual formula designs in individual states, primarily by virtue of two decisions that had to be made: whether the state should set expenditure levels and tax rates, or whether the state should let districts set their own tax-and-spend limits. Major kinds of equalization plans flowing from these decisions became known as minimum foundation plans and resource accessibility plans.

Foundation plans were based on a minimum concept. This meant several things. First, a foundation is politically and factually effective in that equality is met by initial expenditure and tax rate uniformity. Second, the state requires districts to provide a minimum educational program. Third, a minimum foundation encourages additional local spending discretion. Fourth, the costs are better equalized because aid is inversely granted on local ability to pay. On the downside, foundation minimum expenditure and state shares must be high enough to encourage local effort above the minimum. The foundation has been the most popular equalization formula, and many states currently use some form of foundation as the primary means to distribute state aid. Several states also use a foundation in combination with other aid programs.

Resource accessibility plans also have sought to equalize revenues by taking a different approach. Where a foundation seeks statewide minimum standards in tax rate and expenditure levels, resource equalization tries to empower districts to make their own fiscal and program decisions unhindered by wealth limitations. This means that variability in programs and expenditures are acceptable so long as availability of revenue is not the reason for such variability. Thus, whereas foundation plans promote minimum equality, resource accessibility plans attempt to balance wealth, or ability to pay, in each district through formulas that adjust for tax base differences. The vehicles have been various percentage equalizing (PE) plans, and these plans have been further refined to include variations such as guaranteed tax base (GTB), guaranteed tax yield (GTY), and district power equalization (DPE). Each resource equalization plan approaches the problem of unequal resources uniquely. PE plans guarantee a constant percentage of budget from the state based on local ability to pay with the local district setting costs and programs. GTB and GTY equalize revenues by assuring districts the same tax capacity as every other district. DPE carries the resource accessibility concept to its ultimate potential of recapture of excess revenue capacity by requiring that districts with wealth greater than the state's guarantee must pay money back to the state for support of poorer districts. Compared to the popularity of foundation plans, fewer states have adopted resource accessibility, and most states have limited the politically risky features. Almost no states have adopted power equalization, at least on a long-term basis. Yet equalization schemes have served a useful purpose, in that school finance reform in the 1970s gave impetus to self-scrutiny by states of their aid formulas, with resulting improvement of equalization that has carried forward to the present day.

The operation and effect of a simple equalization plan is illustrated in Figure 3.3. The graph shows a foundation plan, with a uniform tax rate and with an expected $5,000 per pupil expenditure target. The poorest district raises only 20% of the target, and the state is obligated to provide the other 80%. Conversely, the wealthiest district raises 100% of the target at the uniform tax rate. As we said earlier, countless variations on this scheme are possible. Some states provide local option leeway above the minimum expenditure, and the leeway may or may not qualify for state aid depending on the state's preferences. Recapture might be built in by setting the statewide tax rate high enough to produce more revenue than districts can legally spend per pupil. The variations are too many to illustrate here, but the effect of aid inversely related to ability to pay is clearly the aim of any equalization formula. Equalization plans are costly to states, both in terms of actual dollars when setting adequate resource levels and in political terms because concepts like low aid, zero aid, or recapture (negative aid) can take a toll over time if wealthy communities resent sending their tax dollars to support other school districts (see earlier discussion in Chapter 2 on long-term political consequences of aggressive attempts at equalization).

Figure 3.3. Effect of an Equalized Foundation Grant

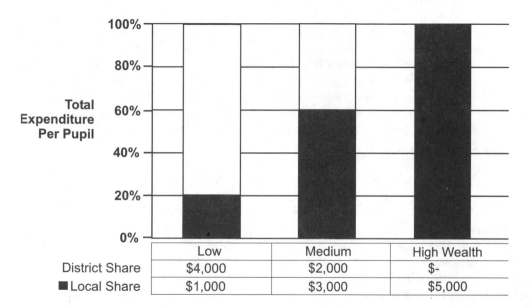

	Low	Medium	High Wealth
District Share	$4,000	$2,000	$-
■ Local Share	$1,000	$3,000	$5,000

Multi-Tier Grants

Because all aid plans have politically objectionable features or inherent weaknesses, policy makers have sometimes created state aid formulas that combine parts of several plans. For example, an astute legislature might enact a foundation program combined with local leeway. Variations might include capping local leeway, equalizing the local leeway portion at the same aid ratio as the foundation amount, or equalizing the local option only to a certain point after which no cap and no aid apply. Other pieces, such as flat grants or incentive aid, could also be attached. Such designs are known as multi-tier grants. Combinations of multi-tiering are limited only by good sense and money.

Several states use multi-tiering to set the state's share of education's costs. The most common mixture combines flat grants or foundations with some form of percentage equalization. As a general rule one scheme provides base aid, whereas the other formula is added for political reasons. Figure 3.4 illustrates a very simple multi-tier aid formula by combining a base mandated (foundation) per pupil amount under uniform tax rate, with an additional 25% local option leeway aided at the same aid ratio as the foundation amount. In this example, districts can choose to spend up to $6,250 per pupil, but they must tax themselves voluntarily for the portion identified as the local share of local option. The state's aid ratio, however, is guaranteed up to the maximum per pupil expenditure level, so choosing to exert higher local tax effort means more aid in exchange for additional local spending on children's education. Of course, districts can choose to not exert the required extra tax effort and thereby forego the enticement of additional state aid. Many policy decisions are imbedded in these designs: for example, Figure 3.4 contains a concession to wealthy districts, as it has been designed to provide an additional 25% spending window for any district that opts for additional local tax effort—a disequalizing but politically smart move. In essence, multi-tiering has seemed to some states to be a palatable alternative in a world where politics and fairness must be closely balanced.

Full State Funding Grants

We noted earlier that full state funding has never been accepted in the real-world policy arena. Regarded as radical and inimical to local control of schools, full state funding has received little support except in a couple of instances. The best defense of full state funding is its strict observance of education as the state's inescapable duty, but that has not been enough to offset the drawbacks associated with loss of local control.

Operationally, full state funding is extremely simple. It places all the resources of a state within reach of every child by requiring a statewide tax, apportioned equally without regard to location or wealth. The plan is different, however, in that there can be no local leeway because localities no longer factor into the plan. Further, the tax is statewide and is not considered to be a local resource. Finally, recapture is inherently included because uniform statewide taxes will produce differing amounts from the various communities, with some exceeding uniform expenditure requirements. These features are radically different from all other plans, particularly running contrary to local control—a feature confirmed in that all revenues collected locally are sent to the state for redistribution on a statewide basis—that is, local tax resources actually belong to the state.

Under these stipulations, only a few states (under very rare conditions) have adopted full state funding. Hawaii's single school district structure has permitted full state funding, and the unusual nature of the District of Columbia's dependence on Congress for funding describes the only other true case. Some people would argue that their states are "nearly full state funded" because of high levels of state aid with only small local tax contribution. But for

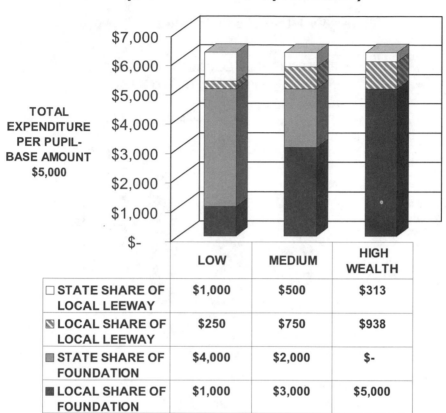

Figure 3.4. Effect of a Foundation Grant with Equalized Local 25% Option Leeway

	LOW	MEDIUM	HIGH WEALTH
☐ STATE SHARE OF LOCAL LEEWAY	$1,000	$500	$313
◩ LOCAL SHARE OF LOCAL LEEWAY	$250	$750	$938
▣ STATE SHARE OF FOUNDATION	$4,000	$2,000	$-
■ LOCAL SHARE OF FOUNDATION	$1,000	$3,000	$5,000

the most part, full state funding has been antithetical to the American ideal of local control, despite the plan's ability to eradicate wealth-based differences.

Figure 3.5 illustrates the ideal full state funding plan, although oversimplified here by a lack of vertical adjustments such as diseconomy of scale (discussed in the next section). Figure 3.5 shows a mandate that each district spend exactly $5,000 per pupil, and the local share is financed by a uniform 20 mills. The poorest district can raise only $40 per pupil in local revenue, whereas the wealthiest district's tax yield per pupil exceeds the minimum/maximum expenditure per pupil. The result is that the state must provide aid to all districts in the exact amount of $5,000 per pupil, but it does so in part by taking $6,000 away from the wealthiest district (recapture) and giving $4,960 of that amount to the poorest district—a balancing act that involves state-level decisions on whether to set the statewide mill rate high enough to cover the cost of education in all districts, or whether to supplement educational expenditures by tapping other state sources such as sales and income taxes.

Figure 3.5 Effect of a Full State Funding Grant

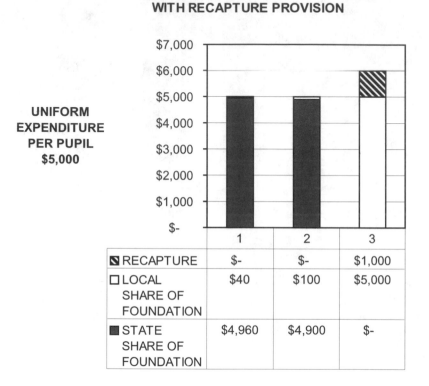

UNDER 20 MILLS LOCAL TAX EFFORT
WITH RECAPTURE PROVISION

UNIFORM
EXPENDITURE
PER PUPIL
$5,000

	1	2	3
RECAPTURE	$-	$-	$1,000
LOCAL SHARE OF FOUNDATION	$40	$100	$5,000
STATE SHARE OF FOUNDATION	$4,960	$4,900	$-

Adjustments to Basic Formulas

Our discussion to this point has only considered regular programs, without consideration for any special adjustments to aid formulas based on inequality of the human condition. In its most basic form, this simply means that *horizontal* fairness requires all children to be considered as equals, but that children are not equally advantaged physically, economically, and so on. States have increasingly come to aid such inequalities, and a common vehicle is through *vertical* adjustments to the basic basic-aid formulas we just described. As a generalization, vertical adjustments fall into categories of *need* equalization or *cost* equalization.

Need Equalization

The concept of need speaks directly to the inequalities among children relating to physical and economic disadvantage. Anyone who has spent time around children realizes that they have complex needs that cannot be addressed simply by an equality based on blind neutrality. Although there is much disagreement about how to address children's needs on physical, psychological, emotional, and many other dimensions, inequality of the human condition is undisputed. Need equalization has therefore become a critical player in state aid to schools. A huge outlay of programs has sprung up around the concept of special needs, most of which fall into categories relating to *compensatory education, bilingual education,* and *special education,* with the recent addition of *early childhood education.* It is a modern reality that most states provide some additional support to these areas in an effort to equalize fundamental inequalities.

Compensatory education primarily tries to redress social and economic inequality, a concept familiar now in this book because the social context of education in Chapters 1 and 2 particularly spoke to social and economic disadvantage. The federal government has long had an interest in compensatory education through many kinds of legislation, ranging from school lunch to special reading programs. In addition, many states provide aid to compensatory education in some way. Compensatory aid usually is added above the cost of regular education, either by a weighting scheme that increases per-pupil costs, or by a flat grant tied to regular education costs. Local districts often are required to share in the extra costs. At the present time, a majority of states provides some kind of compensatory education services.

With growth in immigration, aid to *bilingual education* has become increasingly important to states and local districts. Various court rulings have spurred the need for bilingual programs, in that civil rights legislation has been held to encompass language barriers. Court rulings and other federal legislation have caused states to provide bilingual programs or risk lawsuits or loss of federal funding for failing to meet bilingual mandates. The response has been varied, as states have taken very different approaches to aiding bilingual programs. States with larger bilingual populations often spend the most and usually provide more extensive programs, whereas less affected states spend less and sometimes provide more limited services. More than two-thirds of all states now aid bilingual education (up from only about 50% at the first edition of this book), although aid formulas and amounts of funding still vary considerably. The most common methods use additional pupil weights or provide flat grants beyond regular education costs.

A relatively recent concern has been exhibited for *early childhood education.* Various states have implemented programs, both on the basis of preschool mandates and due to a belief that early intervention may have a positive return in later years of schooling. A large majority of states now provides some type of early childhood education services, although data are sparse on funding methods.

Special education has been the most visible vertical need program for many years. Although special schools have been around for many decades, special education has taken on new meaning in the last four decades with enactment of federal special education legislation and an aggressive history of litigation surrounding the rights of special needs children (see Chapter 2 earlier). Although other vertical needs adjustments receive at least modest attention in most states, special education has been the center of intense activity, with every indication of continuing far into the future as a powerful political and legal force.

States generally fund special education in much the same way as other special needs programs, but the mandated nature of special education and the vast amount of money involved result in strict governmental monitoring, particularly because special education funding involves a mix of federal, state, and local monies. States typically fund special education by providing additional per-pupil or per-teacher weighting or by using restricted or categorical grants to reimburse districts for the excess costs of special education. Many states either weight pupils by handicapping condition or make other weighted provisions for instruction such as funding special teacher costs or classroom units up to a capped amount. Other states pay all excess costs for special services or reimburse some percentage of total costs. A few states use flat grants or combinations of aid plans. An arena in which constant change prevents up-to-the-minute accuracy when reporting funding plans in a textbook, all states now provide some method of aiding special education.

Cost Equalization

Unique conditions in states have encouraged other concerns for equalization as well. In particular, state responsibility for education has caused states to pay attention to other pupil inequalities that may arise related to geographic and economic conditions. Often these issues go to economy of scale, as districts may experience higher costs because of their very urban or very rural circumstances. Cost equalization in school funding usually takes two forms. One form recognizes that different costs may arise due to economy or diseconomy of scale. The other form considers the marketplace. For example, higher costs may stem from the price of urban life. But conversely, rural districts may face higher costs when trying to attract and retain personnel. Similarly, rural school districts may face higher costs related to distance education and travel.

States choosing to engage in pupil cost equalization do so on political and educational bases. Politically it makes sense to take care of a state's constituents, and it is as educationally sound to care as much about unequal scale or market costs as it is to care about other kinds of special needs. Cost equalization is addressed most often through categorical aid or by pupil weightings attached to the regular aid plan. A majority of states provides aid for extra cost factors such as enrollment density or sparsity, declining or increasing enrollment, grade level differences, and so forth. A few states have tried to approach price indices based on market differences, although the complexity and political explosiveness have made it difficult to achieve on a wide scale.

HOW DO STATES FUND SCHOOLS?

Our discussion has indicated that states have many goals when creating school aid formulas. At the most basic level, aid formulas are an attempt to redress tax base (wealth) inequality. Such inequality, if not abated, would result in horrendous variations in educational program quality because money is linked to student achievement in a complex and poorly understood fashion. It is at least linked in that less money buys less instruction, and it is sufficient to say that less instruction is unacceptable to nearly everyone. The first goal of aid formulas, then, is to make more money available to all districts using state resources. Other goals are equally important. Among those goals are the need to address special human conditions, to reflect the unique problems of individual states, and to convince taxpayers that their voices are heard. At the same time, state aid formulas must satisfy external legal mandates based in constitutional equality. And certainly, states are attuned to political philosophies as they seek to create aid plans that are neither overly intrusive on local control nor too benign to be effective.

Although attempts to publish absolutely current funding information is impossible in a textbook because of the constantly changing political arena, Figure 3.6 (pp. 96–97) is excerpted from the most recent authoritative compilation of modern state aid features. Foundation schemes remain by far the most popular type of aid formula, with only two states claiming to provide full state funding. Aid ranges widely across the 50 states, although how states accumulate and report these data leave much room for interpretation (e.g., a high level of aid to a low dollar amount of state support is misleading). Although the data are too complex and too subject to change to publish in a textbook, states also show a common concern for both cost differentials and other vertical adjustments, usually by attaching these features to the basic state aid plan in some manner. Although schools in all states would opt for more money if asked, the data in this chapter indicate an awareness of states' educational obligations, leaving only the details and amounts of aid open to serious debate.

ARE THERE INNOVATIONS ON THE HORIZON?

The issues in this chapter are very complex from economic and sociopolitical perspectives and do not have simple solutions. And the question of whether there will soon be new ways to fund schools does not have a very satisfying answer. More appropriately, it is correct to consider the weight of all the material in this chapter so that an understanding of the barriers to innovation can be understood.

The short answer to promising innovation is that there is little reason to anticipate major breakthroughs. The reasons are simple. We already know how to build an equitable formula, at least on the surface, for distributional

Figure 3.6. State Aid Plans

State	Formula Type	Required Local Tax Effort for Aid	Aid Recapture in Wealthy Districts
Alabama	Foundation	Yes	No
Alaska	Foundation	Yes	No
Arizona	Foundation	No	No
Arkansas	Foundation	Yes	No
California	Foundation	No	No
Colorado	Foundation	No	No
Connecticut	Foundation	Yes	No
Delaware	Flat grant/equalized	Yes	No
Florida	Foundation	Yes	No
Georgia	Foundation/equalized	Yes	No
Hawaii	Full state funding	N/A	N/A
Idaho	Foundation	No	No
Illinois	Foundation/flat grant	No	No
Indiana	Guaranteed tax base	No	No
Iowa	Foundation	Yes	No
Kansas	Foundation	Yes	Yes
Kentucky	Foundation	Yes	No
Louisiana	Foundation	No	No
Maine	Foundation	Yes	No
Maryland	Foundation	Yes	No
Massachusetts	Foundation	Yes	No
Michigan	Foundation	No	No
Minnesota	Foundation	No	No
Mississippi	Foundation	Yes	No
Missouri	Foundation	Yes	No
Montana	Foundation	No	No
Nebraska	Foundation	Yes	No
Nevada	Foundation	Yes	Yes
New Hampshire	Foundation	No	No
New Jersey	Foundation	No	No
New Mexico	Foundation	Yes	No
New York	Foundation/percentage equalizing	No	No
North Carolina	Foundation	No	No
North Dakota	Foundation	No	No
Ohio	Foundation	Yes	No
Oklahoma	Foundation	No	No
Oregon	Foundation	No	No
Pennsylvania	Foundation	Yes	No
Rhode Island	Foundation	Yes	No
South Carolina	Foundation	Yes	No
South Dakota	Foundation	No	No
Tennessee	Foundation	Yes	No

State	Formula Type	Required Local Tax Effort for Aid	Aid Recapture in Wealthy Districts
Texas	Foundation/guaranteed yield	Yes	Yes
Utah	Foundation	Yes	Yes
Vermont	Foundation/guaranteed yield	No	Yes
Virginia	Foundation	Yes	No
Washington	Full state funding	No	No
West Virginia	Foundation	Yes	No
Wisconsin	Guaranteed tax base	No	No
Wyoming	Foundation	Yes	No

SOURCE: *Education Week*, "Research Center: Education Counts." Excerpted and compiled November 2004.

fairness purposes. We know far less about the impact of money on student achievement, which creates some hesitation in saying that the problem is solved in every way except politically. We therefore need to be a little cautious in saying that a better aid formula could not be built, but we are deceiving ourselves if we deny that good formulas are within reach—it is political barriers that prevent them from being adopted. Very specifically, equalization formulas and full state funding have the necessary mechanical elements to be distributionally fair. But it is in enactment that problems arise. These problems relate to rewriting state aid formulas to protect constituencies and to under-funding. We've often wryly observed that any problem can be solved by throwing money at it, and consequently we believe an adequate and equitable formula is not an unreachable goal given the right mindset and determination. In other words, the two problems faced by state aid formulas today are under-funding and the political tampering that thwarts how the aid formula should operate.

Under these conditions, innovation is unlikely for several reasons. First, politics cannot be removed from state school aid plans because representative government reasonably requires legislators to represent their constituents' interests. Second, no amount of formula refinement can offset under-funding. Third, a perpetually under-funded climate is likely far into the future as Americans aggressively seek to limit and control the influence of government. Because local government is more reactive to criticism, school revenues are a likely target for constriction as patrons vote in school budget referenda and school bond elections. We're reminded of a signboard near one of our universities that says, "Vote for responsible education: just say no to tax increases!" Of course, we don't mean that the points we make in this paragraph are applicable to all communities everywhere, but there is an enduring antitax, antigovernment sentiment that has been building for decades starting with the 1978 property tax rollback in California in Proposition 13. These conditions do not suggest that some new funding formula is waiting to miraculously solve education's fiscal problems if only it could be discovered. Rather, it suggests that educators, policy makers and taxpayers have a hard road before them if they are to resolve their political differences in ways that bring harmony instead of more shrill partisanship.

At the same time, we should give credit when due. We should celebrate the long way that school aid formula fairness has come, and we should give credit to educators, policy makers, and laypeople alike who have struggled to produce a system that works surprisingly well despite its evident problems. As we've said before, the job faced by legislators is overwhelming as they try to balance increasingly vocal advocacy groups from all walks of life who compete for the same finite tax resources—a condition under which a gain by one group always results in a loss by another group when no new revenue is available. Educators deserve praise, too, as public schools have become vast social providers with broad missions far surpassing basic teaching and learning. Taxpayers deserve understanding, too, as it must be admitted that government has grown by leaps and bounds with staggering monetary outlays. Society simply has not reconciled its insatiable appetite for entitlements with the cost of such convenience. Accordingly, no magic school aid formula exists: Fairness, or the lack thereof, is both to the credit and discredit of the same players.

Basic funding structures are in place for the support of public schools and have been developed over a long period of time. These structures are not without justification and relate closely to the political and social context of the nation. They are connected intimately to the tax system history of the nation and to the sovereignty of states in the Union. Although there are problems, there are reasons to celebrate. The overarching context is simply that educators, board members, policy makers, and laypersons must work to preserve and increase fairness in school funding, to make sure funding is adequate, and to actively try to minimize partisanship. But to remove partisanship is an unrealistic goal because that is not the nature of a representative democracy—its destructive side, however, should be actively guarded against.

SUGGESTED FOLLOW-UP PROJECTS

♦ Obtain documents explaining the state aid formula in your state. Identify broadly how the state views aid to local school districts. Identify how the state primarily funds its educational obligations (e.g., state general fund transfers, income tax, sales tax, etc.). Identify the type of aid formula used in your state.

♦ Develop a list of methods used in your state to address fairness through the aid formula. Consider how horizontal equity is addressed, and identify any vertical or other special adjustments related to need and/or cost equalization. Identify the amounts of money earmarked for general aid, categorical aid, and need or cost adjustments. Make a judgment about whether these amounts are adequate to meet educational needs—explain how you reached your decision.

♦ Talk to representatives of educational organizations (e.g., school board, teachers' union, administrators, state agencies, professional associations) to learn what these persons see as positives and negatives of your state's aid formula. Ask what needs to be done to improve adequate and equitable school funding in your state. Find out whether major changes may be on the horizon.

♦ Watch for meetings addressing school funding you can attend. These might include legislative committee meetings, legislative issues town meetings, teacher association meetings, local school board meetings, and so forth—any place where school funding will be discussed. Capture the issues and attitudes, including a sense of favorableness or resistance to change. Identify the barriers to change and the players who are most influential in presenting the pros and cons of the issues voiced.

♦ Compare how your state funds education to several other states in your region. Consider numbers of students to be educated, dollars legislatively appropriated, choice of state aid formula design, and so forth. Give your opinion regarding which state in your region does the best job of funding schools and justify your conclusion.

Part II

OPERATIONALIZING SCHOOL MONEY

4

SCHOOL FUNDS: ACCOUNTABILITY AND PROFESSIONALISM

SETTING THE STAGE

The first three chapters in this book sounded a warning about public trust and confidence in schools. In fact, we argued throughout the first chapter that citizens are increasingly involved in school affairs in ways best described as voting with their feet. We argued in the second chapter that there are different legitimate views on the value of schooling, and the third chapter laid out the highly complex problems faced by federal, state, and local units of government in trying to satisfy the demands of all constituents while still providing equal educational opportunities to all children. Our point in all three chapters was that schools are part of the fabric of the larger society, and citizens hold the power to cause enormous and lasting change, either by forcing change or by resisting it. Many school leaders have learned the hard way that the public is becoming much bolder about voicing disagreement with what educators have long regarded as standard policy in revenues, expenditures, curriculum, and so forth. Our warning that school leaders must listen carefully to their constituents could not be truer than in relation to financial accountability and the fiduciary trust. A point we will return to frequently is that far more school leaders have been fired for lack of good sense in handling money than for incompetence in teaching and learning.

Our discussion until now has focused on the broader principles of school funding. With this chapter, we begin considering the implementation of school budgets; that is, putting money to work in schools. It is appropriate to begin with money as an issue of accountability and trust because, unfortunately, only a few people in a school system really understand the complex expectations to which school leaders are held when dealing with public funds. Although we cannot address all such complexities in a single chapter, we can have a useful discussion about school funds *accountability* and *professionalism.* As in other chapters, we are again faced with questions having practical implications. For example, what is fiscal accountability? What is the level of trust to which administrators, teachers, board members, and other policy makers are held? How do good fiscal practices help ensure that the public trust is upheld? What kinds of money do schools receive, and what types of restrictions are placed on sources of revenue? How does money flow through a school system from beginning to end? Are there ethical standards to which people with fiduciary responsibilities must conform? We tackle these and other questions in this chapter, providing blunt answers because too many good school leaders get into serious trouble in this arena, either as a consequence of ignorance of competent professional practice or as the result of improper conduct.

SCHOOL FUNDS ACCOUNTABILITY

The concept of accountability for school funds is intimidating to many people, and it is a concept worthy of the fear it creates. We've started a practice in this book of laying out our biases, and it is time to do so again. Our strong bias is that there is no defense for people who do not take time to grasp the serious weight of accountability for public money—in fact, it is our belief that such people should be run out of the profession to make room for smarter people. It is our firm belief that all aspects of education suffer irreparable harm when proper accountability measures are not in place, so much so that the concept of "spillover" can be applied to almost everything in education—in sum, failure to observe good fiscal accountability results in pervasive distrust of everyone touched by schools. In the context of public education, particularly in the general social climate of today, it makes sense to turn our attention to laying a foundation for the highest ethical standards and understanding in general terms of how money is tracked in schools.

WHAT IS ACCOUNTABILITY?

Accountability is a term that currently is much overused in educational settings these days. This does not imply that too much accountability exists, but rather that the word is applied too casually to a wide scope of activities ranging from curriculum to student achievement to mapping bus routes and winning ball games. In essence, this means that accountability is not always well defined, and its meaning is elusive because of a lack of precise tools to measure what people are hoping to achieve when they think about accountability. In the fiscal world, however, accountability has a much clearer meaning. Fundamentally, accountability in fiscal terms means that people responsible for some activity involving money must provide evidence of appropriate care as conservators, which is now taken to include *wise use* of all resources. Importantly, the definition of accountability continues to expand so that wise use is being redefined constantly.

Accountability can be conceptualized on many levels. At its root, it describes observance of good business principles when handling money, regardless of whether the source of such money is public or private. This definition can be traced back for centuries. Growth in schools in the United States has forced special recognition of the importance of good business practice in education, with the first known business manager's position created in 1841 when Cleveland, Ohio, hired a manager to care for the accounting functions of the school district. The ever-increasing complexities of managing the millions of dollars now characterizing virtually every modern school district have added greatly to the need for accountability because the rising price of education continually increases the need for confidence that good business procedures are being followed.

At broader levels, accountability has come to mean wise use of all resources purchased by the district. This includes the accounting function, but it also includes the decision-making process by which funds are spent and the outcomes resulting from such expenditures. It is easy to know that squandering resources on things that hold little hope for helping students is not a wise business practice. Yet the issues discussed in the first several chapters have great implications for wise resource utilization. In other words, an increasingly sophisticated public is no longer satisfied with just good accounting, choosing instead to ask significantly more difficult questions about whether increasing teacher pay or creating new programs is wise fiscal and educational accountability. Struggles over which programs get funded or eliminated stand as proof of emerging definitions of accountability, as do legislative and local debates on the relationship between funding and student achievement. This latter issue has reached historic proportions, as the No Child Left Behind Act has caused states to require schools to meet minimum performance standards and as states have simultaneously enacted their own reforms that are often based in sanctions, loss of funding, and school district consolidation for academic nonperformance or other efficiency reasons. The topic of resource decision-making and fiscal accountability is something we will return to frequently, particularly in later chapters when we address budgeting for educational programs.

What Are Fiduciary Responsibilities?

The easiest way to understand the weightiness of this chapter is to contemplate the definition of a fiduciary. As a noun, a fiduciary is a *trustee*. Trusteeship is itself a colorful word, having a heavy weight attached by virtue of trust as its root. More specifically, fiduciary responsibility carries many pointed elements, with dictionaries all defining it as "…a trust, a thing held in trust, such as designating a person to hold something in trust for another … and valuable only because of public confidence and support." The seriousness needs little development except to underscore the weighty language. For our purposes, a person with fiduciary responsibility is someone placed in charge of any kind of property in whom others—the public, in schools' case—have placed trust, so much so that one's personal reputation and professional livelihood are dependent on public confidence and support in wise use and conservatorship. Under these conditions, the level of trust is enormous—in fact, it is hard to imagine a more serious charge than that of a fiduciary, and the responsibility for millions of dollars entrusted to schools and their leaders is truly staggering.

As accountability has increased, so have the duties and responsibilities of persons with fiduciary obligations. In other writings, we have detailed the duties of a fiduciary from the perspective of a school business manager. Although limited in that case to a specific role inside a school system, it is easy to see that responsibility is equally shared by administrators, boards, teachers, policy makers, and laypersons to varying degrees, because everyone touches school resources in some way. We identified those duties as the following:

- *Planning:* the process of looking to the future, identifying resources and needs, and creating a master plan to follow
- *Decision making:* the process of choosing among options, based on knowing that setting a course of action is not easy to reverse and that making choices precludes other options
- *Organizing:* the process of preparing a plan for identifying needed human and fiscal resources and a sequence of events to reach a set of stated goals
- *Directing:* the process of accepting responsibility for seeing that plans are implemented and carried out
- *Controlling:* the process of monitoring progress against the original goals so that errors can be corrected during the implementation phase
- *Evaluating:* the ultimate responsibility for determining if goals were met and whether resources were wisely used.[1]

These responsibilities have direct application to the business of schools, so that only the level of involvement of a fiduciary varies based on formal roles. For example, administrators, teachers, and other school personnel have a shared responsibility for making schools successful—only the level of involvement differs. As a general rule, instructional personnel carry out these duties in ways related to teaching and learning, although site councils, decentralized budgeting, salary negotiations, and other aspects of participatory management have diffused formerly centralized fiduciary responsibilities. Administrators and boards have more direct hands-on control of resources, although limited substantially by laws governing resource utilization and shared decision-making. At the same time, policy makers are involved in setting guidelines and controls, in many instances providing primary impetus and leadership for more accountability. Lay people are increasingly involved, particularly by approving or rejecting budgets, serving on site councils, and either directly or tacitly controlling all planning activities through the democratic process. Indeed, planning, organizing,

---

1. R. Craig Wood, David C. Thompson, and Lawrence O. Picus, *Principles of School Business Management*, 3rd ed. (Reston, VA: Association of School Business Officials, International, 2005).

directing, controlling, and evaluating are no longer discrete tasks, as these critical functions have increasingly involved interactions by interest groups.

Although people's roles drive their level of direct involvement, interest in the fiduciary trust relating to schools and money eventually comes to the same end. Ultimately, such interest relates to fulfilling the primary mission of schools—an accountability question—that is, are schools doing what is expected? The fiduciary path to answering this question also answers a second query: What are the essential fiduciary duties associated with schools? The following bulleted list clearly indicates that meeting schools' primary mission is complex and, as we saw in earlier chapters, involved more than $400 billion for schools in late 2004—an issue of significant public trust.

- Financial planning and budgeting
- Fiscal accounting and financial reporting
- Cash management
- Fiscal audits and reports
- General management
- Payroll management
- Purchasing
- School insurance and risk management
- Debt service and capital-fund management
- Legal control
- Office management
- School activity and student body funds
- Personnel management
- School plant maintenance
- School property management
- School plant operations
- School-community relations
- Collective negotiations
- Plant security and property protection
- Data processing
- School transportation services
- School construction management
- School food services
- Staff development
- Grants and contracts
- Educational facility planning
- Educational resource management

Under these conditions, the level of fiduciary trust is enormous and requires "accounting" in a multitude of ways. The answer to what level of trust is required, then, is only the highest, because educational resource management is an all-encompassing term describing the entire educational system and society itself.

How Does the Accounting Process Help?

Although not widely understood, the accounting process is *the* vehicle by which a substantial portion of accountability is carried out. Although this is not sufficient alone to get at issues of school effectiveness under the heading of broader accountability, the accounting process serves a critical function by managing the single resource (money), which controls the purchase of all other human and material resources used to carry out the educational mission. Importantly, emerging developments suggest that linkages will be increasingly established between the financial data examined in accounting and other forms of public calls for accountability. In other words, tying money to outcomes continues to grow in importance.

What Are the Purposes of Accounting?

On a broad scale, people think that accounting is used by businesses to summarize their financial profits or losses and to detect wrongdoing. That perception is accurate, although it sells short the range of benefits gained from the accounting process, and it suffers from lack of awareness that accounting also applies to nonprofit organizations. Although this book cannot go far into fiscal analysis tools, it is important to lay out the purposes of accounting, to identify the uses of accounting in schools, and to provide some indication of how budgets, accounting, and accountability will be linked in the future.

We have held for many years that a budget is the fiscal expression of the educational philosophy of a district and its schools. That is, a budget is the implementation of the *educational plan*. By setting up a budget, districts identify how money will be spent to achieve their educational goals. Only by accounting for how the budget is spent can it be known whether, in fiscal terms, the district is living up to its expectations. These realities establish at least five purposes for the accounting function, all of which are meant to keep the organization focused on its mission.

The first purpose of accounting is to set up a procedure by which all fiscal activities in a district can be accumulated, categorized, reported, and controlled. Each of these terms has specific meaning. *Accumulating* transactions sets up a method of data collection in one location (set of books) to view the district's fiscal activities. Categorizing transactions separates the various fiscal activities in terms of similarities, and it implies that grouping transactions will provide useful analysis about where money is going. Reporting transactions makes the results of all activities known. Controlling transactions is essential because resources are finite whereas needs are infinite.

The second purpose of accounting is to provide a means to judge progress toward goals. This is a cornerstone of the accountability issue, as schools are increasingly expected to show wise use of resources beyond their traditional methods that have relied on standardized testing and other locally constructed achievement measures. The accounting function can provide a tool for assessing progress in several ways, and new directions are being sought constantly, particularly in public debates on school funding policy. One way in which the accounting function is able to help assess goal attainment is by tracking the financial condition of a district. For example, the accounting function monitors changes in balances of all funds and accounts held. To illustrate, if only 10 percent of instructional supply money remains by the end of the first month of the school year, the accounting function will flag a serious problem unless, for example, there has been a decision to spend money down to capture some other benefit such as bulk purchasing that offsets the otherwise alarming rate of spending. Similarly, later chapters will discuss performance budgeting—an activity aided by the accounting function that can help judge progress on academic goals by tying fiscal information to student achievement data. The accounting function thus helps assess whether expenditures and educational programs are in proper alignment.

The third purpose of accounting is complementary by providing evidence to the state that schools are fulfilling their statutory educational responsibility. This purpose has an even more basic goal whereby accounting helps the state judge whether districts, as legal extensions of the state, are fulfilling the state's constitutional duty to educate. In other words, all states have inescapable duties to educate children, and accountability data, including financial data, are indicators against which states themselves may be judged. States' interest has increased as state aid to schools has grown, with states now requiring extensive reporting of educational revenue and expenditure data, from which many policy decisions are ultimately based, including future amounts of state aid. These realities have shaped uniformity of reporting requirements through standardized state budget documents and other reports, for the sole purpose of gathering comparable data across districts for the multiple aims of accountability at state and local levels. States themselves also face upward accountability in the form of federal reporting to qualify for federal grants and federal revenue sharing, and to satisfy federal laws relating to educational equity.

The fourth purpose of accounting is budget preparation. As shown in later chapters, the task of building a budget at district and school levels requires historic data for baseline purposes. Indeed, budgeting is the act of placing money on line items in the budget for the express purpose of carrying out the district's educational plan. The process is bidirectional: The accounting function is satisfied in part by budgeting, and budget preparation fails without accounting information. More specifically, accounting sets up both initial and end products by creating the funds and line items to which budget allocations are made, whereas the process of spending down a budget creates the data needed to carry out the accounting cycle *and* establish a baseline for the next budget cycle.

The fifth purpose of accounting is to ensure proper handling of money and to guard against misuse of public trust. This aspect of the accounting function is crucial to many of the issues discussed in earlier chapters because of growing dislike by the public toward government. One direct outcome is skepticism aimed at public officials, making it essential for schools to observe the highest standards of openness and integrity. All of us know of cases of real or imagined abuse of public trust, and headlines speculating about misuse of public money are commonplace. A critical aspect of the accounting function is to provide clear *proof* that public confidence is deserved. The role of accounting is a powerful tool for carrying out educational planning, control, and stewardship because accounting provides budgetary structure and organization, whereas the budget simultaneously is the vehicle on which all accountability turns. As a result, accounting accomplishes a major accountability feature when it does the following:

- *Creates a complete record* of all financial transactions at district and school levels
- *Summarizes activities* of the schools in financial reports required for proper, effective, and efficient administration
- *Provides information* used in budget preparation, adoption, and execution
- *Provides safeguards* on use of money and property, including protection against waste, inefficiency, fraud, and carelessness
- *Creates a longitudinal record* to aid administrators, teachers, boards, and laypersons in program decision processes

How Are School Budgets Allocated?

The previous section introduced reasons and benefits of an accountability structure to track money, but it said nothing about what happens to money when it comes into the school district. The question of how school budgets are allocated actually has several embedded questions that are discussed in greater detail in other chapters. For example, related questions arise regarding how to determine amounts of money to be assigned to budget lines during the budget-building process. Those are detailed questions that interweave the accounting and budgeting functions to make them work together—but, for now, we need to first understand the big picture of how money comes into a school district before getting more specific about budgeting behaviors.

Fund Structure

As shown in Chapter 3 when we discussed revenue plans, schools receive money from several sources, including federal, state, and local units of government. Regardless of how revenue distribution happens in a given state, however, certain accounting principles apply that make it possible to record revenues and expenditures. For accounting and accountability purposes, we refer to the overarching system as a *fund structure*. Within the fund structure are the broad categories of *governmental* funds, *proprietary* funds, and *fiduciary* funds. Each of these must be identified to grasp the big picture of how school money is allocated.

As a preface to looking at each fund's purpose, it is important to note that we're actually saying that schools operate under a system of fund accounting. Fund accounting is a term that describes how the types of revenue and expenditure are organized and reported for (in this case) an educational organization. Its primary value is based in the requirement that each fund be used only for specific purposes and that the various funds not be commingled. For example, schools must deposit state transportation aid only to the transportation fund for exclusive use in transportation-related expenditures. Analogously, special education money must not be commingled with other money. The purpose of fund accounting is to recognize segregated fiscal operations, to track revenues and expenditures by function, and to provide accountability for these functions according to intended use.

Governmental Funds

The broad fund structure is actually composed of individual funds. Governmental funds make up most of the various funds in educational organizations receiving most of the actual money receipted and spent by schools. Most districts operate four types of governmental funds:

- ◆ *General fund.* All money not reserved to other funds is placed in the general fund—hence its name, which implies a general use fund. The general fund is the largest of all funds because most current instructional expenditures are made from it, including teacher and administrator salaries, teaching supplies, and so forth.

- ◆ *Special revenue fund.* Money that is restricted to specific purposes, such as compensatory education or special education programs, is placed in special revenue funds. The purpose is to earmark monies to ensure they are spent only for specified purposes.

- ◆ *Capital projects fund.* A capital projects fund allows deposit and expenditure of money from a variety of sources (usually bond revenues) used to finance long-lived assets such as buildings, equipment, land, or other facilities. A capital projects fund is distinct from other operating funds such as capital outlay and debt service funds.

- ◆ *Debt service fund.* A debt service fund allows receiving and expending money used to pay off long-term debts, including bond issues for school facilities. Bond issues usually require establishment of debt service funds, and a separate fund is established for each bond issue.

Proprietary Funds

Not all money received by schools is governmental, thereby requiring that nongovernmental money be accounted for separately. The convention for depositing and spending the most common type of nongovernmental monies is by creating separate *proprietary* funds. Proprietary funds often involve fees for services or provide a method of internal billing; as implied by its name, these are monies generated and "owned" differently than governmental money, which is more globally the property of the state or other taxing unit. Such funds are created to fit local needs and ways of doing business. They are further identified as either *enterprise* or *internal service* funds, a distinction made clearer as follows:

- *Enterprise funds.* These funds handle money from activities such as athletics, school newspapers, student bookstore operations, and so forth. The idea is that these activities are like private enterprises, with services provided in return for charges. As a result, enterprise revenues and expenditures are maintained separately.

- *Internal service funds.* Larger school districts often produce goods or services within the organization that are consumed by other parts of the same organization. Examples include central printing or maintenance. Such districts may have an internal charge-back system. This also assists in cost accounting to track the cost and profitability of these various services.

Fiduciary Funds

Not all revenues fall neatly into governmental or proprietary funds. One type of revenue of growing importance is money received from external nongovernmental organizations such as business partnerships, gifts, and donations, and other charitable trusts. Although the vast majority of school districts likely do not have such funds, the structure is available if needed. Such funds are known as *fiduciary* funds.

Districts managing fiduciary funds are actually only trustees, as the name implies. Revenue is deposited to a fiduciary fund, and expenditures are controlled by an agreement detailing the purpose of the fund, how the fund is to be managed, and the disposition of the proceeds if the agreement is ever dissolved. In general, fiduciary funds include two basic types:

- *Trust funds.* These may be of several different types. In all cases, the district has trusteeship and acts as the fund's manager. A pension trust fund is a common type and may exist when the district offers local pension benefits in addition to, or in lieu of, a state retirement system. An investment trust fund is another type and is used to account for the external portion (the part that does not belong to the school district) of investment pools operated by the district. Private-purpose trust funds are the final type: These may include nonexpendable trusts where the principal amount must remain intact, whereas the interest may be spent for district benefit—similarly, an expendable trust fund may be set up, wherein the principal and interest are available for district use.

♦ *Agency funds.* Agency funds are monies held in a custodial capacity by a school district for individuals, private organizations, or other governments. Examples include accounting for student activities or taxes collected for another unit of government. A historically common use of agency funds has included setting up a central payroll fund to reduce the number of accounts needed for payroll transactions to the various entities in a district, for example, teachers, administrators, support staff, and food service workers. Under one central fund, all data on wages, fringe benefits, tax withholding, and workers' compensation may be more efficiently monitored.

An Intermediate Overview

As we said at the outset, accounting is complex, and exhaustiveness is not within the scope of this textbook. Yet it is critical for everyone to understand that there is a structure for depositing school money so that it may be tracked and used for its intended purpose. The picture is clearer if the accounting system is regarded as an inverted pyramid, starting at the broadest perspective. From the broadest view, we see that the total accounting system is first made up of various funds. Districts in all states operate governmental funds made of up a general fund and special revenue funds, and most districts also have capital project and debt service funds. Similarly, all districts use proprietary funds to some extent, particularly for common operations such as enterprise funds, and many districts also have internal service funds. Fewer districts have extensive fiduciary funds. It is important to remember that the fund structure is the starting place for school accounting and that everyone associated with schools is touched by fund structure. More specifically, central administrators and boards of education are the custodians of all funds, and building administrators are charged with administering activity funds. Similarly, teachers want adequate funding for salaries and instruction, and policy makers and units of government rely on fund structures to direct the flow of money and to judge the impact of educational and tax policy decisions. And, of course, laypersons depend on fund structures to assure educational experiences for children and to preserve the public trust. In essence, accounting through the fund structure is truly part of accountability.

HOW DOES SCHOOL MONEY GET TRACKED?

Discussion to this point has illustrated how easy it is to become extremely complex when trying to provide an uncomplicated view of financial accountability in schools—and that is just the financial side without consideration for using money as a tool for educational decision-making! But one more introductory step is needed: We should briefly explore how money is handled within the fund structure once it is received. First, we turn to the twin concepts of *revenue* and *expenditure*. Second, we look at the *accounting cycle*. These concepts are foundational to the actual budget process discussed in later chapters because we need to understand the conceptual underpinnings to appreciate how resources are assigned in the budget.

Revenue Structure

For accounting purposes, we need to consider a district's fiscal affairs as a two-dimensional plane—revenue and expenditure—(even though we already moved beyond this when we conceptualized the budget as expressing the district's educational plan). This parenthetical point argues that the budget is actually three-dimensional—a budget triangle—when accountability for program planning is linked to revenue and expenditure. For present purposes, however, we need to see revenue simply as money going into schools, as contrasted with expenditure, which is that same money going back out in support of teaching and learning. As we've already noted, there is useful information about the educational process to be gleaned from revenue and expenditure data.

Revenue to education generally involves a three-tiered classification. The first tier is the fund, which we've discussed. The second tier is the source of revenue. The third tier is the type of revenue. The concepts are interrelated.

Our earlier discussion about fund structure reenters the picture, in that revenue received must be placed in one of the *funds* operated by the district. For example, revenue earmarked for transportation must be placed in the transportation fund, and revenue for any other categorical purpose must be put in its appropriate special fund. Similarly, revenue not reserved to special funds is usually placed in the general fund, and it follows that expenditures must come from that same fund.

When we look at budgeting in later chapters, it will be evident that the revenue side of a budget requires placing each revenue receipt on a line noting its source. Each state has its own specific budget forms, but the practice is universal in that placing money on a source line is important because it allows the district to report fiscal data to the state, to establish lobbying positions during legislative sessions, and so forth—that is, it is required by law, and data tell many tales. Three revenue sources apply to school budgeting and accounting[2]:

♦ *Local and intermediate sources*—local sources include money raised by the district, usually from local property taxes. Intermediate sources include money from governmental units that stand between the local district and the state, such as cities and counties.

2. U.S. Department of Education, Office of Educational Research and Improvement, *Financial Accounting for State and Local School Systems, 2003 Edition* (Washington, DC: U.S. Government Printing Office, 2004).

- *State sources* include money raised within the state in which the district is located, generally state aid, but excluding funds passed through the state from the federal government.
- *Federal sources* include direct federal aid or state flow-through money, usually categorical aid.

Type of revenue refers to both source and purpose. Local revenues often include property taxes, tuition, student transportation fees, investment earnings, student organization fees, revenue from textbook rentals, and so forth. Intermediate and state revenues may include unrestricted grants-in-aid and revenue in lieu of taxes under tax exemptions or abatements granted by other taxing units. Types of revenue from federal sources include unrestricted grants-in-aid received either directly from the federal government or as restricted grants-in-aid from the federal level distributed through the state. Figure 4.1 (p. 116) illustrates how fund, source, and type of revenue are placed in the revenue side of a district's budget. In Figure 4.1, the *fund* is the general fund. *Sources* include local, intermediate (county in this case), state, federal, and other. *Types* include *ad valorem* property, motor vehicles, and so forth. Source codes are part of the system for reporting to the federal government.[3] Budget documents in the various states may look different from Figure 4.1 because of differences in funding scheme, but the essential elements apply.

The system of revenue structure is important because it is used to allocate money to the different funds comprising a school district's budget. Revenues are thus first classified by fund and source, and then broken into governmental, proprietary, and fiduciary groups for further distinction by fund, source, and type. Not all of this is apparent in Figure 4.1, which only shows governmental general fund revenue, but it illustrates that the first step to creating an educational plan is receiving and depositing revenue so that an expenditure plan can be built.

Expenditure Structure

Expenditure structure is significantly more complex than revenue for good reason. Revenue sources typically fit into three categories, whereas expenditures can be broken into many different classifications. This means that districts have only a few sources of revenue, but they have many ways to spend.

Budget documents in every state classify expenditures in a program budgeting format. Expenditures are classified by *fund, function,* and *object,* and may be further broken down by project, instructional level, operational unit, subject matter, and job classification if desired. States and local school districts vary in amount of detail, although each state specifies a minimum amount of coding that must occur. Such a classification schema permits

---

3. U.S. Department of Education, Office of Educational Research and Improvement, *Financial Accounting for State and Local School Systems, 2003 Edition* (Washington, DC: U.S. Government Printing Office, 2004).

Figure 4.1. Revenue Side of a Sample Budget

GENERAL		12 mo. 2002–2003 Actual (1)	12 mo. 2003–2004 Actual (2)	12 mo. 2004–2005 Budget (3)
Unencumbered Cash Balance July 1				
Unencumbered Cash Balance from Transportation, Bilingual Education and Vocational Education Funds				
Cancel of Prior Yr Enc				
Revenue: 1000 Local Sources 1110 Ad Valorem Tax Levied 2001 $				
2002 $				
2003 $				
2004 $				
1140 Delinquent Tax				
1300 Tuition 1312 Individuals (Out-District)				
1320 Other school district In-State				
1330 Other school district Out-State				
1410 Transportation Fees				
1700 Student Activities (Reimbursement)				
1900 Other Revenue From Local Source 1910 User Charges				
1980 Reimbursements				
1985 State Aid Reimbursement				
2000 County Sources 2450 Recreational Vehicle Tax				
2800 In Lieu of Taxes IRBs				
3000 State Sources 3110 General State Aid				
3130 Mineral Production Tax				
3205 Special Education Aid				
4000 Federal Sources 4590 Other Reserve Grants in Aid 4591 Title I (Formerly Chapter I)				
4592 Title (Math/Science)				
4599 Other				
4820 PL 382 (Exclude Extra Aid for Children on Indian Land and Low Rent Housing) (formerly PL 874)				
5000 Other 5208 Transfer From Supplemental General				
Resources Available				
Total Expenditures & Transfers				
Excess Revenue to State (recapture)				
Unencumbered Cash Balance June 30				

accumulation of data that may be used for a wide variety of purposes, the first of which is tracking expenditures for program accountability. Each level in the expenditure classification scheme has discrete codes hierarchically arranged to track expenditures from broad to narrow. For example, the general fund is very broad, whereas the object breaks a function into various subcodes for detailed reporting and analysis.

Extensive details of how far down expenditures can be broken is beyond the scope of this discussion. For general purposes of understanding expenditure structure, however, consider the following statements that go from the broad to narrowly specific:

- *Fund.* Expenditures are first classified as an expenditure from a governmental fund, proprietary fund, or fiduciary fund. The purpose of starting with the fund should be clear: Revenue is first assigned to a fund on the basis of use in support of some educational activity. Expenditures therefore must be assigned to the corresponding fund—for example, Code 01 to designate general fund.

- *Function.* Expenditures can be classified by function, which refers to the general activity for which a purchased good or service is acquired. Function describes the areas of instruction, support services, operation of noninstructional services, facilities acquisition and construction, and debt service. These codes track expenditures more closely by identifying functions carried out—for example, Code 2300 to designate an expenditure for general administration support services within the general fund.

- *Object.* Finally, expenditures are classified by object, or the item or service acquired. This includes nine major object categories, which can be further subdivided. The major categories include salaries, employee benefits, purchased professional and technical services, purchased property services, supplies, and so on. Using our previous example, Code 310 to designate a board-level salary expense within the general fund.

Figure 4.2 (pp. 118–122) helps illustrate this complex structure. Figure 4.2 is the expenditure side of one state's general fund budget document. Assume the district has received and deposited revenue to each of its funds. Assume also that the budget process is complete and that a legally adopted budget is in place—something we explore in other chapters. Now the district has authority to spend money. More importantly, several other things are in place. In Figure 4.2 , we can see expenditure classification as follows: The *fund* is the general fund. *Functions* in the general fund include instruction (Code 1000), support services (Code 2000), school administration (Code 2400), operations

(Text continues on page 123.)

Figure 4.2. Expenditure Side of a Budget

GENERAL EXPENDITURES		12 mo. 2002–2003 Actual (1)	12 mo. 2003–2004 Actual (2)	12 mo. 2004–2005 Budget (3)
1000 Instruction 100 Salaries 110 Certified				
120 NonCertified				
200 Employee Benefits 210 Insurance (Employee)				
220 Social Security				
290 Other				
300 Purchased Professional and Technical Services				
500 Other Purchased Services 560 Tuition 561 Tuition/other State LEAs				
562 Tuition/other LEAs outsid the State				
563 Tuition/Priv Sources				
590 Other				
600 Supplies 610 General Supplemental (Teaching)				
644 Textbooks				
680 Miscellaneous Supplies				
700 Property (Equipment & Furnishings)				
800 Other				
2000 Support Services				
2100 Student Support Services 100 Salaries 110 Certified				
120 NonCertified				
200 Employee Benefits 210 Insurance (Employee)				
220 Social Security				
290 Other				
300 Purchased Professional and Technical Services				
500 Other Purchased Services				
600 Supplies				
700 Property (Equipment & Furnishings)				
800 Other				
2200 Instr Support Staff 100 Salaries 110 Certified				
120 NonCertified				
200 Employee Benefits 210 Insurance (Employee)				
220 Social Security				
290 Other				

GENERAL EXPENDITURES		2002–2003 Actual (1)	2003–2004 Actual (2)	2004–2005 Budget (3)
300 Purchased Professional and Technical Services				
500 Other Purchased Services				
600 Supplies 640 Books (not textbooks) and Periodicals				
650 Audiovisual and Instructional Software				
680 Miscellaneous Supplies				
700 Property (Equipment & Furnishings)				
800 Other				
2300 General Administration 100 Salaries 110 Certified				
120 NonCertified				
200 Employee Benefits 210 Insurance (Employee)				
220 Social Security				
290 Other				
300 Purchased Professional and Technical Services				
400 Purchased Property Services				
500 Other Purchased Services 520 Insurance				
530 Communications (Telephone, postage, etc.)				
590 Other				
600 Supplies				
700 Property (Equipment & Furnishings)				
800 Other				
2400 School Administration 100 Salaries 110 Certified				
120 NonCertified				
200 Employee Benefits 210 Insurance (Employee)				
220 Social Security				
290 Other				
300 Purchased Professional and Technical Services				
400 Purchased Property Services				
500 Other Purchased Services 530 Communications (Telephone, postage, etc.)				
590 Other				
600 Supplies				
700 Property (Equipment & Furnishings)				
800 Other				

(Figure 4.2 continues on next page.)

GENERAL EXPENDITURES		2002–2003 Actual (1)	2003–2004 Actual (2)	2004–2005 Budget (3)
2500 Operations & Maintenance 　100 Salaries 　　120 NonCertified				
200 Employee Benefits 　210 Insurance (Employee)				
220 Social Security				
290 Other				
300 Purchased Professional and 　Technical Services				
400 Purchased Property Services 　411 Water/Sewer				
420 Cleaning				
430 Repairs & Maintenance				
440 Rentals				
460 Repair of Buildings				
490 Other				
500 Other Purchased Services 　520 Insurance				
590 Other				
600 Supplies 　610 General Supplies				
620 Energy				
621 Heating				
622 Electricity				
626 Motor Fuel (not school bus)				
629 Other				
680 Miscellaneous Supplies				
700 Property (Equipment & Furnishings)				
800 Other				
2600 Operations & Maintenance 　(Transportation) 　100 Salaries 　　120 NonCertified				
200 Employee Benefits 　210 Insurance (Employee)				
220 Social Security				
290 Other				
300 Purchased and Professional 　Technical Services				
400 Purchased Property Services				
500 Other Purchased Services				
600 Supplies 　610 General Supplies				
620 Energy				
621 Heating				
622 Electricity				
626 Motor Fuel (not school bus)				
629 Other				
680 Miscellaneous Supplies				

GENERAL EXPENDITURES	Code 06 Line	2002–2003 Actual (1)	2003–2004 Actual (2)	2004–2005 Budget (3)
700 Property (Equipment & Furnishings)				
800 Other				
2700 Student Transportation Services 2710 Supervision 100 Salaries 120 NonCertified	652			
200 Employee Benefits 210 Insurance	654			
220 Social Security	656			
290 Other	658			
600 Supplies	660			
730 Equipment	662			
800 Other	664			
2720 Vehicle Operating Services 100 Salaries 120 NonCertified	666			
200 Employee Benefits 210 Insurance	668			
220 Social Security	670			
290 Other	672			
442 Rent of Vehicles (lease)	674			
500 Other Purchased Services 513 Contracting of Bus Services	676			
519 Mileage in Lieu of Trans	678			
520 Insurance	680			
626 Motor Fuel	682			
730 Equipment (Including Buses)	684			
800 Other	686			
2740 Vehicle Services & Maintenance Services 100 Salaries 120 NonCertified	688			
200 Employee Benefits 210 Insurance	690			
220 Social Security	692			
290 Other	694			
300 Purchased Professional and Technical Services	696			
400 Purchased Property Services	698			
500 Other Purchased Services	700			
600 Supplies	702			
730 Equipment	704			
800 Other	706			
2790 Other Student Transportation Services 100 Salaries 120 NonCertified	708			
200 Employee Benefits 210 Insurance	710			

(Figure 4.2 continues on next page.)

GENERAL EXPENDITURES	Code 06 Line	2002–2003 Actual (1)	2003–2004 Actual (2)	2004–2005 Budget (3)
220 Social Security	712			
290 Other	714			
300 Purchased Professional and Technical Services	716			
400 Purchased Property Services	718			
500 Other Purchased Services	720			
600 Supplies	722			
730 Equipment	724			
800 Other	726			
2500, 2800, 2900 Other Supplemental Service 100 Salaries 110 Certified	730			
120 NonCertified	735			
200 Employee Benefits 210 Insurance	740			
220 Social Security	745			
290 Other	750			
300 Purchased Professional and Technical Services	755			
400 Purchased Property Services	760			
500 Other Purchased Services	765			
600 Supplies	770			
700 Property (Equipment & Furnishings)	775			
800 Other	780			
3300 Community Services Operations	785			
4300 Architectural & Engineering Services	790			
5200 TRANSFER TO: 932 Adult Education	795	0	0	0
934 Adult Suppl Education	800	0	0	0
936 Bilingual Education	805	0	0	0
938 Capital Outlay	810	0	0	0
940 Driver Training	815	0	0	0
943 Extraordinary School Prog	823	0	0	0
944 Food Service	825	0	0	0
946 Professional Development	830	0	0	0
948 Parent Education Program	835	0	0	0
949 Summer School	837	0	0	0
950 Special Education	840	0	0	0
951 Technology Education	842	0	0	0
952 Transportation	845	0	0	0
954 Vocational Education	850	0	0	0
955 Area Vocational School	852	0	0	0
963 Special Liability Expense Fund	855	0	0	0
972 Contingency Reserve**	885	0	0	0
974 Textbook & Student Materials Revolving Fund	889	0	0	0
TOTAL EXPENDITURES & TRANSFERS*	xxxx	0	0	0

and maintenance (Code 2600), and so on. These expenditure codes are broken down further by *object*, as with teacher salaries (Code 1000–110), teacher benefits (Code 1000–200), general administration salaries (Code 2300–100), and so on. The benefits are multiple. First, federal and state data-tracking is satisfied by uniform reporting methods. Second, the district may choose to analyze the minimum required data further by expanding it to include codes that report at progressively more incremental levels, wherein the purchase of teaching materials can be tracked to each school and each classroom—an activity that, accumulated, shows the cost (and potentially impact) of instructional expenditures. In other words, accounting is not just an assurance against ineptitude, carelessness, or fraud—it is the other dimension of accountability in that costs of programs can be calculated, and costs can be linked to student achievement data if the system is properly structured. For example, if low performance and under-funding simultaneously appear at an identifiable grade level, the data can call attention to both facts. At that point, good educational decision making must be engaged—perhaps more money for new textbooks is needed, teachers may need professional renewal, or additional teacher aides might be needed because of large class sizes that result in inadequate individualized attention—in other words, a host of options can be explored based on data available only through accounting and accountability, all of which can be derived by tracking revenue and expenditure in schools.

The Accounting Transaction

Although this textbook avoids becoming mired in the details of advanced school business management, a brief description of the accounting transaction is important to have a complete overview of how money is tracked in schools. Administrators and school board members need such knowledge because they are ultimately the responsible agents. Teachers seldom understand accounting, yet they are negatively affected if someone engages in bad financial management—for example, providing cash for school field trips or tossing athletic gate receipts into the car trunk over the weekend are two examples of poor business management and accounting practices. The list of bad examples can be long, but the point is that virtually everyone is touched by the accounting transaction—and it would not do much good to understand the big picture of accounting without the important detail of how money actually gets handled from beginning to end. Unfortunately, there is no easy way to explain the accounting transaction. A broad brush, however, can paint a useful description.

Earlier discussion in this chapter illustrated how the various funds provide a structure for grouping the financial activities of a school district along both revenue and expenditure dimensions. This is an important first step in the accounting process because it segregates money according to its use. The next step, however, is to establish individual *accounts* within each fund wherein the actual fiscal transactions occur. These accounts make up the record of assets, liabilities, revenues, and expenditures that occur in the broader fund context.

Generally, five classifications of accounts are established within a given fund such as the general fund. The five accounts are *expense, income, asset, liability,* and *net worth* or *fund balance* accounts. Their purpose is singular: All transactions involving revenue or expenditure or increases or decreases in the value of assets are entered (posted) to these accounts. Schools use the *double entry* method of posting transactions to the various accounts in a fund. Double entry involves entering both a *debit* (an entry on the left-hand side of the account ledger) to one account and a *credit* (entry on the right-hand side) to another account for each transaction. Asset and expenditure accounts (left-hand side accounts) are increased by debiting and decreased by crediting. Conversely, an income account (a right-hand side account) is decreased by a debit and increased by a credit.

An example of double entry posting of a transaction can be illustrated using a district that has received a general fund tax distribution of $1,000,000. Using a double entry system, this payment involves two general fund account groups: the income account and the asset account (the cash account). The income account increases as the transaction is entered as a credit. The cash account also increases as the transaction is entered as a debit to its side of the ledger. If the district then hires a new teacher at a salary of $35,000, a new transaction in the general fund occurs. Categories affected are the cash account and the appropriate expenditure account containing teacher salaries. As a result, cash balance in the asset account is credited (decreased), and the expenditure account for salaries is debited (increased). The purpose of this seemingly complex process is important: Double entry is a tool that creates a self-balancing set of books, so that the assets of the district are not inflated. If this were not done, assets and liabilities would not balance, misrepresenting the actual cash position of the fund because appropriate additions and subtractions would not cross-balance revenue and expenditure activity.

The individual accounts in each fund are listed in the *general ledger,* a set of books that keeps all records in a single location. Each transaction is recorded in the general ledger by a complicated process. Before being entered in the general ledger, revenue and expenditure transactions are first recorded in a *general journal,* which is a chronological listing of transactions as they were initiated. Transactions are transferred from the general journal and posted to the appropriate accounts on the general ledger using double entry. This process brings together (summarizes) all similar accounts. Figure 4.3 is a sample journal entry for a given day that shows the unpaid bills and charges to the appropriate expense and asset accounts. Figure 4.3 also shows how double-entry creates a self-balancing set of books: That is, expenses are debited in the amount of $3,238.84, thus increasing the expense account, whereas assets are credited $3,238.84, thereby decreasing the district's assets. From this transaction, the district can know exactly how much it owes compared to its assets—a reflection of true cash position.

Figure 4.3. Typical Journal Entry

For the Journal Period Ending June 1, 2005

Expense Accounts

Debit No.	1	Supplies	$3,175.63
	18	Miscellaneous	63.21
			$3,238.84

Asset Account

Credit No.	20	Accts. Payable	$3,238.84

This process is repeated for each fund and transaction during the accounting cycle. Each accounting transaction is one part of 10 steps:

1. Journalizing transactions
2. Posting transactions
3. Preparing a trial balance
4. Preparing a work sheet
5. Preparing financial statements
6. Journalizing closing entries
7. Posting closing entries
8. Balancing, ruling, and bringing forward balances of balance sheet accounts
9. Ruling temporary accounts
10. Preparing post-closing trial balances[4]

The complexity of the accounting cycle underscores the need to account for all fiscal activity in a tax-based organization. Obviously, administrators and other school leaders and policy makers do not have the time or expertise to actually carry out these tasks, making it critical to secure qualified outside assistance and to provide good training for the employees who perform the daily entries in books of record—an assurance that makes it possible for school leaders to spend their time using fiscal data to make educational program decisions.

---

4. R. E. Everett, R. L. Lowes, and D. R. Johnson, *Financial and Managerial Accounting for School Administrators* (Reston, VA: Association of School Business Officials, International, 1996), 17.

Auditing

Finally, we need to give attention to auditing to round out the discussion of tracking money in schools. Fortunately, auditing is easier to understand and absolutely vital to understanding schools and money because accounting and reporting would have no authority without the critical element of auditing. Auditing is the independent examination of accounting systems generally, and specific accounts in particular, to ensure the accuracy and completeness of the accounting records in a school district.

Most people are unfamiliar with audits, although the word strikes fear on a wide scale. Auditing conjures up images of fraud, embezzlement, or other wrongdoing. Although audits may reveal problems in accounting, including wrongdoing, they are actually the best protection for anyone in a fiduciary role because without auditing, innuendo and accusation gain very strong footholds—suspicion that may be unfounded but difficult to disprove.

The purposes of audits are several. First, audits are meant to detect errors in accounting. With the enormity of fiscal data in a modern school district, errors can occur easily. Errors can be accidental or intentional. Auditing serves a second purpose of recommending changes to accounting procedures and improving fiscal operations. Finally, auditing demonstrates to states, the federal government, and local taxpayers that the educational mission is being fiscally supported according to law. Audits therefore are not to be feared unless wrongdoing is present—rather, audits advance the educational mission and serve to protect professional reputations.

Types of Audits

Auditing is a protection for school districts, boards, administrators, and everyone affected by the business of education. Several types of audits have been devised, each serving a different need. Audits fall into two broad categories of *internal* and *external*. Audits are also known by their timing as *preaudits*, *postaudits*, or *continuous* audits. Finally, all external audits are *general comprehensive* audits, *state* audits, or *special* audits. Each type has a unique purpose based on the data being sought.

Internal Audits

Internal financial auditing within a school organization provides a system of self-checks. Internal auditing ranges from basic monthly board reports, to a full system of continuous internal monitoring, with accountants employed by a district to study and improve accounting systems. All systems engage in some amount of internal auditing. For example, budget reports on the financial status of the district sent to board members prior to each meeting is a kind of internal audit. Internal auditing is required to produce monthly financial statements because journals and ledgers must be examined to generate income and expense statements. Mandatory state reports require internal auditing to produce and verify the data on which state aid requests are based. Internal auditing exists in all districts, although the extent varies by individual district.

Internal audits are usually either *preaudits* or *continuous* audits. A preaudit ensures proper accounting procedures in advance of a transaction. A continuous audit implies constant observation of the accounting system. Continuous auditing occurs through the system of checks and balances in place in most districts, whereby multiple approvals must be secured to spend. The hierarchy from one actual district, shown in Figure 4.4 (pp. 128–129), shows protections in place to guard against error or wrongdoing. Although internal auditing is never sufficient alone, it is an important tool of good management.

External Audits

Most people are more familiar with the *external* audit. External auditing is a formal examination of financial records in a district by a qualified outsider to verify accuracy and legal compliance. External audits are always conducted by an independent auditing organization such as a certified public accounting firm or, in some instances, by state auditors checking for compliance with regulations.

External audits are exhaustive, yielding an audit report with recommendations on the audit findings. External audits are accompanied by a letter of transmittal stating the purpose of the audit, procedures followed, a statement of findings, and a list of recommendations. In most instances, the audit is conducted at the same time as preparation of the district's annual financial report. As a general rule, most external audits are *general comprehensive audits* occurring at the close of an accounting period, usually an entire year. The report generally contains summaries of revenues and expenditures and compares cash balances against encumbrances to determine if statutory requirements were met. Governmental funds are examined separately under statements of budgetary accounts, and other funds such as fiduciary expendable trust funds and proprietary funds are also separately examined. If no problems are noted, the report is an *unqualified opinion* because its findings are not qualified by any *audit exceptions*. If concerns are present, the report is a *qualified opinion*. Audit reports are presented to the school board, with the board required to show receipt of the audit in its minutes and to show action to correct exceptions.

Although developed over many years, the audit process is not static and is subject to change. At the external audit level, perhaps the most significant change in many years occurred in 1999 when the Governmental Accounting Standards Board (GASB) adopted Statement No. 34, which changed how school districts issue financial statements in conformity with generally accepted accounting principles (GAAP). Statement 34, entitled *Basic Financial Statements—and Management's Discussion and Analysis—for State and Local Governments*, required that by the year 2003 all school districts' presentation of financial information must meet new standards aimed at improved fiscal

(Text continues on page 130.)

Figure 4.4. Accounting Checks and Balances

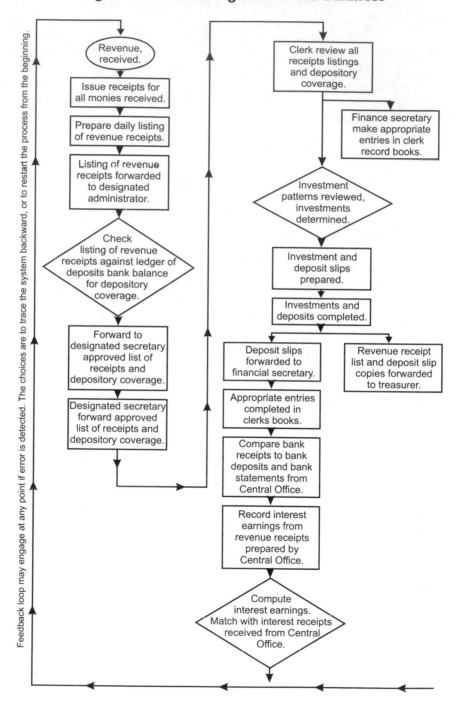

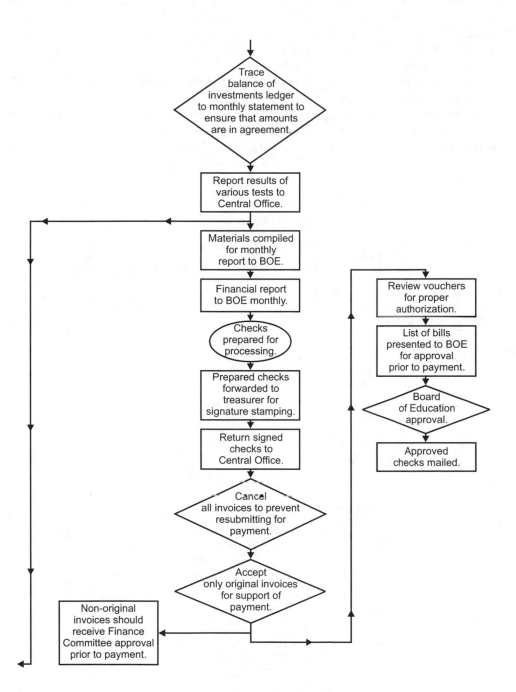

and operational accountability. According to the Association of School Business Officials International (ASBO), GASB Statement No. 34 was designed to require "...that a district demonstrate the extent to which it has met and can continue to meet its operating objectives in an efficient and effective manner into the future."[5] GASB Statement 34 moved schools closer to a business accounting model through its focus on cost data and through its efforts to make financial statements clearer to the taxpaying public by requiring, among other things, information about the cost of delivering services to students and information about general infrastructure assets of the school district. ASBO illustrated the major changes to district accounting and auditing procedures brought about by Statement 34, as seen in Figure 4.5.

Figure 4.5. Major Changes to Financial Statements in School Districts Under GASB Statement 34

Changes to Enhance Financial Accountability		Changes to Enhance Operational Accountability	
Previous Model	New Model	Previous Model	New Model
Information in basic financial statements aggregated by fund type	Information in basic financial statements presented separately for major governmental and enterprise funds	All reporting based on fund and fund types	Introduction of district-wide financial statements
Budgetary comparisons associated with the basic financial statements aggregated by fund type	Budgetary comparisons associated with the basic financial statements presented for general fund and each major special revenue fund with a legally adopted budget	Information on governmental activities limited to near-term inflows and outflow of spendable resources	District-wide financial statements provide additional long-term focus for governmental activities
Budgetary comparisons report only final amended budget	Budgetary comparisons report both original and final amended budget	Cost data available for business-type activities	Cost data provide for both governmental and business-type activities

Source: ASBO International, *GASB Statement No. 34 Implementation Recommendations for School Districts*, 2nd ed. (Reston,VA: ASBO, 2003), ix. By permission.

---

5. ASBO International, *GASB Statement No. 34 Implementation Recommendations for School Districts* (Reston,VA: ASBO, 2000), 5.

Accounting and auditing affect everyone connected to schools. Trouble-free audits are the ultimate affirmation of trust, in that administrators, boards, teachers, staff, children, and the community are well served by good financial management. On the other hand, everyone suffers if bad fiscal management goes undetected. The price paid for accounting and auditing is money wisely spent, although these tools still do not ensure accountability for wise educational decision-making. Nonetheless, accounting and auditing play an important part in overall accountability by assuring educational stakeholders of absolute conformity with the law. In other words, it is much easier to closely monitor financial affairs than to explain errors that cast a dark pall on professional and personal reputations.

State Audits

In addition to internal audits and external general comprehensive audits, a variety of *state* audits may occur in school districts. State audits serve a different purpose and are designed to monitor compliance with statutes and regulations involving state or federal money.

The variety of individual state audit requirements makes it hard to generalize about the details. Many differences rest primarily in how states choose to control education. In states emphasizing local control, state audits may only serve to meet a minimum compliance standard. In states where education is strongly vested at the state level, state audits may be interested in more exhaustive review of finances and programs.

All state audits have a common goal of determining whether the state's financial interest in schools is protected. State audits thus focus particularly on those funds to which the state either supplies aid directly or to which the state acts as a channel for federal aid to local districts. In the case of federal funds, states are interested in maintenance of applications, expenditure reports, and transmittal documents. In the case of state funds, states are interested in all documentation related to state aid claims. For example, transportation claims are often closely examined because many states invest large sums in student bus services. Likewise, states closely audit schools to ensure that federal monies are not commingled or improperly spent. State audits are state-specific, although their goal is always to verify that the state's educational obligations and priorities are met.

Special Audits

Finally, school districts can be subject to *special* audits. Although fairly uncommon, the purpose of a special audit may relate to suspicion of serious error or fraud. One of the logical ways special audits occur is as an offshoot of a normal state audit. For example, a transportation audit might reveal that a district was claiming more children than were actually being transported. Likewise, internal auditing might cause a district to seek a special audit; for example, inability to reconcile expense claims with receipts could result in a special audit. Other events such as inventory loss might result in special audit at the local level. Unfortunately, these examples are not implausible as it is not possible to completely control individual behavior.

Accounting and accountability are constant companions affecting school administrators, board members, policy makers, teachers, and laypersons on a daily basis. The right way to do business requires at least:

♦ Strong internal accounting procedures, including segregation of duties based on checks and balances (see Figure 4.4 earlier)

♦ Competent employees with sufficient time to do the work of accounting so that errors of haste are not made

♦ Extensive documentation based on a system that includes the following:

- Proof of school board approval of expenditures
- Statements showing receipts and disbursements
- Reconciled bank statements, including all canceled checks
- A system of purchase orders
- A strict no-cash disbursement policy

A FINAL WORD ABOUT PROFESSIONALISM

In this chapter, we have made clear that the gravity of fiduciary trust cannot be overstated. This is the issue of professionalism in handling school money. Although we already addressed professionalism in the broad context of harsh warnings, we should take one further step by looking at published ethical standards that should be followed.

Ethical standards exist in most professions. Administrators, teachers, and many community people belong to professional or trade organizations that have adopted written ethical conduct codes. Standards are essential to the integrity of the entire social order, but we believe people with fiduciary capacity for public money have an extraordinary duty to ethical conduct. The Association of School Business Officials International takes the same stance and has established a code of ethics that should be seen as fundamental to fiduciary relationships—a code applicable far beyond just those persons whose professions lead them to be ASBO members. Figure 4.6 excerpts key parts of the ASBO Code of Ethics. The preamble states:

> In this age of accountability, when the activities and conduct of school business officials are subject to greater scrutiny and more severe criticism than ever before, Standards of Conduct are in order. The Association cannot fully discharge its obligation of leadership and service to its members short of establishing appropriate standards of behavior.

The preamble captures the point of this chapter—that is, increasingly broad definitions of accountability, including student outcomes, are the defining feature of the future of education.

Figure 4.6. ASBO Code of Ethics and Standards of Conduct—Condensed and Paraphrased

♦ In relationships within the school district it is expected that the school business official will:

- Support the goals and objectives of the employing school system.
- Interpret policies and practices of the district to subordinates and to the community fairly.
- Implement the policies and administrative regulations of the district.
- Assist others as appropriate in fulfilling their obligations.
- Build the best possible image of the school district.
- Refrain from publicly criticizing board members, administrators, or employees.
- Help subordinates achieve their maximum potential through fair and just treatment.

♦ In the conduct of business and the discharge of responsibilities, the school business official will:

- Conduct business honestly, openly, and with integrity.
- Avoid conflict of interest situations by not conducting business with a company or firm in which the official or any member of the official's family has a vested interest.
- Avoid preferential treatment of outside interest groups, companies or individuals.
- Uphold the dignity and decorum of the office in every way.
- Avoid using the position for personal gain.
- Never accept or offer illegal payment for services rendered.
- Refrain from accepting gifts, free services, or anything of value.
- Permit the use of school property only for officially authorized activities.
- Refrain from soliciting contributions from subordinates or outside sources for gifts/donations to a superior.

♦ In relationships with other colleagues in other districts and professional associations, it is expected that the school business official will:

- Support the actions of a colleague whenever possible, never publicly criticizing.
- Offer assistance and/or guidance to a colleague when such help is requested or needed.
- Actively support appropriate professional associations.
- Accept leadership responsibilities, but refrain from "taking over" any association.
- Refrain from using any organization or position of leadership in it for personal gain.

SUGGESTED FOLLOW-UP PROJECTS

♦ Obtain a copy of your school district's budget and identify the fund structure for revenues and expenditures. Familiarize yourself with the operational funds in your district and determine the number of dollars and uses for each fund and account group.

♦ Closely examine the general fund in your district. Talk to your chief fiscal officer about what activities are paid from general fund and how the district finances its daily operations. Discuss cash flow and fiscal resource management to determine how the district optimizes its assets. Ask about what kind of problems the district encounters in this area.

♦ Find out which funds beyond the general fund your district operates. Identify their uses and how they are administered. Ask about special revenue funds, capital projects funds, and any debt service funds. Be sure to ask about proprietary and fiduciary funds and their uses and any restrictions.

♦ Obtain a copy of the monthly revenue and expenditure report in your district. Identify account codes and learn how the district accumulates and reports its revenues and expenditures, including any program planning uses. In particular, learn how the district uses the accounting transaction to provide both fiscal and program accountability.

♦ Talk to your district's accounting clerk, tracing one or more receipts and disbursements through the entire accounting cycle. Ask about how the district ensures safeguards in the context of this chapter—for example, handling of money, disbursements, auditing. Ask what audits are conducted in the district and how auditing has helped to improve the accounting function. Ask how the district's business office engages in regular training activities.

5

BUDGET PLANNING

BUDGETS AND SCHOOLS

Our discussion in the last chapter laid the groundwork for the next several chapters on principles of budgeting. In retrospect, the whole book has been building toward this point. We now understand the social context of schools, which increasingly includes a demanding and dissatisfied public. We also have gained respect for the seriousness of handling school money, and we understand how money flows through the fund structure as revenues and expenditures. We also have been exposed to the many policy decisions underlying state aid formulas. In sum, we built a framework for the context of money in schools. Now we need to address the many details of budgeting.

We start our journey in this chapter by examining school district budgets from a broad context. Later chapters will explore additional aspects of budgeting in greater detail, but this chapter provides the foundation to which we will return often. In this chapter we gain an overview of how budgets are built, with some attention to how money is directed toward individual schools. As always, questions guide the way. For example, what is a budget at its most basic conceptual level? What are some common approaches to budgeting? What is a good budget framework? What is the general budget process? What are the roles of teachers, principals, central office administrators, school boards, and other stakeholders in budget building? Asking these and other questions will help clarify a very complicated process.[1] As we progress, we should keep our central goal clearly in mind—to leave this chapter with a better understanding of how district and school budgets are put into place.

CONCEPTUALIZING BUDGETS

Almost every idea in this book has been couched in terms of increasing competition for scarce resources. Earlier chapters revealed that education is undergoing enormous change related to populations served, increased understanding of differing needs of children, and greatly increased expecta-

---

1. For extended discussion on this topic, see generally David C. Thompson, R. Craig Wood, and David Honeyman, *Fiscal Leadership for Schools: Concepts and Practices* (New York: Longman, 1994). See also R. Craig Wood, David C. Thompson, and Lawrence O. Picus, *Principles of School Business Management*, 3rd ed. (Reston, VA: ASBO, 2005).

tions that schools become a major caretaker of children in our society. Schools have not been able to meet such demands easily because, despite greater state assumption of education's costs, demands on government at all levels have resulted in scarcity of funds for schools. At the same time, disenchantment with educational outcomes has joined with taxpayer resistance toward the cost of government, creating an atmosphere of hostility toward government and taxation for any purpose.

The result has been greater scrutiny of the fiscal operation of schools. As citizen participation in school budgets has grown, everyone associated with educational policy making has had to become more skilled in the language of budgets. As we just noted, that is our thesis in this chapter: How budgets are built is a topic of real importance to educators, policy makers, and laypersons because these groups must work in a tense and risk-laden environment.

What Are the Basic Budget Concepts?

As we have built budgets and worked with educators and communities for many years, we have observed a singular lack of understanding regarding the basic budget concepts that underlie everything else that goes into a financial plan for school districts and individual schools. These concepts fall into general categories of *old assumptions, budgetary purposes, the need for strong leadership,* and *uses of budgets.* Taken rightly, together they enable the district's mission and educational plan. Taken wrongly as they sometimes are, they are the source of much misunderstanding.

The realities of life as we begin a new century deny many old assumptions about school budgets. Many people relegate school finance to relatively low priority and believe that budgets can be handled by noneducators, who only need accounting skills. We have long resisted that mistaken attitude, arguing that *everything* in education is driven by school finance and wise budgeting. This does not deny that teaching and learning are the most critical activities in districts and schools, but it does say that no teaching and learning would occur without sound funding and competent budgeting because no one works for free. Even if such persons could be found, no school buildings would exist and no supplies, equipment, or textbooks would be available. Although it seems obvious to say that the first and most basic concept of school budgets is that educational programs cost money, it is a fact that escapes many educators who seem to want this little problem to just go away so that they can claim *their* role in education is most important. Unfortunately, reality does not respect idealism, so it is a basic fact that without good budgets, there are no schools.

Although many people do bow to the supremacy of money, a large number of people seem to have missed a second fundamental concept that says that the primary purpose of a budget is to translate educational priorities into programmatic and financial terms. Most people know the phrase "money talks," and the concept is entirely true in schools. Although educators should be praised for focusing on learning as the primary mission of schools, it is important for *everyone* to internalize the view that the budget is a statement of *priorities.* This seems simple, but it goes much deeper. Very simply, because programs cost money, a budget is the execution of the individual and collective programs in a district or school. Likewise, because money is finite whereas needs are infinite, prioritization occurs wherein top priorities are funded first when other programs fall victim to economic change. It is not merely philosophical to say that a budget is the translation of a district's educational goals: In other words, programs that are valued are funded better, making it true that the budget is a fiscal expression of the educational philosophy of the district.

A third fundamental concept is that budgets do not just happen. Budgeting is a deliberate act of establishing priorities and educational plans. Budgets are created by people, whose charge is to carry out the educational duties of a district. It is important to remember that those obligations are both constitutional and statutory, and they are influenced by philosophical and fiscal realities that have their truest expression at the local level. Although it is true that all districts must provide programs conforming to state laws regarding days, hours, and minutes of instruction and various required and elective courses, the budget that supports any program is greatly affected by the attitude of those in leadership positions. Leadership includes the community at large, which approves (or disapproves) of total school operations; the board, which is legally charged with school operation; and school personnel who design and carry out the educational programs. These persons play crucial roles. For example, administrators are hired to build the district's financial plan and to provide philosophical leadership and technical expertise—leadership that should be influenced by the teaching staff. Board members bring their views, which are often influenced by the community, and ultimately only the board can enact a fiscal plan. As a result, it is critical to remember what enables educational programming—it is money, pure and simple—money taken from a public whose desire to support schools depends on confidence in leadership. As a result, educational leaders should never underestimate the power of their expertise and influence.

A fourth fundamental concept is similar in that budgets should be seen as a powerful political tool in schools. Again, money talks loudly, and the process is highly political. Anyone experienced in school fiscal affairs understands that the budget is the means by which public approval or disapproval is expressed, that board attitudes about budgets are determined in the political arena, and that individual programs rise or fall based on these realities. Although politics are often viewed negatively, in many instances these earthy realities are opportunities. For example, failure to engage the public in the budget process is a serious mistake because ownership and approval of schools is vital to school success—in fact, politics are very useful because a disengaged community is often apathetic or hostile. The political side of budgets can be dysfunctional, of course, but politics can be useful when remembering that budgets are the fiscal expression of an educational philosophy. The key is accepting and ethically utilizing the political benefits of the budget process.

These concepts are the basis for many misperceptions about school budgets. It is unfortunate that so many people see budgets as dry financial documents interesting only to accountants and clerks because budgets are the enabling tool by which schools function. It is also unfortunate that so few people realize that the budget is the fiscal expression of the educational philosophy of the district, so that it becomes even more critical to engage staff and patrons at every opportunity. It is further unfortunate that many school administrators fail to appreciate their own importance in the budget process, or, alternatively, refuse to use their power by keeping budgets at a level that discourages wide involvement. And it is finally unfortunate that so many school leaders have viewed the politics of budgets with distaste, instead of learning to take ethical advantage of political systems.

These concepts actually define a budget. First, a budget is a *description of a desirable educational program*. Second, a budget is an estimate of expenditures needed to carry out the program. Third, a budget is an estimate of revenues available to meet expenses. Our definition is thus three-sided. Although different from the accountant's view that sees only revenue and expenditure, the three-dimensional view best expresses our budget philosophy, which states that programs should drive both revenues and expenditures.

Figure 5.1 illustrates how we view the budgeting process, and it is intentional that the educational program is the base of the budget triangle. Although fiscal problems often cause the sides to reverse as programs are restrained by resources, it is important for community members, parents, boards, administrators, teachers, and others to not lose sight of the goal that budgets should be built on the basis of program needs. As the budget triangle illustrates, the definition of a budget is first based on quality programs and then well supported by revenue and expenditure plans that make envisioned outcomes possible.

Figure 5.1. Ideal Budget Triangle

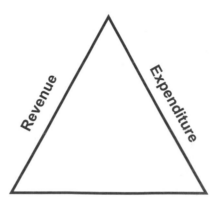

Program

ORGANIZING FOR BUDGETING

Our discussion to this point leads to one result: Budgeting is critical to the success of everything that happens in schools. Needless to say, something so important demands a high degree of organization, attention to detail, and fundamental accuracy.

Unfortunately, the importance of budgeting has gone unrecognized, at least until recently. This has coincided with the fact that budgets have been an intensely local affair, with only minimal state control relating to a few reporting procedures to qualify for state aid. Yet while state requirements have increased, the budget process has continued to be somewhat unsophisticated in many school districts. Various efforts to devise budgeting systems have been made, however, whereby districts can adopt a budget framework consistent with their vision and operational philosophy. A brief look at the most common budget models helps to understand the various ways in which districts seek to organize budgeting activities.

What Are the Common Approaches to Budgeting?

Efforts to improve budgeting have led to common approaches at the district level. These include *incremental* budgeting; *line-item* budgeting; *program, planning, and budgeting* systems; *zero-based* budgeting; *school-site* budgeting; and emerging models like *outcome-focused* budgeting. The order relates to their chronological appearance and to the political processes that have increasingly impacted the school setting. The main purpose of any approach to budgeting is to detail where resources are targeted to address children's needs, but there is a corresponding level of politics in each model that ultimately affects distribution. As a result, each approach has benefits and drawbacks inherent to the model itself and to its political viability, so much so that adoption of a model should include consideration of both technical benefits and whether the model will fit local belief systems.

Incremental Budgeting

Incremental budgeting historically has been the most common way to build budgets. Incremental budgeting is a simplistic model that assumes the previous year's expenditures are an adequate base for building the next budget. Incremental budgeting takes its name from the assumption that each budget line should receive the same increment as a percentage increase or decrease during the next budget cycle.

Incremental budgeting appeals to common sense. For example, there is sensibility to believing that next year's legislative allocation will be based on the prior year's funding. Legislatures themselves often couch new funding as percentage increases or decreases from the prior year. Additionally, there is common sense in thinking about budgets in terms of comparing multiple years to measure changes in revenue and costs. Many states' budget documents also require districts to show several prior years' data by line item to help the state assess fiscal health of districts and to alert taxpayers to the

[handwritten margin note: Previous year's expend. are adquate base for building next yrs' budget]

ever-changing amounts of money sent to schools. As a result, incremental budgeting has had an alluring simplicity in a complex world.

Although incremental budgeting still forms the basis for some decisions, there are drawbacks. Obviously, it focuses on aggregate trends and fails to analyze revenue and expenditure changes unless extra effort is made. Incremental budgeting also has paid no attention to the selective impact of money because it was developed at a time when there was low concern for measuring educational outcomes. Finally, it is obvious that incremental budgeting results in unquestioned equal increase to each budget line, potentially causing over-funding or under-funding of individual areas. This approach does little more than reveal gross trends and does not speak to strategic allocation or returns on investment in educational programs. Still, some districts continue to believe that incremental budgeting is fair in that no area of the budget can be said to receive less than another area.

Line-Item Budgeting

An improvement to incremental budgeting is development of line-item budgeting. This tool has been widely used for many years to assign different amounts to each line of the budget. In line-item budgeting, emphasis is placed on the specific objects for which funds are spent, wherein each line item in the budget is seen as the proper base for expenditure decisions. As a result, budgets are planned around each line, and the new budget is based on increases to each line's base—usually last year's spending level. For example, lines for instructional salaries, administrative and clerical salaries, repair, upkeep of grounds, supplies, and capital construction might be increased unequally.

Line-item budgeting has several advantages. The major benefit is that the budget is viewed as a sum of its parts. Additionally, each part is considered separately in terms of some measure of need. Finally, line-item budgeting suggests some consideration of program needs, although the concept is unsophisticated. Because line-item budgeting has been in place for many years and because it is easily understood, it has survived despite the availability of newer budgeting tools.

Despite its popularity, line-item budgeting has drawbacks. One drawback is that it depends on the budget document almost entirely for decisions. Most state budget documents are not very informative because they are quite general, only providing broad lines such as teacher salaries, supplies, or miscellaneous "other" expenses. Too little information is given on how decisions are made, the process depends too much on experience, and little or no record of decision processes is evident; for example, it is impossible to determine what kind of thinking relates to levels of expenditure for particular grades, programs, or projects. Such a method of allocating money fosters secretiveness in budgets, vests power in only a few select persons, and does not encourage accountability. By far the most popular method until the 1960s, use of line-item budgeting has faded, although it is still more prevalent than it should be.

Program Planning Budgeting Systems

Program planning budgeting systems (PPB) arose from a realization that the budget should be more clearly related to the educational program. This approach requires each unit in a district or school to establish goals through systematic planning that first sees the program's goals before considering the object of expenditure. The process requires an educational plan where each unit makes plans to meet instructional objectives, underlain by a plan for spending justified by needs. Funds then follow the plan.

The benefits of PPB are real. This model represents a major conceptual shift by deliberately linking programs and expenditures to a presumed cause-and-effect of money. PPB contributes to accountability, both by its focus on programs and by its potential to use object-function codes to include productivity analysis. This conceptual framework includes projecting long-term costs of programs, so that advocates of PPB believe that organizations are more likely to reach their stated goals and objectives when program is the first consideration in building a budget.

Not surprisingly, there are drawbacks to PPB, particularly as both thinking and technology can outpace organizational readiness for change. Historically this was true of PPB, as schools have had a hard time being prepared for the dramatic philosophical shift underlying program budgeting systems. This continues to plague PPB, as it is difficult to smoothly connect budget goals, organizational patterns, and the many new structures needed by PPB. Yet schools have had to consider program budgeting at increasingly greater levels, as newer accountability structures have taken this concept to a new intensity (see outcome-focused budgeting later in this section).

Zero-Based Budgeting

As we said earlier, political overtones often overshadow school finance and budgeting. Politics clearly apply to zero-based budgeting (ZBB), as ZBB has been a case of external politics pressing change on schools during an era of fiscal austerity.

The advent of zero-based budgeting in schools coincided with fiscal problems that began to surface during the high inflation years of the 1970s. ZBB was first instituted in the federal government under President Jimmy Carter as an effort to control federal spending using sunset laws to zero out unproductive government programs. Popular with antitax constituencies, ZBB was also implemented by many local governments in response to taxpayer unrest, and it was only a matter of time until schools experimented with the concept. The basic premise of ZBB is that budgets must be justified each year with the goal of cutting waste and improving efficiency.

Many school districts have adopted a modified ZBB model. A typical procedure is to build new budgets based on a percentage reduction from the prior year, where maintenance of prior year funding requires extensive justification. The rationale is that greater efficiency can be injected into any district, and reductions as a matter of course help to achieve that end. New resource requests are closely scrutinized. Another form of ZBB requires staff to prepare multiple scenarios and to justify each scenario. The first scenario requires extensive description of the educational plan, with the new budget set at a specified percentage below current funding. The second scenario requires maintenance of both the educational plan and the budget at the same level as the current year. The third scenario allows improvement and expects the budget to increase more than the current year. In all instances, each scenario must detail any difference between the current year and the next budget cycle, with full expenditure justification.

Benefits of ZBB are obvious. The product of an era of high inflation and perceived government waste, ZBB represents a chance to mollify taxpayers by giving the impression of strong action to reduce waste and growth. Particularly sound is the idea that budget growth should not occur absent questions about actual contribution to the organization. The idea of multiple spending scenarios is sound, in that planning may improve if growth is restrained. Finally, common sense dictates that districts may be better prepared for reductions if systematic groundwork is laid ahead of actual need. On the other hand, drawbacks are real because the process of zeroing budgets is complex. ZBB is a cost reduction tool that can require more resources for effective strategizing than is saved in the end. The problem of internal strife also applies to ZBB, as elective and enrichment courses must make the same justification for existence as core areas. The notion of zeroing core courses is impossible, creating both incredulity and requiring substitution of a modified zero-based budget model. Although most people see ZBB as an intrinsically good idea, its problems are so great that many districts are wary. Vestiges still linger, however, as many districts continue to use best/no growth/worst case scenarios in the uncertain revenue context commonly faced by schools and when faced with unavoidable cuts.

School-Site Budgeting

In contrast to centralized budgeting methods, a currently popular trend is school-site budgeting. School-site budgeting is a school-based management tool following closely after the popularity of decentralized administration, where budget decisions are made at individual school levels. It can be said that school-site budgeting is a variant of program budgeting applied to each individual school within a district. Under this plan, each site is assigned resources based on some district-level formula that takes into account the number of students at each site in each grade level and program. The principal and a school site council made up of patrons, parents, and staff are given responsibility for developing and managing the budget within limits of the total allocation. These persons may have authority to make decisions in such areas as salaries, supplies, activities, and so on—all within the requirement of not violating bargaining agreements, regulations of federally funded programs, statutory requirements such as class size, and district policies such as school calendar or length of school day.

Advantages of school-site budgets are appealing because they complement the philosophical underpinnings of site-based management. In concept, site budgeting supports recent advances in learning theory because it values the impact of resources at the point of utilization; that is, resources are only meaningful at the individual classroom level under the care of the teacher as applied to students. Site budgeting is sound in that it involves all stakeholders, especially parents and teachers, in the education of children. The concept is especially attractive in an era when parent involvement is at an historic low, and it acknowledges the role of the home and community in each child's progress. The special value, then, is in providing a more holistic and inclusive view of education, making school-site budgeting a viable option long into the foreseeable future.[2]

School-site budgeting has some drawbacks. A primary disadvantage is its complexity, wherein schools are once again asked to take on new roles and to accept new power brokers. Throughout history, schools have been semiclosed social systems, and the addition of community members and parents to complex decision making is stressful. Site-based budgeting requires much training for stakeholders, as administrators, teachers, and parents must learn about organizational and technical aspects of funding and must learn to work together cooperatively. And there are real dangers in the concept, that is, unless close attention is paid, equity among schools within a district may be endangered through site-based budgeting in that some schools will have greater participation and advocacy. Similarly, some schools simply will do a better job at teaching and learning, making a child's education even more dependent on a given attendance site. Likewise, there is danger to site decisions in personnel matters, raising legal, ethical, and moral questions. But given current trends, school-site budgeting is a likely companion for the foreseeable future—a fact borne out in that we return later to a more intensive look at implementing site-based budgeting.

Outcome-Focused Budgeting

All the various budget models examined so far have attractive features as well as drawbacks. All models represent emerging thought and amalgamation either as a result of forward progress or as a consequence of adaptation to individual school districts' needs. The political aspects of budgeting have been important as well, and outcome-focused budgeting is a good representation of all such realities.

Outcome-focused budgeting has grown in popularity in governmental circles in recent years in direct response to interest in accountability. Fiscal austerity, along with competition for finite resources, has only served to

---

2.   For models on productivity and site-based budgeting, see Allan Odden and Sarah Archibald, Reallocating Resources: How to Boost Student Achievement Without Asking for More (Thousand Oaks, CA: Corwin Press, 2001). See also *School Based Financing: 20th Yearbook of the American Education Finance Association* (Thousand Oaks, CA: Corwin Press, 1999).

increase the model's attractiveness. Outcome-focused budgeting is the practice of connecting the aims of the organization to the allocation of resources and finally to measurable outcomes such as test scores.

Patterns in state aid allocations across the last decade have all headed in this direction. The sanctions in the new *No Child Left Behind Act* go directly to implications for outcome-focused budgeting. The advantages are clear: It is intuitive that an organization whose financial support depends on adequate performance will be much more attuned to actually meeting the standard, and it is unarguably legitimate to demand performance in exchange for continued fiscal support. The disadvantages are equally clear: Organizations in survival mode are likely victims of unhealthy stress, and the unintended consequence of a slavish devotion to singular measures of outcomes is to slight or ignore the grander aims of developing the whole child. Notwithstanding, outcome-focused budgeting combined with site-level issues is the harbinger of the future.

What Is a Good Budget Framework?

Although budgeting approaches are increasingly mandated by federal and state governments, school districts still must approach the total budget process from a perspective that makes sense locally. The various choices in budget philosophies demand that school leaders individually develop a framework for budgeting; similarly, others such as board members and laypersons serving on site councils should understand the issues affecting budgeting. Many questions about each type of budgeting philosophy must be asked, and leaders must ensure that both the district's temperament and their own values are served. As a consequence, there are several considerations in adopting a budget framework to ensure that districts and schools do not naively seize on a good idea that later proves unworkable.

The set of issues to be considered when choosing a budgeting philosophy cautions against an uncritical attitude. Although one may ask why a personal philosophy about budgets is important, it should be clear that participants' attitudes toward fiscal control must be in agreement, or chaos and discontent will follow. Because administrators, boards, staffs, and communities must work cooperatively to assure success in schools, it is essential to adopt a framework that meets the expectations of stakeholders.

Hartman long ago proposed issues to be raised when adopting a financial structure at either district or individual school levels.[3] These relate to style, preference, and congruency of stakeholders in the budget process. Hartman proposed that consideration must be given to the district's history, in that rapid or abrupt changes in budget policies and operations will be met with resistance. For example, if the district has a history of constituent apathy in budget affairs, opportunity for dramatically increased patron involvement is

---

3.   William T. Hartman, *School District Budgeting* (Englewood Cliffs, NJ: Prentice Hall, 1988), 28–29.

unlikely except over a long time. Decisions must be made in light of the historic role of the board, in that districts with a history of strong board control will experience strife when trying to move quickly to decentralized models such as site-based budgeting. Likewise, the fiscal condition of the district must be analyzed, as districts in poor economic health should not decentralize because of high costs and inefficiency of broad-based decision making. As Hartman warned, these and other issues should be considered before jumping on the bandwagon of any new innovation.

The inherent problems in each budget philosophy give rise to another option if carefully structured. As an alternative to strict adherence to any one philosophy, districts can take the best aspects of each framework and meld them into a workable compromise. Although there is danger to assembling incompatible elements, there is value to applying the benefits each philosophy has given to the field. The value of incremental budgeting is clear in working with legislatures, although leaders should encourage legislators to understand the value of looking at the various tasks of schools. Line-item budgeting has value in that every budget ends up with money assigned to each line. Program planning budgeting is basic to the work of schools, and the focus on program in PPB has brought budgeting into the modern era. Zero-based budgeting also helps by questioning protectionism. Site-based budgeting is consistent with new designs of schools and is a likely companion of outcomes-focused budgeting as accountability demands continue to escalate. Although inconsistency is always a risk, the best parts of each model are useful in the hands of skilled leaders. For example, regardless of whether a district is centralized or decentralized, the benefit of function-object code tracking for productivity analysis should not be ignored and ties neatly to the growing focus on measurable student achievement data.

Organizing for budgeting and developing a philosophy are essential parts of educational leadership. Organization and philosophy are consistent with the purpose of budgets, which is to identify and prioritize needs, match resources with needs, and make educational goals operational. Although there is no way to become so skilled that there is no room to improve, leaders who operate from an informed framework for budgeting are better positioned to see opportunities and problems arising during the actual building of school budgets. With growing public interest in school funding, budgeting skills are a critical element of leadership.

CONSTRUCTING BUDGETS

Our discussion leads to how school district budgets are actually built. Constructing a budget demands three kinds of knowledge. The first is a general appreciation for the critical impact of budgets on the educational process. This is crucial if leaders are to work effectively with legislatures and local boards and communities to provide good educational experiences. The second kind of knowledge is understanding of the technical process of budget-building on a general level. Although budgeting is state-specific, a good grasp of procedures can be gained because there are common elements that apply irrespective of location. The third kind of knowledge is understanding of specific state practices. In the last case, no textbook can cover the complexity of state-level budgets. But by establishing knowledge in the first two areas, all leaders can prepare to add state-specific details at the appropriate time. As a result, our study of budgets here focuses on the process of budget construction in a general context.

What Is the Budget Model?

Budget construction follows a similar pattern in most states. Although states have specific timelines and forms that budgets must follow, the process uses the format of the model in Figure 5.2. The model includes much of the information we saw in earlier chapters, wherein the interdependent nature of schools and external agencies such as federal, state, and local government is apparent. Because Figure 5.2 includes both the political and technical dynamics of the budget process, the model frames our discussion throughout the remainder of this chapter.

Figure 5.2. The Budget Model

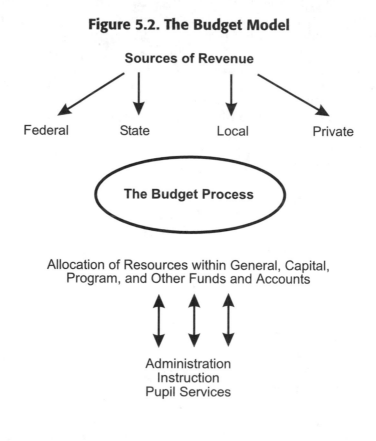

Sources of Revenue

Federal   State   Local   Private

The Budget Process

Allocation of Resources within General, Capital, Program, and Other Funds and Accounts

Administration
Instruction
Pupil Services

The model reflects a common belief that school budgets are built locally. Most people believe that the process is basically carried out as the local school board and administration work together to determine needs and set the budget. The budget model in Figure 5.2, however, argues that the budget process is much more complex because it actually begins long before the amount of revenue available to a district is knowable. The model reaffirms our learning in prior chapters by showing that money flows to districts from a variety of sources. Although districts receive the largest share from state and local governments, aid amounts vary greatly in individual states, so that the budget process is unique to each state and district. Districts with high concentrations of federal land, for example, may receive a large proportion of revenue from federal sources. Similarly, the balance between state and local revenue varies among states. The mix of revenue sources has a powerful impact on budgeting, and mixtures are determined long before funding is ever known in any district.

The budget model also illustrates that revenue balance among sources is achieved entirely by the political process. We noted earlier that federal aid has been indirect and tied to special interests. Federal aid has also varied with changes in Congress and presidential administrations. Under President Lyndon Johnson, federal aid increased as a result of liberal social programs; under President Ronald Reagan significant conservatism ruled the day; and today's version of the political process observes the powerful fiscal and programmatic impacts of *No Child Left Behind*. Similarly, state budget processes depend on the political will of state legislatures. States using a full state funding formula will differ greatly in type and amount of aid to school districts, compared to states using minimum foundations. Economic health of states also determines revenue balance, as states with stagnant or depressed economies are more likely to shift costs of schools to local districts. In all instances, balance is determined at political levels far above the local district, making local participation in politics a necessity.

The model notes that federal and state aid is beyond local control and that this process is necessary in order for three other events to follow. The first event follows in that the amount of federal and state revenue is the engine that drives local revenue requirements because the balance to fund programs must be raised by local taxes. The second event follows in that local revenue drives many program decisions because there are both legal and practical limits on the amount of local taxes that can be raised. The third event follows in that when federal, state, and local revenues are set, budgeting at the local level finally can be undertaken by assigning resources to the educational plan. Figure 5.2 shows that the process results in direct impact on instruction. The model notes that although amounts of federal and state aid are beyond the control of local districts, in many states the local share varies by local taxpayer willingness to fund the balance. In other words, voter approval sets local spending priorities.

The budget model finally illustrates that, depending on the amount of local discretion, determination of the local share can be complex. The process is simplest in the few states using full state funding. In states where a uniform local tax rate is required with no local option leeway, the process is also simple in that federal, state, and local amounts are easily known, leaving discretion only in allocation to lines within a budget document. In states where local option leeway exists, determining local shares can be a sensitive political process. For example, some states require local budgets to be voted on by the public. Other states grant districts authority to increase budgets subject to protest referenda. Other states permit boards to raise budgets without taxpayer recourse. The process is more difficult in states that allow tax rates to vary, because taxpayers often pay more attention to changes in tax rates than to total dollars in the budget.

Figure 5.2 (p. 146) effectively portrays the politics of budgeting. Budgets are intensely complex creations, with multiple players having different interests and operating at different levels of power and influence. Budgets at the local level are externally driven in that revenues are determined in large part prior to local choices and limited by restrictions placed on districts by the state. Budgets also depend on the willingness of local patrons to support proposed spending levels because residents will make their satisfaction—or dissatisfaction—widely known. Except for the opportunity to politically influence appropriations at each of the three primary revenue source levels, district budget processes generally center on allocational issues in providing the best educational program possible under revenue constraints, thus creating the impression that school budgets are a local affair.

What Is the General Budget Process?

At the local level, the budget process usually consists of four sequential and interrelated activities. The first activity is determining revenue for the new budget year. Envisioning the educational program is usually the second step. The third step is determining the expenditures required to support the program. The fourth step is a set of decisions designed to balance program needs against revenue and expenditure realities. Consequently, the general budget process is the *operationalization of the budget triangle.* Ideally, programs should be determined first, but very often revenues drive both expenditures and programs. Although this should be resisted to keep focus on a district's fiscal beliefs, leaders know that the budget process first calls for revenue estimation.

Estimating Revenues

Although states use their own special forms to calculate federal, state, and local funding, revenue is known by local districts in a typical pattern. Federal revenues are determined at the national level and usually flow through a state agency, with notice of entitlement sent to qualifying districts. State revenues are determined through the legislative process, and districts are run through the state aid formula with notice sent to each district of entitlement. A district then calculates its local tax requirement, subject to state limits.[4]

For example, states with aid formulas based on a classroom unit may permit total instructional costs of $30,500 per unit, with the state aid formula supplying $20,000 per classroom. If federal aid were equal to $500 per classroom, then $10,000 must be raised locally. A variation achieving the same result might be through an aid plan requiring a uniform local tax rate of 20 mills paid to the state with state aid returned to the district through a statewide staffing formula and salary schedule paying for 55 professional staff positions per 1,000 students. If local leeway is permitted, other costs would be funded by local option levy. Likewise, in states funded on a per-pupil basis, the formula might determine the local tax requirement by providing aid in an equalized ratio between 0% and 100%; where the unfunded portion must be met by whatever local tax rate is required to raise the necessary funds. Many other highly state-specific configurations exist, in that each state's funding mechanism determines how resources are raised. An example of revenue estimation for a hypothetical school district is shown in Figure 5.3, where $433,712 is raised from local property tax, $4,005,159 from state aid, and so forth, to complete its general fund budget of $4,998,854.

In most states, revenues are estimated by individual funds using state worksheets and information from other agencies. As we saw in Chapter 4, fund accounting sets up multiple separate funds for revenue and expenditure purposes. For example, a state may require that all financial transactions be made from one of the following funds: general, vocational education, special education, capital outlay, bond and interest, food service, transportation, adult education, bilingual, or in-service. As we also saw earlier, fund-based budgets permit analysis of how money is spent and further permit states to categorically aid districts based on state educational philosophy. For example, rural states often place priority on aiding transportation to improve educational opportunities for children in sparsely populated areas. Fund-based budgets permit the state to choose to aid transportation at a high level, while aiding some other aspect, such as general fund, at a lower level. Similarly, urban states may provide greater aid to an adult education fund to improve adult literacy or to aid in dropout recovery. As a result, districts must repeat the revenue estimation process for each fund the district operates.

In many states, revenue estimation by fund may also include the ability (or necessity) to levy different amounts of local taxes for each individual

---

4.   Local tax effort is calculated in most states using mill rates. A mill is 1/1000 of a dollar or $1 of tax yield for every $1,000 of assessed valuation. A property valued at $100,000 market value and fractionally assessed at 12% for tax purposes and to which a 20-mill tax rate is applied would result in a tax bill of $240 (i.e., $1,000,000 × 12% = $12,000 × 0.020 = $240). A district's tax rate is found by dividing the local tax requirement by the sum of the district's assessed valuation (e.g., $5,000,000 local share ÷ $250,000,000 assessed valuation = 0.020 mill).

Figure 5.3. Sample General Fund Revenue Structure

GENERAL	12 mo. 2002–2003 Actual (1)	12 mo. 2003–2004 Actual (2)	12 mo. 2004–2005 Budget (3)
UNENCUMBERED CASH BALANCE JULY 1	683,202	4,657	13,893
UNENCUMBERED CASH BALANCE FROM TRANSPORTATION, BILINGUAL Education AND VOCATIONAL Education FUNDS	2,368	12,368	0
Cancel of Prior Yr Enc			
REVENUE: 1000 LOCAL SOURCES 1110 Ad Valorem Tax Levied 2001 $	407,781		
2002 $	435,968	199,680	
2003 $		414,810	262,990
2004 $			433,712
1140 Delinquent Tax	14,897	16,648	6,779
1300 Tuition 1312 Individuals (Out District)			
1320 Other school district In-State			
1330 Other school district Out-State			
1700 Student Activities (Reimbursement)			
1900 Other Revenue From Local Source 1910 User Charges			
1980 Reimbursements			
1985 State Aid Reimbursement			
2000 COUNTY SOURCES 2400 Motor Vehicle Tax	276,484	258,224	252,155
2450 Recreational Vehicle Tax		6,642	14,166
2800 In Lieu of Taxes IRBs			
3000 STATE SOURCES 3110 General State Aid	2,298,537	3,620,788	4,005,159
3130 Mineral Production Tax			
4000 FEDERAL SOURCES 4590 Other Reserve Grants in Aid 4591 Title I (Formerly Chapter I)			
4592 Title (Math/Science)			
4599 Other	14,365	15,864	
4820 PL 382 (Exclude Extra Aid for Children on Indian Land and Low Rent Housing) (formerly PL 874)*	39,642	42,888	10,000
5000 OTHER 5208 Transfer From Local Option Tax	0	0	0
RESOURCES AVAILABLE	4,173,244	4,592,569	4,998,854
TOTAL EXPENDITURES & TRANSFERS	4,168,587	4,578,676	4,998,854
EXCESS REVENUE TO STATE ***			0
UNENCUMBERED CASH BALANCE JUNE 30	4,657	13,893	

fund. For example, the uniform tax rate common to many states usually refers only to the general fund from which the bulk of educational costs are paid. Many states that do not aid capital outlay or bond indebtedness therefore permit or require districts to levy a special tax for these funds. As a result, the series of funds operated by school districts can result in several revenue estimations and multiple tax levies. Revenue estimation by fund is also political, in that it must be remembered that other governmental units also levy taxes for services and operate on fund-based budgets that may require numerous tax levies. Aggregate tax rates assessed by all units of government may be lengthy, underscoring the importance of remembering that the school tax is only one of many types of taxes citizens pay. In other words, revenue estimation by fund can result in an aggregate tax rate for services including city, county, township, and special assessments two or three times higher (or more) than the school tax.

Revenue estimation is usually the first step in preparing a school district budget. This process is the simplest of the four budget steps because federal and state revenues cannot be altered except by the political process, and legislative decisions are usually complete before districts estimate revenues or calculate local tax requirements. Revenue estimation thus generally comprises estimating federal, state, and local revenues by fund and entering amounts into the state budget document for comparison to program description and adjustments based on program expenditures.

Envisioning Educational Programs

The second activity in the budget process is review and establishment of the educational program. The process calls for maintaining the present program and considering new improvements. At times, fiscal issues may force program reductions, but districts try to maintain or improve services.

Envisioning programs takes many forms. One method is to assume the present program is adequate and that the budget should be built around the price of program maintenance. A second method is to propose improvements based on consultation with various constituencies. This method has gained popularity with the advent of school reform, so that many districts have school improvement plans linked to current research aimed at increasing excellence or targeting high-risk populations. Such designs may include school curriculum committees, task forces, site councils, community-school models, business or industry partnerships, and a host of other arrangements. Generally such efforts intend to look at the schools' program, with improvement and redesign as major goals. As a rule, envisioning programs is undertaken to better align curriculum and to specify outcomes in return for resources invested.

Regardless of how schools assess their programs, the underlying issue is that programs cost money. The purpose of program description in budgeting is to identify the physical needs of programs to translate them into fiscal terms in the budget. If program maintenance is the goal, the district can use prior year data as the basis, with allowance for increased costs in the new year. If improvements are being considered, the district generally turns to its proposed program description, which should include statements about resources. A budget development calendar may be used to gather input and build the vision. The district's fiscal philosophy, such as site budgeting, will have a powerful impact on designing educational programs. The budget triangle seen earlier in Figure 5.1 (p. 138) is a good illustration of how curriculum goals are translated into statements that can be quantified for budgetary purposes.

Envisioning the educational program is a process that can be complex. But it should be the heart of budgeting because unless program vision is thoughtfully carried out, nothing more than maintenance will occur. In sum, envisioning the program is the link between estimating revenues and estimating expenditures.

Estimating Expenditures

Estimation of expenditures needed to support the program is the third activity in preparing a budget. Like revenue estimation, expenditure plans must follow state requirements. Although many unique features of expenditure estimation apply to different states, the process generally calls for placing revenue on the various lines of each fund in the budget. Although it is difficult to say that any one step is most important, expenditure estimation is one of the most critical because underestimation of costs is disastrous. For example, failure to accurately calculate the costs of a new salary schedule could result in unmet payroll, suit for breach of employment contract, and force school closures because revenues must cover all expenditures.

Expenditure estimation identifies the major cost determinants and makes best estimates of all changes for the new year. Estimating general fund expenditures, for example, requires negotiating salaries and benefits for employees, determining the number of positions required, determining movement of each staff member on the salary schedule, determining quantities and costs of supplies, determining equipment costs, and finding costs of services such as professional in-service, legal fees, auditing, insurance, printing, security, data processing, and so forth. The exhaustive nature of these activities is seen in Figure 5.4 (pp. 153–156), which shows the expenditure side of a hypothetical district's general fund budget document. Of course, the steps are repeated for each separate fund the district operates.

In most states, every item in the budget is driven by enrollment. Staff, supplies and equipment, size and number of buildings, and so forth are an absolute function of the number of children in school.[5] As a result, estimating

(Text continues on page 156.)

---

5. This is qualified by uncontrollable changes in enrollment. For example, sharp increases or decreases in enrollment can cause imbalances in staffing and school facility needs on a year-by-year basis that may eventually lead to decisions to open or close buildings and to hire or reduce staff. The following statement, however, is true: Enrollment drives all current and future resource decisions.

Figure 5.4. Sample General Fund Expenditure Structure

GENERAL EXPENDITURES	12 mo. 2002–2003 Actual (1)	12 mo. 2003–2004 Actual (2)	12 mo. 2004–2005 Budget (3)

1000 Instruction
  100 Salaries
    110 Certified
	1,688,504	1,799,864	1,872,000

120 Noncertified	25,682	28,243	29,000
200 Employee Benefits 210 Insurance (Employee)	28,949	33,640	34,000
220 Social Security	131,083	138,764	140,000
290 Other	3,039	3,642	3,800
300 Purchased Professional and Technical Services			

500 Other Purchased Services
    560 Tuition
    561 Tuition/other State LEAs			

562 Tuition/other LEAs outside the State			
563 Tuition/Private Sources			
590 Other	9,241	10,953	9,000
600 Supplies 610 General Supplemental (Teaching)	85,984	102,760	104,000
644 Textbooks	52,486	62,384	65,000
680 Miscellaneous Supplies	4,685		3,960
700 Property (Equipment & Furnishings)	51,863	5,543	6,000
800 Other			62,000

2000 Support Services
2100 Student Support Services
  100 Salaries
    110 Certified
	60,504	64,164	65,500

120 Noncertified			
200 Employee Benefits 210 Insurance (Employee)	562	699	750
220 Social Security	4,630	4,984	5,200
290 Other	59	100	100
300 Purchased Professional and Technical Services	7,982	9,641	10,000
500 Other Purchased Services			
600 Supplies			5,000
700 Property (Equipment & Furnishings)	4,291	5,007	
800 Other			

2200 Instructional Support Staff
  100 Salaries
    110 Certified
	91,860	96,541	98,000

120 Noncertified			
200 Employee Benefits 210 Insurance (Employee)	1,072	1,286	1,400

(Figure continues on next page.)

GENERAL EXPENDITURES	12 mo. 2002–2003 Actual (1)	12 mo. 2003–2004 Actual (2)	12 mo. 2004–2005 Budget (3)
220 Social Security	7,070	7,509	8,500
290 Other	112	148	200
3300 Community Services Operations	3,064	3,704	4,000
3400 Student Activities	28,564	34,296	35,000
4300 Architectural & Engineering Services			
300 Purchased Professional and Technical Services			
500 Other Purchased Services			
600 Supplies 640 Books (not textbooks) and Periodicals	14,389	16,841	18,000
650 Audiovisual and Instructional Software	12,684	15,092	17,000
680 Miscellaneous Supplies			
700 Property (Equipment & Furnishings)	4,066	4,905	5,000
800 Other			
2300 General Administration 100 Salaries 110 Certified	38,184	40,448	41,500
120 Noncertified	49,860	53,624	54,600
200 Employee Benefits 210 Insurance (Employee)	984	1,206	1,300
220 Social Security	7,115	8,492	9,000
290 Other	103	200	200
300 Purchased Professional and Technical Services	17,054	20,384	21,000
400 Purchased Property Services			
500 Other Purchased Services 520 Insurance			
530 Communications (Telephone, postage, etc.)	4,643	5,605	5,900
590 Other			
600 Supplies	8,106	9,653	10,000
700 Property (Equipment & Furnishings)	7,964	9,582	10,000
800 Other	13,165	16,769	16,000
2400 School Administration 100 Salaries 110 Certified	211,864	220,843	227,000
120 Noncertified	84,286	89,300	91,000
200 Employee Benefits 210 Insurance (Employee)	4,995	6,001	6,500
220 Social Security	2,505	26,984	28,000
290 Other	324	411	500
300 Purchased Professional and Technical Services			
400 Purchased Property Services			
500 Other Purchased Services 530 Communications (Telephone, postage, etc.)	1,793	2,174	2,200

GENERAL EXPENDITURES	12 mo. 2002–2003 Actual (1)	12 mo. 2003–2004 Actual (2)	12 mo. 2004–2005 Budget (3)
590 Other			
600 Supplies			
700 Property (Equipment & Furnishings)	4,001	4,624	5,000
800 Other			
2600 Operations & Maintenance 100 Salaries 120 Noncertified	192,386	200,784	205,000
200 Employee Benefits 210 Insurance (Employee)	1,995	2,396	2,500
220 Social Security	15,750	16,863	18,000
290 Other	209	255	500
300 Purchased Professional and Technical Services	1,248	1,498	1,500
400 Purchased Property Services 411 Water/Sewer	8,150	9,750	10,000
420 Cleaning			
430 Repairs & Maintenance	161,745	188,640	264,860
440 Rentals		61,980	42,840
460 Repair of Buildings	218,714	251,574	388,431
490 Other	37,984	45,472	55,000
500 Other Purchased Services 520 Insurance	32,345	36,542	37,000
590 Other		13,052	
600 Supplies 610 General Supplies	42,387	50,845	51,000
620 Energy 621 Heating	45,190	46,842	48,000
622 Electricity	67,810	69,742	71,000
626 Motor Fuel (not schoolbus)			
629 Other	22,196	32,482	26,000
680 Miscellaneous Supplies		12,052	1,000
700 Property (Equipment & Furnishings)	4,284	8,244	6,000
800 Other	2,361	2,876	3,000
2500, 2800, 2900 Other Supplemental Service 100 Salaries 110 Certified			
120 Noncertified			
200 Employee Benefits 210 Insurance			
220 Social Security			
290 Other			
300 Purchased Professional and Technical Services			
400 Purchased Property Services			

(Figure continues on next page.)

156   Money and Schools, Third Edition

GENERAL EXPENDITURES	12 mo. 2002–2003 Actual (1)	12 mo. 2003–2004 Actual (2)	12 mo. 2004–2005 Budget (3)
500 Other Purchased Services			
600 Supplies			
700 Property (Equipment & Furnishings)			
800 Other			
5200 TRANSFER TO: 932 Adult Education			3,000
934 Adult Suppl Education			
936 Bilingual Education			
938 Capital Outlay	75,246	94,400	97,315
940 Driver Training	5,000	5,000	5,000
942 Education Excellence Grant Prog		10,000	5,000
943 Extraordinary School Prog			
944 Food Service			
946 In-service Education	5,136	4,533	11,798
948 Parent Education Program			
949 Summer School		10,000	10,000
950 Special Education	130,000	100,000	125,000
951 Technology Education			
952 Transportation	313,080	323,070	360,000
954 Vocational Education	6,000	12,864	15,000
955 Area Vocational School			
956 Disability Income Benefits Reserve			
958 Health Care Services Reserve			
959 Group Life Insurance Reserve			
960 Risk Management Reserve			
962 School Workers' Compensation Reserve			
968 Cooperative Elementary Guidance			
972 Contingency Reserve			
TOTAL EXPENDITURES & TRANSFERS	4,168,587	4,578,766	4,998,854

enrollment is the most important and difficult task in budgeting because no single system is always 100% accurate. Even with powerful population mapping tools, sudden in- and out-migrations due to human factors and economic shifts can hamper accuracy. Enrollment projection techniques are remarkably useful, however, because they are all based on two important features. The first feature is an expectation that the conditions characterizing the past will continue. The second feature mitigates the obvious error in that assumption by requiring constant reevaluation and updating of the assumptions underlying the model. Tracking shifts in population over time provides a smoothing effect to the data, a technique used in the most common methods of enrollment estimation—that is, trend analysis and cohort survival.

Trend analysis is the application of statistical regression to predicting enrollment based on previous years. In its simplest form, trend analysis predicts the future based on the manner in which previous enrollments deviate from a straight line. The formula for the regression line (straight line) is $Y = Mx + b$ where Y is the future enrollment, M is a coefficient used in the regression, x is some future year, and b is a constant showing the relationship between enrollment and year. Using multiyear historic data, a future year is entered, and the result is a predicted enrollment. Figure 5.5 shows a sample trend analysis. The regression formula casts a line of best fit, yielding projected enrollment for next year (Year 6). Results for these data indicate a steadily increasing enrollment trend, with Year 1 enrollment at 1,990 students and increasing to 2,710 by Year 5. Although Figure 5.5 only projects ahead one year, substituting other years for the x variable obtains projections for additional years—in this case, 2,900 for next year.

Figure 5.5. Trend Line Analysis of Enrollments

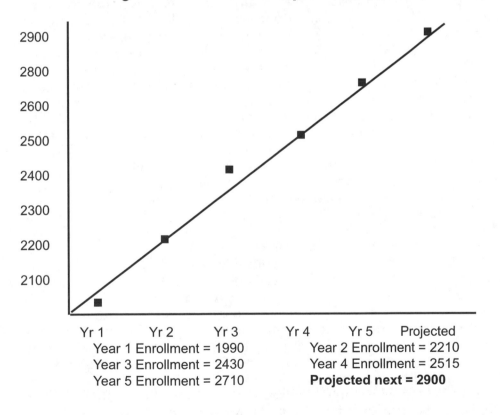

Year 1 Enrollment = 1990   Year 2 Enrollment = 2210
Year 3 Enrollment = 2430   Year 4 Enrollment = 2515
Year 5 Enrollment = 2710   **Projected next = 2900**

Trend analysis is useful in larger districts because the averages in a regression line do not harm the district to the extent that would be true for smaller districts, where the loss of each student has a larger impact because each student is a greater part of the budget. As a result, medium and smaller size districts often prefer other techniques that are more arithmetically straightforward, more intuitive, and more sensitive to changes in head count.

Cohort survival is an enrollment projection tool that groups students according to grade level at entry to school and tracks them through each year they remain in the school district. In concept, cohort survival looks at entering kindergarten students in Year 1 and calculates how many enter first grade in Year 2, second grade in Year 3, and so on, until graduation. Such a system more closely accounts for grade failures, dropouts, and migratory trends impacting student population.

Cohort survival requires enrollments from the previous and present years for each grade. It calculates the percentage of change and survival as a percentage of the previous year's grade. For example, the middle part of Figure 5.6 (pp. 159–160) shows that, historically, enrollments from first to second grade averaged only 94% of the prior year's population. This means that outmigrations or grade failure resulted in a ~6% average loss between first and second grade. This allows entry of the multi-year average into the bottom part of the analysis, where current first grade enrollment can be multiplied by 94% to project 376 students in second grade next year compared to 400 students in first grade in the present year. This process is repeated for each grade for several years into the future, and enrollments are totaled by grade level. One additional point should be made, however. Kindergarten estimation is very unreliable and constitutes a special case, requiring use of birth records, roundups, knowing local preschool numbers, and so on. Except for kindergarten, the data are smooth, and these numbers are used with relative confidence to assign staff, purchase supplies, plan facility use, and calculate other aspects of revenue and expenditure estimation. Virtually all budgeting is based on enrollment, making cohort survival a good choice because of its sensitivity to changes in population.

The sheer volume of activities involved in estimating expenditures precludes their explanation in a single textbook chapter. For example, the next major activity after enrollment projection is projecting staffing needs. This is a complex set of events involving labor negotiations, salary schedules, and so on—topics that take up at least the same amount of space already used in this chapter! Enrollment and staff numbers also drive the purchase of teaching supplies, equipment, and facilities. As a result, we cover other aspects of estimating expenditures in other chapters; for example, Chapter 6 covers budgeting for personnel, Chapter 9 discusses budgeting for facilities, and so forth. For our purposes in this chapter, however, expenditure estimation is broadly detailed and begins with enrollment projection because accurate revenue and expenditure estimates must combine in the final budget and ultimately must be balanced.

Figure 5.6. Cohort Survival Technique

Part I Historic Enrollments

Grade	1999–2000	2000–01	2001–02	2002–03	2003-04	2004–05	Average
Pre-K	500.0	500.0	499.0	502.0	500.0	503.0	500.7
One	490.0	501.0	498.0	499.0	501.0	400.0	481.5
Two	627.0	499.0	478.0	466.0	489.0	410.0	494.8
Three	590.0	611.0	497.0	477.0	477.0	488.0	523.3
Four	491.0	593.0	601.0	488.0	482.0	469.0	520.7
Five	399.0	478.0	578.0	615.0	479.0	489.0	506.3
Six	617.0	389.0	502.0	477.0	610.0	477.0	512.0
Seven	591.0	616.0	399.0	499.0	470.0	600.0	529.2
Eight	499.0	588.0	618.0	381.0	489.0	479.0	509.0
Nine	650.0	482.0	549.0	729.0	377.0	488.0	545.8
Ten	533.0	623.0	492.0	532.0	716.0	369.0	544.2
Eleven	811.0	540.0	622.0	499.0	415.0	616.0	583.8
Twelve	710.0	815.0	539.0	627.0	481.0	421.0	598.8
TOTAL	7508.0	7235.0	6872.0	6791.0	6486.0	6209.0	6850.2

Part II Survival Ratio

Grade	1999–2000	2000–01	2001–02	2002–03	2003–04	2004–05	Average
Pre-K		100%	100%	101%	100%	101%	100%
One		100%	100%	100%	100%	80%	96%
Two		102%	95%	94%	98%	82%	94%
Three		97%	100%	100%	102%	100%	100%
Four		101%	98%	98%	101%	98%	99%
Five		97%	97%	102%	98%	101%	99%
Six		97%	105%	83%	99%	100%	97%
Seven		100%	103%	99%	99%	98%	100%
Eight		99%	100%	95%	98%	102%	99%
Nine		97%	93%	118%	99%	100%	101%
Ten		96%	102%	97%	98%	98%	98%
Eleven		101%	100%	101%	78%	86%	93%
Twelve		100%	100%	101%	96%	101%	100%

(Figure continues on next page.)

Part III Enrollment Projection through 2010

Grade	Multi-year Average	2004–05 (actual)	2005–06	2006–07	2007-08	2008-09	2009–10
Pre-K	100%	503.0	503.6	504.2	504.8	505.8	506.4
One	96%	400.0	482.5	483.1	483.6	484.2	485.2
Two	94%	410.0	376.5	454.2	454.7	455.3	455.8
Three	100%	488.0	409.2	375.8	453.2	453.8	454.3
Four	99%	469.0	484.5	406.3	373.1	450.0	450.6
Five	99%	489.0	466.0	481.4	403.6	370.7	447.1
Six	97%	477.0	473.2	450.9	465.8	390.6	358.7
Seven	100%	600.0	475.8	471.9	449.7	464.6	389.5
Eight	99%	479.0	594.3	471.2	467.4	445.4	460.1
Nine	101%	488.0	485.4	602.2	477.5	473.7	451.3
Ten	98%	369.0	479.1	476.6	591.2	468.8	465.1
Eleven	93%	616.0	344.4	447.1	444.8	551.8	437.5
Twelve	100%	421.0	614.7	343.6	446.2	443.8	550.6
TOTAL		6209.0	6189.0	5968.4	6015.7	5958.4	5912.3

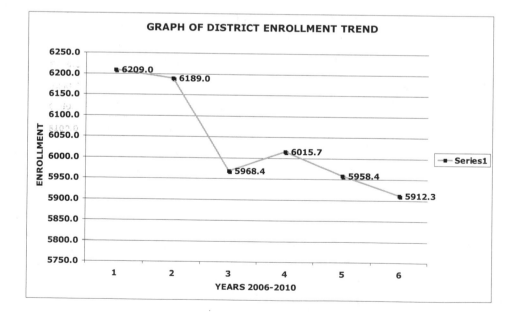

Balancing the Budget

The fourth step in the budget process aligns estimated costs for each fund with anticipated revenues. Again, the process is easier in states that tightly control revenues by mechanisms such as allocating classroom units to each district. For example, it takes little time to find salary costs if the state allocates 55 professional positions per 1,000 pupils. In such states, school districts will spend more time deciding how to meet all their instructional needs given a set staff size because no options regarding staff size are available. Where less state control exists, districts may spend time playing with reallocation of money to various lines in the budget to achieve the best balance. In states where tax rates can float more freely through local tax leeway, districts may also consider raising taxes to fund the desired educational program. The process in all states, however, calls for aligning the revenue and expenditure sides of the budget because most states forbid deficit spending in schools.

Balancing revenues and expenditures results in cause-and-effect scenarios, usually impacting instruction. For example, revenues may need careful review if program needs exceed available funding. Ultimately, programs may have to be scaled back if it is clear that revenues are inadequate. Although state-specific conditions sometimes limit the options, these activities, called budget adjustments, usually involve one of three common scenarios. The first scenario happens when legislation results in increased revenue, although other factors such as increased property wealth can cause tax windfalls as well. The second scenario occurs when revenues are static. The third scenario appears when revenue declines. Each of these situations has been faced at some time by every school district, and the process for dealing with each one can be difficult and complex.

Increased Revenue

The problem of new revenue is a dilemma that schools often like. Although thought to be the least common scenario, the history of funding for schools suggests that revenue increases have been the case until very recently. For example, revenues increased by 100% from 1920–30, another 67% in the 1960s, and 36% in the 1970s. But it must be remembered that revenue increases result in offsetting expenditures that are most often cumulative, as in the case of teacher salaries—if salaries go up a modest 3% annually, the cumulative result is a startling +130% of base over only a decade, and that amount is surely compounded by events such as additional college credits earned, experience step increases, and so forth that add to teacher salary costs. Indeed, the meager 3% step increase is not just the 30% gain—it is more likely in the neighborhood of 50% or even more. It is no surprise, then, that school costs can rise so rapidly because about 80% of budgets are in personnel costs, of which teacher salaries are the vast bulk. Districts thus need a plan for dealing with revenue increases, especially because a revenue increase eventually results in an expenditure increase that is difficult to back away from later.

Big revenue increases typically follow from unusual events. For example, in the 1950s and 1960s, the Cold War and social programs drove huge revenue spikes. In the 1980s and 1990s, revenue increases often accompanied legislative efforts aimed at school reform. Revenues were targeted at special areas meant to strengthen the quality of education. Dealing with new revenue often meant spending in categories the state had targeted. For example, much money in recent years has been poured into at-risk programs and timely curricula such as special education, staff development, human sexuality, and parent education. Similarly, since the year 2001 hundreds of millions of new dollars have been earmarked for support of the *No Child Left Behind Act*. Despite inflation, net dollars flowing to education have greatly expanded due in part to school reform. Increased revenues have also stemmed from growth in tax base, as school tax rates often fail to drop despite rapid increases in property values. This phenomenon has had negative implications, however, as taxpayer protests have occurred throughout the nation and, in the worst instances, have resulted in tax limitation referenda. In states escaping tax protests, schools have sometimes profited by these tax windfalls. In such cases, schools have the option of committing extra dollars to various funds in the budget or building capital and contingency funds.

Notwithstanding, the need to increase revenues is a far more common problem. Highly specific to state laws, increasing revenue can be difficult. Increasing revenues is easiest in states permitting local tax leeway options. Even yet, choices are usually limited due to state interest in equalization and because equalization is less expensive to the state if it caps local leeway at some ceiling rather than providing open-ended aid to poor districts under cost-share or power equalization formulas. Beyond local tax leeway, districts must turn to improved cash management, student fees, partnerships with businesses or other groups, and volunteers in lieu of purchased services. Unless wide tax latitude exists, the most profitable option is improved cash management, with the goal of increasing investment income and under-spending the budget to build cash reserves and offset tax increases for the next year. In hindsight, districts have experienced revenue increases mostly through inflation, state aid, and wise management, but they have generally had to spend any new money rather than build cash reserves.

Static and Declining Revenue

The scenario of static revenue is not unlike the problems that occur when revenues actually decline. In fact, it may be argued that the difference is only one of degree, as static revenue in a growing economy results in decline. The problems are so similar that static and declining revenues can be discussed simultaneously.

Static or declining revenue is a dreaded event. Although the history of revenue growth might suggest that the problem is uncommon, the reverse is true; remember that trends are a summation of gains and losses in all the districts in a state or nation. The impact on individual districts yields a highly varied picture. In many states, districts have experienced static or declining revenues in response to poor state economies, enrollment losses, depressed land prices reducing tax bases, decreased sales and income taxes, and a host of other elements that impact school revenue. For example, energy-dependent states have had a particularly hard time in recent years because of low oil prices, and agricultural states have seen dramatic losses in property values as inflated land prices from the 1980s have collapsed. Similarly, more populous states have seen a massive influx of student enrollments outstripping revenue growth, and rural states have experienced sharp enrollment declines. Although revenues have grown rapidly overall, it is small comfort to individual districts because such growth is like the old saying that a "hand in the fire and a hand in the freezer on average is quite comfortable."

Regardless of cause, static or declining revenue forces the need to devise methods to balance the budget. There are few ideal solutions. From a practical perspective, often only two solutions are available: Districts must find replacement revenue from other sources or reduce expenditures. The best approach is to combine these strategies, but limits on revenue enhancement in many states often result only in expenditure reductions. The unfortunate reality is that personnel reduction-in-force (RIF) is the most significant tool, simply because salaries make up 80–85% of a typical district's budget. Such decisions are more than fiscal considerations because budget reductions cannot violate federal employment law, state employment statutes, district personnel and instructional policies, collective bargaining agreements, or other legal and moral obligations to the people who carry out the business of educating children. Such realities make it difficult to settle satisfactorily on any single reduction strategy. As a result, educational decision makers should involve as many staff and community members as possible because decisions made from a single point of view (e.g., the superintendent or the school board) can have severe legal and political repercussions.

Although RIF is the major way to balance revenues and expenditures, other efforts should be made that can amount to real savings. Under the best conditions, the preferred way is to cut costs by improving the efficiency of the district. Examples of strategies actually used by districts have included:

- *Energy conservation:* adjusting thermostats in winter and summer, reducing the number of cooled or heated spaces, turning out lights, or making new energy-efficient expenditures such as thermal retrofitting to reduce costs in the long run. The latter is problematic in that the need to reduce budgets hardly places a district in a position to spend its way out of a budget deficit.

- *More efficient purchasing:* streamlining by not purchasing elective items, bulk discount buying, or "just-in-time" purchasing. Many districts claim significant savings from these strategies.

- *Improved cash management:* investing idle funds wisely, underspending the budget to build cash reserves, reducing annual cash carryover, and so forth. Some strategies, however, have negative long-term impact (e.g., reducing reserves) and, importantly, may actually starve instruction.

♦ *Improved risk management:* raising insurance deductible amounts, assessing the potential benefits and risks of self-insuring, bidding insurance coverage, and so forth.

♦ *Deferral or elimination:* delaying purchases of equipment, supplies, and maintenance, although the strategy creates new problems—for example, delaying bus purchases results in old and possibly unsafe buses, raising liability questions and increasing maintenance, as well as higher replacement cost later. Similarly, under-maintained facilities are proof of what deferral can mean. A variation on this strategy includes make-or-buy decisions, where the district keeps more tasks in-house.

♦ *More efficient equipment and technology:* replacing buses with more economical units, using environmentally smart thermostats, automating some tasks to reduce personnel costs, and so forth. But care should be taken to calculate the cost-benefit ratio, including political ramifications.

♦ *Refinance long-term debt:* refunding bonds to cash in on lower interest rates can save many thousands of dollars if care is taken not to increase costs in the long run by extending bond payments over a longer period of time.

♦ *Implementing early retirement programs:* buying out high-cost teachers nearing retirement by replacing these persons with new teachers at lower salaries or, alternatively, leaving the positions vacant.

♦ *Changes to bargaining agreements:* negotiating salaries and benefits downward, although difficult, is based on the theory that a job at a lower salary is better than a RIF.

♦ *Reduction-in-force:* reducing staff in the knowledge that the vast majority of costs are for personnel, leaving no option if deep and permanent cuts must be made.

Although listed from most to least desirable, even these measures may not be sufficient to balance the budget. In that case, the only remaining alternative is to cut programs. These include reductions in course offerings, changes in length of the school day, increased class size, and reduction of nonessential services not legally mandated in a given state, such as extended day programs or extracurricular activities. Care must be exercised, however, not to violate contracts or state laws. For example, in many states length of school day, hours of work, and class schedules are part of negotiated agreements, and many states have mandated preschool and extended day programs. Although cuts are never easy, reductions in staff and program are the most painful. As a result, such measures should be used only as a last resort.

Completing the Budget Process

Budget construction is nearly complete when programs are envisioned, revenues and expenditures are estimated, and a balanced budget is achieved. The budget still must be approved, however. Approval steps differ among states, but the process always results in legal adoption of the budget under statutory requirements. For example, in states where school districts are fiscally dependent on some other unit of government, approval usually means that the budget is forwarded to a higher authority, often a city or county board. In states where districts are fiscally independent, approval is more complex in that several events usually occur sequentially. Although highly state-specific, a general procedure calls for official publication of a budget summary, usually in a newspaper of general local circulation, followed by a waiting period, public hearing, formal adoption of the budget, and certification of the proposed or amended budget to some other governmental unit such as a county taxing authority. Publication is meant to give notice to the public of the budget hearing, with the waiting period to allow citizens a chance to prepare comments and to be present at the hearing. Statutes usually call for the school board to vote in open meeting. The budget, if adopted, must be certified according to statute. Because these laws are meant to guard against improper behavior, they must be rigidly observed or angry taxpayers could conceivably force school closures until a budget is properly adopted under statutory requirements.

How Are Individual Schools Funded?

The process discussed to this point tracks money into school districts, but it says nothing about funding individual schools. As can be imagined, this is a difficult topic because no state has enacted true statewide school-level funding laws, leaving each of the nation's more than 14,000 districts free to adopt its own budget philosophy. That is exactly the point of earlier review of budget philosophy: Districts have great freedom in how they decide to create internal budget structures, and the decisions they make have a tremendous impact on individual schools. As a result, how individual schools are funded is as different as the number of districts that exist. Nonetheless, some common ways that districts fund schools can be reviewed.

Most districts create a budget calendar such as the one in Figure 5.7 (p. 166). Budget calendars range from very simple to highly complex. Figure 5.7 is fairly uncomplicated and is taken from a district of about 7,000 students. The calendar identifies all areas of the budget, assigns responsibility to an administrator, and lays out the budget process with deadlines. An important feature is that budgeting is a multi-month process that includes a flow chart of responsibility and involves many people, including principals and other staff. Budget calendars are unique to individual districts and are based on organizational design. The processes of estimating revenues, envisioning school programs, estimating expenditures, and balancing the budget are all evident in the sample budget calendar, as is the overall coordination of the budget process, which brings these separate activities into a completed budget prior to a new school year.

Figure 5.7. Sample Budget Calendar

Budget Area	Staff Responsible
General Fund	Board/central administration
Administration	Superintendent
School budgets	Principals
Travel: admin and teacher	Director of Personnel
Special programs	Director of Special Services
Adult education	Coordinator Adult Education
Bilingual programs	ESL Coordinator
Capital outlay	Director of Maintenance
Driver education	Business Manager
Food service	Director of Food Service
Transportation	Transportation Director
Special education	Director of Special Education
Bond & interest budgets	Business Manager
In-service budget	Director of Curriculum
Vocational school budget	Director of Curriculum
Special projects and grants	Business Manager
Other budgets	As assigned

Preparation Calendar

Date	Description	Responsible
January	Distribute planning guide Meet with principals and program directors	Business Manager
March	Requests for new programs and personnel due	Superintendent, Business Manager, and Personnel Director
April	Seek board input on programs and new personnel	Superintendent, Curriculum, and Personnel Director
April	Building, program, and capital repair/improvements due	Directors and Principals
May	Bid capital outlay, instructional items and advise of bids	Principals and Business Manager
June	First draft of total budget	Superintendent and Business Manager
July	Board budget workshop	All administrators
July	Budget publication and hearings	Admin, Board, public
August	Adoption and certification	Business Manager

The budget calendar in Figure 5.7 also notes another aspect of school budgeting, in that building principals are assigned a formal role. Although again entirely dependent on local district preference, this budget calendar shows principals involved at most stages including the initial planning stage, program envisioning, preliminary budget review, requisitioning and purchase order preparation, and the administration of school budgets. Figure 5.7 might be used in a relatively central office-controlled district, or it could apply just as easily to a district using site-based budgeting. In the first case, principals would be asked about program needs, supplies, equipment, and facilities. In the latter case, principals would have significant control over daily resource utilization, including decisions about whether to buy teachers, aides, and so forth—in essence, the school would operate as a mini-district with ultimate accountability for productivity. We will explore these and other ideas later when we look at budgeting for instruction, and again when we look more extensively at site-based leadership and the future.

The process of budgeting at this point can be viewed as a pyramid turned upside down, flowing mostly from state to local. It begins with the federal and state policies that make revenue available to school districts. Each district simultaneously determines its program requirements and desires and matches revenues and needs, adjusting local revenue and programs to fill the deficit. Districts then apportion revenue to individual schools based on a budget philosophy, using such concepts as fairness, horizontal and vertical equity, and preferences about decentralization and accountability. For example, a district may decide it wishes to make block grants to each elementary school in exchange for the promise to increase student achievement on test scores by 5% next year. Principals and staffs may then consult with site councils and opt for more teacher aides instead of new playground equipment in hopes of meeting achievement goals. Another district, however, might take a different path by hiring a grant writer to seek additional funding and using the enhanced revenue to provide extra supplies, equipment, and instructional staff to meet some other set of learning goals. The range of possibilities depends on state laws and available revenues, in combination with local ingenuity.

What Is the Role of Stakeholders?

Every chapter in this book has strongly implied that school money is a legitimate place for multiple stakeholders to freely make their voices heard. This chapter is no different. We have underscored that there is a place in school budgeting for everyone, including administrators, boards, teachers, policy makers, and laypersons. If the purpose of budgets is to identify the needs of schools, prioritize those needs, match resources and needs, and make educational goals operational, there can be no good reason to exclude any of these persons, and there is much to be gained by their informed participation.

Although we believe everyone should take initiative and responsibility for budgeting, we especially believe that good administrators should deliberately use the budget for specific stakeholder benefits. Administrators should use budgets to structure the educational plan, to read progress toward outcomes, to evaluate achievement of the plan, and to make adjustments when discrepancies arise. Budgeting is not only a central office function, as principals must increasingly account for program decisions with greater responsibility for money under site-based leadership. Boards are legally charged with responsibility for expending funds and must take responsibility for wise policy making. Teachers consume most of the budget, and their expertise in educational program planning should be used in building the educational plan expressed by the budget. Policy makers need knowledge about educational programming, and feedback loops help them reach the decisions they are constitutionally required to make. And no audience is more crucial than laypersons, as these are the parents and community members whose taxes pay for schools and whose approval every district must have to continue operating. The interaction of these constituent roles is clearly evident in Figure 5.8—it is not by accident that the link between strategic planning influences and school budget outcomes are the multiple decision makers that ultimately decide how well schools are funded.

The consequences of this chapter and our beliefs about budget construction have real implications. Carrying out the educational plan requires resources, forces value decisions, and requires linking inputs and outcomes in an integrated budget plan. Unfortunately, the budget triangle is often turned on its side by economics in an imperfect world. Leaders must therefore guard against losing sight of the purpose of budgets and be true leaders, rather than accountants and clerks. As Ward suggests, the field of education finance is not a "...technical and sterile area of study employing complex mathematics, arcane algebraic formulas [nor] a refuge for the methodologically minded to be avoided by those humanists in education who see their emphasis as being on children, instruction, and qualitative aspects of schooling."[6] Instead, a budget is the fiscal expression of the educational philosophy of a school district.

SUGGESTED FOLLOW-UP PROJECTS

♦ Make an appointment with a senior central office leader to discuss budgeting from the strategic planning perspective. Explore how the district conceptualizes its budget and the processes by which budgeting occurs. Discuss the overall process of estimating revenues and expenditures, including how the district involves employees and the school board in the process. Discuss the act of balancing the budget, looking for ways in which the district tries to maintain and improve instructional programs.

---

6.   James G. Ward, "An Inquiry into the Normative Foundations of American Public School Finance," *Journal of Education Finance* 12, no.4 (1987): 463.

Figure 5.8. School Budget Arena

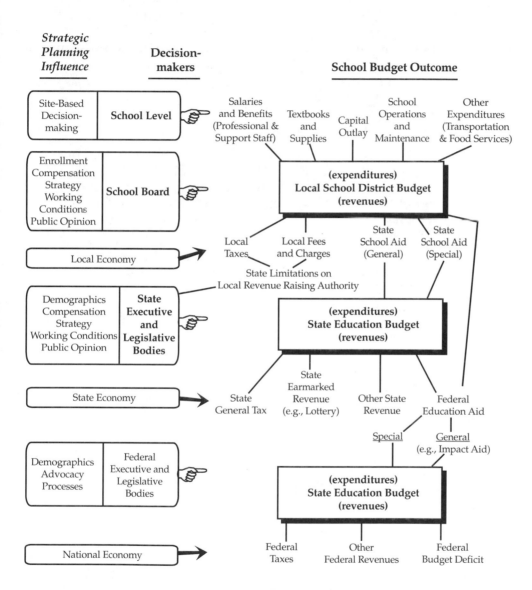

♦ Obtain a copy of your district's enrollment projection and try to replicate its results. Experiment with different assumptions based on current conditions in your district. Include appropriate consideration for any unusual factors, such as demographic changes that may cause instability in historic data. Consider how this entire process might affect your budget planning attitudes if you were in charge of these kinds of decisions.

♦ Talk to school site administrators to determine how they are involved in the budgeting process. Ask how they involve their staffs and how they prioritize requests when expenditures exceed budget allocations. Inquire about the extent of their involvement, their frustrations, and ask how they would improve the budget planning process.

♦ If your state, district, or school uses school site councils, find out the extent to which councils are involved in budget planning activities. Form a personal opinion on the desirability or undesirability of lay involvement in budget planning and defend your reasons.

♦ Determine how your district obtains public input into the budget process at both formative and final stages. Consider how the district tries to ensure smooth passage of the final budget.

6

BUDGETING FOR PERSONNEL

THE GENERAL LANDSCAPE

Our introduction to the overall budgeting process in Chapter 5 taught us that the greatest portion of education's price is concentrated in the form of personnel.[1] It has always been the case that education is labor-intensive: In fact, personnel costs make up about 80% of most school districts' budgets. A flavoring of these massive costs is seen in data on teacher salaries in public schools. In 1869, salaries averaged about $189 per year; by 1900, salaries had risen only to $325. But by 1930, salaries had quadrupled to $1,420, and the number of teachers was growing rapidly. By 1950, salaries again more than doubled to $3,010 and nearly tripled to $8,840 by 1970. By 1990, salaries quadrupled again to $33,084 and had reached $45,822 (+39%) by 2003. These salaries paid 3.4 million public school teachers in 2003 (up from 2.8 million in the last edition of this textbook) with the demand for teachers expected to continue rising despite fears of reduced supply.[2]

Sustained growth in staff and salaries suggests that school budgets are under genuine stress. Actual expenditures for instruction in 2000 totaled nearly $200 billion, whereas the need for staff is expected to grow from the current 3.4 million teachers to 3.6 million by the year 2013.[3] Additional salaries for new staff have an effect on salaries of experienced teachers, a reality evident during recent decades as overall staffing grew while salaries increased only modestly in inflation-adjusted dollars. Projections of teacher salaries to 2013 suggest that while schools will spend considerably more

---

1. For a different and fuller discussion of these concepts, see David C. Thompson, R. Craig Wood, and David Honeyman, *Fiscal Leadership for Schools: Concepts and Practices* (New York: Longman, 1994); see also R. Craig Wood, David C. Thompson, and Lawrence O. Picus, Principles of *School Business Management*, 3rd ed. (Reston, VA: ASBO, 2005).

2. U.S. Department of Education, National Center for Education Statistics, *Mini-Digest of Education Statistics 2003* (Washington, DC: National Center for Education Statistics, 2005).

3. U.S. Department of Education, National Center for Education Statistics, *Projections of Education Statistics to 2013* (Washington, DC: National Center for Education Statistics, 2004).

across the next several years, average salaries are projected to reach only $47,200 in constant 2001–2002 dollars, an increase of only 6% in the 10 year period 2003–2013.[4] Budget stress is seen in these data, as hiring more staff will require more money, while at the same time existing staff may see only small increases in nominal dollars—and potentially a decrease in real purchasing power.

Under these conditions, it is easy to see that personnel costs are the single most expensive (and most important) item in school budgets. In fact, we noted that after estimating enrollment and envisioning programs, costing out salaries is the next most important task in successfully balancing revenues and expenditures. As a result, we need to study the act of budgeting for personnel. Once again, our discussion is shaped by key questions. What is the scope of the personnel function? How are staffing needs determined? What goes into staff recruitment and selection? What are the issues in personnel compensation? What is current thinking about alternative reward systems, especially merit pay? What are the fiscal and legal ramifications of staff reductions? How does due process play into personnel issues? And, as always, what are the roles of administrators, staffs, boards, and laypersons? These questions help us better understand the relationship of the budget to all areas of school operations.

THE PERSONNEL FUNCTION

We have already established that the bulk of school district budgets is consumed by salaries and benefits. Most people probably see these expenditures as costs, a view that cannot be fully dismissed. At the same time, however, many costs in education are actually purchased benefits. In the case of the personnel function, the cost of salaries and fringe benefits actually can be seen as having a positive effect on the total economy because teachers and other school personnel are active consumers whose salaries are returned to the local economy in exchange for housing, clothes, cars, food, and luxuries. An additional point often missed by education's critics is that school personnel also pay taxes to support schools. In a complex cycle, the personnel function represents a cost to the public because money is taken from taxpayers and used for a public service, but the money is invested (rather than spent) because most school dollars pay the salaries of people who buy within the same district and may actually create more employment than they consume. As a result, the personnel function is both a human and a fiscal resource issue, combining to create human capital as a purchased resource.

What Is the Scope of the Personnel Function?

The personnel function takes into account everyone who is employed by a school system. Yet, when most people think of school staffs, they immediately think of the teaching faculty. Although teachers are at the core of what

---

4. NCES. *Projections of Education Statistics to 2013.*

schools do, this view is inadequate because the personnel function embraces a much larger group that includes both certified staff (teachers and other certified employees) and classified staff (custodians, bus drivers, teacher aides, cafeteria workers, and other noncertified service personnel). All these persons have indispensable roles in operating a school district. As districts have become more organizationally complex and inclusive of the many definitions that contribute to equal educational opportunity, the number of certified and noncertified staff has increased dramatically.

The size of the personnel function is exceeded only by its importance to successful district operation. In fact, regardless of how well the fiscal operations of a school district are managed, the true success of a school finally depends on the people who work with children each day. Selection, employment, and retention of competent staff are the keys to *cost-effective* operation of schools. The critical role of the personnel function has led most districts to centralize this operation, with one person having line authority over all personnel matters. Although titles vary with local custom and even by school district size, an assistant superintendent for personnel, a director of human resources, or the superintendent may have direct responsibility for the personnel function. In large districts, the responsibility often is further subdivided. For example, the chief fiscal officer may also serve as the personnel director for support staff, whereas a director of human relations may serve as personnel officer for certified staff. In such cases, certain aspects may be coordinated between the two offices, while others remain separate. The purpose of a coordinated office, however, is to ensure appropriate linkages among all vital aspects of the district.

Regardless of how the personnel function is structured at the local level, good personnel administration expects certain characteristics that assist in furthering the work of the district and link all operations under one umbrella. The umbrella and linkages should be provided in a policy manual that sets out all aspects of personnel policy. Good policies assure uniform communication and help monitor relationships between the goals of the district and the expectations of personnel. Policies must be clearly stated to avoid confusion for either the employer or employee and to form the basis for interpretation and legal evaluation in the event of disagreement. An added benefit of policies is to provide a blueprint for action, which in turn has a greater opportunity for consistent actions that will enhance employee morale and productivity. Because program quality is a result of the skill of all certified and classified staff working in unison, an effective and efficient district wisely spends time and money on creating and maintaining sound personnel operations.

When the personnel function is formally assigned to an individual or office, governed by written policies and procedures, and organized efficiently, the result is strong leadership and good management. Leadership is apparent, in that a district that merely maintains the status quo cannot consistently improve programs. Alternatively, reliance on charismatic leadership to the neglect of proper management of the personnel function endangers the district in many ways, including liability for the many problems that can arise in a highly peopled organization. The district's overall goals and objectives cannot be met except by proper control and management of all instructional and support staffs. Although it is sometimes hard to distinguish between the nuances of leadership versus management, the point here is that the organizational and directive functions of personnel must be carefully structured if the district is to function well because schools rely on competent personnel to fulfill their goals.

The scope of the personnel function is extremely broad, encompassing six major task areas:

1. Determining staffing needs
2. Recruiting and retaining the most competent staff
3. Assisting in individual development of competencies
4. Assuring that staff are assigned and used efficiently
5. Increasing and improving staff satisfaction
6. Establishing clear expectations and ensuring competent performance evaluation

The critical nature of these tasks underscores the need for both leadership and management. The personnel function requires leadership for educational improvement, and management is needed to ensure useful performance assessment. The personnel function thus assesses staffing needs and recruits, selects, inducts, compensates, evaluates, and retains employees. The personnel function also embraces other duties, including dismissal of unsatisfactory staff. Although many of these duties are beyond the scope of this book, the tasks of determining personnel needs, recruitment, selection, compensation, and dismissal are explored more fully here because of their close relationship to the act of creating a good budget.

Determining Staffing Needs

We noted in Chapter 5 that enrollment drives staffing. This concept requires more development because the basic budgeting task of estimating revenues and expenditures is based entirely on enrollment and staffing.

Ability to properly determine staffing needs is a function of organizing and using information about the district and its current and prospective staff. All districts maintain a database of employee information, if for no other reason than reporting for state aid purposes and information needed to calculate payroll taxes. The database includes basic and descriptive information such as each individual's salary, insurance and other fringe benefit costs, record of leave days, and even projected retirement information for predicting voluntary and induced staff changes. More detailed information is less likely to be well organized, however, because many districts believe they are too small to spend the time and money to extensively forecast district needs. Although school districts are required to maintain information on employees, most districts still need to develop wide-ranging staff data because the lack of comprehensive information automatically limits good decision-making, and because the uses for data nearly always rise to meet its availability. Although other chapters in this book discuss the importance of data on other budget items such as transportation, it is unfortunate that many school districts do not spend enough time setting up staffing files.

Information about the district and staffing is interrelated and should be planned to permit electronic linking because, in every instance, the district's profile drives staffing needs. The database should contain much information, including population of the community, population of the schools, percentage of households with school-age children, ages of children in preschool through twelfth grade, in- and out-migration patterns, commercial and industrial characteristics of the district, major sources and types of employment, income and age of residents, and, of course, fiscal data on the district. This information is useful as a general backdrop to the actual population projections the district must make each year. In most states, enrollment is the basis for funding, and it is clear that the population of a community drives student enrollment. Also, it should not be missed that demographic data are highly useful in predicting community attitudes toward school budgets.

Determining staffing needs is thus largely a function of predicting the profile of a community. But while many districts keep much employee information on file, it is often not preplanned or organized for projecting staffing needs. In thousands of small districts, information on employee certification is largely kept on paper and accessed only if needed. In larger districts, electronic databases are standard and contain information on staff qualifications, including professional certification or other qualifications and experience useful when considering noncertified staff. In larger districts, these files typically contain information on prospective employees and may also contain projections of staff attrition by area and level.

Regardless of district size, an effort to create community profiles and employee databanks must be made because databases can be used to project whether staffing needs can be met internally, whether it will be necessary to look outside for new employees, or (under the worst conditions) whether it will be necessary to reduce staff at some future point. The employee database should be much broader than simple retrieval of areas of certification and should permit other projections, such as calculating the cost of early retirement incentives. Such information overlaps with the budget function, in that the cost of early retirement compared to other alternatives such as hiring less experienced staff must be available when making long-term staffing decisions. Likewise, projections indicating a need for new staff also require budget input. Use of databases makes it possible to descriptively assess present reality and future scenarios—an obviously critical function for the budget side of planning and organization. In most instances, the basic database is built and maintained in the personnel office and electronically linked to the budget office.

Although districts develop databases to meet their unique needs, the goal is always the same. The personnel and budget functions must share information on many occasions, but the most frequent interaction is when staffing needs are reviewed. For current staff, the personnel function annually considers whether they will be rehired, and decisions must be coordinated with the budget office, which must find money for salaries. There are, of course, times when the scenario is reversed, as the budget office finds that staffing is too expensive and the personnel side must find ways to deal with economic reality. But although these functions are codependent, the realities of the modern comprehensive school district cause the personnel function to most often drive the fiscal side by telling the business office what the staffing needs will be for the next school year.

Although a comprehensive community and staff database is essential, the technical side of determining staffing needs is different among states and individual districts. For example, some states calculate the number of pupils at each grade level and allocate funds to districts on a per-classroom basis. In this case, the district has little meaningful control over the most basic personnel function of determining how many teachers it will hire because it can obviously afford to hire only those teachers that the state aid formula reimburses. In other states, districts are free to decide how many staff to hire by choosing among the many competing expenditure categories within overall budgetary constraints; for example, a choice to reduce overall class size may be at the expense of expanding athletic or academic programs. Decisions are driven by many factors, including locally negotiated agreements and board policies. These differences make a thorough discussion impossible, but it is clear that the personnel and budget functions are mutually affected by staffing needs and are sometimes driven by outside forces beyond local control. The fact remains, however, that all such forces greatly affect staffing needs.

State and local governments also powerfully influence staffing patterns. As a general rule, either or both governmental units tend to adopt some kind of staffing ratio for determining staff needs. At the state level, an example of a strongly centralized system is Washington's recent state aid plan, which converts full-time equivalency (FTE) students into staff units, which are then multiplied by a statewide salary and benefits schedule, with additional allocations for nonpersonnel-related costs. This formula, in response to legal battles over equitable funding, has had the practical effect of leveling expenditures (with staffing implications) downward in some districts to bring greater fiscal parity across school districts. At the opposite extreme are states that have tried to reduce class sizes, as in Oklahoma, where state-initiated reform in the early 1990s mandated lower pupil-teacher ratios with the practical effect of causing higher staffing needs. A more middle-ground example of local decisions driving staffing needs is seen in districts with board policies or negotiated agreements seeking to limit class sizes. Most boards have tried to reduce pupil-teacher ratios, and in many instances have adopted policies requiring new staff when class size in a grade level exceeds some cap. A more complicated but typical situation is when boards have either been required by state law to negotiate class size or have voluntarily negotiated such agreements. In all of these examples, it is clear that personnel and budgets are tightly linked.

Regardless of local circumstance, once a policy or law governing staffing is set, it is easy to apply the staffing formula to actual enrollments. After projecting enrollment, the process calls for applying the staffing formula, usually by dividing the number of students at each grade level by the approved ratio, yielding the number of staff needed. The process is usually carried out at the district level, with input from individual schools. A simple illustration using a single high school might result in the following staffing pattern:

Enrollment + Approved Ratio = Staffing Needs

or

421 ninth graders + 20:1 ratio =	21 ninth grade positions
373 tenth graders + 20:1 =	18.6 tenth grade positions
297 eleventh graders + 20:1 =	14.8 eleventh grade positions
312 twelfth graders + 20:1 =	15.6 twelfth grade positions
1,403 FTE	70.0 FTE

Of course, funding these positions is harder than simply calculating staffing needs, at times requiring adjustments to the staffing formula if funding is unavailable. The comprehensive database should be designed to aid this process when combined with other personnel and budget activities such as long-term enrollment projections. This is especially true when enrollment fluctuates between grades or school buildings. If the data reveal, for example, that other schools in the district will lose enrollment, and our sample high school actually has 78 existing faculty (instead of the 70 needed), the district can use the personnel database to reassign surplus teachers to other schools if their professional licensure matches vacancies. Obviously, this solution is more feasible as district size increases because small districts may have only one teacher per grade or only one high school. It is more likely that other enrollments will not offset a surplus, triggering other decisions about reassignment or reduction-in-force.

Determining staffing is thus simple and complex. It is mathematically easy, but it is complex because decisions affect real people and because layers of governmental policy may limit the options. Regardless, good decisions cannot be made without a comprehensive database that takes into account both community and employee profiles. For example, a district in the scenario just described might be able to lessen the impact of staff reductions if the database holds information on retirements or early contract buyouts. In a more positive vein, data can be used for targeted information sharing such as in-house mailings to employees when vacancies arise. For many reasons, an orderly plan for determining staffing needs is the next step after projecting enrollment.

Recruitment and Selection

When staffing needs are known, the next major task is recruitment, followed by selection of personnel. Regardless of the type of position, every employee classification should have a formal recruitment plan. The district needs to make decisions regarding number and type of positions, as well as minimum and preferred qualifications for each employee classification. The budget and personnel functions overlap here again, particularly regarding pay for current staff and whether the district must hire beginning teachers or whether it can afford more experienced staff.

Although in many states pay scales are largely a function of collective bargaining laws and how the negotiations process plays out in individual school districts, the ultimate goal is to attract and retain the most highly qualified people. This goal is difficult to reach because the purpose is at odds with another competing goal of minimizing taxpayer costs. Although there are no good solutions, there are certain procedures in the recruiting process that may soften the harshness of these realities.

At the outset of the recruiting process, the budget and personnel staff should jointly produce a guidebook for the district. This guidebook is so important that it should be given to all current and prospective employees to familiarize them with the terms and benefits of employment. This document should contain a clear description of the hiring process, starting with application procedures and continuing through descriptions of how screening committees, interviews, contract offers, and pay periods and amounts will occur. Every current and prospective employee should be informed of training requirements and opportunities, and this information should convey a high level of standardization within each employee classification. These procedures should be closely tied to job advertising by the district and should be standardized with regard to internal and external search procedures consistent with equal opportunity selection of the best candidate for each vacancy.

When policies and procedures for recruitment have been determined, the district is ready to recruit. For larger districts, this may mean hiring on the basis of anticipated vacancies. Large school systems visit teacher recruitment fairs across the nation every year, hiring candidates for vacancies that have not yet opened but that the district knows from experience will become available. In many instances, these districts are taking little risk because they know that they will not be able to hire staff for all openings. In other areas of the country, the process is simpler, as districts advertise via university placement offices and wait for applications to arrive. Even here, however, the personnel and budget functions continue to overlap, as success in recruiting is related to how well the salary schedule is designed and funded. Because many states do not have uniform or statewide teacher salary schedules or, in some cases, allow districts to exceed the statewide salary schedule, recruitment is the joint responsibility of wise personnel and budget planning.

When the district has successfully calculated its staffing needs and recruited as effectively as it can, the selection process begins. Because the success of district goals depends on the quality of personnel, selection is a critical responsibility. Even though the depth of the candidate pool and the marketplace affect who is hired, it must be recognized that the first obligation of the district is to select employees on the basis of skills. Skills must be judged on the basis of documented training, relevant experience, and satisfactory performance. Additionally, many positions, whether certified or not, require specific licensure from a state agency. Every position should be filled only after the appropriate person, often the superintendent, has made a final recommendation to the board. As we will see later in the chapter on legal liability, a valid offer of employment usually cannot be made unless the board has made the offer in a public meeting in a lawful manner.

The overlapping and conflicting goals of the personnel and budget functions are most apparent at the time of selection. The goal of the personnel function is to select the most qualified person to perform the duties of a specific position. This applies whether the person is being interviewed for a teaching position or a custodial position, and unqualified people should not be considered. The goal of the budget function is to hire that same person as well, but under impossible terms. The old adage, "...20 years old with 20 years experience and willing to work for $20,000..." accurately describes these terms. Of course, this is impossible, and some middle ground must be found that assures selection of quality staff within budget limits. Selection thus involves many steps, all aimed at hiring the best candidate at the least turnover. From the beginning of the process to the end, the relationship between the personnel and budget functions is apparent in that whatever employee is chosen, that person will have to be funded.

Other Personnel Budget Issues

Although it is beyond the scope of this textbook to delve deeply into the personnel side of district operations, it is important to note that there are other issues of budgeting for personnel that go beyond recruitment and selection. The most obvious of these is compensation policies and procedures, a topic we spend much time developing in the last half of this chapter. Other personnel tasks including induction, orientation, assignment, evaluation, staff development, and so forth—all these areas overlap with the budget because these activities are expensive, although failure to take control of these duties carries a high price in lost opportunity and lowered job performance. These issues are so important that although nothing is more crucial to the success of district mission than recruitment and selection, it is these other issues that consume most of the time of the personnel office.

The scope of the personnel function is thus complex and overlapping. In general, it can be described as working closely with the budget office to determine staffing needs based on enrollment projections in the context of salaries and operating costs. Salaries take in a full range of certified and classified employees. More specifically, the personnel function in tandem with the budget function is usually responsible for:

- ♦ Recruitment and selection
  - Describing role expectations for positions
  - Assessing personal characteristics needed to fit the role
  - Compiling appropriate information on candidates

- Evaluating candidates on role and personal expectations
- Rating eligible candidates on the criteria
- Making the employment decision from among choices

♦ Compensation policies and procedures
- Placing the employee in the most appropriate position
- Determining appropriate pay structures

♦ Personnel development
- Inducting new staff to the district
- Assigning staff to positions based on program needs
- Orienting staff to the position and role
- Evaluating staff on objective performance criteria
- Developing staff through additional training

PERSONNEL COMPENSATION POLICIES AND PROCEDURES

As we have noted often in this book, enrollment drives revenue, which in turn drives expenditures. We have also noted that these realities sometimes drive program decisions. But as we have further noted, expenditures primarily support personnel costs because for most schools about 80% of the budget goes to salaries and benefits. As a result, we now turn to compensation policies and procedures because this is the most critical budget activity that takes place—that is, inability to fund an outstanding staffing plan will invariably limit the quality of services available to children, and error in this activity will result in inability to serve the district's clients.

What Is the Role of Compensation?

The role of employee compensation is clear in the preceding bulleted list. Compensation is the reason people work in a school—it provides their livelihoods and rewards their professional achievements. Compensation forms the basis for purchased services and covers a range of work including administrative leadership, instruction and instructional support, transportation, food service, repair and maintenance, and so on. Compensation must be viewed as more than salaries because the money a district pays employees is much larger than just earned income. For example, compensation includes workers' compensation coverage, unemployment insurance, and social security, to name just a few. Additionally, employee compensation includes other negotiated benefits such as various kinds of health insurance and leave benefits. For example, there is often time away from the job not deducted from pay, including sick leave, bereavement leave, and personal leave. There are also many other kinds of direct and indirect compensation such as overtime pay, supplemental salaries, and performance pay. Additionally, state retirement systems and school district benefits add to a long list of compensation that people forget to include as nonsalary income for public school employees. In sum, compensation provides an important reason for why people work, and the relative strength of compensation structures is often the basis for employee willingness to remain in an employment contract.

General Issues

Longitudinal data on teacher salaries at the beginning of this chapter do not leave much room for surprise at the high cost of compensation. Growth in salary costs will continue, as new positions are needed to serve a growing population. At the same time, staff expect more pay while inflation takes its toll. The important missing observation, however, is that these amounts do not include the vast expenditures for nonteaching personnel or for fringe benefits, bringing the total to a very large sum. Yet, although the dollars are vast, on a personal level there is no capturing of great wealth by individual school staff employees, as seen in Figure 6.1, which depicts trends in average teacher salaries for the last three decades. The data show that salaries have not changed much in constant dollars since 1970, even wavering back and forth in purchasing power over time. The difficulty of recruiting and selecting new teachers is striking, at least on a financial level. Yet the sum of education's costs indisputably makes staff compensation a critical problem in the face of an increasingly stingy public.

Figure 6.1. Average Annual Salary for Public School Teachers 1970–2003 in Constant Dollars

Year	All Teachers	Elementary	Secondary
1970–71	$42,489	$41,356	$43,964
1975–76	$41,377	$40,326	$42,483
1980–81	$37,094	$36,224	$38,141
1982–83	$38,399	$47,531	$39,505
1985–86	$42,173	$41,368	$43,256
1990–91	$44,992	$44,184	$46,096
1995–96	$44,370	$43,776	$45,260
1999–00	$44,996	$44,457	$45,796
2000–01	$45,141	$44,660	$45,084
2001–02	$45,667	$45,284	$46,243
2002–03	$45,822	$45,658	$46,119

SOURCE: U.S. Department of Education, National Center for Education Statistics, *Mini-Digest of Education Statistics 2003* (Washington, DC: National Center for Education Statistics, 2005), 20.

When the topic of public school pay is broached, most people think first of direct salaries. All school districts pay salaries, and by far the majority reward staff, particularly teachers, on a single salary schedule. Historically, single salary schedules were a means to correct pay inequities that discriminated unfairly among minority, male and female, and elementary and secondary school teachers. Additionally, in many rural and urban districts, teachers were paid based on political party affiliation or other nonmeritorious bases. The practice was so prevalent that in 1918 the National Education Association noted that no single salary schedule existed in a city school district anywhere in the nation. Although the single salary schedule has many modern opponents who argue that lockstep schedules invite a flat organization and discourage individual merit, proponents have long held that it is superior to other choices because it fosters better working relationships, is relatively inexpensive to administer, and avoids serious problems such as favoritism and retaliation. The concept has spilled over into state government, as many states use minimum salary schedules for state employees.

The administration of all forms of employee compensation begins with determination and formulation of a job description for each position in a district. Complete and detailed written job descriptions should be developed for every classification of employee. If done properly, descriptions are based on surveys, interviews, and assessments of what every job classification is expected to contribute to organizational goals. Job descriptions should be very clear so that all parties can agree on the nature, duties, and expectations of each position. Each position should have a performance-based job description that includes statements about the method and amount of compensation. Evaluation of performance based on goals can then follow, and performance should form the basis for an employee's location on the salary schedule. Obviously, descriptions vary by position. For example, the job description of a school principal is different and far more complex than the job description for a secretary. Examples of real job descriptions and their differences are shown in Figures 6.2 and 6.3 (p. 184).

Although job descriptions should result in neutral salary decisions based on placement of employees according to district salary schedule policies, the actual salary structure is usually a function of two realities. In some states, collective bargaining applies to both certified and classified employee groups. In other states, teachers bargain under collective negotiations, while classified employees and administrators are outside the negotiations law. In such instances, nonteaching staff salaries are often a function of prevailing wages obtained by informal comparisons between competing school districts. Once salaries are in place, however, annual adjustments across employee groups are likely to be a function of similar percentage increases. For example, it is unlikely that administrators will receive a much higher salary increase than teachers simply because of the negative aspect of public relations. In states where nonteaching staff have no legal bargaining status, it is likely that salaries will be decided after collective negotiations for teachers are complete, with percentage increments closely conforming.

Figure 6.2. Sample Job Description for High School Principal

Position Title: Elementary School Principal

Basic Function: Administers the school under the supervision of the Assistant Superintendent. Provides leadership to faculty and students; manages and directs all activities.

Performance Responsibilities:

♦ Demonstrates leadership through beliefs, skills, and personal characteristics.

♦ Ensures that teachers plan and provide effective instruction.

♦ Monitors, assesses, and supervises the approved district curriculum.

♦ Develops an effective staff development program.

♦ Promotes positive school climate by encouraging capabilities of all individuals.

♦ Uses a variety of data to improve the school's instructional program.

♦ Coordinates development of a written statement of the school's beliefs and goals.

♦ Determines whether the individual educational needs of pupils are being met.

♦ Evaluates the performance of the certified and classified staff members.

♦ Interprets, implements, and maintains Board policies and state school laws.

♦ Develops a program of public relations to further community support.

♦ Administers the school's budgeted allocations.

♦ Directs activities involving pupil/parent contacts concerning registrations, credits and transfers, suspensions, expulsions, pupil progress, placement, guidance and counseling matters, and other matters of a personal nature.

♦ Possesses a thorough understanding of child growth and development.

♦ Engages in a program of continuing professional development.

♦ Orients newly assigned staff members and ensures their familiarization with school policies/procedures, teaching materials, and school facilities.

♦ Creates a strong sense of togetherness through human relations techniques.

♦ Possesses skill in conflict resolution, decision-making, and consensus building.

♦ Performs other related duties as requested.

♦ Requirements: Valid certificate and five years teaching experience. Salary commensurate with experience.

SOURCE: Adapted and modified from the Denver Public Schools, Division of Personnel Services.

Figure 6.3. Sample Job Description for Secretary

Qualifications: Type, file, keep records, and take shorthand at 80 wpm

Reports to: Principal

Job Goal: Provide secretarial services to operate the school

Job Functions:

1. Assigns duties to and supervises work of clerical personnel in the school.
2. Provides input to the administrator on evaluations of clerical personnel.
3. Is responsible for typing and processing all confidential correspondence.
4. Provides the technical skills of typing, filing, record keeping and taking and transcribing shorthand and all other means of communication.
5. Maintains and updates reports, lists, inventories, attendance records, and other similar records that are modified frequently.
6. Serves as one of the school office receptionists and as the first-line public relations staff member when answering phone calls, responding personally to staff, students, parents, and community members, when greeting people in person.
7. Understands and is able to operate equipment including computers, typewriters, dictating equipment, duplicating machines, photocopiers, calculators, and other similar equipment.
8. Prepares certain administrative reports, communications, memoranda, legal notices, employment and vendor contracts, purchase orders, and work orders.
9. Coordinates the activities and schedule of the supervising administrator, permitting the administrator to perform as efficiently and effectively as possible.
10. Responds appropriately to all concerns and complaints from the public and staff and assists in providing an answer or remedy.
11. Conducts special activities in accordance with the specific job assignment, such as the annual school election and graduation.
12. Has a working knowledge of the business and budgeting procedures, as well as the legal obligations of the specific department.
13. Receives and distributes mail and other messages.
14. Provides other necessary secretarial services as requested by the supervising administrator.
15. Salary shall be paid according to years of experience and educational training in strict accordance with the district's board-approved secretarial salary schedule.

SOURCE: Adapted and modified from Galloway Township (NJ) Public Schools.

Negotiations

The fiscal aspect of collective bargaining can be very time-intensive and complex. Because so much is at stake, both financially and in terms of human relations, it is important for all parties to develop trust and respect for each side's information and position. Many districts hold informal contract discussions during the year about concerns, including compensation. Discussions should always be with appropriate association or union leaders to not commit an unfair labor practice. Throughout the school year and in multi-year contracts as well, dialogue with all groups eases the negotiations process by not allowing tensions to grow and fester.

The negotiations process is unique in each state because of different bargaining laws. In principle, however, the steps are similar depending on the extent to which arbitration is required. At whatever time of year discussions begin, the budget office is called on by the personnel division to provide salary data for use in making fiscal projections and to provide cost analyses of all salary proposals. The reason is that short- and long-range costs must be known for all proposals before the board can agree to a compensation plan. The budget office must include not only all direct costs of salary and fringe benefits, but it also must consider cash flow, cost of employee time, and any other items on the negotiations table. Each of these issues must be analyzed for present and future costs and for the long-range impact on district financial health. The essence of all these activities is to conduct negotiations in good faith and to accurately anticipate all costs of salaries to balance revenues and expenditures in the final budget.

Basic Elements

After the relevant data are collected and verified by both sides, the negotiations process is ready to begin. Agreement on the facts makes bargaining easier because the district's position at the bargaining table, the potential for favorable review at impasse or arbitration, and the union's receptiveness are all enhanced. Items on which initial agreement should be sought include cash projections, the impact of these data on the district, historical data related to the issues, and data showing how the district compares to other school districts of similar profile in the state and region. Careful preparation and presentation always increases the potential for success at the bargaining table, as well as aiding favorable treatment if fact-finding and arbitration are eventually required.

The goal of both sides in negotiations is to have a reasonable discussion about the facts to agree on a fair compensation package. When agreement is struck, any changes are applied to the appropriate salary and benefit schedules. For example, for certified teaching staff the most direct impact is on adjustment to the single salary schedule, both in dollars and in changes to the structure of the schedule itself. For noncertified staff, the impact occurs either in similar application to a salary schedule or by adjustment to each individual's contracted salary. The goal of fairness must be extended to the fringe benefit package as well. Thus, data reflecting the need to attract and retain high quality staff, as well as promoting professional growth for all employees, must be balanced with the ability of the district to fund the contract.

During negotiations, both sides come to the bargaining table with items they want to negotiate. Preparation on the part of the district focuses on collecting and examining fiscal data and any other concerns of the district. The employee organization also has interest in these same items, although for different reasons. Items brought to the table by both sides are fairly common and include:

♦ *Strengths and weaknesses* of the entire contract

♦ *Salary schedule*, including number and costs of each cell of the matrix over the life of the contract and a projection into the near future

♦ *Basic data* on minimum, maximum, and actual average cost per employee over the life of the contract

♦ *Comparative salaries* in competing districts and industries

♦ *Living standards* of the local community

♦ *Personnel turnover*, as well as pending retirements

♦ *Movement on the salary schedule* because of advanced training, as well as experience movement

♦ *New programmatic needs and curtailments*

♦ *Future revenues and expenditures,* including tax levies and state aid projections

In addition, the district and employee groups will need to gather and bring other nonfinancial data. Generally this consists of such issues as:

♦ Are there parts of the contract that have not worked well?

♦ Is there a pattern of grievances over parts of the contract?

♦ Should parts of the contract be modified or dropped?

♦ What new issues may prove problematic?

These data are critical to the negotiations process and to compensation policies because, without good data, the proposed costs are unobtainable and capability to fund a future contract is unknown. In fact, it is easy to see that the fiscal integrity of the district may be at risk by lack of such data. Data must be continuously updated based on the latest information for accurate decision making.

Costing-Out Salary Proposals

Although terms and conditions of employment make up a large part of the total negotiations process, the most elemental aspect comes when salary is discussed. It is at salary time when the personnel and budget functions are most closely related because, if contract agreement is not reached, the district is likely to suffer low staff morale.

For certified staff, discussion of salary is likely to center on changing the basic structure of the salary schedule and on increasing the dollar amount of the base. Figure 6.4 illustrates a salary schedule for a district and provides an illustration of how contract negotiations occur in the majority of cases. Most of us are familiar with single salary schedules, but three observations should be made before examining likely scenarios involving salary negotiations. First, the top portion of Figure 6.4 (pp. 188–189) shows the index that computes the dollars seen in the center portion. Second, Figure 6.4 is actually two different versions of the same salary schedule; that is, the first half shows the current year, whereas the second half calculates a change in base salary. Third, the bottom portion of each half of Figure 6.4 uses a few staff members from the district to show how a salary schedule is costed out. Figure 6.4 thus provides a basis for some extended discussion of the negotiations process.

Although no two districts negotiate exactly alike, it is almost certain that teachers will propose three changes to the salary schedule in Figure 6.4. The first proposal will be to increase the base salary. Both the teachers and the district know this has the effect of increasing all other steps in the schedule because salary schedules are always step-dependent. In other words, a change in base salary will increase all salaries. The second proposal will be to increase the number of columns. In districts without a doctorate degree column, the proposal will likely seek more columns beyond the master's degree. In Figure 6.4, such a proposal would have to seek columns beyond the doctorate. The third proposal will be to add steps at the bottom of some or all columns as a reward for longevity. Board proposals, on the other hand, will seek more restrictive language on nonsalary items such as discretionary leaves and will further seek to minimize increases to the salary schedule. Almost everyone recognizes the futility of board efforts to negotiate most other items: For example, negotiating a salary decrease is highly unlikely.

Some of the changes proposed by teachers have a fair chance for success because these changes seem reasonable to most people. But all changes must be considered carefully. The effect of increasing the base is seen in the second half of Figure 6.4 where a $1,000 increase (+4%) raises the base to $26,000. But increasing the base by a modest amount causes a ripple to occur throughout the schedule, as all other steps take at least the same increase. This is because each step in Figure 6.4 is indexed to the prior step. For example, a teacher on step 1 will get not only the 4% base increase, but also another 2% for a year's longevity. For just this one teacher, the cost of raising the base 4% is actually 6%. Step increments are often progressively greater with more years of experience. Given the relative maturity of teaching staffs in the United States, care must be taken because as salary schedules load on experience, they become expensive. The first change proposed by teachers is thus far more costly than the $1,000 base increase might suggest, costing $13,940 to fund only seven teachers in our sample group (note that we added $300 to fringe benefits as well in recognition of rapidly rising health care costs).

Figure 6.4. Sample Salary Schedule

BASE=$25,000

YEAR	BA + 0	BA + 15	BA + 30	Masters	MS + 15	MS + 30	Doctorate
1	100%	102%	104%	106%	108%	110%	112%
2	102%	104%	106%	108%	110%	112%	114%
3	104%	106%	108%	110%	112%	114%	116%
4	106%	108%	110%	112%	114%	116%	118%
5	108%	108%	112%	114%	116%	118%	120%
6	110%	112%	114%	116%	118%	120%	122%
7	112%	114%	116%	118%	120%	122%	124%
8	114%	116%	118%	120%	122%	124%	126%
9		118%	120%	122%	124%	126%	128%
10		120%	122%	124%	126%	128%	130%
11			124%	126%	128%	130%	132%
12			126%	128%	130%	132%	134%
13				130%	132%	134%	136%
14				132%	134%	136%	138%
15					136%	138%	140%
16					138%	140%	142%
17						142%	144%
18							146%

YEAR	BA + 0	BA + 15	BA + 30	Masters	MS + 15	MS + 30	Doctorate
1	$ 25,000	$ 25,500	$ 26,000	$ 26,500	$ 27,000	$ 27,500	$ 28,000
2	$ 25,500	$ 26,000	$ 26,500	$ 27,000	$ 27,500	$ 28,000	$ 28,500
3	$ 26,000	$ 26,500	$ 27,000	$ 27,500	$ 28,000	$ 28,500	$ 29,000
4	$ 26,500	$ 27,000	$ 27,500	$ 28,000	$ 28,500	$ 29,000	$ 29,500
5	$ 27,000	$ 27,000	$ 28,000	$ 28,500	$ 29,000	$ 29,500	$ 30,000
6	$ 27,500	$ 28,000	$ 28,500	$ 29,000	$ 29,500	$ 30,000	$ 30,500
7	$ 28,000	$ 28,500	$ 29,000	$ 29,500	$ 30,000	$ 30,500	$ 31,000
8		$ 29,000	$ 29,500	$ 30,000	$ 30,500	$ 31,000	$ 31,500
9		$ 29,500	$ 30,000	$ 30,500	$ 31,000	$ 31,500	$ 32,000
10		$ 30,000	$ 30,500	$ 31,000	$ 31,500	$ 32,000	$ 32,500
11			$ 31,000	$ 31,500	$ 32,000	$ 32,500	$ 33,000
12			$ 31,500	$ 32,000	$ 32,500	$ 33,000	$ 33,500
13				$ 32,500	$ 33,000	$ 33,500	$ 34,000
14				$ 33,000	$ 33,500	$ 34,000	$ 34,500
15					$ 34,000	$ 34,500	$ 35,000
16					$ 34,500	$ 35,000	$ 35,500
17						$ 35,500	$ 36,000
18							$ 36,500

Projections based on zero dollar increase on base (see asterisk note below).

Name	Current salary	Current benefits	Current pkg.	New salary	New benefits	Proposed pkg.	% increase
Mary A.	$ 25,000	$ 3,000	$ 28,000	$ 25,500	$ 3,000	$ 28,500	1.8%
Bob B.	$ 29,500	$ 3,000	$ 32,500	$ 30,000	$ 3,000	$ 33,000	1.5%
Julie C. (frozen)	$ 31,500	$ 3,000	$ 34,500	$ 31,500	$ 3,000	$ 34,500	0.0%
James D.	$ 26,500	$ 3,000	$ 29,500	$ 27,000	$ 3,000	$ 30,000	1.7%
Janet E.	$ 33,500	$ 3,000	$ 36,500	$ 34,000	$ 3,000	$ 37,000	1.4%
Bill F. (frozen)	$ 36,500	$ 3,000	$ 39,500	$ 36,500	$ 3,000	$ 39,500	0.0%
Paula G.***	$ 35,500	$ 3,000	$ 38,500	$ 36,500	$ 3,000	$ 39,500	2.6%
and so on...							
TOTALS	$ 218,000	$ 21,000	$ 239,000	$ 221,000	$ 21,000	$ 242,000	1.28%

COST TO FUND $ 3,000

***will obtain doctorate by end of current school year.

Base= $26,000

YEAR	BA + 0	BA + 15	BA + 30	Masters	MS + 15	MS + 30	Doctorate
1	100%	102%	104%	106%	108%	110%	112%
2	102%	104%	106%	108%	110%	112%	114%
3	104%	106%	108%	110%	112%	114%	116%
4	106%	108%	110%	112%	114%	116%	118%
5	108%	108%	112%	114%	116%	118%	120%
6	110%	112%	114%	116%	118%	120%	122%
7	112%	114%	116%	118%	120%	122%	124%
8	114%	116%	118%	120%	122%	124%	126%
9		118%	120%	122%	124%	126%	128%
10		120%	122%	124%	126%	128%	130%
11			124%	126%	128%	130%	132%
12			126%	128%	130%	132%	134%
13				130%	132%	134%	136%
14				132%	134%	136%	138%
15					136%	138%	140%
16					138%	140%	142%
17						142%	144%
18							146%

YEAR	BA + 0	BA + 15	BA + 30	Masters	MS + 15	MS + 30	Doctorate
1	$ 26,000	$ 26,520	$ 27,040	$ 27,560	$ 28,080	$ 28,600	$ 29,120
2	$ 26,520	$ 27,040	$ 27,560	$ 28,080	$ 28,600	$ 29,120	$ 29,640
3	$ 27,040	$ 27,560	$ 28,080	$ 28,600	$ 29,120	$ 29,640	$ 30,160
4	$ 27,560	$ 28,080	$ 28,600	$ 29,120	$ 29,640	$ 30,160	$ 30,680
5	$ 28,080	$ 28,080	$ 29,120	$ 29,640	$ 30,160	$ 30,680	$ 31,200
6	$ 28,600	$ 29,120	$ 29,640	$ 30,160	$ 30,680	$ 31,200	$ 31,720
7	$ 29,120	$ 29,640	$ 30,160	$ 30,680	$ 31,200	$ 31,720	$ 32,240
8	$ 29,640	$ 30,160	$ 30,680	$ 31,200	$ 31,720	$ 32,240	$ 32,760
9		$ 30,680	$ 31,200	$ 31,720	$ 32,240	$ 32,760	$ 33,280
10		$ 31,200	$ 31,720	$ 32,240	$ 32,760	$ 33,280	$ 33,800
11			$ 32,240	$ 32,760	$ 33,280	$ 33,800	$ 34,320
12			$ 32,760	$ 33,280	$ 33,800	$ 34,320	$ 34,840
13				$ 33,800	$ 34,320	$ 34,840	$ 35,360
14				$ 34,320	$ 34,840	$ 35,360	$ 35,880
15					$ 35,360	$ 35,880	$ 36,400
16					$ 35,880	$ 36,400	$ 36,920
17						$ 36,920	$ 37,440
18							$ 37,960

Projections based on $1,000 increase on base plus $300 fringe.

Name	Current salary	Current benefits	Current pkg.	New salary	New benefits	Proposed pkg.	% increase
Mary A.	$ 25,000	$ 3,000	$ 28,000	$ 26,520	$ 3,300	$ 29,820	6%
Bob B.	$ 29,500	$ 3,000	$ 32,500	$ 31,200	$ 3,300	$ 34,500	6%
Julie C.	$ 31,500	$ 3,000	$ 34,500	$ 32,760	$ 3,300	$ 36,060	5%
James D.	$ 26,500	$ 3,000	$ 29,500	$ 28,080	$ 3,300	$ 31,380	6%
Janet E.	$ 33,500	$ 3,000	$ 36,500	$ 35,360	$ 3,300	$ 38,660	6%
Bill F.	$ 36,500	$ 3,000	$ 39,500	$ 37,960	$ 3,300	$ 41,260	4%
Paula G.***	$ 35,500	$ 3,000	$ 38,500	$ 37,960	$ 3,300	$ 41,260	7%
and so on...							
TOTALS	$ 218,000	$ 21,000	$ 239,000	$ 229,840	$ 23,100	$ 252,940	5.87%

COST TO FUND

***will obtain doctorate by end of current school year. $ 13,940

The cost of the second teacher proposal to increase the number of columns cannot be calculated quickly from the data in Figure 6.4 because decisions would need to be made about how a new column should be built. The general impact can be seen, however. For next year, only those teachers with college credits beyond the doctorate degree would qualify for movement to a new column. Assuming some teachers would be able to move, an expensive result follows. Again, the dollar effect is even larger when the base increases simultaneously. As expected, teachers who qualify for extended columns are experienced and better educated—needless to say, salaries at the top end are much more expensive. Although boards often want to increase the base, there are practical barriers.

The third proposal to add steps to existing columns is also costly. The purpose, of course, is to unfreeze teachers who have bottomed out on experience. Adding steps, however, multiplies against their salaries and the cost may be much higher than it first appears. Before making such an agreement, it must be known how many teachers would qualify for movement. Additionally, the district must know how many of those persons also returned to a university campus during the year and would further qualify to move horizontally. In other words, the district might have to pay newly unfrozen teachers twice—once by adding steps and again by moving to a new column, all of which has a cumulative effect.

The data in this example have many benefits. One of the most important benefits is the ability to automate the salary schedule for instant "what-if" scenarios. Figure 6.4 was prepared in a spreadsheet with interactive cells, so that if the base changes, all other cells update. Also, when the data are agreed on, both sides can see the effect of new proposals. Both sides also profit from the entire negotiations process in that, although the board will have to increase salaries next year, it does so in exchange for the least amount possible at which it can still hire happy employees. It is important for board members, administrators, teachers, and the public as a whole to understand that collective bargaining is a series of compromises and that one side rarely has complete success. By anticipating staffing needs, recruiting and selecting the best staff, and preparing and using data for personnel compensation policies, both sides have a better chance of reaching an acceptable compromise.

Whatever proposals come to the table, several features must be recognized and accepted. It must be recognized that negotiations can be very confrontational, but the risk can be minimized by openness and trust. It also must be recognized that the personnel and budget functions should take negotiations seriously because the costs interweave throughout the district's budget; that is, a decision to meaningfully improve the salary schedule will negatively impact other operations. However, failing to improve salaries is destructive to long-term district health. It further must be recognized that an average increase of 3% in teacher salaries, for example, will probably also result in a 3% increase for all nonteaching staff, including administrators. The multiplicative nature of these events can be costly when a simple 3% increase is costed across vertical and horizontal dimensions of the teachers' single salary schedule, across noncertified salary structures, and across all administrators. In most cases, state aid increases are not sufficient, making it necessary to either raise taxes or reduce other operations.

Instead of sitting on the sideline, the personnel and budget functions are directly involved in the negotiations process through production of data, costing out proposals, and working with both sides in search of agreement. In many instances, the board's negotiator may be an administrator. In some districts, the superintendent serves as chief negotiator, although the field and the professional literature suggest this may be risky. In other cases, the assistant superintendent for personnel and/or finance may serve in the lead board role. In other instances, the chief negotiator is an attorney, selected for adroitness or benefit of impartiality. Regardless of who serves as the board's spokesperson, the personnel and finance functions should be aware of the progress of negotiations and should be consulted to determine the viability of any proposed actions.

No matter who serves in the lead role, there are skills and knowledge that must be present. The chief negotiator must be knowledgeable of collective bargaining statutes, be familiar with unfair labor practices, and have experience in such matters in the public sector. Additionally, personal skills including maturity, articulation, flexibility, and the ability to reject ideas without alienating the opposing side are valuable.

Beyond the spokesperson, the board team often consists of the chief fiscal officer for the district, a recorder, a board subcommittee, and others as appropriate. Team composition varies by custom. Teachers are often represented by an attorney, a professional association or union official, or other such person. Each district differs in the culture of negotiations. As a generalization, most negotiating sessions follow custom wherein only spokespersons may speak, that written initial nonexpandable proposals must be exchanged in advance, and that each team keeps good notes. Generally, caucuses may be unlimited unless agreed otherwise. Again, it must be stressed that each state varies in statutory guidelines and local custom; for example, in some states sessions may be closed. The scope of a sample state negotiations law is provided in Figure 6.5 (p. 192).

Impasse Resolution

Despite best efforts, negotiations may fail and move to impasse. Under most states' laws, districts are required to recognize impasse and to engage in fact-finding, followed either by binding arbitration or by unilateral board contracts. Generally, impasse and fact-finding occur when the parties cannot reach agreement on terms and conditions of a new employment contract by some date specified in law. For both the personnel and budget functions, failure to successfully negotiate a contract is a stressful event that introduces uncertainty and tension into employer-employee relations that are difficult to heal.

When negotiations reach impasse, most states' statutes invoke a timeline calling for a third party to examine the last best offers from both sides and to

Figure 6.5. Sample Negotiations Law

Mandatorily Negotiable*

1. Salary	14. Jury duty
2. Wages	15. Grievance procedure
3. Pay under supplemental contracts	16. Binding arbitration
4. Hours of work	17. Discipline procedure
5. Amounts of work	18. Resignations
6. Vacation allowance	19. Contract termination
7. Holiday leave	20. Contract non-renewal
8. Sick leave	21. Reemployment
9. Extended leave	22. Contract terms
10. Sabbatical leaves	23. Contract form
11. "Other" leaves	24. Probationary period
12. Number of holidays	25. Evaluation
13. Retirement	26. Insurance benefits
	27. Overtime pay

Permissibly Negotiable*

1. Academic and personal freedom (except constitutional)	7. Teacher copyrights
2. Assignment and transfer of personnel	8. Facilities, equipment, materials, supplies
3. Association rights (in excess statute)	9. Grading frequency
4. Class size	10. Security
5. Classroom management	11. Substitutes
6. School library hours	12. Teacher aides

Nonnegotiable*

1. Number of days or total hours of school	5. First Amendment issues
2. Nondiscrimination	6. Affirmative action
3. Special education placement procedures	7. Student discipline if constitutional issue
4. Teacher discipline if constitutional issue	8. Federal programs

* Negotiations items cited are taken from one state's statutes. No inference to all states can be made.

review the facts and issue a report. This person, depending on state law, may be a state employee of the employment relations board or a person approved by some other state agency. Generally, fact-finding in most states is not binding, but it is persuasive to the parties. If the two sides still cannot reach agreement after fact-finding, some states require mediation and/or binding arbitration. Mediation usually precedes arbitration, although in practice each state's statutes are unique. In several states, binding arbitration is immediately invoked wherein an impartial panel issues a report and both sides must accept the decision. Such a ruling cannot be challenged unless it can be successfully argued that the arbitrator exceeded legal authority. In other states, the process only calls for impasse, fact-finding, mediation, and issuance of unilateral contracts if agreement is still not reached. In all instances, a statutory timeline applies (Figure 6.6).

Figure 6.6. Sample Negotiations Timeline

Feb 1	Exchange of notices and proposals. A petition to the state to declare impasse may be filed.
Jun 1	Notice of impasse must be filed if applicable.
Jun 5	Five days set aside for consultation with state on impasse.
Jun 15	State issues findings. Arbitration process begun if needed.
Jun 20	Fact-finding board appointed with 5 days.
Jul 10	Fact-finding report issued within 20 days.
Immediate	Parties must meet to discuss fact-finding results.
Jul 20	Report made public after 10 days.
Jul 30	Board may issue unilateral contracts if no agreement.

In states where binding arbitration exists, the budget and personnel functions are prevented from issuing contracts, setting budgets, and engaging in other activities until negotiations are settled. This can be uncomfortable for both sides, who often must continue to work together, especially in states where public employee strikes are prohibited. Even more complex, however, is the total subjugation of the district to the will of an arbitrator who may make a decision that is financially difficult to obey. In states without binding arbitration, issues are also tense, but the budget and personnel functions can resume operations earlier, and the issue of salary costs in unilateral contract states is obviously under far greater control.

Depending on the state, negotiations are repeated with each employee group. But when contracts are finally settled, a major task of the budget and personnel functions is finished and these divisions can resume employer-employee relationships in which the new contract must be administered on a daily basis. At this point, yet another budget-building block is in place.

OTHER ISSUES OF
PERSONNEL BUDGETING

Although contract negotiations are the most important element of budgeting once projecting enrollment and estimating staff needs are complete, there are other important issues in budgeting for personnel. For legislators, school boards, administrators, staffs, and communities, three particular areas are important because they impact compensation structures and financial liability for court awards. These areas are proposals for merit pay, reductions-in-force and other dismissals, and due process concerns.

What About Merit Pay?

A recurring issue related to compensation in schools is the concept of merit pay. Attempts to introduce merit pay have been around for a long time, first dating from 1908 in Newton, Massachusetts. In the 1920s, interest grew rapidly but peaked in the 1950s. Although interest has followed cycles, the concept has neither died out nor been widely adopted. Merit pay has received recent attention, though, as accountability and antitax sentiment have gained momentum.

Merit pay does not merely provide additional compensation for more duties. That approach is better described as career ladders or similar devices. Career ladders are intended to encourage outstanding teachers to stay in classroom service by increasing their responsibilities in exchange for more pay. In contrast, merit pay rewards superior performance on school or district goals by creating a hierarchical performance difference between people with similar jobs. The basis for merit pay has been sensible, but its application has been inconsistent. Some of the call for merit pay has been laudable, such as Cubberley's view in 1916 that merit pay would provide better distribution of rewards and reverse the 25–50% staff turnover in teaching at that time. More recently, national reports have called for teacher evaluation systems designed to reward superior teaching in response to declining student achievement. On the downside, however, have been critics who widely condemn schools for low performance, calling for dismantling the system as the only solution to a poor investment.

Proposals for merit pay vary greatly. Generally, merit pay plans have arisen from renewed interest in accountability among state legislators who are being pressured for reform. The plans are often responses to crises of a moment and are not accompanied by stable funding. As a result, the structure of many merit proposals is based on a one-time performance award, although outstanding work may be repeatedly rewarded based on annual evaluations. The problem is not so much that legislators have not wanted to fund long-term merit pay, but rather that merit pay can be costly. Additionally, there is some belief that merit is best evaluated on an annual basis because increases to single salary schedules reward people in perpetuity—an idea antithetical to merit pay goals.

Despite interest, there has been only limited trial and success. In fact, merit pay has been abandoned almost every time it has been tried in schools, largely because of the difficulty of measuring good teaching or because of unrest among teachers. Other problems have included harming a cooperative environment, subjective observation, invalid evaluation, lack of accord. on goals, and no agreement on the elements of good teaching. Critics have found many flaws with merit pay, particularly in implementation and maintenance, and in the inflexibility of most school aid plans, all of which are said to siphon money from base salaries whenever merit pay is implemented.

Despite low enthusiasm, merit pay is in place in several states and continues to interest many legislators. In most cases, however, existing plans are not true merit plans because the majority only provide more pay for extra duties or professional growth. Research has indicated that merit plans are few in number due partly to the fact that many districts simply do not have the extra money. Only when merit plans are state-funded does research indicate that they are viable within a state.

The message is mixed on the wisdom of merit pay. On the one hand, it is wise to believe that interest will continue and that districts should study the issues, if for no other reason than legislative interest may reduce revenues for schools if educators resist too much. Additionally, as states experience slow economies and as the demographic changes noted in this book continue, powerful private interests may bring pressure on legislatures to improve schools through merit pay. On the other hand, there is much literature suggesting a low return on investing in merit pay. Although clear data do not exist, the budget and personnel functions continue to be faced by both sides on the issue, giving rise to two concerns that need to be briefly developed here.

The first concern is whether merit pay can be forced on schools. Under private sector guidelines, issues affecting wages and working conditions are covered under collective bargaining. This arises from regulations of the National Labor Relations Act (NLRA), where it is an unfair labor practice to refuse to bargain on wages, hours, terms, and conditions of employment. A board's attempt to force merit pay would seem to demand negotiation, and alternatively, a request by employees to implement merit pay would have to be negotiated. However, NLRA does not apply to schools. In fact, in at least one instance, a court has reasoned that a school district does not have to negotiate merit pay. The court stated:

> In municipal employment relations the bargaining table is not the appropriate forum for the formulation or management of public policy. Where a decision is essentially concerned with public policy choices, no group should act as an exclusive representative; discussion should be open; and policy should be shaped in the political process. Essential control over the management of the dis-

trict's affairs must be left with the school board, the body elected to be responsible for those affairs under state law.[5]

In other states, legislatures at times have passed laws encouraging or even requiring merit pay in schools. Recent examples of legislative interest include a 2004 Arkansas law establishing a knowledge and skills-based pay system for teachers and providing for school-based performance awards.[6] Similarly, the state of Delaware required that beginning in 2002 at least 20% of an educator's performance evaluation must be tied to student improvement and further expanded the salary system to include compensation for skills and knowledge.[7] Recently, numerous states have passed legislation providing additional compensation for teachers achieving National Board certification. Other states such as Iowa, however, have both embraced and simultaneously softened merit-based plans, as in a 2003 Iowa law in which that state affirmed interest in comparing student achievement gains across districts while striking language in the same law that had required the state department to allocate funds for performance pay.[8] Under these varying conditions, the opinion of the court cited earlier is clearly not binding in other jurisdictions, so that state legislatures can drive development of public policy at the negotiations table. As with many other points of law, forcing merit pay depends heavily on state statutes and subsequent legal scrutiny.

The second concern relates to the wisdom of attempting to force merit pay. There has been no overwhelming enthusiasm in schools for merit pay, and doubts about such plans are widespread. For example, in 2003 a national study by the Public Agenda, a opinion research group, reported that teachers were cautiously supportive of merit pay but simultaneously viewed it with grave reservation. On the positive side, 70% were willing to support incentives for teachers in low-performing and physically dangerous schools, and 67% indicated that teachers who work harder and work longer hours should be paid more. Likewise, 57% supported extra pay for teachers who achieve national certification. But support stops suddenly when tying pay to student achievement measures, with only 38% favoring merit pay linked to test scores. Worries about implementation were strong as well, with 63% believing that merit pay would result in competition and jealousy.[9]

Although there is no doubt that critics are correct in charging that single salary schedules provide no motivation for high performance, reason suggests that abandoning pay systems that promote apathy will only lead to pay systems that promote resentment. Additionally, with little legal sympathy for boards and legislatures bent on eliminating or diluting single salary

---

5. *Unified School District v. WERC*, 81 Wis.2d 89, 259 N.W.2d at 730–31 (1977).

6. Arkansas. S.B. 42. Signed into law January 2004.

7. Delaware. S.B. 260. Signed into law May 2000.

8. Iowa. H.B. 549 (omnibus bill). Signed into law May 2003.

9. The Public Agenda, *Stand by Me. America's Teachers—Don't Make Us Scapegoats*, June 4, 2003.

schedules, there is potential for disruption of the personnel and budget functions if merit pay is forced. A better path may be through the literature, which offers alternatives to merit pay based on job redesign—a strategy more compatible with the norms of autonomy, equality, and civility that have long been entrenched in schools. All that may be said with confidence is that great care must be taken before merit plans are implemented because of risk of violating statutes and bargaining agreements and the negative impact on morale that haunts merit pay.

What about RIF and Other Dismissals?

The second area of concern for the personnel and budget functions involves reduction-in-force (RIF) and other dismissals. Reductions-in-force occur when districts have more staff than are needed, and other dismissals occur for cause, including poor performance or uncooperative behavior. In both cases, it is necessary for the budget and personnel functions to minimize the damage and to estimate the impact of these actions.

In contrast to merit pay, which offers more money for certain behaviors, RIF reduces money in a district's instructional or operations budget. In some instances, merit pay and RIF may be joined, but the concept behind RIF is reducing expenditure, often in response to enrollment decline or other fiscal distress. Because these problems may continue indefinitely, some districts have had to reduce staff because state aid is always enrollment-driven and because aid formulas do not respond to all types of financial distress unless legislatures choose to intervene through hold-harmless or other kinds of emergency provisions.

Reduction-in-force cuts tenured or nontenured staff for reasons unrelated to performance. Conversely, if performance led to program enrollment decline, dismissal or nonrenewal may still be treated as RIF. The usual reason for RIF is insolvency. It must be understood that when fiscal insolvency is claimed by a board, counterclaims by the teachers' association will center on the validity of the board's data. The board must be able to substantiate its actions based on clear evidence. In this arena, the need for clear and precise data is paramount. When data are clear, boards will be supported by the courts.

When RIF is invoked, employee rights to seniority and "bumping" come into play along with state statutes and local collective bargaining agreements. A majority of courts have held that teachers must be treated alike, regardless of program issues. As a result, seniority and bumping are concepts to be kept in mind when the personnel and budget divisions decide which teachers will be nonrenewed. Importantly, courts have extended rights to nontenured staff in some cases. Other courts, though, have ruled that nontenured teachers possess no seniority rights. Within professional certification areas, teachers may bump other teachers with less seniority. Again, these issues depend on state statutes and local bargaining agreements. Courts have also ruled that once RIF is declared, the district must complete the task and not create new positions. Thus, educational leaders must be familiar with the negotiated agreement, as well as statutory requirements.

In addition to RIF, other dismissals occur. Although it is commonly believed that a teaching job is a life appointment, reality is that both tenured and nontenured staff are dismissed. There should be no misperception about local boards' power in personnel matters. Boards and supervisors have the authority to evaluate and dismiss, and these powers are by virtue of state legislatures granting implied and delegated authority to operate the schools.

Even though boards can dismiss staff, termination under either RIF or other conditions must not be undertaken lightly. This is true because, in the vast majority of states, significant differences exist between dismissal procedures for nontenured versus tenured staff. Tenure grants a continuing contract and entitles the staff member to due process. In contrast, nontenured teachers are given only a term contract under whatever employment and dismissal processes are granted under contract law. This does not mean nontenured staff have no rights or protections because no one can be denied constitutional rights, that is, nontenured staff may demand full due process if allegations are made that fundamental rights such as freedom of speech have been violated. In addition, statutes in each state govern other rights of nontenured staff, making it mandatory to understand state law, the termination process, and terms of the employment contract.

Although our discussion accurately gives the impression that it is easier to dismiss nontenured staff, and despite the belief that tenure is a life contract, there are many cases where tenured faculty have been successfully dismissed. The task is more difficult because state statutes generally provide very specific reasons for termination of tenured employees, and by logic no dismissal can occur except for cause. Cause includes incompetence, immorality, insubordination, felony conviction, unprofessional conduct, incapacity, and neglect of duty. Within limits of seniority and bumping, fiscal exigency is a defensible cause for tenured dismissal. When any of these reasons is invoked, the right of termination falls to employers if the claims can be substantiated. Failure to substantiate, however, will likely result in a lawsuit and liability for various types of compensation and restitution. As a result, care should be taken in choosing the reason for dismissal.

Dismissal for incompetence depends on state statutory definition. However, courts have allowed broad definition of incompetence. Incompetence is often defined as lack of ability, legal qualification, or fitness to discharge any required duties. Generally, proof of incompetence is measured against others having similar duties. Incompetence may be proved by any one of the following criteria or some combination thereof:

- Lack of a proper teaching certificate
- Lack of knowledge of subject matter
- Lack of ability to establish reasonable discipline in class

- Deficiency in teaching methods
- Emotional instability demonstrating inability to effectively teach

Both nontenured and tenured staff may be dismissed for these reasons. In dismissing tenured staff, however, care must be taken to document any charges in case litigation ensues. Additionally, in nearly all states there is a duty to remediate before dismissal. Remediation must also be documented and should include a variety of activities designed to bring the employee up to at least an adequate level of performance. Remediation should help employees to be successful in the specific job, define activities and duties of all parties, and demonstrate good faith by the district to salvage the contractual interest of the employee. Documentation of failure by the employee to respond must be thorough because the first defense will be to say that the employee is not the worst case in the district. It is easy to see that serious liability accompanies improper dismissals.

Staff may also be dismissed for immorality. In the modern context, immorality is not confined to sexual misconduct. In a court, immorality generally is based on prevailing community standards, in which the test is whether the act is inimical to public welfare. Actions such as corruption or indecency constitute immorality, in that the standard has been defined as conduct that offends the morals of the community and that sets a bad example for the youth whose ideals a teacher is supposed to foster.

Although immorality is broadly defined, care must be taken not to expose the district to liability for misapplication of the standard. For example, one of the touchy areas is unwed pregnant teachers. Generally, courts have not supported claims of immorality in such cases because of a lack of irrefutable proof of immorality. This simply means that it is difficult to prove in the majority of communities that such pregnancy results in damage to students in the learning process, or that the teacher's respect in the community has been affected. The issue is made more difficult because in 1978 Congress passed the Pregnancy Discrimination Act, amending Title VII to include pregnancy as covered under equal benefits.

Dismissal without liability is much easier in the case of insubordination. Willful disregard or refusal to obey reasonable directives constitutes insubordination. As always, however, courts place the burden of proof on the district, particularly with tenured staff, because of property rights inherent to a contractual relationship. A hasty decision to charge insubordination can be devastating, as insubordination as cause for dismissal has *not* been upheld when:

- The alleged misconduct could not be proved.
- Existence of a pertinent rule or verbal order was not proven.
- The teacher's motive for violating a rule was admirable.
- The rule or order was unreasonable.
- The rule was invalid and beyond the authority of the maker.

♦ The enforcement of a rule or order revealed possible bias or discrimination.

♦ The enforcement of a rule violated constitutional rights.

If the employee can show that one of these reasons led to the action, courts will not support dismissal because directives must be reasonable. Insubordination and willful neglect must be proved and not assumed. It is appropriate to take great care in dismissing for insubordination because, under an adverse ruling by a court, liability can follow.

Finally, employees may be discharged without liability for neglect of duty. In practice, neglect of duty may be part of a claim of incompetence. For example, neglect of duty might include failure to follow curriculum guidelines, lack of discipline, failure to follow teaching lessons, and other similar actions or inactions. Neglect is distinct from insubordination, however, where an employee blatantly disregards directives. To withstand judicial challenge, charges of neglect of duty or insubordination must reflect prior notice and established policy or directive. Finally, other dismissals for acts such as conviction on felony charge likely will be upheld because such offense may have an impact on the performance and standing of a teacher in the community. In many states, statutes declare that felony conviction is evidence of unfitness to teach. As always, lack of care in substantiating dismissals for due process purposes may result in great harm to the district.

What About Due Process?

The seriousness of discussion in this chapter is evident when it is remembered that districts are liable for wrongful acts. Liability for improper dismissal places a heavy burden on the personnel and budget functions because a wrongful dismissal impacts both personnel policy and the fiscal welfare of the district due to probable claims for reinstatement, back pay, and damages for violating the rights and reputation of accused persons. These realities place a grave duty on boards and administrators to discharge their duties properly and to assure procedural and substantive due process. Procedural due process ensures that parties are entitled to notice and hearing. Substantive due process is a constitutional guarantee that no one may be arbitrarily deprived of life, liberty, or property and must be protected from unreasonable action.

The personnel division should have responsibility for developing due process guidelines conforming to the requirements of law. Guidelines should be written, reviewed by all divisions including the budget office, approved by the board, and made known to the staff. Due process consists of four elements that also apply to dismissal. First, the employee must receive written notice giving specific reason(s). Notification must conform to all state statutes on timing and method of delivery. Second, an impartial hearing is required so the employee can have a chance to hear, examine, and refute any evidence. Third, the employee must have an opportunity to challenge these statements and to call witnesses. Fourth, hearings must occur at several levels within the district. The process begins with the immediate supervisor and administratively ends with the board. This ensures that the employee will have opportunities to be heard and to challenge the actions at each level. Failure to provide these proceedings is almost certain to result in severe consequences.

Determination of whether due process has been accorded is a function of the external mechanics of proceedings and closer scrutiny of the total process. The administration and board must be careful to deal objectively with the facts and to procedurally follow due process steps. This is critical for tenured employees because these persons have property rights to continued employment, and procedural and substantive due process must be accorded in that property rights may not be removed arbitrarily. The duty of the district is grave, as the U.S. Supreme Court has ruled that such interests of employees are "broad and majestic."[10] Yet appropriate dismissals should not be avoided because, notwithstanding the seriousness of violating rights and due process, failure to correct poor employment decisions also causes great harm over time. All that is required is that dismissal be reasonable, that reasons are not arbitrary or capricious, that documentation exists, and that procedural and substantive due process is observed. Although courts can be severe, they are also perceptive in that dismissal may stand even when constitutional infractions were merely incidental.

WHAT IS THE ROLE OF STAKEHOLDERS?

Our discussion in this chapter has great consequence for boards, administrators, staff, and community laypersons. The most obvious consequence relates to the massive costs of personnel that drive approximately 80% of every school district's budget. An equally important consequence is that personnel decisions represent the true resources of a district, so that human capital is the most effective investment a district can make. At the same time, the district's ability to reach its goals depends entirely on staff.

So what is the role of stakeholders? When viewed as a process, the events examined in this chapter (projecting enrollment, determining staffing needs, recruiting, selecting, compensating, and retaining quality personnel) are much of the essence of budgeting. When these elements are done right, the opportunity for success in providing good education for children is greatly enhanced. When done poorly, disaster is certain. For boards, a constitutional obligation to carry out education rests in the relationship between the budget and staffing. For administrators, the success of creating and balancing the budget is at stake, along with having to live with bad decisions if staffing and budgeting are badly done. For teachers, career success and stability and happiness are the sum of budgeting for personnel. And for laypersons, the climate of the community and the economic and personal vitality of everyone, including children, is at stake. In essence, *budgeting for personnel drives reve-*

---

10. *Board of Regents v. Roth,* 408 U.S. 564 (1972).

nues, expenditures, and programs at the most fundamental level—a level that interests all stakeholders who increasingly expect to participate in school decision making.

SUGGESTED FOLLOW-UP PROJECTS

♦ Talk to your district's personnel director to outline the functions of that office. Make a list of duties, prioritizing from highest to lowest, including estimates of time spent on each of these functions. Explore the coordination between the personnel and budget offices.

♦ Obtain a copy of your district's salary schedule(s) for employee groups and analyze the structure of each. Experiment with changes to the salary schedule structure, noting the impact of changes that would be popular in your district—for example, use changes proposed during last year's negotiations or the current year, depending on when you are carrying out this project.

♦ Obtain a copy of your state's professional negotiations law and familiarize yourself with the mandatory and permissive aspects.

♦ Obtain negotiations documents from your local teachers' association and analyze the impact of proposals being offered for consideration.

♦ Talk to your local teacher union representative and a school district representative to obtain a balanced view on the positive and negative aspects of personnel-related budget issues.

♦ Volunteer to serve on your school district's negotiations team.

7

BUDGETING FOR INSTRUCTION

THE BIG PICTURE

Our journey in this book has provided us with an understanding of broad school funding concepts, with the ultimate goal of examining the individual tasks of budgeting. A look back across the first six chapters confirms our progress: That is, we have spent much time considering the modern context of schools, the dynamic social milieu in which school funding policy is made, the sources of school funding, the gravity of handling school money, the general process of budgeting, and the major costs associated with personnel. The big picture has been steadily narrowing the examination of each specific element of budgeting. And so it is that we arrive at budgeting for instruction, because it is sensible to turn next to a look at money and classrooms—a topic of intense interest to education's stakeholders.

As always, our discussion is framed by a series of questions progressing from general to specific. It makes sense to begin by asking: What is instructional planning? Where do mission and goals fit, and what is the role of districts and individual schools in instructional planning? At least part of the answer to such questions lies in other issues of organizational structure. Most importantly, how are schools in a particular district organized? Answering this question drives many other decisions, including choices about budget practices. Once these items are laid out, we should ask questions about actual instructional budgets. For example, what is the role and size of instructional budgets? What are the sources of instructional revenues? What are the elements of budgeting for instruction? What does an instructional budget look like? With these questions, we continue deeper into the world of school money.

THE PLANNING FUNCTION

Our emphasis in this book on strategizing for positive learning organizations makes it clear that planning is a significant activity in successful school districts. The ability to see ahead and plan accordingly was strikingly clear in Chapter 6, when we said that once enrollment is known, staffing is also known, and that once staffing is known, most costs are automatically known. These are strong arguments for planning, that is, careful planning for instruction because students and teachers are the key actors in the teaching and learning process. To successfully plan for instructional budgeting thus requires an understanding of planning generally and of the instructional mission of schools.

What Is Instructional Planning?

Our experience as administrators has taught us many lessons about organizing and operating schools, with three overriding realities. The first reality is that good instructional planning comes only as the result of hiring experts who envision and direct the teaching and learning process. The second reality is that good instruction cannot happen without the support of a deliberate financial plan. The third reality is that good instruction requires something that is inseparable from the first two realities—that is, the ability to plan based on mission and goals.

District Mission and Goals

Mission and goal statements have become cornerstones of education in the last several years. Although everyone probably always knew or assumed the value of guiding statements, positive benefit has come from consciously focusing on mission and goal statements. The primary value has been that once such statements are made publicly, the performance burden increases noticeably. Although some people may question the broad sweep of mission and goal statements, suggesting that anybody knows them to be true, there is an increased duty to the district when it professes mission statements, such as "All Children Can Learn." Although such beliefs should be the firm conviction of all stakeholders in education, history reveals that schools and society have not always believed that all children can learn, and the proof lies in the heated debates about the inherent value of special education and compensatory programs. Those debates are beyond the scope of this textbook, but it is sufficient to say that a mission statement frames the attitude of schools, so that the whole mindset of an organization can be driven by a mission that sounds simplistic but has the effect of focusing attitudes and performance on a promise made publicly.

The same is true of goal statements. Although a mission statement is meant to be broadly exhortative, goal statements become specific and are often performance-based. For example, districts may adopt goal statements such as, "all children will reach at least the 50th percentile on grade-level standardized tests before passing to the next grade," or "all high school seniors will pass a criterion-referenced test with a state-approved minimum score permitting entry into the state's higher education system without remediation." The range of possibilities for goal statements is endless, but the purpose is simple: to focus the district on outcomes in the larger context of its overall mission. Obviously, both mission and goal statements have strong budget implications, so much so that budgeting for instruction becomes the centerpiece of all planning aimed at carrying out mission and goal statements.

School Mission and Goals

Mission and goal statements are typically extended to individual schools within a district. Although somewhat redundant to restate goals, it is important to spend time and energy building commitment to organizational and school goals. Very often, mission and goal statements in individual schools are more specific than at the district level because schools have unique personalities and needs that vary substantially across the same district. Although individual school mission and goal statements should not run counter to district objectives, school statements should extensively reflect program strengths and target the particular needs of their populations.

The budgetary implications of school mission and goal statements are significant. As we will see later, districts often provide great latitude for individual schools to pursue their goals. It is reasonable to believe that because schools have different needs, expenditures may differ because of those needs and preferences. Just as at the district level, mission and goals are useful planning tools in individual schools by focusing on outcomes, which in turn should drive instructional costs.

The planning function is thus one of determining district and school mission and goals, supported by other activities in the district that determine how it spends money. Clearly part of a district's money is spent for noninstructional purposes, but the majority is tied up in costs relating directly to teaching and learning. As we saw in Chapter 6, the bulk of those costs is for personnel, but there remains a significant portion that goes to nonsalary instructional expense. These latter costs are the focus of this chapter, together with how instructional expenditure decisions are made—decisions based in significant part on how school organizations are structured.

ORGANIZATIONAL OPTIONS

Instructional planning raises the issue of how schools are structured. We alluded to organizational options in Chapter 6 when we talked about budgeting strategies. It is clear, for example, that schools involved in site-based leadership will be structured differently from schools operating under a more centralized hierarchy. Because instructional decisions are strongly influenced by organizational design, it is important to examine some options before considering how instructional budgeting might occur.

How Are Schools Organized?

Instructional budgeting is highly dependent on district organizational design. Although there are many variations, districts are fundamentally driven by administrative leadership style. The most common organizational designs include varying degrees of centralization, management teams, and site-based leadership. These designs drive most planning and decision-making processes.

Centralized Structure

Predictably, in school districts that are highly centralized, most decisions are made in a closely controlled central office environment at the superintendent's level, and budgets are tightly controlled. As a general rule, centralized organizations are committed to line item or program budgeting, and there is usually an attempt to make uniform allocations to schools as an expression of even-handedness. Centralization usually is not complete, however, in that it is often characterized by degrees of delegation. But in all cases, delegation of decision-making ultimately is accompanied by strict reporting and accountability.

Centralized control has sizable benefits and drawbacks. Among the benefits is the concept that the central office is ultimately responsible and that top leaders should have the necessary expertise to make the most important decisions. An additional benefit is organizational efficiency, as there is no room for indecisiveness if leaders are strong individuals. On the downside is the obvious fact that decision-making and ownership are not shared, so that endorsement of mission and goals by those who are not the decision makers is more mandated than voluntary. In such organizations, there is typically little involvement of staff at any level in budgeting and only marginal involvement in instructional planning.

Management Teams

Although there are relatively few highly centralized districts still in existence, use of management teams has grown rapidly. Management teams represent a middle ground between complete centralization and decentralization. This concept argues that more heads are better than one, although many earmarks of centralization remain. The basic structure finds most big decisions made by central office staff who advise the superintendent. Central office staff, however, may often seek advice from groups within the district.

Management teams also carry benefits and drawbacks. A clear benefit comes from advice more broadly gathered, often by floating trial balloons among senior officials before any controversial decisions are made public. Benefits also include the checks and balances of constituent consultation, and much efficiency of central decision-making is preserved. On the downside, people may complain that input is not taken seriously, or that advisement is designed to seek preferred answers. In such organizations, centralization is still very evident, but budgets and instructional decisions are more widely delegated.

Site-Based Management

Although no data indicate how many districts are still highly centralized, many districts have tried to step away from that image; indeed, it is difficult to imagine that such organizations could exist for long given demands by today's employees and other stakeholders to have a voice in organizational decision-making. Participatory expectations have given rise to site-based management (SBM) on a fairly wide scale, including instances where SBM has been written into law.

Perhaps the biggest modern impetus for SBM in schools began with the massive education reform legislation enacted in Kentucky in 1990, as that state was ordered to fix a constitutionally flawed education system. In responding to the state supreme court, the legislature ordered total restructuring of schools. The Kentucky Education Reform Act of 1990 was a monumental piece of legislation that required local school boards to implement school-based decision-making vested in site councils comprised of parents, teachers, and principals. These persons were given substantial responsibility, including management of schools on a daily basis. For example, the Kentucky law charged site councils with the following:

- Setting school policy to provide an environment to enhance student achievement
- Dividing the staff into committees by areas of interest for the purpose of making recommendations to the council
- Determining the number of persons employed in each job and making personnel decisions on vacancies
- Determining instructional materials and support services
- Determining curriculum, including needs assessment, curriculum development, alignment with state standards, technology utilization, and program appraisal
- Assigning use of staff time
- Assigning students to classes and programs
- Determining the schedule of the school day and week
- Determining use of school space during the day
- Planning and resolving issues of instructional practice
- Implementing discipline and classroom management
- Selecting extracurricular programs and determining policies relating to participation
- Administering the school budget, including discretionary funds, activity and other school funds, maintenance, supplies, and equipment
- Assessing student progress, including testing and reporting to parents, students, board, community, and the state
- Creating school improvement and professional development plans
- Coordinating parent, citizen, and community participation

The demands by the Kentucky legislature left no question about its dramatic intent. The rules had changed, and the purpose of putting stakeholders in charge of a decentralized system was clear. Similar legislation passed in

Texas in 1990, and numerous other states copied the basic design in subsequent years. Although the form varies among states today, the principles of SBM underlie many current laws and practices, and the underlying rationale is always the same: Stakeholders want a strong voice in schools; expertise exists among educators and noneducators alike; and effective decisions are often best made at the school site.

Predictably, site-based leadership designs have benefits and drawbacks. A clear benefit is that it stands as the epitome of the concept of shared decision-making in which all stakeholders are extensively involved. Although not all states mandating SBM nor all school districts voluntarily adopting it have gone to the lengths seen in Kentucky, it is also a real benefit that parents and communities have little ground to stand on when complaining that schools are unresponsive. On the downside, the efficiency of professional decision-making is lost as inexpert people become intimately involved in complex decisions. Additionally, the many sensitive areas in SBM can be a source of legal and ethical concern as, for example, personnel decisions are made by site councils. Further, the potential for inequity may increase as some schools will inevitably perform better and create better financial and parental support structures.

Budget implications of SBM are self-evident and applicable regardless of how completely the model is implemented. Although the model varies according to local preference or state statute, schools must take far more responsibility for revenues and expenditures—tasks that were formerly a central office domain. Individual schools may have to choose between supplies and personnel, or between facilities and student activities, and greatly increased emphasis is placed on school performance and partnership. As a consequence, decision-making latitude is gained, but a heavy burden falls on individual schools and stakeholders (boards, central office administrators, principals, staffs, parents, and other site council members) to agree on mission and goals, to gather and distribute resources, and to produce outcomes in response to new latitude. The shift is fundamental at all levels: that is, under SBM the central office takes on a role of broad oversight, whereas the individual school becomes the nucleus of authority, power, and activity.

In sum, individual schools are taking on new powers, even under more centralized organizational designs because laws and the public are seeking more control of educational priorities and outcomes. Stakeholders are now a familiar group—indeed, this entire book speaks to school boards, policy makers, administrators, staffs, parents, and laypersons as leaders in schools. It accordingly behooves all leaders to understand issues of organizational design to identify the parameters of appropriate and effective leadership, including determinations of the following:

♦ Who has responsibility for establishing the overall level of expenditure in a district and school?

♦ Who has responsibility for establishing expenditures for each major program or organizational unit?

- Who has responsibility for selecting specific resources within the allotted dollar amounts for each program?
- Who has responsibility for curriculum selection?
- Who has responsibility for new programs or for eliminating current programs?
- Who has responsibility for establishing salaries and benefits?
- Who hires personnel?
- Who decides which items and amounts will be cut if needed?
- Who establishes capital budgets and decides how facilities and equipment are allocated?
- Are there serious disagreements on these or other questions?

These critical issues drive all aspects of budget planning. But regardless of district structure, there are common elements to budgeting for instruction that extend beyond organizational design. As a result, we should take additional time to continue with budgeting issues that affect instruction.

INSTRUCTIONAL BUDGET CONCEPTS

As we have said repeatedly throughout this book, all parts of a budget are linked together. Numbers of students drive staffing patterns, both of which in turn drive revenues and expenditures. We actually began discussing instructional budgets when we first studied demographic needs of children, state aid formulas, envisioning educational programs, compensating staff, and so forth. In truth, we covered a huge part of instructional budgets when we considered personnel costs. The next step is to make sure our discussion has considered the total picture of instructional costs.

What Are Instructional Budgets?

We can begin by asking, exactly what are instructional budgets? The question can be answered in several ways.

One reply is that the instructional budget is that portion of the total budget that remains after excluding noninstructional costs. By answering this way, the costs of food service, capital outlay, in-service education, transportation, debt service, and most other separate operating funds are excluded. As such, the definition defaults to the general fund as the best description of instructional expense. Although not entirely accurate, it is useful to think of instructional costs in this way because direct instructional expense is what most people really mean. Using this logic, it is accurate to think of the general fund in this manner because the general fund in fact pays the vast majority of certified and classified staff salaries, buys instructional supplies, and pays for a large part of other operating expenses associated with daily operation of school buildings and instructional programs. By this definition, about 87% of a typical district's general fund budget goes to instruction (excluding business operations and maintenance) as seen in Figure 7.1.

Figure 7.1. How Does a District Spend Its Money?

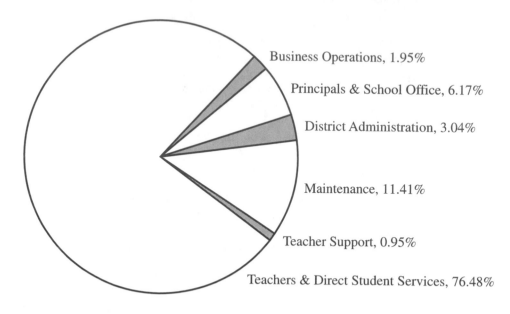

A second answer is to say that the instructional budget is that portion of a total budget after subtracting all salary and nonteaching supply costs. By this definition, instructional budgets are not as large, but it neatly underscores the reality that the vast majority of education's costs lie in instructional staff, and it also illustrates that all other operations are funded by very low percentages of the budget. In fact, logic again dictates that if instructional salaries and other direct instructional costs are removed, schools operate all current noninstructional services on only a small fraction of total general fund budgets.

A third answer is to say that the instructional budget includes all costs going directly to students. This includes teachers, supplies and equipment, special education, and other essential services such as librarians, counselors, and nurses, as well as transportation—all of which make up about 76% of the budget, as seen in Figure 7.2. Including the professional and physical environment changes the mix and makes it fuzzier (Figure 7.3), but has merit in that students clearly receive benefits greater than just direct instruction, further illustrating that the cost of education is more complex than just teacher salaries. In fact, the strongest argument for an inclusive view is that all parts go together so tightly that direct instruction would not be very effective if it were not for each of the many contributions such as warm classrooms, safe and clean buildings and grounds, nutrition and health services, and other system costs as finally seen in Figure 7.4 (p. 212).

(Text continues on page 212.)

Figure 7.2. Direct Student Costs

Direct Student Costs = 76.48%

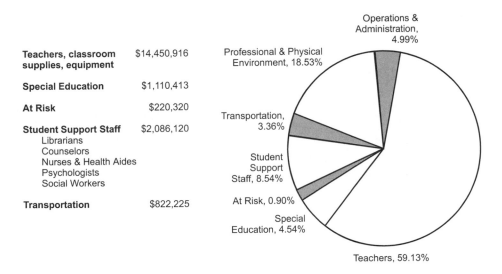

Teachers, classroom supplies, equipment	$14,450,916
Special Education	$1,110,413
At Risk	$220,320
Student Support Staff	$2,086,120
Librarians	
Counselors	
Nurses & Health Aides	
Psychologists	
Social Workers	
Transportation	$822,225

Figure 7.3. Professional and Physical Environment

Principal & School Office
- Principal
- Vice Principal
- Secretary & Clerks
- Office Supplies

Improving Teaching
- Staff development workshops
- Curriculum
- Inservice

Maintenance & Utilities
- Director of Plant Facilities
- Custodians
- Maintenance & Grounds Crew
- Utilities
- Water & Trash
- Security Officers
- Insurance

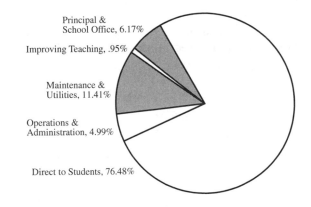

Figure 7.4. Running the System

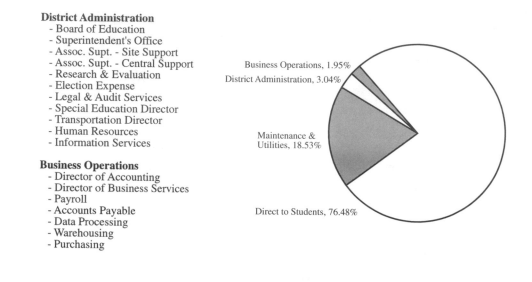

District Administration
  - Board of Education
  - Superintendent's Office
  - Assoc. Supt. - Site Support
  - Assoc. Supt. - Central Support
  - Research & Evaluation
  - Election Expense
  - Legal & Audit Services
  - Special Education Director
  - Transportation Director
  - Human Resources
  - Information Services

Business Operations
  - Director of Accounting
  - Director of Business Services
  - Payroll
  - Accounts Payable
  - Data Processing
  - Warehousing
  - Purchasing

Business Operations, 1.95%
District Administration, 3.04%
Maintenance & Utilities, 18.53%
Direct to Students, 76.48%

Although there are other useful ways to look at instructional budgets, the most important features have already been laid out. Probably the most productive way to think of instructional budgets is to use the ≥80% method, remembering that all remaining money must cover other general fund costs, including teaching supplies. This view is also helpful because it shows that the role and size of instructional budgets are very significant, in that instruction (broadly defined) is almost everything in the current operating budget and is supported by other funds that carry out the "other" business of schools. In contrast, our view in this chapter is narrower because we are concerned for the moment with only that portion after salaries and some operating costs are known. In essence, instructional budgets are partly defined by a district, with the most salient fact resting in how money is allocated to people in decision-making roles because this determines how any available funds get spent.

What Are the Sources of Revenue?

The discussion in earlier chapters of revenue sources deserves some expansion, in that we are now in the operational phase of budgeting. Our discussion laid out a revenue scheme made up of federal, state, and local money. However, these sources only represent money coming into a district from external sources in the macro-perspective and did not develop the impact of such money on individual schools. These and other sources actually make up a range of revenues that school districts receive and allocate, using one of the budgeting philosophies discussed earlier as well.

External Sources

Most external revenue comes from three sources. Federal aid to education is mostly categorical, targeted at special federal interests such as compensatory education, special education, desegregation, and so forth. At times federal aid has been in the form of a block grant, in which Congress has determined that districts should have fewer restrictions on how money is spent, provided it can be shown that the money benefits children. General federal aid also exists, although the vast majority of federal funds are targeted to Congressional interests. Almost all federal money is "flowthrough" funding, meaning that states are the intermediary recipients and are required to pass revenue on to districts under federal regulations. Additionally, districts must be able to show that money reached individual schools and students and was not commingled with money from other sources. The most distinguishing feature of federal aid, however, is its relatively minor status in the total revenue scheme, with a national average of about 7%. State revenue comes to qualifying districts through a state aid formula. As we saw in Chapter 3, state aid formulas generally are meant to grant aid inversely to ability to pay—that is, poor districts often receive greater aid than wealthier districts. The entirety of Chapter 3 was devoted to describing variations on aid formulas, noting that states rely on property, sales, and income taxes to fund the state's share of aid formulas. The distinguishing features of state aid are the growing dependence of districts on such aid and the laws in some states on how districts must account for expenditures, either as discussed in Chapter 4 or as a consequence of site-based management as seen earlier in this current chapter. At the present time, state aid ranges from a low 29% to 90%, with an average 50% across all states (see Chapter 2).

Local revenue comes to districts primarily through property taxes. As seen earlier, local revenue is frequently contentious because citizens are tempted to regard local taxes as the last chance to protest the cost of government. It has been a documented fact that tax levies have been increasingly difficult to pass in the last few decades, with no sign of lowered resistance. In a few states, local districts have the authority to levy income, sales, or sumptuary taxes—such authority, however, is rare and relatively unproductive because of tax limitations and tax base overload. Obviously, the distinguishing feature of local revenue is its visibility to patrons, a feature that can be a double-edged sword. At the present time, nationally about 43% of school revenue is raised locally, although varying widely within states.

District Revenue Structures

The previous section was a short review of what we learned in earlier chapters. The unexplored feature of revenue now enters, in that money coming into the district must be distributed. Again, familiar concepts enter into play. In a centralized district, money is gathered into the central office and distributed using a philosophy such as line item budgeting or program planning and budgeting systems. In more decentralized districts, site-based budgeting may be used. But in all instances, care must be taken to provide an overarching structure to guard against unfairness in distribution, ensure that all programs are coherent, and guarantee that all children's needs are met.

To meet this goal, districts have options. Highly centralized budgeting makes initial sense, as this structure efficiently allows the district to meet all its obligations for fairness and control. Under this plan, principals gather input from staff and forward purchase requests or work orders to the central office, where senior administrators carefully prioritize requests making sure that each school receives approximately the same overall budget allocation. This process continues by spending down available money according to the priority list. The benefit is clear: Control is present, efficiency is maximized, staff is not burdened with noninstructional financial duties, and all schools are treated neutrally. The drawbacks are equally clear: Control at individual sites is lacking, decisions are made far from the point of need, uniform neutrality may not be what is fairest, and staff is uninvolved.

Another option is to provide block grants to individual schools for selected purposes, although the district continues to keep some items centrally funded. This seeks a middle ground between centralization and site-based budgeting by arguing that some tasks are best handled at the school level, whereas other costs are uninteresting to the individual schools. Maintenance of buildings and grounds, utility costs, transportation, personnel compensation, and so forth are good candidates for centralization. Under this plan, block grants tend to be solely instructional budgets, as does any discretionary money sent to individual schools. The benefits are clear: Individual schools are not saddled with tasks that can be handled more efficiently at the district level, a degree of uniformity across the district is upheld, and individual schools have latitude within the block grant to fund local priorities. The one drawback is significant: Because salaries consume most of a district's budget, block grants may not entail really big money, and schools still queue up for capital projects and other large purchases such as textbooks and major equipment.

The third option, of course, is site-based budgeting. In its purest form, the district merely acts as a funnel, flowing most available dollars to schools. Under this plan, the board gives a charge to each school based on the mission and goals of the district, although schools create their own financial plans to carry out district and school objectives. Although intriguing, reality usually moderates the concept so that site-based budgeting often becomes more an issue of the degree to which centralization is relinquished—that is, it is often the case that site-based budgeting is really an enhanced block grant. The benefits are clear: Moving money and freedom to the individual site confers power on the people who have first-hand knowledge of needs and who have the skills to address local problems. The drawbacks are clear as well: If the district overdoes the concept, staff may rebel against noninstructional duties, some bad decision making is inevitable, and there is real danger that unequal resources and performance will follow—after all, freedom is antithetical to uniformity!

Regardless of which option districts choose, the flow of money is clear. Federal and state monies flow through formulas to local districts, which in turn decide whether to centralize or decentralize fiscal decision-making. Resources at the district level are basically limited to tax dollars, although districts may benefit from gifts, foundations, and partnerships. As we noted very early in this book, however, on the whole, revenue sources are few whereas expenditure opportunities are unending.

School Revenue Structures

It is only reasonable to expect that revenue structures at the school level are fundamentally determined by district revenues and by board policies on distribution. Other revenue that falls outside traditional thinking, however, also may be available to schools. As a result, school revenues derive from two basic sources, one of which has not yet been discussed. These sources are the district and the individual school site.

District revenues have been addressed already in this chapter. The issue, as we detailed, is how much revenue is allocated to individual schools to be used at the discretion of the staff and administration and how that revenue can be used. As we also discussed, this often takes the form of a uniform amount (e.g., a per-pupil dollar amount) to which some restrictions apply. Figure 7.6 (located at the end of this chapter) explores this idea more fully.

Site revenue refers to money generated at the school level beyond what is normally distributed by the district. Most schools receive some site revenue. Schools often apply for state department grants, and states often participate in national grant legislation. In addition, foundations are a source of site revenue. Districts receiving grants could then hold subgrant competitions within the district, with individual schools competing for funds. Schools can also apply directly to corporations, many of which have a good record of funding innovative school projects. Many other grants are available to either districts or school sites, such as those advertised in the Federal Register. Foundations listed in the National Directory of Corporate Giving also fund both site and district projects. Site revenue can also come from local businesses that set up partnerships with individual schools, donating money, time, or materials for good causes. Schools and districts also raise money from internal foundations, booster clubs, and parent organizations. But although site revenue can be both a benefit and concern by creating unequal resources within districts, it nonetheless represents an important funding source.

What Are the Elements of Budgeting for Instruction?

Regardless of whether a district chooses to centralize or decentralize instructional budgeting, there are elements common to the process. In fact, these elements are repeated to some extent at all levels in a district—something we will see later in this chapter when we illustrate an instructional budget for a hypothetical district. Let's assume in advance for the purpose of this analysis that our hypothetical district has chosen to engage in some decentralization and at the same time, retain several efficiencies at the central office level. Our interest, therefore, is fourfold. First, a needs assessment is required to create the educational plan for both the district and each school. Second, the district must determine its revenues and inform schools of allocations. Third, schools must create individual educational and expenditure plans. And fourth, the district must provide overall coordination of these activities.

Needs Assessment

Figure 7.5 identifies many of the important data elements required to build an instructional budget. Figure 7.5 sets out an environmental scan that should be prepared for both the district and each individual school. The scan seeks data targeting many of the conditions we discussed in Chapter 1 and shows how available resources should be prioritized. The scan creates a portrait of the community, the district, and each school so that people in leadership positions can understand the common and unique needs of children. Assuming that our sample district has as a goal to raise student performance on standardized tests and to increase entry rates into colleges and universities, the environmental scan should help identify weaknesses that should become prime targets for increased resources. The political viability of the educational plan also can be tested through the demographic data in the scan. Results of these activities will be used in our sample district at the district level in setting district financial support for programs and by the individual schools in deciding how to spend discretionary funds to meet district goals.

Determining Revenues and Educational Plans

As noted earlier, revenues flow from federal, state, district, and site sources. Chapter 5 identified the steps in creating district budgets, and this chapter points out additional decisions resulting in revenue to individual schools. In our sample district, assume that the district has set uniform per-pupil allocations and further assume that individual school sites have taken the initiative to secure some external funding for enhancement purposes. At this point, the educational plan can be built and should address the priorities of the district and school site, as well as any concerns identified by the environmental scan. In effect, the process calls for setting short-term, intermediate, and long-range priorities for the district, each school and grade level, programs, departments, and classrooms in such a way that resources are matched to needs by creating program based budgets.

District Coordination

Regardless of the degree of budget decentralization, all districts must assume responsibility for overall coordination of every aspect of the budget. Only school boards may spend money, and the law assigns responsibility for all educational programs to the board. Additionally, efficiencies are gained through central coordination and management, and budgets are finally the district's responsibility. The budget calendar in Chapter 5 (Figure 5.7, p. 166) provided a clear understanding of the district's role in coordination. In our

Figure 7.5. Environmental Scan

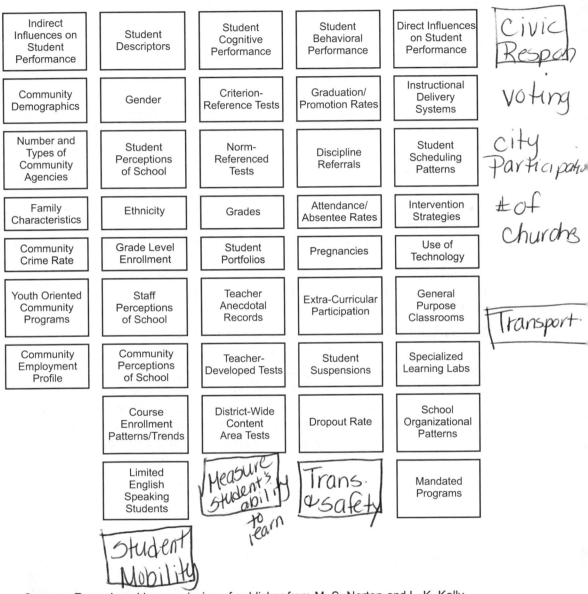

Indirect Influences on Student Performance	Student Descriptors	Student Cognitive Performance	Student Behavioral Performance	Direct Influences on Student Performance
Community Demographics	Gender	Criterion-Reference Tests	Graduation/Promotion Rates	Instructional Delivery Systems
Number and Types of Community Agencies	Student Perceptions of School	Norm-Referenced Tests	Discipline Referrals	Student Scheduling Patterns
Family Characteristics	Ethnicity	Grades	Attendance/Absentee Rates	Intervention Strategies
Community Crime Rate	Grade Level Enrollment	Student Portfolios	Pregnancies	Use of Technology
Youth Oriented Community Programs	Staff Perceptions of School	Teacher Anecdotal Records	Extra-Curricular Participation	General Purpose Classrooms
Community Employment Profile	Community Perceptions of School	Teacher-Developed Tests	Student Suspensions	Specialized Learning Labs
	Course Enrollment Patterns/Trends	District-Wide Content Area Tests	Dropout Rate	School Organizational Patterns
	Limited English Speaking Students			Mandated Programs

Handwritten annotations: Civic Respon., voting, city Participation, # of Churches, Transport., Measure student's ability to learn, Trans. & safety, Student Mobility

SOURCE: Reproduced by permission of publisher from M. S. Norton and L. K. Kelly, *Resource Allocation: Managing Money and People.* The School Leadership Library (Larchmont, NY: Eye On Education, 1997), 39.

sample district, the board has centralized some district-wide activities but has chosen to grant substantial sums of instructional money to individual school sites.

What Does an Instructional Budget Look Like?

As we warned at the outset of this chapter, instructional budgeting cannot be easily examined one piece at a time. The parts of instructional budgeting join tightly—demographics and student needs are revealed through scanning environments and other data collection mechanisms; fund accounting tracks and reveals how money is spent; aid formulas cause educational programs to flourish or wither; liability reduces available revenue; personnel costs and enrollments drive resource levels; and district budgeting philosophies determine how much money is available, how it is spent, and who makes spending decisions. As we also noted, all aspects of the entire budget of a school district can be viewed as the instructional budget, although fund accounting conventions do not regard budgets that way.

Figure 7.6 (pp. 222–227) presents data on our hypothetical district and combines concepts from our study of accounting with the concept of instructional budgeting. In fact, Figure 7.6 is completely comprehensive by going to all issues in all chapters thus far—it even goes beyond by looking at capital outlay and transportation. Figure 7.6 focuses us on the budgeting implications of the chosen organizational structure in our sample district, in that the district has decided to do the following:

♦ *Track* instructional budgets with accounting codes that permit accumulation of data by program

♦ *Decentralize* many budget aspects and retain central office coordination through the board and directorships

♦ *Allocate* uniform amounts per pupil for instructional program purposes

♦ *Retain* overall transportation services at the board level and allocate discretionary transportation budgets to schools

♦ *Decentralize* some aspects of capital outlay and equipment purchases

♦ *Link* expenditures to expected outcomes in a program budgeting model

Consequently, Figure 7.6 illustrates a school district that has acted to locate considerable program and budget authority at the individual school site. Much efficiency is gained through overall district coordination and control of uninteresting topics like maintenance, repair, and construction of buildings. School sites are free, however, to determine how programs are executed, including responsibility for sizable amounts of discretionary money. In our sample district of about 7,700 pupils, total discretionary money assigned to all sites is $892,278—a sum meant to be spent on strategically targeted school needs. The fund accounting structure permits program and expenditure analysis, and proposed expenditures are justified by indicating expected outcomes resulting from purchases. School staffs, administrators, and site councils have authority to move money among funds within reason.

Figure 7.6 appears complex, and it is—in the sense that it carries out a very important task of creating the educational plan for the district and multiple school sites. It makes sense, however, when viewed first in terms of the overarching scheme and then in terms of what it means to each individual school. A school principal receiving this document should see it as a planning guide to direct the educational process in the district and each individual school. Assuming principals will work with their staffs and school site councils to create the instructional budgets for the schools, the following series of questions makes a complex task and a lengthy planning document much more manageable:

- ◆ General Background Questions
  - What is the district's overall mission?
  - What are the district's goal statements?
  - What is my school's overall mission?
  - What are my school's goal statements?
  - What were the results of the district's environmental scan?
  - What were the results of my school's environmental scan?
  - Does my school's educational plan reflect these needs?
  - How can I spend my school's budget to address these needs?
- ◆ General Budget Questions and Answers
  - Where are the account codes I need to make purchases? (See the beginning of Figure 7.6, p. 222)
  - Can I accumulate program costs? (Use the account codes)
  - What does my budget have to cover? (See the instructions in Figure 7.6, p. 223)
  - How much money do I have for instructional programs? (See the remaining portions of Figure 7.6, pp. 224–227)
  - What if I need more money? (Generate site revenue or seek more district funds)
  - How will I be accountable for outcomes? (Provide program outcomes for each purchase. Account codes will accumulate costs over time. The district will help determine if outcomes are being met)
  - What do I do when I have a question? (Contact the central office)

The budget structure in Figure 7.6 is general in scope, but it clearly lays out the underlying philosophy and facts. From Figure 7.6, the principal, staff, and school site council know to turn to board documents to learn about the district's mission and goals. They know they must be intimately familiar with the school's environmental scan, and they know to link the scan to student needs and to use these elements to construct the educational plan. They also know that many resource needs will be handled by the district such as text-book adoptions, and that each school site has been allotted money on a per-pupil basis—in fact, principals can find their schools listed, know the exact amount of discretionary funds for instructional programs, transporta-tion, and capital outlay, and understand that uniform per-pupil allocation is the basis for all funding. Principals also know that program budgeting is fun-damentally at their discretion and that accountability, tied to mission, goals, and school profile, will follow for decisions that are made at the site level.

WRAP-UP

Obviously, not all school districts are ready to follow the hypothetical site-based organizational design set out in Figure 7.6. District structure drives all resource decisions, and available revenue curtails all decisions. The important thing is that instructional budgeting consumes most school resources, leaving only the details of how to slice the pie—that is, district choices about local preference in resource allocation.

Regardless of whether districts choose to become more accountable or whether they are forced to do so through legislation mandating constituent involvement in site councils or other structures, the budget will be the focus of increased interest and accountability because the surest way to get atten-tion is to talk about public money. In the case of budgeting for instruction, it should not be otherwise: Money pays for schools, and schools provide opportunities for children. In truth, instructional budgeting is the heart of education.

SUGGESTED FOLLOW-UP PROJECTS

- Make an appointment with your district's curriculum director to discuss the nature of instructional budgeting in your school dis-trict. Obtain a copy of the district's mission and goal statements and ask if or how the district goes about curriculum-based budgeting.

- In your interview with the curriculum director, use the series of planning questions appearing in this chapter as a discussion guide. For example, ask questions about who has responsibility for establishing the overall level of instructional spending, who sets budgets for each major program or school, who selects the curriculum, who has responsibility for new programs or for eliminating current programs, and so on.

- If your district uses site-based budgeting, obtain a copy of your school's building-based budget (e.g., see Figure 7.6, p. 224, which is a sample instructional building budget). Talk to the school principal to analyze how decisions are made at the individual school site. If your district does not use school-site budgeting, explore the level of discretionary funding available at each school site and discuss the decision-making process with your principal.

Figure 7.6. Sample Instructional Budget

General Fund: School Program Codes

Line items can be refined or expanded in monitoring activities in your school or program. Contact the Director of Business for information.

ELEMENTARY	Year	Fund	Funct.	Obj.	Bldg.	Prog.
Kindergarten	1	-00	-1000	-610	-xx	-01
Reading						-02
Math						-03
Language Arts						-04
Social Studies						-05
Science						-06
Textbooks						-07
Tchg supplies						-08
School office						-09
Postage						-10
Site council						-11
Grants (list)						-31

JUNIOR HIGH						
Phys. Ed.	1	00	1000	610	xx	-01
Voc. Arts						-02
Home Ec.						-03
Art						-04
Science						-05
Band						-06
Vocal music						-07
Languages						-08
Math						-09
Social Studies						-10
Publications						-11
Tchg. supplies						-12
School office						-13
Postage						-14
Site council						-15
Grants (list)						-31

HIGH SCHOOL						
Phys. Ed.	1	00	1000	610	xx	-01
Voc. Arts						-02
Home Ec.						-03
Art						-04
Science						-05
Band						-06
Vocal music						-07
Languages						-08
Math						-09
Social Studies						-10
Publications						-11
Tchg supplies						-12
School office						-13
Postage						-14
Site council						-15
Grants (list)						-31

INSTRUCTIONS TO PRINCIPALS

You are responsible for all instructional money assigned to your school as outlined in this document. You should gather input from staff members and your site council. All budget requests and expenditures should be tied to the site plan for your school.

These instructions provide: (a) account codes used by central office to track cost of programs in schools—any purchase request needs to show the right codes; (b) general notes to guide you on how the district expects you to code your purchases; (c) a list of instructional programs that have separate budgets; (d) a listing of all general fund budget allocations—it is here that you know how much you have for your school for all accounts; and (e) sample budget request forms.

GENERAL NOTES

1. Teaching supplies includes general supplies, paper, folders, ink cartridges, etc.
2. School office includes general office expenditures, professional materials, printing, student assemblies, and reserve funds.
3. Materials should be purchased from program budgets: examples include magazine subscriptions, and other direct program expenses. Do not include textbook or equipment purchases here.
4. Remember to include shipping and handling when preparing purchase orders.
5. Transportation costs for program use will be charged to your school. This does not include transportation on regular routes before/after school.
6. Advance payment purchases are not allowed. Staff may not be reimbursed for out-of-pocket purchases.
7. No purchase will be approved without a purchase order in advance.
8. Repair of district-owned equipment will not be charged to schools. Routine expenses like reeds, pads, printer cartridges, etc. will be charged to programs.
9. Major purchases such as textbooks, curriculum adoptions, achievement tests and so forth are budgeted separately—see OTHER PROGRAMS below.

OTHER INSTRUCTIONAL PROGRAMS

CURRICULUM AND INSTRUCTION

Major purchases district-wide are budgeted separately, rather than charged to school budgets. The following categories are developed and administered by the Director of Curriculum and the Directors of Elementary and Secondary Education:

TEXTBOOKS	STAFF DEVELOPMENT	SPECIAL EDUCATION
CURRICULUM	GUIDANCE	TESTING

INSTRUCTIONAL MEDIA

The Director of Media Services coordinates all media services through school principals and librarians.

STUDENT ACTIVITIES

Athletics, debate, forensics, music contests, dramatics, and equipment purchases will be subsidized by the district. Separate line items will be set up for each activity. Submit all purchase requests according to the budget calendar.

GENERAL FUND INSTRUCTIONAL BUDGETS BY SCHOOL

The board of education annually sets the per-pupil allocation based on revenue availability and the recommendations of principals, staff and site councils. It must be understood that the board pays many other expenses centrally— amounts shown here should be considered discretionary in terms of how schools expend.

ELEMENTARY INSTRUCTIONAL PROGRAMS ($27.50 per pupil)

Washington School	(230 pupils)	$6,325
Adams School	(326 pupils)	$8,965
Jefferson School	(270 pupils)	$7,425
Madison School	(189 pupils)	$5,198
Monroe School	(276 pupils)	$7,590
J. Q. Adams School	(250 pupils)	$6,875
Jackson School	(479 pupils)	$13,172
Van Buren School	(159 pupils)	$4,372
Harrison School	(233 pupils)	$6,408
Tyler School	(362 pupils)	$9,955
Polk School	(198 pupils)	$5,445
Taylor School	(289 pupils)	$7,948
Fillmore School	(432 pupils)	$11,880
Pierce School	(459 pupils)	$12,622
Buchanan School	(316 pupils)	$8,690
Instruction-Elementary Totals:		$122,870

JUNIOR HIGH INSTRUCTIONAL PROGRAMS ($58 per pupil)

Lincoln School	(601 pupils)	$34,858
Johnson School	(598 pupils)	$34,684
Instruction-Junior High Totals:		$69,542

HIGH SCHOOL INSTRUCTIONAL PROGRAMS ($75.18 per pupil)

Hayes High	(1076 pupils)	$80,894
Garfield High	(986 pupils)	$74,127
Instruction-High School Totals:		$155,021
INSTRUCTION TOTAL	7,729 pupils	$347,433

INSTRUCTIONAL MEDIA ($19.25 per pupil)

Books, periodicals, AV supplies, teacher center, staff $148,783

HIGH SCHOOL ACTIVITY PROGRAMS (each school)

Debate and forensics	$10,500
Dramatics	$1,000
Music contests	$3,250
Band uniform rotation (carries over budget years)	$5,000
ACTIVITY TOTAL 2 HIGH SCHOOLS (×2) =	$39,500

TECHNOLOGY REQUESTS

Instructional technology and computer services will be coordinated through the IMC coordinator, in cooperation with the District Technology Committee.

FURNITURE AND OTHER EQUIPMENT

Direct all requests to central office for district-wide purchasing.

TRANSPORTATION BUDGETS BY SCHOOL

EDUCATIONAL FIELD TRIPS ($3.20 per pupil)

Washington School	(230 pupils)	$736
Adams School	(326 pupils)	$1,043
Jefferson School	(270 pupils)	$864
Madison School	(189 pupils)	$605
Monroe School	(276 pupils)	$883
J. Q. Adams School	(250 pupils)	$800
Jackson School	(479 pupils)	$1,533
Van Buren School	(159 pupils)	$509
Harrison School	(233 pupils)	$746
Tyler School	(362 pupils)	$1,158
Polk School	(198 pupils)	$634
Taylor School	(289 pupils)	$925
Fillmore School	(432 pupils)	$1,382
Pierce School	(459 pupils)	$1,469
Buchanan School	(316 pupils)	$1,011
	Field Trips-Elementary Total:	$14,298

JUNIOR HIGH FIELD TRIPS ($3.85 per pupil)

Lincoln School	(601 pupils)	$2,314
Johnson School	(598 pupils)	$2,302
	Field Trips-Junior High Total:	$4,616

HIGH SCHOOL FIELD TRIPS ($3.85 per pupil)

Hayes High	(1076 pupils)	$4,143
Garfield High	(986 pupils)	$3,796
	Field Trips-High School Total:	$7,939
FIELD TRIP TOTALS		$26,852

ATHLETICS

Lincoln School	$9,000
Johnson School	$9,000
Hayes High	$27,500
Garfield High	$27,500
ATHLETIC TOTALS	$73,000

ACTIVITIES ($1.90 jr. high, $5.65 sr. high)

Lincoln School	$1,142
Johnson School	$1,136
Hayes High	$6,079
Garfield High	$5,571
ACTIVITY TOTALS	$13,928

DEBATE and FORENSICS

Hayes High	$7,000
Garfield High	$7,000
DEBATE/FORENSIC TOTALS	$14,000

CAPITAL OUTLAY BUDGETS BY SCHOOL

Major capital projects are the district's responsibility. Schools have a small amount available for minor equipment needs. Money for copiers is available as shown here. Direct all items to central office that are not covered below.

MINOR EQUIPMENT ($4.50 per pupil)

Washington School	(230 pupils)	$1,035
Adams School	(326 pupils)	$1,467
Jefferson School	(270 pupils)	$1,215
Madison School	(189 pupils)	$850
Monroe School	(276 pupils)	$1,242
J. Q. Adams School	(250 pupils)	$1,125
Jackson School	(479 pupils)	$2,156
Van Buren School	(159 pupils)	$716
Harrison School	(233 pupils)	$1,048
Tyler School	(362 pupils)	$1,629
Polk School	(198 pupils)	$891
Taylor School	(289 pupils)	$1,301
Fillmore School	(432 pupils)	$1,944
Pierce School	(459 pupils)	$2,066
Buchanan School	(316 pupils)	$1,422
Lincoln School	(601 pupils)	$2,704
Johnson School	(598 pupils)	$2,691
Hayes High	(1076 pupils)	$4,842
Garfield High	(986 pupils)	$4,437
	MINOR EQUIPMENT TOTALS	$34,780

SCHOOL EQUIPMENT BUDGETS

Elementary total	$10,000
Lincoln Jr. High	$13,000
Johnson Jr. High	$13,000
Hayes High	$25,000
Garfield High	$25,000
IMC	$16,000
SCHOOL EQUIPMENT TOTALS	$102,000

COPIER BUDGETS

Elementary total	$16,000
Lincoln Jr. High	$15,000
Johnson Jr. High	$15,000
Hayes High	$15,000
Garfield High	$15,000
Central office	$16,000
COPIER TOTALS	$92,000

GRAND TOTALS

Total Instructional Budgets	$535,716
Total Transportation Budgets	$26,852
Total Athletics, Activities, and Debate	$100,928
Total Capital Outlay Budgets	$228,780
TOTAL SCHOOL BUDGETS	$892,278

PROGRAM BUDGET REQUEST FORM BY SCHOOL

WASHINGTON ELEMENTARY
2005–06 Budget Year

Program Area: Reading

Code: 4-00-1000-610-80-01

Outcomes: Replaces 1995 copyright collection of storybooks. Children will increase reading time by 20 minutes per pupil.

Supplier: ABC Publishers, Inc.
          12345 State Street
          Uptown, NY 00000-0000

Cost per book:	$9.65
Quantity:	100
Freight:	$37.49
TOTAL:	$1,002.49

8

BUDGETING FOR STUDENT ACTIVITIES

ACTIVITIES AND SCHOOLS

The act of budgeting for the total education of children is wide-ranging and includes the need to fund opportunities outside the traditional classroom setting. A major aspect of budgeting is related to providing a sound financial base for the many student activities supported by school districts today.

There is no doubt that student activities demand very large amounts of time and money. In fact, activities are so central to the life of schools that many public attitudes about education are based almost entirely on the countless activities supported by the modern school district. Although it is unusual for books about school funding to contain much, if any, discussion of activity programs, the topic is so important to a comprehensive view of school money that we have devoted an entire chapter to making sure that activities are regarded as an essential aspect of equal educational opportunity.

As in past chapters, a series of questions forms our discussion about activities and schools. We begin by asking, what is the role of activities? From there we go to the questions most interesting to school boards, administrators, staffs, and other stakeholders. What are activity funds? What are student activity funds? How do these differ from district activity funds? What are the controls on activity funds? What lines of authority exist? What kinds of policies are needed regarding segregation of duties, internal controls on handling cash, and disbursement procedures? What about nonactivity funds such as fee funds? What about sales tax and petty cash? And, of course, we end the chapter with a final word of caution because activity funds are one of the greatest sources of financial problems in schools today.[1]

---

1. For fuller development of student activity fund issues, see David C. Thompson, Chapter 8, "Activity Fund Guidelines," in *Financial Accounting for Local and State School Systems 2003 Edition* (Washington, DC: U.S. Department of Education, NCES, 2004), 157–168.

What Is the Role of Student Activities?

The role of activities in the life of a school cannot be overestimated. Although every school and district is different, an immediate sense of the importance of activities can be gained by merely glancing at the long list of student activity programs supported by nearly every school district today. For example, a typical high school in America may support art clubs, auto clubs, camera clubs, cheerleader clubs, chorus clubs, computer clubs, speech and debate teams, drama and forensics teams, drill teams, electronics clubs, foreign language clubs, journalism clubs, math clubs, marching bands, pep clubs, student government, and athletic booster clubs. These are only a few of the student organizations that surround the really big activities such as football, basketball, volleyball, baseball, track, tennis, cross-country, wrestling, soccer, and other athletic and academic competitions—all of which require resources in the form of sponsors and coaching salaries, travel expenses, transportation, equipment, facilities, and so forth. To resurface a track costs well in excess of $100,000, and it must be remembered that track is hardly a sport that generates much in the way of gate receipts. The point is simply that activities represent a huge financial outlay that is typically not self-funding, so that energy, time, money, and many other issues such as risk and good business practices relating to activities quickly become a school funding concern.

There is a second reason why the role played by student activities should not be underestimated, that is, the importance of activities in the lives of young people. Starting with music and class programs at the elementary grades, small children enthusiastically perform for community audiences. Progressing into the high school years, young people form character and learn to work hard and stay in school as a result of athletic and other programs. In addition, activities encompass programs related to academics, so that activities represent an extension of the school day. Whether school leaders enjoy attending activities or not, they generally learn to support activity programs because they believe that activities are not *extracurricular*—rather, they accurately see activities as part of the *cocurriculum* in ways that deserve genuine support.

Beyond the noble reasons for supporting activity programs is a very practical justification for understanding the important role of activities. School leaders sometimes joke (in all seriousness) that the quality of academic programs is judged by the shine on the floor of the school and by the success of athletic and academic competitions. Good school leaders, however, quickly understand that success in activities and shiny floors boost pride in everything else about schools. Because about 70% of all people in a typical school district do not have children in school, it follows that about 70% of all taxpayers see schools only from a spectator viewpoint—as grandparents, sports fans, and so forth. School appearance and activity programs, then, play an important role in the lives of children, boards, administrators, teachers, policy makers, and the public.

BUDGETING FOR ACTIVITIES

The sheer size of school activity programs underscores the fact that a large amount of money goes to support activities. As we will see, budgeting for activities is both similar and dissimilar to other budget issues explored in this textbook. Similarities follow from the fact that many of the accounting principles seen earlier apply to activity funds, so that revenue and expenditure dimensions and various account structures are familiar. Unlike other funds, however, activity funds are more loosely structured in the sense that fewer controls often exist and may be housed in multiple locations. Statutes controlling activity funds often are more loosely written as well, so that many aspects of activity fund accounting are not mandated. The potential for error and fraud is highest in activity funds, making it essential for all stakeholders in education to budget for activities in ways that both appreciate the contribution of activities to school learning and guard against abuse.

What Are Activity Funds?

Activity funds are legal creations set up in statutes in most states for the purpose of separating money for support of student activities. The unique nature of activity funds is emphasized in that statutes often define activities as cocurricular events, which may be further defined as activities outside the classroom that complement the curriculum. Making such distinction has two advantages. First, it creates the basis for expending district funds in support of activities by equating nonclassroom learning with the academic curriculum. Second, it sets up the mechanism for districts to separately support activities and to account for money spent on activities. The first distinction is especially important because it is reasonable to believe that districts are not authorized to spend resources on programs unrelated to some kind of curriculum. The second distinction is less profound, but it does set up useful controls and permits the existence of student-owned organizations, as will be seen later.

Activity funds are thus accounting funds analogous to the general and special revenue funds in the district's regular budget. Each activity fund is an independent accounting entity created to segregate its financial activity from that of other funds, usually because of special restrictions on how money can be spent. Activity funds may only be spent for statutorily approved purposes, which are usually quite broad and limited only by the intent to spend activity funds for such purposes as athletics, music, special projects, and so forth. As such, activity funds may not be appropriated for any other use. Operation of activity funds, however, is very different from the district's regular budget. As we will see later, the collection, disbursement, and accounting for activity fund monies usually is centralized at the school level, with building principals designated as the activity fund supervisor. Further, activity funds are distinguished by ownership, that is, whether the funds are owned by the district or by student organizations. In addition, the activity fund supervisor is usually responsible for accounting for nonactivity fund monies, including many fee collections, sales tax, and petty cash accounts. To make matters more difficult, the ownership distinction creates collection and disbursement issues. To further complicate the mix is a vague and often wrong perception among organizational sponsors and students regarding uses of activity funds. Thus the school principal has a hard task in being responsible for funds belonging to students, funds belonging to the district, administration of nonactivity funds belonging to the district, collecting and disbursing funds from a school base, transferring certain funds to the district for disbursement, and so forth. The potential for real error and misunderstanding is self-evident.

Student Activity Funds

As we just noted, one of the unique features of activity funds is the distinction of who owns them. There is no question of ownership in the district's regular budget, because the school board has total authority and control subject only to applicable statutes on permissible expenditures. Activity funds, however, are of two types. *Student* activity funds are owned by students, that is, students are the legal owners of certain activity funds and have the right to control how the money is spent, pursuant only to statutes, accounting guidelines, and applicable board policy.

Student activity funds consist of those student activities that involve a student organization. Operationally, students in the organization not only take part in the organization's activities but also are involved in the management of the organization. Examples include many of the clubs and organizations listed earlier. The definition is important for several reasons. Most obvious is that no one in the district other than students can legally expend money from a student activity fund account. In other words, money on deposit in a district-maintained activity fund is not always owned by the district. The other critical reason is subtler, in that districts must be very careful in subsidizing activities because district money could come under student control if not carefully guarded.

The distinction of student ownership is not trivial. For example, on a broader scale many schools have experienced legal problems trying to control organizations like booster clubs and religious groups. Boards have often included such groups in activity fund charts of accounts, but it is best to require groups not directly sponsored by the district to maintain separate bank accounts because inclusion gives the appearance of sponsorship and raises questions of control and ownership.

District Activity Funds

In contrast, *district* activity funds belong to the district. District activity funds support cocurricular activities in which students actively participate but are administered by the school district. Examples of district activities include the many district-sponsored organizations such as choir, band, orchestra, speech and debate, team sports, and so forth. The definition is again important in that the distinguishing feature is that approval to expend these monies rests with the board, rather than students. The accounting process is different also, in that it may be centralized in the district's books, rather than housed in the schools. This structure avoids the problems cited earlier, in that activities supported by the district are accounted for at the district level, and all money is deposited through the district treasurer to the district's bank account.

Again, the distinction of district ownership is not trivial. Boards should maintain control of district resources used to support student activities, and control would be lost by moving district funds into school-level student activity funds. Although parallel activity funds may be redundant, the wise rule is to remember that ownership determines who decides how money is spent within board policy and administrative guidelines.

What Are the Controls on Activity Funds?

The issues raised here suggest that large amounts of money are involved in student activity budgeting and that a complicated process governs what happens at both the district and individual school levels. This raises questions of controls on activity funds, which logically go to further examination of issues such as lines of authority and wise policy development meant to make budgeting and administration easier. Almost nowhere in school budgeting is the word "control" more welcome than in activity funding—all controls are for the welfare of everyone involved. Our years of experience tell us that more administrators are fired for activity fund incompetence than for any other reason.

Lines of Authority

The need for clear lines of authority in handling activity budgets is underscored by our discussion to this point. Segregating activity funds from all other funds in the district and the complications invited by numerous school sites indicate a real need to maintain strict control—for example, gate receipts at an athletic event on a given night may exceed $10,000—assuring that activity budgeting and accounting is no small matter. In fact, it is not unusual for the activity fund chart of accounts at a typical high school to have a fund balance in excess of $100,000. There is almost no smear on a professional reputation as bad as violating a fiduciary trust, and one penny mismanaged is cause for suspicion.

The general guideline for lines of authority for activity funds calls for the board of education to adopt sound policies governing the establishment and operation of all activity funds. Of course, heat always rises, placing the superintendent in charge of administering all board policies. The district treasurer, as the fiscal officer of the district, should be appointed to implement and enforce a system of valid internal control procedures. These persons are responsible for all activity funds in the district, because both student and district activity funds are held by the district and must be reported in the district's financial statements—that is, student-owned funds are agency (fiduciary) funds wherein the district acts as agent for these funds, while district-owned funds are classified as special revenue funds intended for support of student activities.

At the school level, each principal should be designated as the activity fund supervisor. Supervisory designation means the principal is responsible for overall operation of activity funds housed in that school, including collection and deposit of activity fund monies, approval of disbursements from the activity fund, and all bookkeeping responsibilities. The burden is a weighty one because, although custodial duties may be delegated, final responsibility may not. It is precisely this point that gives rise to many of the policies we will note shortly regarding handling of money and multiple safeguards against misuse and embezzlement.

Multiple levels of ownership, responsibility, and other sponsorship give rise to yet one more set of players in the line of authority. Organizational sponsors are often the first line of people to initiate an activity fund transaction, and very often these people do not understand either the process or reasons for the many controls on activity funds. Sponsors need to understand the process of approved purchases, purchase orders, handling of cash, receipts, and so forth—items covered later in this chapter. Although sponsors have no direct line of authority, their presence is necessary but represents still another opportunity for problems if proper procedures for receiving and expending activity funds are not observed.

Suggested Activity Fund Policies

The size of student activity funds and the potential for wrongdoing or error demand that professional accounting and auditing help be obtained to set up effective controls. Nonetheless, a set of general policies should be followed by everyone who deals with student activities and school money. Although an inclusive list is not feasible in a textbook of this nature,[2] useful insights can be given into policies on overall activity fund operation, segregation of duties, internal controls on handling cash, and disbursement of money, because these are the areas representing daily operation and likely pitfalls.

---

2. Individual states may have directive legislation and/or advisory guidelines regarding treatment of activity funds—see each state's statutory requirements for accounting for activity fund monies. More generally, useful references related to activity fund accounting include the following: R. E. Everett, Raymond L. Lows, and Donald R. Johnson, *Financial and Managerial Accounting for School Administrators* (Reston, VA: Association of School Business Officials International, 1996); Governmental Accounting Standards Board, *Guide to Implementation of GASB 34 on Basic Financial Statements—and Management's Discussion and Analysis—for State and Local Government* (Norwalk, CT: GASB, 2000); Association of School Business Officials International, *GASB Statement No. 34: Implementation Recommendations for School Districts, Second Edition* (Reston, VA: Association of School Business Officials International, 2003); and of course, *Financial Accounting for Local and State School Systems 2003 Edition* (Washington, DC: U.S. Department of Education, NCES, 2004).

General Policies

Creation and operation of activity funds require sound controls to ensure safe and effective management of student and district monies. Several of the following bulleted items have already been discussed, whereas others are added to call attention to other potential problems:

♦ *Professional accounting services should be obtained* to set up the activity fund accounting system. All staff and sponsors should be given proper training on activity funding.

♦ *The district treasurer should set up a system of forms and procedures.* Because the district accumulates all student and district activity fund transactions, the district should satisfy itself that controls are in place.

♦ *All activity funds must be approved by the board.* Any request to create a student organization should include a statement of purpose and potential fundraising activity. To avoid confusion and to aid organizational goals, the name of the organization should be descriptive of its purpose.

♦ *The board should formally designate an activity fund supervisor.* Usually there should be only one supervisor at each school or attendance center.

♦ *All fundraising should be approved in advance by the district.* Any group included in the district's chart of accounts for the activity fund should expect the district to approve its activities, including fundraising. It is well known that schools are assumed to have approved all activities, and unauthorized fundraising can create real community relations problems.

♦ *Activity funds should be spent on students.* Although this seems obvious, and it is unlikely that anything else would occur, problems arise when organizations expire with unspent monies on deposit (e.g., senior class). Insofar as possible, money should be spent on those students who raised it.

♦ *Cash basis should strictly apply.* Cash basis requires that no money be spent or encumbered unless an equal or greater amount is already on deposit. This rule is often violated when sponsors or students place phone orders or seek reimbursement on good deals while shopping out of town. Strict adherence to advance purchase orders resolves this problem.

♦ *All activity funds must be audited* along with other funds in the district.

♦ *Activity funds should never be used for any purpose that results in a benefit, loan, or credit* to anyone.

Segregation of Duties

The importance of good general policies on handling student activity funds is underscored by sound business practices relating to segregation of duties. Many errors in bookkeeping can occur inadvertently, and the potential for deliberate mishandling is always in the realm of possibilities. Risk of error and theft can be minimized, however, through a segregation of duties that reinforces general policies, cash controls, and disbursement procedures.

Segregation of duties relates to internal control and speaks to both inadvertent error and to the fact that no one person should be solely responsible for handling money. Daily instances of cash handling occur in all schools, and segregation of duties helps reduce many problems. The activity fund bookkeeper, appointed by the principal, should take the lead on most operations, including collecting activity fund money, preparing deposit slips, making deposits, preparing the fund accounting records, and preparing checks written on the activity fund account. These activities will be examined during an audit and should be periodically reviewed internally as well. In addition, four particular duties need attention. First, although a bookkeeper can prepare checks, no check should bear the bookkeeper's signature. Second, the principal as activity fund supervisor should be the primary signature on checks—in some states, it is required by law that the principal sign all checks. Third, all checks should bear two signatures. Fourth, bank statements must be reconciled monthly with the fund accounting records, and someone other than the bookkeeper should perform this reconciliation. These procedures protect against error and deliberate wrongdoing on the accounting side and serve to back up other internal controls on cash.

Internal Controls on Cash

Modern schools frequently handle large amounts of cash. Yearbook sales, gate receipts, fundraisers, student pictures, and student projects such as vocational and industrial arts result in many thousands of dollars in cash transactions. Cash represents an even greater risk of loss, requiring additional internal controls.

The most important aspects of internal cash controls are well-trained employees and establishing an audit trail to provide physical evidence for each step in all cash transactions. In fact, the audit trail gives more insight to what might be missing rather than showing something was incorrectly done. Although professional accounting advice is required to correctly handle cash, at least the following cash controls must be in place:

♦ *All fund supervisors and sponsors* should be trained and provided with written guidelines on handling cash.
♦ *All forms, receipts, and tickets* should be prenumbered.
♦ *Prenumbered items* should be safeguarded.
♦ *Prenumbered items* should not be printed in-house.
♦ *Persons collecting cash* should be rotated regularly.

♦ *More than one person* should be present when cash is collected.

♦ *No cash collections* should be given to another person without a receipt.

♦ *The bookkeeper* must use prenumbered, bound receipts for all currency and checks received.

♦ *Cash receipts* should be kept intact and may not be used to make change or to make any kind of disbursement.

♦ *The bookkeeper* should make daily deposits. Any undeposited cash should be kept locked safely away.

♦ *Everyone* handling cash should be bonded.

These guidelines seem simple, but it is appalling how often they are violated. Any experienced school leader has seen each of these rules badly abused. Actual examples include frightening stories: for example, principals and sponsors sticking school cash into their wallets or purses, ticket-takers tearing off extra tickets to make the cash and tickets balance, blank prenumbered cash receipts lying carelessly on secretaries' desks, and clerks leaving cash unattended even for only a few moments. Especially appalling is the not uncommon practice of tossing a bank bag of athletic gate receipts into a car trunk to be delivered to the school office the next Monday morning. Under these conditions, it is not difficult to see how people in schools get into big trouble quickly when dealing with activity funds.

Disbursement Procedures

The final area we should address in activity funds is disbursement procedures. Disbursing funds refers to any financial activity in which money leaves an account. This discussion can be short, because some of our other discussion involved disbursement as part of the process. As a result, a bulleted list of guidelines makes these points quickly.

As we noted earlier, activity funds are either student-owned or district-owned. We also noted that student funds are handled at the school level, meaning most activity on these accounts occurs at various sites. District funds are more complicated, in that there can be an extra transaction involved because district funds are accounted for at the district level but may have flowed through a school first. An example makes this clearer. Assume the board has agreed to subsidize students' woodworking projects. Materials are ordered, and the bill arrives. The district pays the entire bill and calculates how much each student owes. Students then make payment to the school office, which makes a deposit to the revolving woodworking activity fund account. The activity fund must then transfer these "district-owned" amounts to the district treasurer for deposit back to the district. It is not as difficult as it seems, but the example underscores the meticulous nature of activity fund budgeting and accounting.

A more typical activity fund transaction simply finds a club or organization wanting to buy something. In that case, advance approval is obtained, a purchase order is written, goods are received, and the bookkeeper makes payment. The opposite is true if money is received: Cash is received, receipted, and deposited. Our interest here runs more toward how to disburse money properly. Accordingly, disbursement procedures for student activity funds are:

- Disbursement requires approval of the student group's sponsor and the activity fund supervisor (usually the school principal).
- Disbursements should be backed up by a voucher signed by the sponsor and principal.
- Disbursements should be made by prenumbered check with multiple signatures.
- Documentation must show who requested the purchase, what was purchased, which activity fund account should be charged, the amount, and the check number.

Additionally, it may be wise to establish a dollar limit for student activity fund disbursements that requires higher approval if exceeded.

The elements of activity fund budgeting discussed up to this point are, in many ways, common sense. Yet at the same time, it is easy to see how administrators, staff, and others can get into deep trouble or become confused about the nature of activity funds. Our discussion in Chapter 4 about fund accounting relates closely to this chapter as well. The three big rules to observe are:

- Be very careful when handling money.
- Spend money only for what it is intended.
- Use fund accounting, which is the tool for segregating money, so that the first two rules can be efficiently met.

It is also wise to remember that activity funds may be the greatest source of financial problems for school people.

What About Nonactivity Funds?

In addition to true activity funds, schools often collect other kinds of money that must be handled just as securely. This falls to the same people who are in charge of activity funds, although in a strict sense, we are now talking about nonactivity funds. The money in question often relates to curricular programs and does not belong in the activity fund structure. Examples of this kind of money include fees related to various programs such as class materials, laboratories, physical education, and so forth. Still other kinds of nonactivity money are handled at the school level, such as sales tax and petty cash. Our interest here has less to do with the intricacies of these funds and more to do with making sure that school people know that these funds exist and must be handled differently, because once again the area is fraught with pitfalls.

The following descriptions are meant to introduce different kinds of nonactivity funds that are typically received in most schools. For our purpose, the most important thing to focus on is that these are generally monies that will be transferred to the district because they are almost always district-owned. A more detailed examination is not appropriate for this textbook because these funds are merely tools to satisfy certain accounting principles and do not represent educational planning devices—although they do represent opportunities for mishandling.

Fee Funds

As noted earlier, schools usually have several fee funds. For example, schools collect fees for instructional supplies and materials, enrollment fees, food service fees, lab fees, shop and towel fees, home economics fees, musical instrument rental fees, and so forth. These funds represent user charges and are owned by the district, which will, in turn, credit the appropriate district fund when the activity fund bookkeeper remits collections to the district treasurer. The district then uses fee receipts to continue providing services.

Fee funds do not represent usable revenue at the school level. Fee funds are "receipt-only" funds, and no disbursements can be made from fee funds. The school merely acts to collect fees on behalf of the district for convenience reasons.

Sales Tax

Another kind of nonactivity fund money often collected at the school level is sales tax. This needs little explanation, although at times it becomes confusing about whether schools should be charging sales tax. The universal rule is that when schools do collect sales tax, the school is merely the collection point and acts as the remitter to another level. Districts usually have the freedom to choose whether to let individual school sites remit multiple sales tax collections or whether to centralize tax collection for a single state remittance. The confusing aspect is usually related to individual states' laws, because it is not always clear whether sales tax should be charged. That issue is answerable only in the context of each state, with the guiding principle that items for resale are usually subject to sales tax collection.

Petty Cash

The last area of nonactivity funds common to school sites is petty cash. Probably every school in America has a petty cash account, but it is often misunderstood and likely misused. Petty cash is a source of cash used for making small disbursements without writing checks or, alternatively, making payment more quickly than could be done by going through the normal bill-paying channels. Petty cash accounts do not involve much money as a general rule, although even the smallest sum of money must be handled properly. Examples of uses for petty cash might include paying game referees with a check drawn on the petty cash fund on game night, buying postage stamps, and other small purchases.

Because petty cash accounts represent more opportunity for trouble than may be true for other kinds of money, petty cash accounts are often statutorily limited in amount. In addition, districts should establish clear policies on uses of petty cash due to the ease with which these accounts can be defrauded because it is possible (unlike other district funds) to make actual cash payments. Board policy should include at least the following:

♦ The board should set an amount for petty cash accounts and state the intended uses. A maximum disbursement should be set, above which board approval is required.

♦ The activity fund bookkeeper should act as the petty cash custodian. Only one person should be in charge of petty cash.

♦ The petty cash custodian should require signed receipts from all persons receiving cash to create an audit trail. Receipts should document the purpose of the disbursement and which fund should be charged when petty cash is replenished at month end.

What Does an Activity Fund Report Look Like?

Although the different requirements of state laws and individual organizations supported in school districts prevent a universal format for activity fund reporting, the complex picture and set of responsibilities involved in activity funding can be best conceptualized visually. Figure 8.1 presents a month-end balance report for a hypothetical school district of about 7,000 students. As we've suggested throughout this book, numbers tell great stories, and Figure 8.1 speaks in a telling fashion. First, it can be seen that this district has a wide range of student activities—almost every conceivable organization has a place in this district's schools. Second, it can be seen that some accounts are district-owned (e.g., athletics), whereas others are student-owned (e.g., choir fundraising). Third, it can be seen that fee funds are reported in the activity fund (e.g., parking permits), although the revenue will be transferred to the district at a later time. And fourth, our point about handling large sums of money is highlighted here, as this medium-size district has a month-end cash balance of $69,442.08—no insignificant amount of money for which to take responsibility.

A FINAL WORD OF CAUTION

Cocurricular programs have long been accepted as a key contributor to the total gestalt of educational opportunity. Fiscal outlays for support of student activities are much larger than people often realize, in that district cash subsidies, student-owned deposits, and the value of land, buildings, and personnel required to operate a successful activity program are enormous. But as we argued at the outset, there is a high payoff for everyone involved.

The high profile of student activity programs raises the stakes of budgeting in many ways, however, and memories can be unpleasant. Two such cases illustrate the need for caution. The first case involves a school principal,

Figure 8.1. Sample Cash Balance
Report for Activity Fund Accounts

ACCOUNT NUMBER/TITLE		BEGINNING CASH BALANCE	CURRENT MONTH TRANSACTIONS		ENDING CASH BALANCE
109 .XXXXX.XXX.XX.XXX.X	SEASON TICKETS	$ 1,362.03	$ -		$ 1,362.03
110 .XXXXX.XXX.XX.XXX.X	ACTIVITY TICKETS	$ 11,235.09	$ -		$ 11,235.09
111 .XXXXX.XXX.XX.XXX.X	CONCESSIONS	$ -	$ -		$ -
112 .XXXXX.XXX.XX.XXX.X	PARKING PERMITS	$ 8,739.84	$ 565.00		$ 9,304.84
114 .XXXXX.XXX.XX.XXX.X	FOOTBALL	$ 4,114.05	$ 1,871.20	-	$ 2,242.85
116 .XXXXX.XXX.XX.XXX.X	BOYS BASKETBALL	$ 10,131.35	$ 3,182.17	-	$ 6,949.18
117 .XXXXX.XXX.XX.XXX.X	BASEBALL	$ 161.84	$ 187.10		$ 348.94
118 .XXXXX.XXX.XX.XXX.X	BOYS TRACK	$ 140.00	$ 490.00		$ 630.00
119 .XXXXX.XXX.XX.XXX.X	SOCCER	$ -	$ -		$ -
120 .XXXXX.XXX.XX.XXX.X	WRESTLING	$ 8.42	$ -		$ 8.42
122 .XXXXX.XXX.XX.XXX.X	CROSS COUNTRY	$ -	$ -		$ -
124 .XXXXX.XXX.XX.XXX.X	BOYS TENNIS	$ 308.86	$ 120.00		$ 428.86
126 .XXXXX.XXX.XX.XXX.X	GOLF	$ 17.50	$ -		$ 17.50
128 .XXXXX.XXX.XX.XXX.X	BOYS SWIMMING	$ 2,788.38	$ 109.03		$ 2,897.41
130 .XXXXX.XXX.XX.XXX.X	GIRLS TENNIS	$ 469.02	$ -		$ 469.02
131 .XXXXX.XXX.XX.XXX.X	GIRLS SOCCER	$ 33.68	$ 426.10		$ 459.78
132 .XXXXX.XXX.XX.XXX.X	GIRLS VOLLEYBALL	$ -	$ -		$ -
134 .XXXXX.XXX.XX.XXX.X	GIRLS BASKETBALL	$ 6,745.51	$ 1,282.03	-	$ 5,463.48
135 .XXXXX.XXX.XX.XXX.X	SOFTBALL	$ 32.97	$ 111.32		$ 144.29
136 .XXXXX.XXX.XX.XXX.X	GIRLS SWIMMING	$ 1,603.06	$ 129.45		$ 1,732.51
138 .XXXXX.XXX.XX.XXX.X	GIRLS GYMNASTICS	$ -	$ -		$ -
140 .XXXXX.XXX.XX.XXX.X	GIRLS GOLF	$ -	$ -		$ -
141 .XXXXX.XXX.XX.XXX.X	WEIGHT TRAINING	$ 7,035.23	$ 4,076.40	-	$ 2,958.83
142 .XXXXX.XXX.XX.XXX.X	TOURNAMENT ACCOUNT	$ 925.26	$ 1,008.58		$ 1,933.84
143 .XXXXX.XXX.XX.XXX.X	WRITERS CLUB	$ 1.64	$ -		$ 1.64
144 .XXXXX.XXX.XX.XXX.X	STUDENT SUPPORT GROUP	$ 16,602.31	$ 11,040.44	-	$ 5,561.87
145 .XXXXX.XXX.XX.XXX.X	CITY BASKETBALL	$ 3,551.84	$ 110.00	-	$ 3,441.84
146 .XXXXX.XXX.XX.XXX.X	DRAMATICS	$ 1,834.92	$ 41.00		$ 1,875.92
147 .XXXXX.XXX.XX.XXX.X	DRAMA TRIP	$ 19,998.54	$ 14,780.01	-	$ 5,218.53
148 .XXXXX.XXX.XX.XXX.X	THESPIANS	$ 656.88	$ 16,008.06	-	$ (15,351.18)
150 .XXXXX.XXX.XX.XXX.X	DEBATE	$ 920.35	$ -		$ 920.35
151 .XXXXX.XXX.XX.XXX.X	SCHOLARSHIP BOWL	$ 825.00	$ -		$ 825.00
152 .XXXXX.XXX.XX.XXX.X	CAP AND GOWN	$ -	$ -		$ -
154 .XXXXX.XXX.XX.XXX.X	NEEDY STUDENT	$ 355.42	$ 5.00		$ 360.42
156 .XXXXX.XXX.XX.XXX.X	NEWSPAPER	$ 1,400.00	$ 848.00	-	$ 552.00
158 .XXXXX.XXX.XX.XXX.X	MUSIC CONTEST ACCOUNT	$ 216.12	$ 195.19	-	$ 20.93
160 .XXXXX.XXX.XX.XXX.X	MUSIC SUPPORT GROUP	$ 1,517.89	$ -		$ 1,517.89
161 .XXXXX.XXX.XX.XXX.X	VARIETY SHOWS	$ -	$ 1,347.05		$ 1,347.05
162 .XXXXX.XXX.XX.XXX.X	SPECIAL MUSIC	$ 1,916.19	$ 100.00		$ 2,016.19
164 .XXXXX.XXX.XX.XXX.X	CHORALE	$ 4,817.36	$ 4,817.36	-	$ -
166 .XXXXX.XXX.XX.XXX.X	SCHOOLWIDE TALENT	$ 134.92	$ -		$ 134.92
168 .XXXXX.XXX.XX.XXX.X	JAZZ GROUP	$ -	$ -		$ -
170 .XXXXX.XXX.XX.XXX.X	ORCHESTRA	$ 263.00	$ 50.00		$ 313.00
172 .XXXXX.XXX.XX.XXX.X	CHOIR FUNDRAISING	$ 9,679.28	$ 10,530.00	-	$ (850.72)
173 .XXXXX.XXX.XX.XXX.X	PEP CLUB	$ 1,924.66	$ 192.24		$ 2,116.90
174 .XXXXX.XXX.XX.XXX.X	CHEERLEADERS	$ 598.73	$ -		$ 598.73
178 .XXXXX.XXX.XX.XXX.X	STUDENT COUNCIL	$ 12,338.69	$ 2,104.76	-	$ 10,233.93
			FUND BALANCE=		$ 69,442.08

respected in his state, who lost his job and his professional licensure as a result of cash receipts that were stolen from his unlocked car. The second case underscores the latent power that can be aroused when activity programs are threatened. In that case, a district facing a $5 million shortfall because of state aid rescissions decided to cut several athletic programs—a decision that cost several school board members and administrators their board positions and employment. Everyone has similar stories, but the point is simply that the prominence and size of activity programs make them a poor place to engage in lax fiscal practices or bad decision-making. The critical feature always ties back to wise leadership in the context of fiduciary trust. In the case of activity funds, it is particularly school-level leaders who are on the firing line.

SUGGESTED FOLLOW-UP PROJECTS

♦ Make a list of all student activities in your district and explore how they are funded. Distinguish which activities are student-funded and which are district-owned.

♦ Make an appointment with your district's treasurer to discuss handling of student activity funding. Obtain a copy of your district's board policies and guidelines on activity funding. Discuss the district's procedures for receipting and disbursing student activity monies.

♦ Obtain a copy of an activity fund report from one of the high schools in your district. Analyze it for the number of dollars, number of student groups, and so on. Talk to the principal about how the activity fund is supervised and the lines of authority and control that are in place. Identify any weaknesses in the system.

9

BUDGETING FOR SCHOOL INFRASTRUCTURE

PHYSICAL NEEDS IN PERSPECTIVE

No study of school funding is complete without examining the role of the physical infrastructure in school districts. The high cost of capital outlay, maintenance and operations, debt service, and other physical needs such as technology and general modernization have invisibly influenced the big picture as we have worked our way through the maze of school funding topics. Unstated costs can be more powerful than the most obvious ones—in this case, the role of school facilities is huge, and we now understand that other costs (mostly instructional) consume the majority of education's budgets. The net sum is that too little is left for schools' physical infrastructure needs. As a result, it is time to put physical needs in perspective, that is, we need to consciously articulate education's infrastructure problems and see how the budget addresses this enormously expensive aspect of equal educational opportunity.

As usual, a series of questions charts our way. To begin, what is the role of school physical infrastructure? What is included in infrastructure? What is the current condition of school facilities? This raises the question, how are schools' physical needs funded? At that point, we are ready to examine issues of planning and maintenance and operations—a different, but related, set of issues. How does infrastructure planning occur? What effect do demographics and programs have on facility planning? What is the role of maintenance and operations? How do schools organize for such activities? Although not as high profile as topics like instructional leadership or educational reform, school infrastructure plays a crucial role in budgeting—a topic of vital interest to everyone who makes educational decisions or who uses or pays for schools.

NATURE AND SIZE OF SCHOOL INFRASTRUCTURE

Although it is popular to overly dramatize issues to capture headlines and money, it does not overstate the case to say that school infrastructure needs are a serious problem far into the foreseeable future. This prediction arises from the many demands on school budgets described in this book, combined with the fact that while much effort has been made in recent years to reform schools, less support has been given to the need for effective physical learning environments. As the American Association of School Administrators (AASA) noted long ago, "[F]rom every corner have come reports, articles, speeches and goal statements about student achievement, unmet needs and education reform...but all these pronouncements have been strangely silent about one essential ingredient...that affects every child's health, safety and ability to learn: *the classroom.*[1]

Pronouncements of this nature are not insignificant in a time when reform of failing schools has captured headlines. The source of alarm rests in evidence that education's physical infrastructure is also failing in ways that surely impede general reform. Numerous reports have warned about the condition of school facilities, and school leaders and policy makers have been told of the cost for repair and replacement. As we will see shortly, estimates run into the billions of dollars, mostly because schools have funded other current needs by delaying maintenance and repair to school buildings. As noted long ago in one legislative report and echoed repeatedly around the nation, "Schools are...worn out, and it must be stated in the most serious terms that we are facing a crisis. ...[W]e can no longer guarantee parents their children are safe when they are sent off to school.[2] Although our discussion in this book has been overshadowed by unlimited needs and finite resources, forced choice is most evident when funding infrastructure because schools have had to choose between spending for instructional programs and spending for bricks and mortar in which to house those programs. An ever-spiraling crisis only underscores the crucial role of planning for capital needs, particularly because infrastructure is the single largest investment a school district makes at any one time.

What Is the Role of School Infrastructure?

Different language has been used over the years to describe the physical environment of education. School plant and facilities have been the common terms describing school buildings, and capital outlay usually has referred to all aspects of paying for the permanent facility and equipment needs of schools. In a broader and more recent context, the term "infrastructure" has been used frequently because it captures the whole range of capital needs in a single word. All these terms have been useful in describing the role of physical environments by implying that planning for instructional programs alone is not enough to meet the educational needs of children. The role of infrastructure was captured by AASA when it stated:

> The most exciting curriculum innovations in the world have trouble succeeding in cold, dank, deteriorating classrooms. If the work

---

1. American Association of School Administrators, *Schoolhouse in the Red. A National Study of School Facilities and Energy Use* (Arlington, VA: AASA, 1991), 1.

2. State of Wisconsin, *Children in Peril: A Preliminary Report of the Senate Subcommittee on Aging Schools* (Author, 1989), 3.

environment is unattractive, uncomfortable, or unsafe, school districts have difficulty competing with other sectors of the economy
to woo talented teachers....Students know the difference too!
When *USA Today* polled 72,000 students as to what they would do
with more school funds, their No. 1 priority was school maintenance and construction. Teens responding to the survey called
their buildings "filthy and a disgrace."[3]

Although we do not suggest that poor conditions describe a majority of
schools in the United States, we do argue that needs outstrip resources, and
the data point to ever-mounting infrastructure needs in most districts. Other
chapters in this textbook suggest good reasons for this crisis, as competition
for tax dollars continues to rise. The crisis has worsened as pressure has been
placed on school facilities through the expanding scope of education, and
stress has resulted from the complex and sometimes arcane ways in which
schools are built and maintained. The role of infrastructure is to support good
instructional programs by providing a safe and inviting physical environment for learning—a role that often has taken a backseat to the costs of demographic realities, curriculum reform, staff compensation, and other school
services. Yet it is clear that the best reforms will fail if the physical environment impedes learning. Deferred construction and maintenance may represent a savings, but such decisions also represent a false economy by
impeding the work of schools.

The Condition of Schools[4]

The headlines heralding school infrastructure concerns make it easy to
believe that the poor condition of many schools in the nation is a newly discovered reality. In fact, problems of facilities and capital needs have long
been noted by education critics. In 1831, William A. Alcott graphically
described the problems of school facilities when he stated:

Few, indeed, of the numerous schoolhouses in this country are
well lighted. Fewer still are painted, even on the outside. Playgrounds for the common schools are scarcely known. There is
much suffering from the alternation of heat and cold and from
smoke. The feet of children have even sometimes been frozen. Too
many pupils are confined to a single desk or bench where they jos-
tle or otherwise disturb each other....Hundreds of rooms are so
small that the pupils have not on average more than five or six
square feet each; here they are obliged to sit, breathing impure air,

3. American Association of School Administrators, *Schoolhouse in the Red. A National
    Study of School Facilities and Energy Use* (Arlington, VA: AASA, 1991), 11.
4. The following section draws substantially on Faith E. Crampton and David C.
    Thompson, eds., *Saving America's School Infrastructure* (Greenwich, CT: Information
    Age Publishing, 2003).

on benches often not more than six or eight inches wide, and without backs.[5]

Fortunately, relatively few schools still suffer the full extent of Alcott's criticisms. Students no longer sit on benches, health standards regulate ventilation, and most schools provide tolerable light and thermal environments. Rigid construction standards apply to all new schools, and many schools have been retrofitted to standards.[6] No public school has escaped some regulation because schools must comply with fire and boiler inspection and other standards of the Environmental Protection Agency (EPA) for hazards such as asbestos, radon, and lead; standards of the Occupational Safety and Health Administration (OSHA); and accessibility under the Americans with Disabilities Act (ADA). As a result of efforts to provide a better learning environment, modern schools are largely relieved of the very worst conditions of earlier times.

Simply enacting building codes, however, has not resulted in excellent school facilities across the nation, as regulations have mostly focused on crises such as asbestos or other gross hazards. Furthermore, although physical environments in new schools are legislated, existing facilities generally have not been upgraded to the same standard. The result has been that existing schools remain the object of concern because numerous national reports have concluded that the physical infrastructure still is in a state of emergency. Although many good schools exist, reports have argued that others are badly deteriorated, with many schools too old to safely function or too outdated to meet the demands of modern equal educational opportunity.

Although Alcott's day may be a relic in many ways, in other aspects it lingers on. Recent data on the quality of school environments has exposed substandard school facilities at the turn of the new millennium, painting scenes of unsafe and unhealthy classrooms described by some critics as resembling

---

5. William A. Alcott, "Essay on the Construction of School-Houses," August 1831. Quoted in David C. Thompson, "Educational Facility Equity and Adequacy; A Report on Behalf of the Plaintiffs in *Roosevelt v. Bishop*," (Manhattan, KS: Wood, Thompson & Associates, 1991), 1.

6. A partial listing of such organizations that publish standards includes the American Concrete Institute (ACI), American Institute of Architects (AIA), American Institute of Steel Construction (AISC), Architectural Woodwork Industry (AWI), American Welding Society Code (AWSC), National Building Code (NBC), National Electric Code (NEC), National Fire Protection Association (NFPA), National Illuminating Engineering Society (NIES), National Plumbing Code (NPC), Uniform Building Code (UBC), Underwriters Laboratories, Inc. (UL), American Association for Health, Physical Education, and Recreation (AAHPER), American Association of School Administrators (AASA), American Institute of Electrical Engineers (AIEE), Association of Physical Plant Administrators (APPA), Association of School Business Officials (ASBO), American Society of Mechanical Engineers (ASME), American Society for Testing and Materials (ASTM), Council of Educational Facility Planners, International (CEFPI), National Board of Fire Underwriters (NBFU), and the National Bureau of Standards (NBS).

the conditions of poor third world countries.[7] In addition, recent research describes health hazards associated with indoor air quality in portable class-rooms, a widely used alternative to new construction, usually in response to legislation mandating class size reduction or as a stopgap solution to rapidly growing student enrollments.[8] These conditions are juxtaposed with emerging research linking student achievement and the physical environment.[9]

Even more recent data graphically portray that the depth of needs is larger than previously thought and is growing rapidly.[10] Until recently, best estimates of the backlog of deferred maintenance in U.S. schools dated from the 1980s[11] and was estimated in 1995 at $112 billion.[12] More recent research, however, shows that this deficit is still unfunded, and that true infrastructure needs were actually severely underestimated because the U.S. General Accounting Office (GAO) only inquired about deferred maintenance, safety, and accessibility. The newest data argue that if unmet needs are vast in just the context of general upkeep and repair, they are staggering in the context of

---

7. See, for example, Jonathan Kozol, *Savage Inequalities: Children in America's Schools* (New York: Harper Perennial, 1992); and U.S. General Accounting Office, *School Facilities: The Condition of America's Schools* (Washington, DC: U.S. Government Printing Office, February 1995).

8. See, e.g., Zachary Ross and Betsy Walker, *Reading, Writing, and Risk: Air Pollution Inside California's Portable Classrooms* (Washington, DC: Environmental Working Group, 1999).

9. See, e.g., Glenn I. Earthman, *Review of Research on the Relationship Between School Buildings, Student Achievement, and Student Behavior.* Position paper prepared for the Council of Educational Facility Planners International, Scottsdale, AZ (July 1996); Glenn I. Earthman, "The Best Possible Environment for the Most Productive Learning," *School Business Affairs* 63 (July 1997): 21–24.

10. See, generally, Faith E. Crampton and David C. Thompson, eds., *Saving America's School Infrastructure* (Greenwich, CT: Information Age Publishing, 2003). See also National Education Association, *Modernizing Our Schools: What Will It Cost?* (Washington, DC: NEA, 2000).

11. American Association of School Administrators, Council of Great City Schools, and National School Boards Association, *The Maintenance Gap: Deferred Repair and Renovation in the Nation's Elementary and Secondary Schools* (Arlington, VA: Author, January 1983); Ann Lewis, *Wolves at the Schoolhouse Door: An Investigation of the Condition of Public School Buildings* (Washington, DC: Education Writers Association, 1989); and Sharon J. Hansen, *Schoolhouse in the Red: A Guidebook for Cutting Our Losses* (Arlington, VA: American Association of School Administrators, 1992). See also two special issues of the *Journal of Education Finance* on the status of state and local funding of capital outlay: David S. Honeyman, R. Craig Wood, and David C. Thompson, eds., *Journal of Education Finance* 13, no. 3 (Winter 1988) and David S. Honeyman, R. Craig Wood, and David C. Thompson, eds., *Journal of Education Finance*, no. 4 (Spring 1989).

12. U.S. General Accounting Office, *School Facilities* (Washington, DC: U.S. Government Printing Office, February 1995); and Laurie Lewis, Kyle Snow, Elizabeth Faris, Becky Smerdon, Stephanie Cronen, and Jessica Kaplan, *Condition of America's Public School Facilities: 1999* (Washington, DC: U.S. Department of Education, National Center for Education Statistics, June 2000), a recent update of the General Accounting Office (GAO) study placing the total at $127 billion.

a fuller definition of total infrastructure and equal educational opportunity. Figure 9.1 illustrates the modern definition of infrastructure and embraces the costs of improvements associated with educational program adequacy.

Figure 9.1. Comprehensive Definition of Infrastructure

♦ *Deferred maintenance.* Deferred maintenance refers to maintenance necessary to bring a school facility up to good condition, that is, a condition where only routine maintenance is needed. If a facility is in such poor condition that it cannot be brought up to good condition, or if it would cost more than to construct a new facility, deferred maintenance can refer to replacement of an existing facility.

♦ *New construction.* New construction may be a response to current overcrowding; to federal, state, or local mandates that require additional facilities, such as class size reduction measures; or to projected enrollment growth. The construction of a new facility includes the building(s); grounds (purchase, landscaping, and paving); and fixtures, major equipment, and furniture necessary to furnish it.

♦ *Renovation.* Renovation of an existing facility includes renovations for health, safety, and accessibility for the disabled. Renovation may also include renovations necessary to accommodate mandated educational programs.

♦ *Retrofitting.* Retrofitting of an existing facility applies to areas such as energy conservation (e.g., installation of insulation or energy-efficient windows) and technology readiness (e.g., electrical wiring, phone lines, and fiber optic cables).

♦ *Additions to existing facilities.* Additions to existing facilities may be necessary to relieve overcrowding; to meet federal, state, or local mandates such as class size reduction; or to accommodate projected enrollment growth. The cost of additions usually includes the fixtures, major equipment, and furniture necessary to furnish them.

♦ *Major improvements* refers to grounds, such as landscaping and paving.

Note: Some states use the term "capital outlay" rather than school infrastructure. In some states, the definition of capital outlay may be broader —for example, in some states, capital outlay includes major equipment and/or equipment costing more than a specific price.

SOURCE: Faith E. Crampton, David C. Thompson, and Janis M. Hagey, *Creating and Sustaining School Capacity in the Twenty-First Century: Funding a Physical Environment Conducive to Student Learning.* A paper presented to the University Council for Educational Administration, Albuquerque, NM (2000).

Data from the most recent comprehensive national study of infrastructure deficit[13] (see Figure 9.2) shows that states' unmet funding needs in 2000 exceeded $266 billion,[14] more than double the estimate provided by GAO only five years before. Total unmet funding need varies dramatically across states, from $220 million in Vermont to nearly $48 billion in New York. When expressed in per-pupil terms, states and local school districts need to spend an average additional $1,100 per student each year over a five-year period to address unmet needs, an increase of 100% more than current actual spending rates—an amount likely to increase again in the near future.

These data join with other reports of troubled school facilities in that shifts in population, issues of economic health, and adequacy of infrastructure are interwoven. Although population in some parts of the nation has grown, schools have continued to age without money to meet the demand for new construction or renovation. In contrast, population in other areas has steadily declined, raising questions about the future of individual schools and districts. In all instances, fully 50% of schools were built approximately 35–45 years ago, and it is not surprising that many buildings are in poor condition because the typical school was built with a life expectancy of 50 years. The general rule is that maintenance costs increase rapidly when a school reaches 30–40 years of age, with accelerated deterioration between 40 and 50 years of age. Although disturbing to people, costs of upkeep on older buildings and technological obsolescence are the factors that underlie the expert view that many schools more than 50 years old should be reconstructed or destroyed. Additionally, 25% of schools now in use were built between 1900 and 1950. Under these conditions, half of all schools have marginal future utility, and another 25% are candidates for reconstruction or abandonment.

Although it is easy to understand that the ultimate impact of infrastructure deficits is deterioration of the learning environment, it is considerably more difficult to address the issue because of limited resources and the tremendous expense represented by bricks and mortar. One of the more aggressive solutions is litigation to force states to absorb the unfunded need, and some success has been experienced by plaintiffs in a small number of states.[15]

---

13. Faith E. Crampton and David C. Thompson, eds., *Saving America's School Infrastructure* (Greenwich, CT: Information Age Publishing, 2003), 17.

14. The total includes $53.7 billion for technology (hardware and software). The total $266 billion contains other technology costs such as wiring and adapting facilities to accept new and emerging technologies.

15. Faith E. Crampton and David C. Thompson, "When the Legislative Process Fails: The Politics of Litigation in School Infrastructure Funding Equity," in *Politics of Education Law: Effects on Education Finance. 2004 American Education Finance Association Yearbook*, eds. Karen DeMoss and Kenneth Wong (New York: Eye On Education, 2004), 69–88. See also David C. Thompson and Faith E. Crampton, "School Finance Litigation: A Strategy to Address Inequities in School Infrastructure Funding," in *Saving America's School Infrastructure*, eds. Faith E. Crampton and David C. Thompson (Greenwich, CT: Information Age Publishing, 2003).

Figure 9.2. Total Unmet
Infrastructure Need by State

State	Total Need ($)	Per Pupil ($)/5 yrs	Per Pupil ($)/10 yrs
Alabama	1,519,210,061	398	221
Alaska	727,014,291	1,074	588
Arizona	4,748,568,494	983	536
Arkansas	1,761,701,495	758	422
California	22,000,000,000	704	386
Colorado	3,805,239,627	1,045	574
Connecticut	5,000,000,000	1,828	1,033
Delaware	1,046,354,648	1,836	1,022
Florida	3,300,000,000	271	151
Georgia	7,061,967,931	942	517
Hawaii	752,533,936	713	386
Idaho	699,469,537	517	278
Illinois	9,213,000,000	824	458
Indiana	2,477,797,613	486	269
Iowa	3,359,129,953	1,386	776
Kansas	1,793,241,845	774	430
Kentucky	2,441,607,196	749	418
Louisiana	3,104,098,619	812	454
Maine	452,064,540	448	253
Maryland	3,891,926,876	905	504
Massachusetts	8,919,014,500	1,822	1,025
Michigan	8,071,127,040	963	541
Minnesota	4,517,232,516	1,068	597
Mississippi	1,038,890,864	406	226
Missouri	3,475,160,989	759	423
Montana	901,492,663	1,101	607
Nebraska	1,608,849,896	1,119	622
Nevada	5,256,000,000	2,888	1,568

State	Total Need ($)	Per Pupil ($)/5 yrs	Per Pupil ($)/10 yrs
New Hampshire	409,511,478	403	226
New Jersey	20,709,650,065	3,247	1,810
New Mexico	1,410,624,747	778	422
New York	47,640,000,000	3,214	1,802
North Carolina	6,210,938,727	902	502
North Dakota	420,000,000	749	420
Ohio	20,900,000,000	2,302	1,291
Oklahoma	2,204,070,041	732	410
Oregon	2,407,425,974	859	475
Pennsylvania	8,465,134,387	927	521
Rhode Island	1,420,952,603	1,882	1,060
South Carolina	2,574,018,400	803	451
South Dakota	498,604,766	706	390
Tennessee	2,273,702,904	466	257
Texas	9,467,620,774	453	248
Utah	8,490,336,757	3,385	1,841
Vermont	220,090,007	425	239
Virginia	5,701,313,528	986	548
Washington	5,478,902,777	1,067	589
West Virginia	1,000,000,000	686	384
Wisconsin	4,762,337,059	1,087	608
Wyoming	530,888,665	1,125	614
Total	266,138,818,788		

SOURCE: Catherine C. Sielke, "Financing School Infrastructure Needs: An Overview Across the 50 States," in *Saving America's School Infrastructure,* ed. Faith E. Crampton and David C. Thompson (Greenwich, CT: Information Age Publishing, 2003), 33–37.

Other proposals have encouraged enactment of special legislation to provide one-time infusions of large amounts of money in states experiencing relatively affluent times, such as during the 1990s, as a large number of states enjoyed sustained economic prosperity resulting in substantial surpluses.[16] But despite favorable economic times, most proposals have focused on only partial or short-term solutions to the problem of infrastructure deficits because the backlog of needs is so great. In many instances, states lack the capacity to deal fully with the enormous costs, particularly because many states do not have permanent funding schemes with the long-term goal of providing the same level of state aid given to school district operating costs (Figure 9.3, pp. 253–257). In fact, only a minority of states fund school infrastructure in a meaningful manner, either in total dollars or in a cost-share ratio.[17]

Although health and safety and construction standards have greatly improved schools, these improvements have required great sums of money. The vastness of infrastructure needs, growth in deferred maintenance, the reluctance of legislatures to embrace infrastructure as an element of equal opportunity, and general budget crises at the local level have all resulted in facility planning that has not been sufficient to provide uniform physical environments for all children. As a result, many districts have had to divert instructional funds to pay for infrastructure needs or, alternatively, have had to watch their deferred needs grow.

How Is School Infrastructure Aided?

The modern condition of education's infrastructure is a cumulative reflection of how well states have chosen to fund school facilities. As we will see, there is a sharp difference in how general education is aided compared to how facilities and capital needs are funded. In contrast to the complex formulas developed to provide state aid to general fund, special education, transportation, and other school services, infrastructure has been neglected at both state and local levels.

An important reason for infrastructure underfunding has been a real reluctance to abandon tradition. School facilities have long been a local expense, dating from an era when far fewer children attended school and facility costs and programs were simpler. Schools stood as symbols of local coop-

(Text continues on page 258.)

---

16. National Conference of State Legislatures, *State Budget Actions 1998* (Denver, CO, and Washington, DC, 1999); National Conference of State Legislatures, *State Tax Actions 1998* (Denver, CO, and Washington, DC, 1999). The National Governors' Association and the National Association of State Budget Officers estimated the average state surplus for fiscal year 1999 at $31 billion (7.1%) of state budgets. See *The Fiscal Survey of States*, National Governors Association and the National Association of State Budget Officers (Washington, DC, December 1998).

17. See Catherine C. Sielke, "Financing School Infrastructure Needs: An Overview Across the 50 States," in *Saving America's School Infrastructure*, ed. Faith E. Crampton and David C. Thompson (Greenwich, CT: Information Age Publishing, 2003), 27–52.

Figure 9.3. State School Infrastructure Funding Programs 2001–2002

State	State Funding Program	Flat Grant	Equalized	Basic Support	Full Funding	Categorical Grant	None
Alabama	Guaranteed tax yield for capital improvements.		X				
Alaska	Grants with required local contribution ranging from 5% to 35%. Reimburses debt up to 70%. Debt must be pre-authorized.	X	X				
Arizona	Full state funding within required state standards. Per pupil amount for "soft," short term capital needs.	X			X		
Arkansas	Provided within basic state aid: Average daily membership (ADM) × wealth index × $39.		X				
California	State provides approximately 55% to 66% of costs.					X	
Colorado	Included in Basic Support Program: $223–$800 per pupil.			X			
Connecticut	Equalized funding for 20% to 80 % of eligible costs. Magnet schools receive 100%. Additional funding for initiatives such as early childhood, reduced class size, full day kindergarten.		X			X	
Delaware	State pays 60% to 80% of costs. Equalized based on taxing ability.		X				
Florida	Public education and capital outlay (PECO) funds projects based on need.					X	
Georgia	Equalized funding based on assessed valuation per pupil, ranging from 75% to 90 %. Special local sales tax (SPLOST) funds are also included in the formula. Grants for new classrooms, reduced class size initiatives. Additional incentives available for low wealth district districts.		X			X X	
Hawaii	Full state funding				X		

(Figure continues on next page.)

State	State Funding Program	Flat Grant	Equal-ized	Basic Support	Full Fund-ing	Cate-gorical Grant	None
Idaho	Subsidies for debt retirement based on mill rate, health & safety issues.					X	
Illinois	Equalized grants based on equalized assessed valuation (EAV) per pupil at the 90th percentile. Grants for debt service equaling 10% of principal × grant index.		X X				
Indiana	Flat grant of $40 per pupil in average daily attendance (ADA) in grades 1–12. Purpose is debt service	X					
Iowa	Grants based on enrollment size and inverse relationship with sales tax proceeds. Required local equalized match based on district fiscal capacity. Minimum match is 20%.		X				
Kansas	Weighting per pupil in basic aid of 0.25 for costs of new facility. Grants for debt service equalized inversely to assessed valuation (AV) per pupil.	X	X				
Kentucky	Flat grant of $100 per pupil. District levy of $0.05 per $100 of assessed valuation (AV) equalized if property wealth is less than 150% of state average. Grants for debt service based on percentage of district unmet needs compared to state unmet needs.	X	X X				
Louisiana	No state funding.						X
Maine	Funding for debt service based on local share for approved projects.		X				
Maryland	Funding based on state share of minimum foundation per pupil. Minimum is 50% of costs.		X				
Massachusetts	Reimbursement of 50% to 90% for approved projects. Funding based on calculation of property value, average income, district poverty level, and incentive points (type of construction, project manager, efficiency, maintenance history).		X				

State	State Funding Program	Flat Grant	Equalized	Basic Support	Full Funding	Categorical Grant	None
Michigan	No state funding.						X
Minnesota	Funding by weighted average daily membership (ADM) × ($173 + district average building age). Equalized debt service aid. Incentive grants such as $30 per year round pupil served, health, & safety issues.		X			X X	
Mississippi	Flat grant of $24 per average daily attendance (ADA). Other grants based on specific needs.	X				X	
Missouri	No state aid.						X
Montana	Funding for debt service only. Based on ratio of district mill value per pupil enrollment and the state mill value per pupil.		X				
Nebraska	Funding for accessibility and environmental issues: $0.052 per $100 assessed valuation (AV).					X	
Nevada	No state funding with the exception of special appropriations for two districts due to extreme need.						X
New Hampshire	State funds 30% to 55% of building costs depending on number of towns. Funding is not equalized.	X					
New Jersey	*Abbott* districts receive 100% funding. Non-Abbott districts receive equalized funding (minimum of 40%) based on district wealth (personal income and property tax base). Some districts may be eligible debt service aid.		X				
New Mexico	Equalized funding for voter-approved 2 mill levy. Grants for critical needs if district is bonded to 65% of capacity.					X	

(Figure continues on next page.)

State	State Funding Program	Flat Grant	Equalized	Basic Support	Full Funding	Categorical Grant	None
New York	Equalized funding based on building aid ratio and approved building expense.		X				
North Carolina	Funding provided based on average daily membership (ADM), growth, and low wealth. Additional flat grant from proceeds of corporate income tax.	X	X				
North Dakota	No state funding.						X
Ohio	Funds Ohio School Facilities Commission. Equity list developed based on 3 year average property wealth; local district must pass levies. State design manual requirements.		X				
Oklahoma	No state funding.						X
Oregon	No state funding.						X
Pennsylvania	Funding (reimbursement) based on the greater of district's market value aid rat o, capital account reimbursement fraction, or density.		X				
Rhode Island	Funding for debt service. State share ratio = 1- ((district wealth per pupil/state wealth per pupil) × 62%). Minimum funding 30% of cost.		X				
South Carolina	Funding allocated per pupil based on available funding divided by K–12 average daily membership (ADM).	X					
South Dakota	No sate funding.						X
Tennessee	Funing through the Basic Education Program. Based on cost per square foot per average daily membership (ADM) + 10%for equipment + 5% for architect fees + debt service at state bond rate.					X	

State	State Funding Program	Flat Grant	Equalized	Basic Support	Full Funding	Categorical Grant	None
Texas	Guaranteed yield funding through the instructional facility allotment which is based on size of district, property value, averge daily attendance (ADA), and amount of annual debt service.						
Utah	Equlized funding based on local effort tax rate of $0.0024 per dollar of taxable value and need.		X				
Vermont	Funds about 30% of cost of project based on prioritized needs. Debt service reimbursed based on the guaranteed yield provisions of the general aid formula.		X			X	
Virginia	Flat grant of $200,000 per district. Remaining amount prorated based on enrollment and ability to pay. Per pupil supplement for maintenance and debt service.	X X	X				
Washington	Funding is based on eligible area, area cost allowance, and matching ratio. Required local effort (matching ratio) is determined by comparing district assessed valuation (AV) per pupil to state assessed valuation (AV) per pupil.		X				
West Virginia	State funding is based on need: efficiency, adequate space, educational improvement, educational innovations, health and safety, and changing demographics. Lottery money is dedicated to debt service.					X X	
Wisconsin	Funding is included in the basic support program.			X			
Wyoming	State supplements mill levy if assessed valuation per average daily membership (AV/ADM) is below 150% of state average.		X				

SOURCE: Catherine C. Sielke, "Financing School Infrastructure Needs: An Overview Across the 50 States," in *Saving America's School Infrastructure*, ed. Faith E. Crampton and David C. Thompson (Greenwich, CT: Information Age Publishing, 2003), 33–37.

eration, often raised by hand with volunteer labor and donated materials and land. Technological obsolescence did not exist, and demands on local tax bases for other services were minimal in a rural nation. Communities were fiercely protective of their schools and rejected outside help. The dawn of the twentieth century, however, marked the end of local tax base sufficiency, as movement from an agricultural to an industrial economy led to rapid growth in cities and schools. Yet despite growing needs of schools for more revenue and broader tax base, many states continued to follow a tradition of local responsibility for funding school facilities. Although other state aids came into being in rapid succession, capital needs continued to depend on local property wealth and were often hindered by low statutory debt limitations, tax rate caps, and other restrictions.

Pressures on local tax base gave rise to a second major cause for school facility neglect. As education grew in importance, students stayed in school longer and were joined by populations needing more instruction and other elements of compulsory education. Early in the twentieth century, educational growth was accompanied by economic prosperity, but the stock market crash in 1929 caused school revenue to falter. The Great Depression nearly halted growth in education, and school construction was nonexistent for nearly a decade. After World War II the backlog of needs was recognized, but it was resolved by rapid construction of cheap facilities that were never meant to last. The result was a backlog of unmet needs, followed by hasty construction and emerging educational technology that quickly made facilities obsolete.

A third source of neglect was that these problems were worsened by slowness on the part of states to become involved in funding school facilities. Although increased costs and demand for new programs severely strained local resources, states were still reluctant to become involved, often citing local control as a reason. As needs grew, however, a few states began providing aid, but often aid was meant to induce other outcomes. For example, in 1901 Alabama began to aid capital outlay—the purpose, however, was to help rural schools and did not suggest a broad state duty to education. Other states followed, with each plan varying in reasons, amounts, and methods. For instance, Delaware and South Carolina began offering capital aid to schools in 1903 for African-American children. Between 1898 and 1927, aid plans were enacted in Arkansas, Delaware, Maine, Minnesota, Missouri, New York, Oklahoma, Pennsylvania, Rhode Island, Tennessee, and Wisconsin—facility aid primarily offered to induce consolidation of tiny school districts. The result of selective aid plans was that as late as World War II, only 12 states gave general aid for capital outlay and debt service to local schools.

Economics, politics, and local control have been the major causes of underfunded school facilities. Yet states have become more aware of school infrastructure needs, especially because some courts have begun to link capital needs and other areas of school finance equity. As seen in Figure 9.3, a large majority of states now provides aid to school facilities (although not adequate or uniform aid). Some states assume a majority of costs, while others provide a smaller share. States actively attempting to aid facilities do so using full state funding or equalization grants or provide aid through the general fund mechanism, whereas states making less intense effort have traditionally used matching grants, flat grants, state loans, building authorities or similar devices, or by allowing districts to incur bonded indebtedness. Although operation of each plan depends on the goals of each state, plans usually resemble the general fund aid schemes from which they derive their names.

Full State Funding

As the name implies, full state funding plans assign total responsibility to the state for the cost of building programs. Under these conditions, the state pays for school facility construction and maintenance, and in return may expect to control many of the decisions previously made at the local level. For example, the process of acquiring new facilities may involve various levels of bureaucracy wherein state resources are allocated first to those districts in greatest need. Although the plan satisfies principles of equity, full state funding of facilities is rare in that most states have not chosen to abandon traditional facility funding practices. Even in those states where full state funding is adopted in name, practice may resemble a modified approach that still uses a local property tax levy rather than a single statewide tax.

Full state funding of facilities has the same advantages found in fully funded general aid formulas (see Chapter 3). Full state support conceptually represents the most equitable system, in that facilities are funded based on the wealth of the entire state. But as expected, disadvantages exist. The difficulty of identifying the full extent of needs typically results in unexpected costs to the state. Similarly, concerns about loss of local control arise whenever centralized authority is imposed. Further, there is a basis for concern about extravagance when districts no longer need to be frugal in assessing needs. Conversely, there is basis for fears about declining local tax initiative when schools are not locally funded. Although several states have experimented with forms of full state support for facilities, there have been only a few states even considering this funding plan.

Equalization Grants

Equalization plans for funding school facilities closely resemble the equalization aid formulas found in general fund financing. Equalization usually involves grants to local districts, wherein facility aid increases as ability to pay declines. Variations on equalized grants have been devised in several states. For example, if power equalization principles (see Chapter 3) are observed, a unique feature may be that a district can choose to increase its share and qualify for more aid. Alternatively, equalization grants, although limited by state definition of an appropriate facility, may aid districts up to a maximum amount based on district wealth. Unlimited variations exist, as states set aid criteria based on attitudes and fiscal realities.

Regardless of how states choose to structure equalization aid, the critical feature is the cost-share based on ability to pay. This feature is its greatest strength, in that aid flows inversely in relation to local wealth. Another advantage may be a greater degree of local control wherein a district can manipulate its tax rate, either to purchase better facilities or to provide tax relief. Disadvantages are few and relate more to political problems such as the difficulty of achieving meaningful power equalization. Similarly, financial constraints and the temptation to thwart equalization by aiding all districts serve to restrict amounts of aid available. Although many states have adopted forms of facility equalization grants, most have capped costs in a modified equalization structure.

General Fund Aid

Only a few states have chosen to build infrastructure aid into their general fund aid programs. Separate from maintenance and operations, which have often been considered current operating expenses and housed in the general fund, general fund aid on a broad scale has been a relatively recent way to channel money to facilities. By default, such programs distribute aid according to whatever equalization principles are included in the general fund. The logic of such programs is simply that facilities are part of the total educational program of the district and equally deserving of support at the same level of aid received by all other general fund expenses. Laudable for its intent, the cost of such plans has prevented widespread adoption.

Matching Grants

Only a few states have chosen to aid facilities using matching grants. First designed to aid general funds, matching grants are an effort to recognize needs and more neutrally aid districts. In its basic form, matching provides aid to all districts by granting a legislatively determined share of costs regardless of need. For example, the state might share costs on a 50% ratio based on legislative attitude and state treasury limitations. Matching plans satisfy three goals. First, matching is recognition of needs. Second, matching is an attempt to provide neutral aid, either from the perspective of not discriminating among districts or recognizing the politics of aiding all districts regardless of need. Third, matching permits the state to limit its fiscal exposure by controlling the percentage required at the local level.

The major advantage to matching grants is political, and the negative aspect of providing aid to wealthy districts is clear. The latter issue has frustrated widespread adoption, so that no state currently offers true matching grants, although at times some states offer equalized grants with minimum aid provisions to all districts regardless of equalized capacity.

Flat Grants

As discussed earlier, flat grants have long been used to grant general aid to schools based on beliefs about both equity and politics. States using flat grants offer districts a set sum of money based on legislative policy decisions and the state's fiscal condition. The formula is simple by granting a flat sum on some basis such as head count or number of classroom units. The result is that local costs are reduced by the state's share, leaving districts free to reduce taxes or enhance programs.

The principle of flat grants has been used to fund school facilities. Under this plan, all districts receive aid and local wealth dependency is reduced. Political realities are aided too, at least in those districts that otherwise would not qualify for aid. Disadvantages exist, however, in that flat grants have not been adequate to meet needs. Although better than no aid, it is well established that flat grants do not reduce wealth dependence because any equity benefits are negligible.

State Loans

Unlike other methods of aiding facilities, loan programs represent one of only two original facility aid inventions. Although other aid plans are an admission by the state of the inadequacy of local tax base to meet districts' capital needs, state loans are a special recognition of the high cost of facilities because state loans are exceptions to the common practice of cash basis. A state loan program fundamentally concedes that current revenues are inadequate to provide facilities and lets districts deficit-spend to provide housing for educational purposes. Loan programs are exactly what the name implies, in that the state loans money to districts for school facility needs. As a general rule, loans carry an expectation of repayment.

State loan programs have advantages and disadvantages inherent to their nature and design. Advantages include better interest rates and strong security ratings for investors because the state itself either makes the loan or guarantees it. Districts can either borrow money at lower cost or buy more facilities for the same cost that would be experienced under traditional debt mechanisms carrying higher interest rates. A second advantage is that some states have structured loans to include forgiveness if the district cannot repay. The disadvantages, however, are meaningful in that wealth and ability to pay are unaffected, as districts in the greatest need may be the least able to afford the cost of borrowing. Historically this method has been fairly prevalent, but its popularity has declined with growing awareness of the depth of school facility needs.

State or Local Authorities

The only other original facility funding invention works much like state loans, although variations have modified this concept. Typically, state or local building authorities are legislative mechanisms seeking to circumvent the normal debt structure of bonding for capital needs, in that authorities allow districts to borrow for capital projects without actually bonding against the wealth of the local district. Building authorities thus encourage use of private capital to construct and lease or lease-purchase schools for several reasons. First, building authorities do not generally involve state monies. Second, the state has the political benefit of liberalizing facility acquisition at virtually no cost to itself. Third, debt limits usually do not apply, making it easier for poorer districts to obtain facilities. Fourth, no bond election is required, avoiding a major obstacle of voter resistance. Under these conditions, building authorities have been used in some states for a variety of reasons relating to districts' inability to fulfill their capital needs.

Advantages to building authorities lie in a unique ability to tap resources without legal debt limitations, and in the ability to obtain needed facilities in a shorter time period because of no referendum requirements—a huge benefit because school bond elections have failed frequently throughout the nation. Opponents, however, have seen authorities as a subterfuge, citing avoidance of referenda and the cost of higher interest rates inherent to using private capital. Although criticism has been significant, school districts have used such mechanisms, with some significant reliance on lease-rent or lease-purchase of school facilities.

Although all states now understand the problem of funding infrastructure needs entirely on the local tax base, eight states still provide no aid (down from 12 states in the last edition of this book). But at the same time, Figure 9.3 suggests that many states still offer relatively low amounts of aid, making clear that local districts still bear much of the cost of school facilities.

Intermediate Summary

Classifying school facility aid types can be elusive, as states do not use comparable language, and hybrid plans defy categorization. Similarly, states may use multiple overlapping plans that make classification a very difficult task. Figure 9.4 (pp. 263–265) provides additional information from the various states about current bond programs and state aid for debt service, and Figure 9.5 (pp. 266–267) offers still a third layer in the form of other school infrastructure programs. Taken conjointly, a wide array of support mechanisms is seen, although again it must be repeated that almost no states support facilities at the same intensity or uniformity seen in other kinds of school aid. The local community remains heavily impacted by infrastructure costs as seen in the next section.

How Is the Local Cost Share Funded?

The cost of school facilities is enormous. In 1999–2000, taxpayers spent more than $31 billion on plant maintenance and operations and nearly $14 billion on capital outlay and interest on debt service.[18] Although state aid no doubt paid some portion of these costs, the vast majority of school districts in the nation have had to finance a large share of capital projects using revenue

(Text continues on page 268.)

---

18. U.S. Department of Education, National Center for Education Statistics, *Digest of Education Statistics 2002* (Washington, DC: National Center for Education Statistics, 2003), 185.

Figure 9.4. Bond Programs and State Aid for Debt Service

State	Bonds	Conditions	Debt Limits	State Aid for Debt
Alabama	X	Municipality may issue bonds; districts may issue revenue warrants	None reported	None
Alaska	X	State approval	None reported	Reimburses up to 70%
Arizona	X	Voter-approved for projects that exceed state standards	10% for unified districts	None
Arkansas	X	Voter-approved second lien bonds	30% of assessed valuation (AV)	None
California	X	Voter-approved	None reported	None
Colorado	X	Voter-approved	None	Part of basic program
Connecticut	X	Issued by municipality, not school district	None reported	Limited
Delaware	X	Voter-approved	10% of assessed valuation (AV)	None
Florida	X	Voter-approved	None reported	None
Georgia	X	Voter-approved	10% of assessed valuation (AV)	Yes
Hawaii		Full state funding		
Idaho	X	Voter-approved with super majority	10–20 years	Partial subsidy for interest
Illinois	X	Voter-approved	None reported	10% of principal × grant index
Indiana	X	No approval but subject to remonstration	2%	Flat grant: $40 per average daily attendance (ADA) in grades 1–12
Iowa	X	Voter-approved with 60% majority	5% of assessed valuation (AV); 20 years	None

(Figure continues on next page.)

State	Bonds	Conditions	Debt Limits	State Aid for Debt
Kansas	X	Voter-approved	None reported	Equalized grants based on assessed valuation (AV) per pupil
Kentucky	X	Districts sell bonds with state oversight	20 years	Yes
Louisiana	X	Voter-approved	10–20% of assessed valuation (AV); 40 years	None
Maine	X	Voter-approved	State approval	Yes
Maryland		Only state issued bonds		
Massachusetts	X	Voter-approved	25% of assessed valuation (AV)	None reported
Michigan	X	Voter-approved	15% of assessed valuation (AV); 30 years	None
Minnesota	X	Voter-approved	15% of market value	Equalized
Mississippi	X	Voter-approved with 60% majority	15% of assessed valuation (AV)	Included in flat grant; $24 per average daily attendance (ADA)
Missouri	X	Voter-approved	15% of tax base; 20 years	None
Montana	X	Voter-approved	45% of assessed valuation (AV)	Yes
Nebraska	X	Voter-approved with 55% majority	None	None
Nevada	X	Voter-approved	15% of assessed valuation (AV)	None
New Hampshire	X	Voter-approved with 60% majority	None reported	None
New Jersey	X	Voter-approved	None reported	Formula considers debt service, district basic aid percentage, eligible costs, and school district fulfillment of maintenance requirements
New Mexico	X	Voter-approved	6% of assessed valuation (AV)	None

State	Bonds	Conditions	Debt Limits	State Aid for Debt
New York	X	Voter-approved	None reported	Equalized funding available
North Carolina	X	Voter-approved	None reported	Yes
North Dakota	X	Voter-approved with 60% majority	10% of assessed valuation (AV)	None
Ohio	X	Not reported	None reported	None
Oklahoma	X	Voter-approved with 60% majority	10% of assessed valuation (AV)	None
Oregon	X	Voter-approved with a 50% majority of 50% of voters	Based on assessed valuation (AV) and school grade level	None
Pennsylvania	X	Voter-approved	No limit	Reimbursement based on approved payment schedule
Rhode Island	X	Not reported	None reported	State share calculated; minimum state funding is 30%
South Carolina	X	Voter-approved	8% of assessed valuation (AV)	None reported
South Dakota	X	Voter-approved	10% of assessed valuation (AV)	None
Tennessee	X	Voter-approved Issued by local municipalities, counties, etc.	None reported	Part of basic state aid
Texas	X	Voter-approved	None reported	Part of instructional facility allotment
Utah	X	Voter-approved	40% of market value	Included in facility funding
Vermont	X	Voter-approved	None reported	Based on guaranteed yield provisions of basic aid formula
Virginia	X	Voter-approved for county schools	None	Lottery allocation & maintenance supplement program
Washington	X	Voter-approved	None reported	

SOURCE: Catherine C. Sielke, "Financing School Infrastructure Needs: An Overview Across the 50 States," in *Saving America's School Infrastructure,* ed. Faith E. Crampton and David C. Thompson (Greenwich, CT: Information Age Publishing, 2003), 40–43.

Figure 9.5. Other School Infrastructure Programs

State	Additional Funding Availability
Alabama	Revenue warrants that do not exceed 80% of pledged revenue
Alaska	None
Arizona	None
Arkansas	State loan program
California	Developer fees
Colorado	Voter-approved mill levies up to 10 mills for 3 years
Connecticut	State loan program
Delaware	May assess a tax rate without referenda for state match requirements
Florida	Up to 2-mill levy without voter approval; voter-approved .005 sales tax
Georgia	Grants; voter approved .001 local option sales tax up to 5 years
Hawaii	None
Idaho	2/3 majority approved tax levies
Illinois	None
Indiana	Leases, rentals
Iowa	County local option sales tax, .005 up to 10 years
Kansas	Additional mill levies with approval of State Board of Tax Appeals
Kentucky	None
Louisiana	None
Maine	State revolving loan fund
Maryland	None
Massachusetts	None
Michigan	State loan fund, sinking funds of 5 mills up to 20 years
Minnesota	State loans
Mississippi	3-mill levy up to 20 years without voter approval; state loan fund
Missouri	Lease purchase up to 20 years
Montana	Building reserves
Nebraska	Voter-approved mill levies

State	Additional Funding Availability
Nevada	Voter-approved mill levies, developer's fees
New Hampshire	None
New Jersey	Lease purchase
New Mexico	None
New York	None
North Carolina	Local option sales tax
North Dakota	Voter-approved building funds up to 20 mills annually
Ohio	None
Oklahoma	Mill levy up to 5 mills annually
Oregon	None
Pennsylvania	Some nonelected debt allowed
Rhode Island	Leases, reserve funds
South Carolina	Children's education endowment fund; funding based on total revenue available, basic aid support formula, weighted pupils, and need
South Dakota	None
Tennessee	Lease purchase, capital outlay notes
Texas	Lease purchase
Utah	Revolving loan fund
Vermont	Sinking funds
Virginia	Revolving loan fund; pooled bond issues
Washington	Fund reserves; special levies
West Virginia	None
Wisconsin	State loan fund; sinking funds
Wyoming	None

SOURCE: Catherine C. Sielke, "Financing School Infrastructure Needs: An Overview Across the 50 States," in *Saving America's School Infrastructure,* ed. Faith E. Crampton and David C. Thompson (Greenwich, CT: Information Age Publishing, 2003), 45–46.

derived from local property taxes. Generally the local share is paid from some combination of three funding methods: *current revenues, sinking funds,* or *bonded indebtedness.*

Current Revenues

We know from our earlier discussion that local school districts generally must supplement state aid to meet their facility needs. Obviously, total responsibility for capital projects rests entirely with the local district in no-aid states. Although several methods of raising local money exist, financing capital needs by current revenues is the oldest method. As the name implies, local revenue is derived on an annual basis from taxes levied during the current year. For example, if a district has an assessed valuation of $500 million and a statutorily permissible tax rate for capital outlay of four mills, it can generate $2 million in current revenues for facility purposes. Similarly, if a district has a valuation of only $7 million and the same maximum tax rate, current revenues for capital projects will raise only $28,000. If in the same example the state were to have no limit on tax rates in local districts, the poorer district would have to levy about 286 mills to obtain the same revenue available to the wealthy district with only four mills of tax effort.

The benefits and limitations of local financing via current revenues are evident in the illustration. The major advantage is that current revenue is a cash basis method that avoids interest costs of borrowing money for capital projects. Additionally, districts are not likely to be extravagant if revenue must be on deposit prior to expenditure. A third benefit is that generations enjoying school facilities are those who also actually pay the bill. At the same time, serious drawbacks exist. The most important disadvantage results from disparate property wealth among districts, in that high wealth districts will have access to outstanding school facilities whereas low wealth districts will not be able to afford equal access.

Few districts are able to effectively use the current revenue method because most local tax bases are far too low to raise enough money to fund all facility needs. In addition, most states limit the maximum millage that can be levied for capital projects. But even if states allowed unlimited local tax leeway, it would be impossible to levy the millage needed to raise adequate funds in poorer districts. As a result, the usefulness of current revenues is mostly confined to small projects and to current maintenance and operations budgets.

Sinking Funds

Because current revenues are insufficient, sinking funds have been permitted in many states. A sinking fund is like a savings account that accumulates until it is large enough to pay for a project with cash. Districts are allowed to levy general or special taxes that are placed in a reserve fund for a specific project or for undesignated purposes. Assuming adequate tax base, sinking funds have the ability to grow rapidly because the money is invested in interest-bearing accounts. For example, an annual tax levy of $1 million per year invested at 5% interest grows to $5.25 million in only five years.

Sinking funds have advantages for both school districts and taxpayers. The obvious benefit is that it encourages saving for public projects. Additionally, a sinking fund is efficient because of immediate and dramatic savings in interest costs since no money is borrowed. Finally, a sinking fund is prudent in that districts can engage in long-range planning without the haste of caring only for daily survival. Predictably, these benefits are seldom realized for several reasons. First, sinking funds still depend on the wealth of the district—as a result, only wealthy districts can really benefit by saving. Second, inflation greatly reduces the future value of money, as a low inflation rate of 2% reduces the value of $1 to only 67¢ after 20 years. Third, gathering large sums not earmarked for specific projects can be a disadvantage in that needs change over time so that voters who originally approved a tax levy might disapprove of eventual uses of the sinking fund. Even if sinking funds are earmarked, needs may change by the time enough money is gathered. As a result, few states allow true sinking funds in the modern watchdog environment.

Bonded Indebtedness

Because current revenues and sinking funds are not good solutions to larger facility problems, school districts often resort to bonded indebtedness. Bonding is a device by which districts are statutorily permitted to incur debt for the purpose of acquiring long-term fixed assets such as facilities. Although debt is prohibited under cash basis laws for current operations in most states, an exception is for acquisition of facilities. Methods by which districts may incur bond debt depend entirely on the laws of each state. In most states, districts are authorized to bond for facility needs, subject only to statutes on referendum and debt limitations. In other states, differences relate primarily to whether districts are fiscally independent or dependent and whether the state controls bonding by a central state authority.

In most states, bonding for facilities is a local affair. Although bonding is a form of borrowing money, it is different from traditional borrowing in several ways. When individuals or businesses want to borrow money, they approach a mortgage lender. A mortgage is a debt instrument that uses the purchased property to secure the loan in case of default. In contrast, governmental units do not operate by these same rules. Although bonds create a legal debt, the mortgage is replaced by the bond mechanism, which has two key features. The first feature is that bonds are sold at open market and purchased by many investors instead of a single mortgage lender. The second feature is that public properties purchased through bond sales cannot be foreclosed. Thus a bond sale for school facility purposes creates neither a mortgage nor collateral. Collateral is theoretical in that the full faith and credit of government, that is, the school district (or other government unit such as the state) is pledged to repay the debt.

Bonding has many benefits. Although collateral does not exist, investors see bonds as attractive investments because the chance of default is very low. In traditional mortgages, a lender risks the principal of the loan on the assumption that the borrower's income is secure and that the property will not drop below loan value in case of foreclosure. Although loan-to-value ratios are not used in bonding, it should be obvious that the borrower's income is the surest risk that can be obtained. This is because the school district generally has taxing authority, and the collateral is future tax revenues. Further, the interest rate paid by schools on bonds is likely to be much lower because of low risk of default, and because bonds are generally tax-exempt. The tax-exempt status of income from school bonds is attractive to investors because lower untaxed earnings may net more income than higher yield investments after taxes.

The Bonding Process

The process of bonding follows similar steps in all states. Most states require a referendum (bond election) whenever a district wants to pursue a facility project that exceeds current revenues or cash reserves. A referendum is a request for approval of facility debt by placing the question on the ballot at a general or special election so that voters in the district can approve or reject the proposed project. The purpose of referendum is to assure that voters are willing to pay the extra taxes needed to retire the debt. Although horror stories of bond election failures abound, and the poor condition of many school buildings is the result of voter unwillingness to pay for schools, the referendum is basic to the democratic process. In most states, a bond election can be held in conjunction with another election such as a presidential or gubernatorial election, or the school bond question may be voted on by special election.

When voters approve a bond issue, they are agreeing to pay taxes over time to repay the many investors who emerge as willing buyers of the bonds. Bonds are like promissory notes in that an investor buys one or more bonds at open sale, often in denominations of $1,000 or $5,000. The investor then expects to be repaid in the form of principal and interest over a set period of time. To amortize the bond schedule, the district levies taxes that are deposited to a special fund from which it makes semiannual or annual bond payments.

When a district decides to initiate a bond sale, a series of steps is required. Determination of the project is usually the first step. As will be discussed later under facility planning, this includes determining needs at school board and community levels and working with architects to describe needs and estimate costs.

When the project is envisioned, and costs are known, the next step requires the district to decide if it can afford to undertake the project. This step is critical because, even though many states do not aid facilities, every state places debt limits on public agencies, including schools. Generally, the debt limitation is expressed as a percentage of the assessed valuation of the school district. For example, if a district were to have an assessed valuation of $500 million with a 10% debt ceiling, total debt in terms of borrowed principal could not exceed $50 million.

The third step is to schedule a bond election. State statutes are very specific. Generally the local district has little responsibility for conducting an election. In contrast, the district usually makes all decisions about the timing of an election, and districts engage in extensive public campaigns to enhance the likelihood of voters approving the bond issue. If the referendum fails, the district must determine cause and decide whether to resubmit the question to voters. Generally, a new election is accompanied by renewed public relations and may include a scaled-down project at a lesser cost.

If the referendum is successful, the district can proceed to the fourth step of preparing the bond sale. Specialized legal counsel is required because of the complexity of bond laws, and financial counsel is required because the bond market is highly complex and competitive. When counsel have prepared for the bond issue, an official advertisement is issued to investors, usually through widely read financial publications and by bond prospectus.

Although the bonding process is normally completed in these four steps, the facility project is just beginning. Bonding merely represents preparing for a facility project because the proposed work cannot begin until the entire bonding process has been carried out. Additionally, the project extends beyond completion and occupancy because the district has committed to long-term debt repayment. Obviously this requires revisiting the financial plan on an annual basis, making tax levies and depositing bond proceeds into special debt service funds until disbursement, and maintaining and protecting the new physical assets. As seen in earlier chapters on budgeting, accounting, and taxation, these processes are important to the successful operation of a district. Because so much money is at stake, facilities and bonding are areas of special care because facilities affect administrators, boards, staff, policy makers, and the community—and of course, children as learners.

FACILITY PLANNING AND MAINTENANCE

Our discussion until now has centered on how schools obtain money for capital projects, primarily from the perspective of building new facilities or major remodeling and renovation or acquisition and accommodation of technology—projects requiring large sums of money. Although big projects can involve current revenues either in the form of local dollars or state aid, there are two other facets to budgeting for infrastructure that must be discussed: facility planning, and maintenance and operations. Although complementary to all other facility issues, a separate examination of these topics is useful in making some additional points.

What Is the Role of Facility Planning?

Although school districts engage in long-range planning in many areas, in some ways facility planning predicts success or failure of other plans made by districts. An excellent curriculum built on the latest technology cannot succeed if facilities are badly designed or maintained; likewise, the most highly skilled teachers cannot succeed in a new facility if it is poorly designed. For example, old buildings with inadequate electrical service and cramped space likely cannot support computer labs. Similarly, old buildings with poor ventilation are dangerous places for chemistry programs. Even new buildings may be unsuitable if crowded or planned without proper thought for the learning environment. Although sparkling facilities will not overcome bad teaching, planning for infrastructure is more than just architectural design—facility planning is the total integration of space with the instructional and support functions of a modern school system.

The value of facility planning has long been recognized. Wise leaders know that poor planning is costly through wasted money, underutilization, lack of long-range flexibility, and the ineffectiveness of bad choices. As a result, good planning requires organization to oversee all aspects of plant planning and operations. Larger districts often hire an assistant superintendent for plant planning who is charged with all facility-related tasks. Often this person has subordinates who perform more specialized functions. In smaller districts, these duties may fall to the superintendent, with greater reliance on contracted services by outside firms. Although district size may help dictate how the school system organizes its planning activities, all districts need a staff person who is knowledgeable about both education and facility management.

In larger districts, an office of plant planning may be created. This office usually has as its major task the ongoing study and analysis of facility needs according to five goals. The first goal is to prepare and maintain a comprehensive analysis of all facilities. The second goal is to assure a well-designed physical plant to enhance teaching and learning. The third goal is to assure that all facilities remain useful over the life of each building because outmoded facilities hurt teaching and learning. The fourth goal is to evaluate facilities for future educational programs in ways that assist in decisions to reconstruct or abandon buildings. The fifth goal is to preserve maximum flexibility in all buildings so that future generations are served. Plant planning should thus reflect careful thought about the following:

♦ School-age population to be served
♦ Location and transportation of school-age population
♦ Programmatic offerings of the district and each school
♦ Overall long-range facility needs of the district
♦ Fiscal ability of taxpayers in the district
♦ Overall organizational structure of the school system
♦ Overall economic and demographic future of the district

These areas make up planning for infrastructure and form a role that includes demographic planning, capital program planning, facility planning, program planning, architectural review, site selection and acquisition, and construction.[19] These factors deserve a brief discussion because they are the factors districts should use to justify many decisions about the total educational program.

Demographic Planning

One of the biggest mistakes in planning for infrastructure is failure to account for demographics in the district. Even the best facilities would be compromised if schools were not convenient to the location of children. Demographic planning is thus the study of a district's profile, including social, economic, and population issues. Demographics drive infrastructure planning because the goal is to serve the needs of clients.

Demographic planning varies greatly based on the unique characteristics of each district. For example, large districts with growing populations must anticipate housing trends so that land can be bought ahead of rising market trends. Smaller districts often engage in demographic planning to predict future facility needs in relation to stable or declining enrollments. A major task of demographic planning is to conduct accurate facility surveys that research the district's profile, analyze findings and propose alternative solutions, and recommend a plan of action. A comprehensive educational survey describes the community's characteristics and educational needs, determines pupil population characteristics, describes the educational program, appraises existing facilities in relation to needs, develops a master plan, assesses resources, and makes recommendations. Because it is comprehensive, the survey forms the basis for careful long-range facility planning.

Description of community characteristics and educational needs is the starting point. The survey should inquire into population characteristics, density, and changes over time. It should examine changes in land use, including zoning and changes that have occurred because of population patterns. Analysis should examine traffic, ways to assess development and land use under growth conditions to predict likely locations for new schools, or continued viability of existing facilities. Socioeconomic status must be studied, in that economics may limit choices. Inversely, rapid population growth in professional communities may result in constant upward mobility requiring new elaborate schools. Other community characteristics should be examined, including vocational opportunities, parental expectations, and public attitudes toward schools and taxes.

The critical element in demographic planning, however, is enrollment projection because quality space must be provided for all students. As discussed in Chapter 5, population projections entail seeing community trends, birth rates, historic and present enrollments, and calculating retention in the district and each attendance center. The most common enrollment projection

---

19. R. Craig Wood, David C. Thompson, and Lawrence O. Picus, *Principles of School Business Management*, 3rd ed. (Reston, VA: ASBO, 2005).

tools include cohort survival and trend line analysis, although large districts may use population mapping, saturation analysis, and other community planning tools to estimate the effect of housing developments. Obviously, accurate data are critical to long-range infrastructure planning, as well as many other aspects of budgeting.

Capital Program Planning

A second activity often known as capital program planning is closely related to demographic analysis. Capital program planning is the anticipation of a district's capital needs in relation to its demographic profile. The purpose is to analyze the district's financial status and characteristics to estimate both the limitations and ability of the district to pay for current and future infrastructure needs. Capital program planning usually involves bonding, sometimes aided by federal impact funds or state aids.

The normal result of capital program planning is creation of a capital improvement program (CIP) that projects all capital needs for the future, usually over a period of 5–20 years. The CIP prioritizes projects, primarily because resources are seldom sufficient to retire all needs at one time, particularly if current revenues are expected to provide a significant part of the money. For example, roof replacement on all buildings more than five years old might be the highest priority, with the CIP targeting buildings with immediate needs. Another example might find the district trying to install computer labs in all buildings according to a priority schedule. Obviously, more aggressive CIPs can occur if bonding is used; for instance, a district might replace all roofs and air handling systems in a single bond issue, or it might retrofit all buildings with electrical service to support hundreds of new computers installed in updated labs built with bond money under the long-range infrastructure plan. When renovation or new construction or major equipment purchases are contemplated, the CIP must analyze revenues over the full period of debt retirement. A feature of a CIP is that its adoption is often considered authorization to proceed with projects. Finally, the CIP should be reviewed and updated as projects are completed or as needs and financial conditions change.

Facility Planning and Programming

The nature of planning for infrastructure does not allow for totally discrete operations in a capital improvement plan. For example, although the sequence calls for first establishing the population base to determine facility needs, it is necessary to overlap demographic planning with capital program planning. Likewise, to envision facilities and educational programs requires knowledge of the financial options and demographic needs of a district. Thus facility planning and programming makes up another task of the plant planning office, along with other activities described in this section.

The purpose of facility planning and programming is to identify the desires and constraints under which an educational facility will have to function. Generally this activity involves consideration of the goals and objectives of the district and each individual school, and it also usually defines instructional and organizational plans. Many constituencies should be involved in facility planning and programming, including the community and staff as well as professional planners such as architects and educational consultants. Although facility programming and planning is complex, the overall goals should include the following:

- Is the facility structurally sound?
- Is it healthful and safe?
- Is it efficient to operate?
- Does it support the program?
- Is it attractive and comfortable?
- Is its location convenient for the users?
- Is its space optimally used?
- Is it the right size?
- Can it be modified?

Answers to these questions, together with demographic and capital program data, are the basis of the CIP. If all the answers are affirmative, the district should keep its course by maintaining its investment and by regular review of the CIP. If, on the other hand, answers are negative, the district must make corrections.

Architectural Planning

Districts that have identified demographic, capital, and programmatic needs must recognize when they have reached the limits of district staff expertise, in that all modern facility projects require professional architectural planning. This has become especially true as concerns about health and safety have surfaced in both litigation and legislation. Consequently, architectural planning represents a fourth activity in school plant planning.

Although architects or engineers must design new or reconstructed schools, it is less well known that many states require architectural services when an educational facility is modified. For example, adding an elevator can invoke other codes on fire protection, electrical service, or other laws that force the entire facility to be brought up to code. Similarly, even the removal or addition of an interior wall may require an entire facility to be made fully accessible under the Americans with Disabilities Act (ADA). The point is that few projects can be done in-house or by phoning a local construction firm because architectural services are pervasive to facility planning.

Selection of an architect is a critical element of facility planning. Most districts use the services of one architect for smaller jobs, but engage in design competition if larger projects are involved. Remodeling jobs like air-handling systems and divider walls to reshape interior spaces are sometimes noncompetitive. Big projects such as renovation, expansion, or new school buildings typically require competition. Because competition is complex and costly, the process is usually reduced to asking architects to submit portfolios on their experience, qualifications, previous examples of similar projects, and rough cost estimates. The board, administrative staff, and consultants make a judgment based on such items as experience of the firm, budget, and overall reputation. As emphasized in earlier chapters, care must be taken to follow all statutory requirements in awarding contracts.

Construction Planning

The value of good architectural services is evident in two critical aspects of facility planning. The first aspect involves planning the project and working to develop project specifications. The role of architects is to work within the physical and fiscal realities of the district and to work with staff to be sure the facility will function well. The second aspect involves actual oversight of the project through completion. These two features are part of the architect's overall responsibility in construction planning, and it should be apparent that the legal liability and technical competency involved in these tasks make architectural services an absolute necessity.

Construction planning thus represents a fifth task in infrastructure planning by combining the services of architects, educational consultants, and school staff in designing a facility project. Because architects are not educators, districts need the services of a consultant to create educational specifications that communicate the district's vision to the architect. Educational specifications are first stated in generalities by local staff and communicated to the consultant. The consultant reviews the statements and examines existing facilities. Depending on the nature and size of the project, the consultant may work with a committee to define needs and expectations. The goal is for the consultant to use the district's broad vision to create a highly specific document that leads the architect to develop an appropriate design. For example, the educational specifications define the school program by classroom and by instructional facility, including requirements for all special areas (e.g., media center, cafeteria, auditorium, physical education, vocational facilities, etc.). The importance of these activities is underscored by the Council for Educational Facility Planners International (CEFPI), which has described educational specifications as the blueprint for the future.

If new construction is required, activities may result in preliminary designs and drawings presented to the school board. Once preliminary plans are approved, actual working drawings and specifications are developed. Plans must be examined to ensure that the design is integrated with curricular and instructional goals, and the facility should embrace other needs of the larger community. Input from instructional leaders is essential during the design phase to avoid inefficiency and waste.

When the design is complete, the physical improvements begin. The major task of schools during the work phase is to be certain that the district keeps close contact with the project. One important reason is that lack of supervision over the project could result in legal problems if it is later found that the district should have kept itself better informed of any problems. A second reason is that the district must state in writing any concerns or changes to the project. A third reason is that payments for work will be made during the construction phase, and the district must be satisfied before any funds are released.

The work phase requires scheduled payments from the district's cash reserves or from bond sale proceeds. These payments satisfy material and labor claims. Architectural fees are usually a percentage of the project, whereas contractor fees are set by competitive bidding. When the project is finished, a percentage is typically held back pending final acceptance and proof that bills, payrolls, and mechanics' liens by all contractors, subcontractors, and vendors have been satisfied. Additionally, the board's attorney must assure that the district will have clear title.

The role of planning for infrastructure is broad and includes demographic plans, capital program plans, architectural plans, and construction plans, all of which apply to both alteration and expansion of facilities and to new construction. All infrastructure projects must be financed by legally permissible methods using cash or debt, and expert counsel ranging from legal and financial services to architectural and construction services must be used. The role of the district is to acquire and coordinate such services—a role that demands sound educational and fiscal planning.

What Is the Role of Maintenance and Operations?

We have stressed the value of planning because the cost of infrastructure and the dependence of educational programs on good facilities are enormous. As we noted earlier, a fine educational program is damaged by poor school facilities, and the same is true for poor maintenance and operations. It should be no surprise that this chapter concludes with the role of planning for maintenance and operations (M&O).

Initial cost of facilities and natural deterioration dictate the need for a good M&O plan. It is the responsibility of maintenance and operations to keep buildings, equipment, and grounds in good condition and ready for use. These tasks are the basis for our closing look at organizing for M&O, determining maintenance needs, and conducting facility operations.

Organizing for M&O

The maintenance and operations function is often organized under a central office administrator with line authority over all physical plant activities and related staff. Obviously, organizational structure depends on district size, with larger districts employing hundreds of plant service workers. A medium-size school district might resemble the organizational chart in Figure 9.6 where both diversification of work and economy of scale are evident. In Figure 9.6, final responsibility rests with the school board, which delegates to the superintendent, who delegates to a general director. As a result, plant planning and operations and maintenance are joined, with a key person coordinating their performance.

Figure 9.6. Sample Facilities Organizational Chart

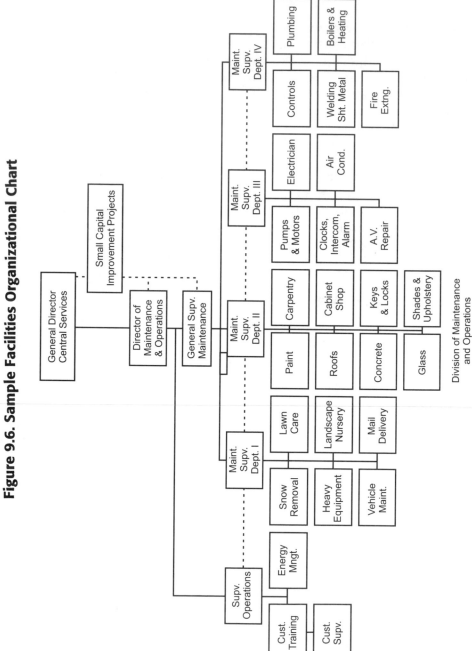

Figure 9.6 develops a central maintenance division that provides services to all schools in the district. These services are often provided on an in-house basis if the district has decided it is more cost-effective to employ permanent staff with specific skills, rather than to contract jobs to outside firms. Figure 9.6 illustrates a school district of approximately 16,000 students and provides an example wherein the district has decided that it has enough work to justify the cost of operating its own maintenance division to perform the many specialized tasks. The plan appoints an assistant superintendent for plant planning to oversee a director of plant services, who oversees a director of maintenance and operations, a general supervisor of maintenance, and so on. Obviously, as district size decreases, the chart becomes organizationally simpler, even though the same tasks still need to be performed.

Organizing for maintenance and operations demands assessing facility needs on the basis of repairing, replacing, and cleaning the district's capital investments. The overarching organizational task therefore includes determining maintenance and operations needs, prioritizing into short-term and long-term plans, and staffing competent and efficient M&O programs. Organizing for these tasks forms the basis of determining maintenance needs and conducting the many facility operations of a modern school district.

Determining Maintenance Needs

As a rule, maintenance of old and new buildings requires skilled evaluation of all component systems. Component systems include footings, foundations, and basements; interior and exterior walls; roofs and flashings; doors, windows, and frames; floors and ceilings; mechanical systems; electrical systems; aesthetics, equipment, and furniture; grounds; and energy conservation. This list points out the need for skilled employees and specialized contracted maintenance. Foundations, footings, and basements should be regularly inspected by staff for any visible problems, and regular evaluation by engineers or architects should be scheduled. Walls and roofs should be inspected regularly, with repairs like sealing cosmetic cracks and light masonry repointing done in-house. Mechanical and electrical systems should be inspected, with problems reported promptly. Painting, refastening trim, cleaning traps, replacing washers in valves, adjusting doors and windows, replacing shades and lighting, and so on can be done in-house. A maintenance plan should include energy conservation, including a formal energy audit and energy-saving steps.

The goal of determining maintenance needs is to identify concerns and prevent new problems. Once needs are known, the district must schedule and fund repair or replacement. As a general rule, districts should spend a minimum 4% to 6% of the general operating budget for maintenance. Unfortunately, much of the facility dilemma today results from failure to follow a program of preventive maintenance. Another contributor is the failure of society to provide sufficient money to protect the enormous investment represented by education's infrastructure. It is a simple fact that no amount of excellent facility operations can overcome the failure to engage in maintenance of basic systems.

Conducting Facility Operations

Although long-term maintenance is key to the financial and instructional health of schools, smooth, day-to-day operation of facilities is equally important to ensure the health, safety, and welfare of everyone in a school. As we said at the outset of this chapter, there are data to show that the physical condition of facilities has an impact on learning. Dirty or badly maintained schools send a message that education is not valued. Although we noted in an earlier chapter that the quality of the educational program is often judged by the shine on the floor, data strongly suggest that students attending clean and well-maintained schools will feel pride, which results in improved teaching and learning. Routine maintenance is essential, and the contribution of polished floors to student achievement should not be devalued.

The maintenance function comprises the tasks of keeping a school open for use. As a rule, the most important skill is organization. Maintenance staff must be organized for efficiency within the limits of cost, labor, and time. Every aspect of maintenance must be organized by a timetable, so that staff know what must be done. Generally, tasks can be broken down into routines of vacuuming, sweeping, mopping, dusting, cleaning glass, and emptying trash; steam-cleaning, buffing, or waxing floors; cleaning chalkboards and trays; cleaning halls including walls, water fountains, and waste containers; and noting damage needing repair. Daily activities include both routine tasks and repairs, although component system evaluation by staff can occur on a monthly or quarterly basis. Minor repairs like fixing trim or changing light bulbs can be scheduled on an as-needed basis, whereas other tasks such as painting can be done during nonschool times. Daily tasks should be done on staggered schedules using a square-foot–acreage formula or by enrollment size of the school. Various formulas for custodial tasks exist, such as the following:

Acreage [1 person per 10-acre site] plus

Square feet [1 person per 15,000 sf of building]

or

Enrollment: [1 person per ~275 elementary students]

[1 person per ~200 secondary students]

Although many activities not described here are needed to ensure a clean and healthful school, no aspect is more important than proper training for custodial and maintenance staff. Training may result in increased efficiency and improvement, including higher standards of service, fewer employees because of efficiencies, less waste, fewer hazards, less deterioration of school plant and equipment, flexibility in shifting employees among buildings, and respect for custodial workers on the part of the public. Facility operations and maintenance are critical to the good work of schools and depend on highly competent staff to create the best possible conditions for equal educational opportunity.

WRAP-UP

Planning for infrastructure is a highly complex operation. As we noted at the outset of this chapter, it is false economy to underspend for facilities, but neglect is a fact that now spans generations. It is also a reality that the age of cheap construction and high maintenance will continue to plague schools because the nation has a long history of underinvesting in education's infrastructure. But as we also said early in this chapter, facilities are the single largest investment school districts make at any one time—an investment that must be protected to provide excellence and equality for children.

SUGGESTED FOLLOW-UP PROJECTS

♦ Identify how capital improvements are financed in your state. This may include obtaining state department documents or examining relevant statutes. If your state uses an aid formula to assist in debt service, analyze it in terms of total dollars, how districts qualify for aid, and so on, including the specific impact of the formula on your district. If your state does not provide aid to facilities, conduct an inquiry into how surrounding states assist districts with capital planning needs.

♦ Explore how infrastructure funding and planning occurs in your district. This may require a meeting with the business office or with the director of facility planning. Learn how your district assesses its short, intermediate, and long-term needs. Identify how much debt your district carries, the amortization schedule, and so on.

♦ Obtain a copy of your district's capital improvement plan (CIP) or long-range capital outlay plan. Analyze it in terms of dollars, how it prioritizes needs, and how the CIP calendar is constructed.

♦ Discuss daily and scheduled maintenance and operations with the appropriate person in your district. Learn how these functions are organized, the amount of budget devoted to M&O, and how it is carried out on a daily basis. Identify any problems associated with this aspect of district operations.

10

BUDGETING FOR TRANSPORTATION AND FOOD SERVICE

SETTING THE STAGE

As we head toward the end of our study of how schools are funded, we should devote some time to the area of auxiliary services. Our goal is twofold. The first goal again is based on a bias, in that we believe there is a tendency in society to see the mission of schools as exclusively instructional, with the unfortunate outcome that other more ancillary areas of school district operations are ignored when they should also be valued for their role in providing equal educational opportunity. Our other goal is that a book examining the many aspects of schools and money would be incomplete if it failed to address auxiliary services, especially transportation and food service, because schools would be negatively impacted without these operations. Our bias is simple: We believe every child has a right to a good education without regard for socioeconomic status, and we believe every child should be able to get to school without hardship and attend classes free from hunger. Because there is no equal opportunity when educational programs are physically inaccessible or when children are underfed, all stakeholders in education should be concerned with organizing and operating efficient systems for transporting and feeding children.

Once again, a series of questions guides the way. We begin by asking, what are the roles of auxiliary services? Related questions arise, including: What are the origins and purposes of transportation? What laws impact transportation services? How is transportation funded? And what other issues are relevant, such as purchasing buses, maintenance, safety, and so on? The same kinds of questions arise regarding food services. We start by asking, what are the general issues? How is food service funded? How is food service organized? And what is important to know about organization and fiscal management? In sum, our view of money and schools is incomplete if we fail to appreciate the impact of auxiliary services on teaching and learning.

The Role of Auxiliary Services

Although auxiliary services can be broadly defined, we use the term to refer to selected noninstructional support services, usually funded under separate fund accounting systems. In a historical sense, this has usually referred to the areas of transportation and food service. These operations are large and complex regardless of school district size. Urban districts use many buses to transport thousands of students over short distances, and rural districts also need many buses, despite low pupil population, to travel over countless open miles. Actual costs may be similar, and large and small systems alike face issues of safety, insurance, and so on. Food service operations in both rural and urban schools employ many staff, with urban schools hiring hundreds of food service workers and rural districts employing large staffs in relation to numbers of students and school sites. Transportation costs in 1999–2000 exceeded $13 billion, a sum just slightly more than the $12.9 billion spent for food service.[1] These sums were spent on about 46.5 million students for an average of $553 per pupil, making transportation and food service major industries. Transportation has become complex as issues of liability, safety, and equal access have arisen, and food service now includes hot lunch and breakfast programs, free and reduced price meals for economically disadvantaged children, commodity support programs to aid schools and to bolster agricultural economies, federal and state lunch subsidies to make meals more affordable, and other aspects of improving learning through health and nutrition.

The role of auxiliary services is thus great and demands efficient organization because noninstructional activities add meaningfully to the social and educational mission of schools.

THE TRANSPORTATION FUNCTION

There is no doubt that the transportation function is one of the most visible services in schools. Bright yellow school buses arrive in front of the homes of more than half of all school children each morning, and the bus is often the last school contact of the day. The transportation function is even larger, however, taking students on field trips and to athletic and academic events, and assisting other services such as special education. It is also like other arguments made in this textbook—when floors shine, the schools seem good. But when buses are late or when problems arise, everything about schools seems suspect. As a result, transportation is one of the most important and visible noninstructional activities of schools.

---

1. U.S. Department of Education, National Center for Education Statistics, *Digest of Education Statistics 2002* (Washington, DC: National Center for Education Statistics, 2003), 189.

What Are the Origins and Purpose?

Transporting students to and from school has largely developed as a result of school district consolidation dating from the early days of the twentieth century. Although assumed to have been an accompaniment of the invention of motor vehicles, the fact is that transportation and state financial support have been in existence since 1869, when Massachusetts became the first state to spend public money for pupil transportation. Although the Massachusetts law was the first of its kind, pupil transportation has had no choice but to grow as compulsory attendance, district consolidation, and the advent of motor vehicles have drastically affected society. Consolidation alone has led to huge change, as between 1917 and 1922 nearly 20,000 small schools ceased to exist and 4,500 one-room schools were closed every year until 1960.

Unlike some aspects of fiscal support for schools, from the earliest days the American public has been willing to spend for transporting students. Support was likely because of recognition that what was difficult for an individual to do could be done by the community much more efficiently. A spurring factor was the remoteness of an agricultural nation, which flourished until only a short time ago. In recent years, however, public school transportation has taken on even more importance because of a host of court rulings on issues affecting equal educational opportunity, including transportation of parochial school pupils and the special needs of physically disabled students. A major role for transportation has also arisen from court-ordered desegregation plans revolving around forced busing, which have added to the size and challenges of transportation. Even more recently, magnet schools and year-round schools have added to the complexity of pupil transportation. With the size of transportation added to burgeoning regulation and insurance costs, the transportation function has experienced huge growth during the last 100 years.

The purpose of pupil transportation is obvious, but its application is complex. As we have stated philosophically, no student has equal educational opportunity if schooling is offered but is physically inaccessible because of lack of transportation. In response, states and local districts have worked to make schools accessible to students who live beyond reasonable distances for which parents can be expected to provide transportation. The cost of providing services, however, is a multibillion dollar industry ranging from employment for drivers to insurance for liability protection. Complicating costs are issues of efficiency and accountability—concepts that are themselves complicated by competing public goals. For example, parents often have one set of expectations whereas the state and school district hold different goals. Transportation may require new facilities, the movement of population within a community may create new transportation demands, racial integration may require new school attendance boundaries, and so on. Additionally each state, as well as each district, has needs confounding the complexity of transportation. For example, no two states or school districts are exactly alike on variables such as population density, number of pupils to be transported, topography, road conditions, and length of routes affecting the size of buses on routes. To make matters more difficult, there are many other decisions at the local level, such as whether a district should operate its own bus system or contract the service out to private companies. Local decisions are even affected by state aid formulas, making transportation a very complex function in contrast to its basic purpose.

Although the origins of transportation can be traced to a simple concept, the implications are so deep that districts have had to create extensive transportation organizations. The result is often a decision to devote a full-time or part-time salary to a transportation director charged with preparing and carrying out bus management policies, establishing controls, arranging driver training programs, and coordinating maintenance service. Often the transportation director also has responsibility for planning bus routes and preparing regular and special route schedules for students and transportation staff.

The job of director of transportation services requires a variety of talents and skills. The knowledge base includes ability to efficiently organize a large transportation fleet and to consistently demonstrate human relations skills in working with personnel problems. Additionally, the director must be skilled in decision-making to manage effectively. The director also must have knowledge of diverse topics, including computer routing, budgeting, labor relations, inventory, drug testing, underground storage tanks, and hazardous materials, to name only a few. Because of liability involved in transportation, the director must demand staff accountability; the director, together with superiors, is responsible for all transportation issues.

Although many people help carry out the transportation function, the director is the one person who oversees all district transportation goals. These goals and attendant procedures and responsibilities should be placed in a comprehensive transportation manual. The manual should be a well-written document open to the public, and in-service should be held with transportation staff to clarify the objectives and policies of the district. All regulations, as well as evaluation policies, should be included. Recruitment plans, job descriptions, training information, and the objectives of each job should be included, and special emphasis must be given to driver training, pupil discipline, energy conservation, disability issues, public relations, bus routes, and bus schedules. Although these elaborate procedures and responsibilities have only a distant kinship to the origins of transporting children at public cost, the basic purpose has not changed—that is, making education available to all children still remains the first goal.

What Is Transportation Law?

Although all transportation issues are complex, none is more serious than the area of transportation law. Many cases have focused on liability in transporting students, and a large body of case law has centered on the issue of authorization to provide transportation.[2] Several cases have addressed the use of public funds to transport private school students,[3] and other cases have addressed who can be transported,[4] as well as authority to deny transportation.[5] Of course, transportation for desegregation has been heavily litigated.[6] Although it is impossible to review all case law here, a quick overview underscores the weightiness of the law's relationship to school transportation.

Educational access via transportation has been the focus of lawsuits at the U.S. Supreme Court level on many separate occasions. In a case seemingly unrelated to busing, the Supreme Court ruled in *Cochran v. Louisiana State Board of Education*[7] in 1930 that public funds could be used to buy books for private school children because it applied a test that became known as the child-benefit theory. According to *Cochran*, courts could relax the church-state entanglement prohibition in the U.S. Constitution[8] by deciding whether the child is the prime beneficiary of a public expenditure in private schools. If children received the benefit, the Court reasoned, the expenditure would not violate separation of church and state if other care was taken. *Cochran* became the basis for a 1947 ruling affecting transportation in *Everson v. Board of Education*[9] where the Court ruled that reimbursing bus fare to parochial and private school children was permissible in that public and private interests are not

---

2.   See, e.g., *Raymond v. Paradise Unified School Dist.*, 31 Cal. Rptr. 847 (Cal. 1963); *Woodland Hills School Dist. v. Pennsylvania Dept. of Educ.*, 516 A.2d 875 (Pa. 1986).

3.   See, e.g., *Board of Educ. v. Antone*, 384 P.2d 911 (Okla. 1963); *Cumberland School Comm. v. Harnois*, 499 A.2d 752 (R.I. 1985).

4.   See, e.g., *Madison County Board of Educ. v. Brantham*, 168 S0.2d 515 (Miss. 1964); *People ex rel. Schuldt v. Schimanski*, 266 N.E.2d 409 (Ill. 1971).

5.   See, e.g., *Shaffer v. Board of School Dir.*, 522 F. Supp. 1138 (Pa. 1981); *Kansas v. Board of Educ.*, 647 P.2d 329 (Kan. 1982).

6.   See, e.g., *U.S. v. Jefferson County Board of Educ.*, 372 F.2d 836 (11th Cir. 1967); *Swann v. Charlotte-Mecklenburg Board of Educ.*, 312 F. Supp. 503 (N.C.1970), aff'd, 402 U.S. 43 (1971).

7.   281 U.S. 370, 50 S. Ct. 335 (1930).

8.   The First Amendment to the U.S. Constitution reads: "Congress shall make no law respecting an establishment of religion, or prohibiting the free exercise thereof; or abridging the freedom of speech, or of the press; or the right of the people peaceably to assemble, and to petition the Government for redress." This has been interpreted to mean that "entanglement" of church and state could follow from involving public funds and private schools, and resulted in the so-called Lemon test of *Lemon v. Kurtzman* (403 U.S. 602, 91 S. Ct. 2105 [1971] rehg. denied), which applies a tripartite test to determine if a law has the effect of (a) advancing the cause of religion, (b) resulting in excessive entanglement, or (c) has a secular purpose. Opponents of "parochiaid" object on the grounds of these three prongs of the *Lemon* test.

9.   330 U.S. 1, 67 S. Ct. 504 (1947), rehg. denied.

crossed with the establishment of religion by applying the child-benefit theory to busing. The Court observed that transportation is like police, fire, and other protections available to private or church organizations, saying that to deny a benefit would make the state an adversary of the church. But despite the Court's rulings in *Cochran* and *Everson,* issues of commingling public funds with private interests have returned many times for further rulings.

The arena of transportation law is still very unsettled as illustrated by a more recent case involving questions of violating equal opportunity when poor people must pay bus fees to ride to school. This issue was taken up by the U.S. Supreme Court in *Kadrmas v. Dickinson Public Schools.*[10] At the root were efforts by the state of North Dakota to encourage school consolidation, which included financial incentives for districts that voluntarily participated. A district chose not to consolidate and also decided to institute fees for bus service. Parents brought suit, claiming a constitutional right to a free public education. The Supreme Court held for defendants in contradiction of the child-benefit theory, stating that the fee was rational and that equal protection was not harmed. The Court stated that the state's financial problems were a rational basis for fees, that transportation need not be provided at all, and that purely economic legislation must be upheld unless it is patently arbitrary. The Court left several issues unsettled, such as whether education is a constitutional right, but it did settle generally that schools may charge user fees. In an unfolding legal world, the child-benefit theory and the right to an education stand in apparent contradiction by allowing charges for a free public education.

Much other transportation litigation financially impacts schools, particularly because transportation is a high-risk activity due to potential liability. School districts serve as a common carrier rather than a private carrier and have the utmost duty to ensure student safety. As a generalization, districts take on many forms of liability when transporting pupils. Liability is controlled by various state tort concepts and is further affected by state statutes regarding transportation of students. Compared to other activities, however, transportation is one of the highest risks—a fact secured by a host of liability cases, particularly involving negligence.

As we will discuss later in Chapter 11, a tort claim may arise when a district or an employee is charged with negligence. For negligence to occur, someone must have been injured, and it must be shown that a reasonable person in a similar setting could have foreseen and prevented the injury. Although the nature of transportation makes prevention difficult, the rules of negligence still apply. For example, the transportation director is normally the person who sets bus stops. If an accident occurs, liability may ensue if hazards were ignored.

---

10. 487 U.S. 450, 108 S. Ct. 2481 (1988).

Liability suits raising such questions have had varying results. In *Vogt v. Johnson*,[11] a 7-year-old child waiting for a school bus at the designated stop tried to cross the highway and was killed. The Supreme Court of Minnesota ruled that the driver of the bus, acting as an agent of the district, was not liable at the time of the accident because custodial responsibility for the child had not yet arisen, and no precaution could have been taken to avoid the accident. Several other cases have upheld this logic, although there have been cases to the contrary, as in the decision in *Brooks v. Woods*,[12] which stands in sharp contrast. In *Brooks*, the district was negligent due to the placement of a school bus stop and the subsequent injury to a student. The bus stop had been established adjacent to a 5-lane highway with a 45-mile-per-hour speed limit, and the scheduled arrival of the bus coincided with rush hour traffic. While waiting for the bus, a child was hurt. A key to the ruling was that the child was known by the school to have physical and mental limitations. The appeals court ruled that the district's legal duty to exercise responsible care extends to any activity of bus transportation that lies outside the control of parents.

No completely exhaustive set of rules can be established for every situation that a bus driver and school district may face. However, in a negligence case, the defendant must show that all actions were those of a reasonable and prudent person under the circumstances. A few more cases illustrate how liability may arise. In *Mitchell*,[13] the district was liable when a child fell on an icy sidewalk and was crushed under the bus wheels. Testimony revealed that the bus was not in its usual pickup spot and that normal supervision was not present. In *Cross*,[14] a bus left the road after failing to make a curve. Testimony revealed that the driver had said he was sleepy, had asked students to talk to him, and that he was seen rubbing his eyes and yawning. Many other cases involving violence, drugs, and unruly activity also exist.

The specifics of each case, state law, and applicability of standard of care based on age of the child are controlling, so that exhaustive discussion is not feasible. What matters most is that districts often have been held negligent in the arena of student transportation. In all such cases, the evidence showed that the potential for injury was foreseeable, and that actions by the board or its agents did not meet the minimum standard of care. As we will see in Chapter 11, failure to protect students may be the causal factor leading to injury, and districts and personnel may be liable. Under these conditions, transportation and the law have become constant companions in the modern world.

---

11. 153 N.W.2d 247 (Minn. 1967).
12. 640 P.2d 1000 (Okla. Ct. App. 1981).
13. 161 S.E.2d 645 (N.C. 1968).
14. 371 N.Y.S.2d 179 (N.Y. App. Div. 1975).

How Is Transportation Funded?

Growth in transportation systems in the United States since the turn of the twentieth century has resulted in vast numbers of children carried in school vehicles at public expense. Costs are even greater than noted at the outset of this chapter, in that no single agency tracks the other transportation costs in schools that fall outside uniform state reporting for instructional programs. Because many states exclude cocurricular programs from transportation aid formulas, part of the cost of transportation goes unnoticed because no central data are collected.

At the start of the new millennium, almost every state provided some form of aid to local districts for regular pupil transportation (Figure 10.1). Like other forms of state aid, transportation aid varies in amount and distribution method from state to state. Formulas include a wide variety of features, with factors such as expenditures per pupil, population density, bus capacities, matching grants, or some combination as common denominators. Formula operation is often complex. For example, many states have a density formula based on an index consisting of the number of pupils transported divided by the eligible bus route mileage. Additionally, many states have an allowable per-student cost, which is usually the actual expense plus cost of bus replacements divided by the number of eligible students in a district. This amount is then plotted against a population density ratio, yielding a permissible cost per pupil as aid.

Beyond these generalizations, formulas differ widely on a state-by-state basis. Some states provide a transportation allowance based on hazardous walking conditions, so that students who live close to school can still be transported with the help of state aid. In other states, transportation aid is tied to the general fund formula, so that there is a relationship between the philosophy of regular education funding and the financing of transportation. In still other states, there appears to be no reason why the state may equalize the general fund and at the same time, aid transportation by a system of unequalized grants. Once basic similarities are noted, the only other commonality is that in most states, transportation aid almost never covers the entire cost.

Although each state calculates transportation aid using its own formula, many states use a concept closely relating to the example in Figure 10.2 (p. 294). The underlying philosophical support is density costs, that is, the ratio of pupils in the district to geographic size. Aid is found by following each step in the formula based on an index of density. In this example, an important point is that while actual transported head count is 583, yielding a density of 3.81 students per square mile (density table not shown), the effect is to weight these pupils higher for transportation aid purposes than would be true in a district where the number of pupils is great enough to result in a higher density factor. When the density factor is tied to the general fund formula in this example (see line 5 of Figure 10.2), the actual number of students

(Text continues on page 294.)

Figure 10.1. Transportation Formulas

State	Aid	Transportation Program	Nonpublic Pupils
AL	6%	Fully state funded categorical aid for students 2 miles or more from school.	N
AK	na	State provides 90% of funding, including air travel or ground transportation to athletic and cultural events.	N
AZ	na	Included in basic program, aids daily route miles; additional funding for vocational, technical, athletic programs.	N
AR	<1%	Expenses divided by ADM with costs of $117 or above receiving aid.	N
CA	2%	Aid for regular and special education through 'mega-item' funding of 32 categorical programs.	N
CO	2%	State pays approved costs at $0.3787 per mile plus 33.87% of excess costs up to 90%.	N
CT	2%	State pays equalized funding 0-60% of eligible costs, minimum $1,000 grant.	Y
DE	8%	State pays full funding, including school choice costs based on miles, fuel and insurance and CPI.	Y
FL	5%	State aid for expenses, bus replacement, density, and route mileage, 2 or more miles or hazardous walking conditions.	N
GA	3%	Aid for special education and regular education pupils more than 1.5 miles based on state determined minimum cost.	N
HI	2%	Transportation provided to all through state or private vendors.	N
ID	5%	State reimburses 85% of allowable previous year costs, including curriculum-related activities.	N
IL	6%	State reimburses over 1.5 miles or more or in hazard areas; reimbursement varies by grade level.	Y
IN	<1%	State pays $280 - ($20 x [eligible pupils + total roundtrip mileage]) over 1 mile. Total aid = per pupil amount times eligible pupils less local cost of $0.43 per $100AV. State pays 80% special and vocational education.	N
IA	na	Included in basic cost.	Y
KS	3%	Included in general state aid as weighted factor.	Y
KY	6%	State pays approved costs for students 1 mile or more from school with density adjustments.	N
LA	na	Included in basic support program.	Y
ME	5%	State pays base year costs plus CPI increase.	N
MD	4%	Previous year's allocation plus lesser of 8% or CPI increase, with guaranteed 3% minimum.	N
MA	3%	State pays 28% aid over 1.5 miles from school. Regional districts receive 80%.	Y
MI	<1%	Included in basic program; partial reimbursement for driver training.	Y
MN	8%	Most funding is provided through the general education revenue program.	Y
MS	nr	Add-on to basic program.	N
MO	4%	State reimburses 75% of approved costs but formula is not fully funded. Districts not exceeding 105% of predicted costs receive 67%; above 105% may receive as low as 56%.	N

(Figure continues on next page.)

State	Aid	Transportation Program	Nonpublic Pupils
MT	2%	State reimburses minimum of $0.85 per mile, extra funding for buses with 45+ capacity; reduced if <50% capacity.	N
NE	2%	Lesser of actual costs or calculated amount on miles transported, in lieu of mileage to parents.	N
NV	nr	Funded through basic support program, 85% of allowable expenditures.	N
NH	nr	State aid only for vocational transportation.	N
NJ	4%	Per-pupil allocations adjusted for average distance pupils reside from school and a incentive factor.	Y
NM	6%	State variably aids average cost per student for each district. Add-on for unpaved and unimproved roads; hold harmless.	Y
NY	7%	Equalized aid to public and non-public school students over 1.5 miles. Sparsity and grade level weightings.	Y
NC	4%	Aid based on pupils transported, eligible expenditures, and number of buses; inefficiency penalty.	N
ND	7%	Maximum 90% reimbursement based on miles, pupils, days, vehicles, distance, and rural/urban setting.	N
OH	5%	Categorical aid provides 50% of costs based on statewide history, adjusted for unique geography.	Y
OK	1%	Supplement to the foundation formula based on Average Daily Haul over 1.5 miles times per capita allowance times factor.	nr
OR	nr	State provides 70% of approved costs over 1 mile for elementary pupils, 1.5 miles for high school students.	N
PA	5%	Subsidy for public and non-public students based on vehicle capacity, mileage, congested areas, service type.	Y
RI	na	Funded through basic support program.	N
SC	4%	State has overall supervision of transportation, including vehicle acquisition, maintenance, training, operational costs.	N
SD	nr	Included in basic support formula.	N
TN	na	Included in basic support formula.	N
TX	na	Maximum rate per mile set by appropriation based on daily cost, maintenance, density, geography.	N
UT	4%	State aids route mileage, transport time, and equipment costs over 1.5 miles grades K-6, 2 miles 7-12.	N
VT	2%	Schools providing transportation eligible for up to 50% reimbursement.	N
VA	nr	Basic support formula considers land area, number of pupils transported, and estimated costs.	N
WA	4%	Based on number of pupils, distance, unique costs, special education, small fleet, special vehicles.	N
WI	<1%	Flat amount per pupil based on distance each pupil is transported.	Y
WY	10%	State pays 100% of transportation and maintenance expenditures for the preceding year and 100% of leases or purchases.	N

nr=not reported; na=not applicable, included in general formula

SOURCE: *The American Education Finance Association's School Finance Programs of the United States and Canada, 1998-1999*, eds. Catherine C. Sielke, John Dayton, C. Thomas Holmes, Anne L. Jefferson, and William J. Fowler, Jr. Washington, DC: United States Department of Education, National Center for Education Statistics (2000). Data excerpted and modified from Table 4.1, authored by Catherine C. Sielke and C. Thomas Holmes.

Figure 10.2. Sample Transportation Aid Formula

Area of district in square miles September 20	=	153.0
All pupils transported living 2.5 miles or more from school	=	583.0
Index of density (Line 2 ÷ Line 1)	=	3.81
Factor from density table (not shown)	=	0.1355
Weighted pupil count 583.0 × 0.1355 factor (to General Fund)	=	79.0

claimed for state aid purposes would be the 583 head count plus 79 more students—in effect yielding extra aid for each of those "ghost" pupils, because the density index is linearly tied to miles traveled and children transported. If the effect of this weighting formula were analyzed, it would be seen that in this instance, the density index grants an extra $316,000 in transportation aid ($4,000 base general aid per pupil times 79 extra transportation weighted pupils) that would *not* have been received if the formula had been distributed on an actual head count basis.

Regardless of the state, transportation aid calculation is a product of legislative decisions. The first decision is adoption of a transportation philosophy. If the state has a high level of commitment, then more aid will be offered than in states where other priorities have been set. The second decision is adoption of an aid formula reflecting that philosophy. The third decision is a product of the first two choices by setting the amount of funding to flow through the formula. Available resources will always determine the amount of aid by "backing into the formula." This means that the formula will be fully funded each year, although full funding could be less than in the prior year. Although this may be semantics, it is reality in an imperfect world in which tax revenues are finite.

Aid formulas therefore grant money to districts based on audited records proving the claims districts make for transportation aid. Aid qualification requires significant recordkeeping, with states closely auditing for overpayment. A set of records for state aid purposes often includes the following:

♦ Area maps and bus route information

♦ Address and destination of all students claimed for aid

♦ List of students using more than one kind of transportation (e.g., vocational or special education)

♦ List of nonpublic school students transported if claimed

♦ Evidence of bus seating capacity for each child claimed

♦ Evidence of bridge or road condemnation or construction if the most direct route from home to school is inaccessible

♦ Evidence of mileage driven on all routes by all buses

◆ Basis and work paper showing calculation for prorated costs
◆ Summary and original documents for all pupil transportation for regular routes, special and vocational education, or other eligible transportation
◆ Claims for payments in lieu of transportation showing dates, mileage, rates, and total payments
◆ Evidence of insurance costs for vehicles
◆ Evidence of price of buses and depreciation history
◆ List of leased or lease-purchase buses and dates of lease
◆ Other as required by state-specific statute

Without records, reimbursement problems arise. Problems range from denial of state aid to liability for negligence or malfeasance if investigation for fiscal impropriety or injury ever occurs.

The key features of aid plans can be stated succinctly. First, almost every state transports students at public expense. Second, aid has become a huge cost to states in the belief that children must get to school to receive the full measure of education. Third, state aid plans generally are tied to density or sparsity of attendance areas. Fourth, there is usually some attempt to judge the fiscal ability of districts, either by tying transportation aid to general fund aid or funding transportation categorically. Fifth, aid is almost always locally supplemented. Sixth, to qualify for aid, states require much documentation. Seventh and finally, these tasks emphasize the value of well-managed transportation systems from both liability and financial perspectives.

What Other Issues Are Relevant?

Several other important considerations should be briefly addressed before leaving this topic. These include the concepts of whether districts should own bus fleets or contract out for bus services, computerization of transportation, bus purchasing, and maintenance and safety.

Owning or Contracting

The merits and disadvantages of district ownership of the transportation fleet versus contracting form an ongoing debate. On one side of the argument are districts that claim to have saved money and time by contracting out transportation services. There are several reasons why these districts may be correct. First, there may be logic to contracting out in districts with cash problems because contracting avoids the cost of buying buses. The average rural district runs 10 to 20 buses ranging from 15-passenger to 66-passenger units or more. The average urban district runs hundreds of such units. At an average cost of more than $50,000 per bus, a bus fleet is a huge drain on cash. Second, districts may benefit because they often cannot afford new buses, and the high maintenance costs of older buses are not a direct consideration if the district does not own the fleet. Third, state laws on bus purchases vary, but in most cases require cash purchase. For example, in some states, buses can only be bought from capital outlay or transportation funds, in effect putting the total cost on the local tax base unless these funds are equalized.

Other arguments are also frequently offered favoring contracting for bus services. These argue that contracting lowers capitalization costs, reduces personnel and administration costs, and provides greater efficiency through contractors whose sole business is transportation. Counterarguments, however, include how to ensure quality performance by a contractor when the district no longer controls the public relations aspect of the contractor's behavior and the need for insuring against liability for acts of contractors. These issues make careful legal and community analysis a prerequisite to contracting out.

In contrast, there are arguments for district ownership of a transportation fleet. Advocates argue that ownership provides more flexibility, provides selection, training, and supervision of transportation employees, and ensures control over changes in operational costs. It may be that there is no one best option, as the right choice may depend on a district's financial position and the community's attitude about this vital service. What must be understood is that if contracting is chosen, written agreements should specify that the contractor is an independent agent and must comply with all state statutes, rules, and regulations. It must also be agreed within state regulations that the contractor will provide insurance for property damage and bodily and personal injury, although the district must still continue to insure itself.

Computerizing Transportation Services

As school system size has grown, and as technology has entered the scene, computerization of transportation services has taken on new importance. Every year more districts are using computerized routing, including many smaller districts. These plans are cost-effective in that they can apply mathematical formulas for routing efficiency. For many districts, especially large ones with mazes of streets to travel, bus routing systems have reduced costs by 15% or more. Software is available to preplan transportation routes in undeveloped areas in advance of actual population movement, and these tools combine with demographic forecasting to help districts economically purchase school sites years before any construction begins. Additionally, many districts use computer-aided techniques in mapping routes, including census data, highway time delay studies, and other devices, along with manual data supplied by demographic, cartographic, and geocoding personnel. Computerized routing systems are complex, but they are easily understood by recognizing that they function from geocoding, that is, manual data entry or data entry from a DIME system (i.e., a computerized filing system maintained via Standard Metropolitan Statistical Areas (SMSAs) as defined by the U.S. Census). Such systems are not cheap and require cost-benefit analysis to justify purchase. The benefit, though, is efficiency and the ability to create "what if" scenarios.

Although computer routing may be best suited for larger districts that must plan migration even before it occurs, computerized fleet maintenance is

common. Such programs incorporate garage operations, vehicle replacement, mechanical repairs and maintenance, and fuel consumption into databases to reveal the relationship between preventive maintenance and emergency repairs. Additionally, the number and type of repairs for each vehicle,
cost per mile, and cost per vehicle repair is tracked. Total and item costs can
be accounted for instantly and used to make decisions about maintenance
and disposal. For example, a district might find that maintenance for one particular bus was $300 in the first year, whereas the same bus consumed $4,117
in its fifth year. This information can be compared with labor costs to determine the true net cost of a new bus. State reports are often prepared with such
programs because the system is useful for maintaining and analyzing data
concerning each bus, number of pupils transported, preventive maintenance,
fuel consumption, and repair records, as well as future inspection and maintenance schedules. The benefit is sizable, in that records can be quickly
gathered, saving many human hours as compared to manual collation.

Purchasing Buses

Our discussion about owning, contracting, and using cost-benefit analysis illustrates the enormity of school bus costs. The price of a typical bus may
average more than $50,000, but the purchase of a bus with a wheelchair lift
can jump by many thousands of dollars. Such large outlays require care to
avoid problems at delivery because of failure to write tight bid specifications
or failure to follow state-specific laws.

Purchase of large ticket items like buses is normally done by the local district using written specifications to detail vehicle features. Specifications are
usually based on state guidelines. In a few states, a state agency prepares the
bid specifications, awards bids, and provides buses to districts. This is not
typical, however, so district personnel must be skilled at these tasks. Buses
are especially complicated because they are purchased on separate chassis
and body bids. That is, the local district bids these items separately, and the
body manufacturer provides a body to fit the chassis at another factory.
Although complex, this provides both economy and specialization that can
be used by both manufacturers because bus body manufacturers can
mass-produce for approximately four standard chassis. Type of motor, that
is, diesel or gasoline, and horsepower rating, can also be bid to make the bus
meet local preferences. In general, most districts find a mix of bus sizes is
appropriate. Larger buses are more versatile, which in turn reduces the number of buses and staff. Smaller buses are used in sparsely inhabited areas or
inner cities on crowded streets.

Most states have competitive bid laws that apply to large purchases,
including buses. The purpose of bidding is to force competition because there
are only a few bus manufacturers in the country, making it possible for lack
of competition to drive prices up. Similarly, in the past some districts have
had favorite suppliers who were able to develop relationships that did not
require them to compete for lucrative contracts. Consequently, many states
require districts to accept the lowest responsible bid for comparable prod-

ucts. As a rule, bid laws set a threshold purchase price above which bids must be taken and set out the conditions of bidding: for example, publication requirements, opening of bids, acceptance of the lowest responsible bid, errors in bids, and procedures for accepting or rejecting bids.

Maintenance and Safety

The importance of bid laws and the rising cost of buses have increased as a result of concern about safety and maintenance of school buses. The National Transportation Highway and Safety Administration (NTHSA) passed new regulations in 1977, which were meant to make buses safer in event of collisions, including requirements for padding the backs and sides of seats. Concern for safety and maintenance of older buses has been so widespread that many states have ordered regular inspections and the scheduled retirement of older buses from service. At the same time, it is clear that maintenance, safety, and staff are inseparable in any discussion of transportation. Obviously, good drivers cannot offset bad buses, nor can new equipment offset bad drivers. Equipment maintenance and staff training are invaluable safety aids, saving lives and prolonging bus life.

Issues of liability underscore the relationship of safety, maintenance, and personnel. Safety includes being certain that loading and unloading zones are protected from traffic, and that students have time to cross streets. Safety includes training for all staff and information for parents and community members. Maintenance includes drivers' daily inspections, including walk-arounds for leaks or tire problems, inoperative lights, flashers, stop arms, and so forth on a daily basis. The director of transportation should establish a regular maintenance schedule that includes oil changes, brake inspections, and all kinds of maintenance to ensure safety and equipment life. In the worst case, accidents will be avoided. In the best case, buses will last longer. Both are excellent outcomes to maintenance and safety programs.

THE FOOD SERVICE FUNCTION

Like transportation, the food service function is a key to effective and efficient operation of schools. Although both these functions are seen as lower in the educational hierarchy because they are less visibly related to the primary mission of schools, these functions provide vital support to the instructional process. This is certainly true for food service because it takes knowledge and skill to plan and conduct a system for meeting the nutritional needs of children. As we said at the outset, it makes no sense to argue for equal opportunity if children come to school hungry. As a result, we need a brief review of the food service function to understand how it operates, how meal prices are set under federal, state, and local participation, and how revenues and expenditures in food service budgets are allocated.

What Are the General Issues?

As we stated at the outset of this chapter, the importance of the food service function cannot be overemphasized because the role of nutrition in schools is fundamental common sense. Data from earlier parts of this book and other sources[15] indicate that schools face tremendous problems, beginning in the home, that are laid on the school as barriers to effective teaching and learning. Most striking is evidence that undernourishment due to poverty and ignorance is still sizable in today's era of economic progress. Data show that many children come to school from impoverished homes, as 15% of all American children fell below the federal poverty line in 2001—down from nearly 18% in 1990—but unimproved from 1970 when the poverty rate stood at 15% as well.[16]

These and other data linking poor school performance to nutrition and social issues have sparked historical interest at all levels of federal, state, and local government. The debate over an appropriate role for government has raged for decades, however, with government aiding health and nutrition in various ways ranging from cash aid to surplus commodity distributions meant to simultaneously benefit different segments of society and the economy. The role of food service in schools has only increased with time, as seen in the fact that most schools now have both breakfast and lunch programs because many children are undernourished. Although food service cannot solve all of society's problems, it can be a positive force by making school a better experience for children.

How Is Food Service Funded?

Food service programs in schools have a long history of federal, state, and local subsidies to supplement meal prices paid by children. These sources make up the revenue side of food service operations and are highly interdependent.

Federal Support

The first federal legislation granting aid to nutrition grew out of economic interests during the Great Depression. In 1935, the Bankhead-Jones Act (PL 74–182) was an act in federal legislation giving grants to states to create agricultural experiment stations. In the same year, Congress approved the Agricultural Adjustment Act (PL 74–320) authorizing 30% of customs receipts for encouragement of exportation and domestic consumption of surplus commodities. The effect was that surplus commodities began to be used

---

15. See generally, Chapter 1 discussion of demographics in David C. Thompson, R. Craig Wood, and David Honeyman, *Fiscal Leadership for Schools: Concepts and Practices* (New York: Longman, 1994), 3–72.

16. U.S. Department of Education, National Center for Education Statistics, *Digest of Education Statistics 2002* (Washington, DC: National Center for Education Statistics, 2003), 27.

in school lunch programs in 1936, wherein both agriculture and schools were beneficiaries in a nutrition agenda linked with a poor market for farm commodities. Not long afterward, Congress enacted the National School Lunch Act (PL 79–396) authorizing grants to states to help provide food and facilities for nonprofit school lunch programs. By 1954, Congress had passed the School Milk Program Act (PL 83–597), appropriating federal funds to buy school milk. Although the economic conditions leading to a federal role are long past, Congressional interest in school nutrition has remained, as it continues to have an agenda in support of farm prices, and as it has pursued an equality agenda focusing on poorer families.

Federal involvement in education has been substantial and broad based, covering a wide array of social and economic national interests. Federal support for education was estimated at $108 billion for fiscal year 2002 (FY 02). Approximately $46.3 billion came from the U.S. Department of Education (DOE), an office created in 1979 to oversee federal education programs. DOE interest has been broad, overseeing programs in the areas of Chapter 1, educational improvement grants, special education, vocational and adult education, impact aid, and other special Congressional interests. All federal interest in education, however, has not come through the Department of Education. Large amounts of money in FY 02 also came from the U.S. Department of Health and Human Services ($22.9 billion), the U.S. Department of Agriculture ($11.9 billion), the U.S. Department of Labor ($6.4 billion), the U.S. Department of Defense ($4.7 billion), and the U.S. Department of Energy ($3.6 billion).[17] When other money and nonfederal funds from federal legislation are included, federal programs provide valuable aid to education.

State Support

A second unit of government that has long participated in food service is the individual states themselves. Historically, in most instances state participation has resulted from three choices states have had to confront. The first choice is whether the state even wishes to participate in the National School Lunch Act of 1946, a federal law that requires matching funds from states to qualify for federal funding. The second choice came as a result of whatever the state chose in its first decision—that is, states could choose to not participate, but refusal would result in loss of important federal funding, forcing the third choice of whether the state would participate at all in local food service programs. State support, then, has been both voluntary and compulsory in the sense that options are available; however, states have had a politically difficult time refusing federal aid.

Individual state participation is harder to summarize because each state has been free to determine the extent of its involvement. Most states have chosen to accept federal food aid, although there is no universal method for

17. U.S. Department of Education, National Center for Education Statistics, *Digest of Education Statistics 2002* (Washington, DC: National Center for Education Statistics, 2003), 419, 429.

structuring state participation. A review of current legislation finds a wide variety in food service program participation, with little uniformity in approach or level of support.

The data illustrate both the importance of food service aid plans and the relationship of amounts of aid to total educational funding. Although the dollars are large, state funding is relatively small compared to both the federal contribution and to the proportion of total spending for school purposes that occurs in the United States. As will be seen later, the large dollar amounts going to food services still represent only pennies per child, as the population is large enough to render aid totals small when viewed on a per-child basis. But as a result of the relationship between federal and state governments to food service, the federal government is the largest contributor to school nutrition.

The Local Role

In contrast to state and federal funding for food service, at first glance the local role seems small. Perspective, however, presents a different picture, especially in food service, because these programs are intended to be self-funding cash operations. The case can be made either way—the local role may be great or relatively minor.

The local role as a minor player flows from the view that if the federal government is the largest contributor, and the states must aid contributions, the local contribution is defined as dividing the unfunded portion of food service costs between the local district and its cash food sales. This view is fundamentally correct, although it understates the local decision making process when dividing the costs out. For example, if federal reimbursement for regular paid meals is 35.25¢ and if the state rate is 4.5¢, then the unfunded portion of a meal is $1.4025 (if the price charged locally is $1.80). Similar calculations occur for free and reduced meals. The local role is thus one of determining how much, if any, the district wishes to further subsidize meals by shifting additional local tax revenue to food service. The view of a minor local role is accurate only if "minor" is defined as dealing with the leftover costs after federal and state revenues are expended.

The view of major importance for the local role is the flip side of the same discussion. Leaving the unfunded part of meal costs to the local district creates a heavy burden for schools, in that such decisions have moral and financial implications. If the district channels all unfunded costs to consumers, then some children may not receive the intended benefits of food service programs. If the district subsidizes meals from tax revenues, a choice to reduce other program expenditures is being made. Fortunately, some of this burden is lifted because federal aid for free and reduced lunch, breakfast, or milk programs is much higher than for regular paid meals. For example, in fiscal year 2004 (FY 04), federal aid for regular paid lunches was 35.25¢ but reduced price lunch reimbursement was $1.8925 and free lunch was aided at $2.2925. Often the biggest problem is rising costs associated with purchasing and preparing food such as supply price increases, labor costs, and equipment and facilities—all of which must factor into what the district ultimately charges for meals. Creating a self-funding program is difficult, and as always, hard choices between competing programs must be made. Costs, efficiencies, and all other aspects of operations are a function of district size and skill in directing food service operations, a fact illustrated in Figure 10.3, which shows (using a sample district of about 1,000 students) how the number of meals and dollars becomes large very quickly.

What Other Issues Are Relevant?

Although entire books exist on food service operations, three additional items need to be examined here. A short look at broad compliance requirements, organizing for food service, and financial management round out this chapter.

Broad Compliance Requirements

Compliance is a common concern whenever outside aid is provided. Granting agencies want assurances that programs align with the grantor's intent. In the case of food service, assurances are directed to the federal government in return for dollars and commodities. Districts must assure states of compliance so the state can provide its own assurances to the federal government. Likewise, states may also aid food service for which the states themselves want separate compliance monitoring.

Eligibility for federal aid has been based on federal rules and regulations. Historically, schools and states have had to agree to the following:

- *Operate a nonprofit program.* Only a three-month operating balance may be kept on hand and still be nonprofit.
- *Serve meals that meet nutrition requirements.* Programs can offer single menu, fast food choice menu, or á la carte menu.
- *Price meals as a unit.* To count as reimbursable, meals must be priced as a unit. This does not prohibit single item sales.
- *Supply free and reduced meals* to eligible needy children.
- *Agree to avoid discrimination.* No child may be refused because of inability to pay, race, gender, or national origin.
- *Keep accurate records of income and expenditures.* Records are subject to intensive state and federal audits.
- *Complete a formal reimbursement claim.* Claims must be sent on a timely basis each month to the state.
- *Distribute applications for free and reduced meals.* Districts must actively inform each student of the program.
- *Review and act on free and reduced applications.* Parents or guardians must be notified regarding decisions.
- *Develop and implement verification procedures.* A method of verifying accuracy of applications must be followed.

Figure 10.3. Sample Food Service Revenue Sheet

		TOTAL ANNUAL MEALS	FEDERAL		STATE		DISTRICT LOCAL		TOTAL 7-1-03 to 6-30-04
			RATE	Reimburse-ment	RATE	Reimburse-ment	PRICE	REVENUE	
LUNCHES									
Paid Elem	1.	64,000	.3525	$22,560	.0450	$2,880	2.00	$128,000	$153,440
Jr. High	2.	35,000	.3525	$12,338	.0450	$1,575	2.10	$73,500	$87,413
Sr. High	3.	33,000	.3525	$11,633	.0450	$1,485	2.20	$72,600	$85,718
Free	4.	20,000	2.2925	$45,850	.0450	$900			$46,750
Reduced	5.	12,000	1.8925	$22,710	.0450	$540	0.40	$4,800	$28,050
Adult	6.	5,000					2.40	$12,000	$12,000
TOTAL	7.	169,000		$115,090		$7,380		$290,900	$413,370
BREAKFAST									
Paid Elem	8.	6,000	.2200	$1,320				$0	$1,320
Jr. High	9.	3,500	.2200	$770				$0	$770
Sr. High	10.	2,000	.2200	$440				$0	$440
Free	11.	1,800	1.1700	$2,106					$2,106
Reduced	12.	900	.8700	$783			0.30	$270	$1,053
Adult	13.							$0	$0
TOTAL	14.	14,200		$5,419				$270	$5,689
SNACKS									
Paid Elem	15.	64,000	.0500	$3,200				$0	$3,200
Jr. High	16.		.0500	$0				$0	$0
Sr. High	17.		.0500	$0				$0	$0
Free	18.	20,000	.5800	$11,600					$11,600
Reduced	19.	12,000	.2900	$3,480			0.15	$1,800	$5,280
Adult	20.							$0	$0
TOTAL	21.	96,000		$18,280				$1,800	$20,080
KINDERGARTEN									
MILK									
Paid	22.		.1350	$0				$0	$0
Free-Avg Dealer Cost	23.			$0					$0
TOTAL	24.	0		$0				$0	$0
OTHER CASH									
Sales/Income	25.								$0
12 Months									
Total Income	26.			$138,7890		$7,380		$292,970	$439,139

◆ *Maintain accurate participation records.* The district must establish procedures for obtaining accurate meal counts.

◆ *Establish and implement purchasing procedures.* Purchasing procedures must comply with state and federal regulations.

◆ *Use federally donated foods or commodities.* This includes the ability to store commodities properly without spoilage.

Federal law also requires food programs to comply with other regulations regarding foods served. The goal is to ensure that approved programs provide meals based on daily nutritional requirements. These requirements are part of the National School Lunch and Child Nutrition programs, which must provide approximately one-third of the recommended dietary allowance (RDA). To receive reimbursement, a lunch must contain a set of specified components and menu items, where components are *meat or meat alternate, vegetable* and/or *fruit, bread or bread alternate,* and *milk.* Similar regulations apply to breakfast programs. The goal is a balanced diet—a goal that has not wavered since the program's inception in the 1940s.

Organizing for Food Service

Growing sophistication of food service programs has led to cost analyses of how districts can better manage programs and costs. Organizing has centered on types of management systems best suited to a district's needs, along with how to manage food service budgets. This has primarily resulted in choosing between contracts for outside management, centralized in-house operations, or decentralized in-house food service systems, all with attendant benefits and drawbacks.

Management Companies

Use of outside management companies has arisen from debate about whether it is more cost-effective to contract out for food service or to handle it in-house. Although districts make different choices depending on circumstances, many districts have decided to contract for food service. The main reason has been a benefit stemming from fiscal and managerial efficiency. Districts that have moved to food contracts have reported benefits including increased and expanded menus, elimination of deficits that have long plagued food service, and improved communication due to the aggressive market responsiveness of vendors who should be more sensitive to clientele demands. The literature reports many instances of district administrators who believe that contracts for food service operations have proved more efficient and less costly. Specifically, advocates have reported five benefits to contracting with management companies:

◆ Administrators have more time for curriculum.

◆ Wage and benefit costs, disputes, and grievances have been reduced because the district no longer handles personnel.

◆ Menu planning is improved by use of food professionals.

♦ In-house record-keeping requirements are reduced.

♦ There is strong incentive for food service to become a profit center with high client satisfaction.

For districts wishing to contract food services, the literature suggests several key elements. Districts should take care to choose from a list of reputable and experienced firms and act from a set of bid specifications to assist bidders in deciding whether to bid, as well as establishing the criteria for evaluating proposals. Because a relationship is likely to last for some time, and because much public harm can be done by poor choices, careful pursuit of the best bid will serve the school district well.

In-House Operations

For districts not choosing outside contracts, the only option is to provide this function in-house. There are only two choices within this option: to centralize or decentralize services. Careful cost analysis should be the basis of the choice because each option has its own problems.

The basis of in-house problems lies in the complex tasks of running a food service program. There is generally so much reporting and supervising that districts operating in-house food service programs usually are forced to hire a full-time director. This person must be highly trained to assure the efficient and cost-effective operation of modern support services. Normally, this person is a certified dietitian who also needs skills to work closely with principals and the central office, as well as taking responsibility for supervising service workers. The position is one of planning, doing, and comparing results because this person is responsible for a full range of menu planning, food purchasing, and hiring and dismissal of staff.

An additional organizing element for in-house programs is consideration for efficiency and cost-effectiveness. This consideration is often the driving force behind how food service is structured and is most apparent as districts choose between centralized and decentralized operations. The debate concerns on-site food preparation versus satelliting from central kitchens, fixed versus free choice menus, and a host of other issues. Satelliting means delivering cooked food with finishing kitchens on-site, in contrast to on-site food preparation. From a cost perspective, central kitchens have proved cost-effective for many districts because the major benefit is mass preparation and nonduplication of full facilities. In well-managed central kitchens, productivity has been shown to increase by large margins. Costs must be carefully watched, however, because the expense of specialized vehicles to transport meals to sites, finishing kitchen equipment, and the use of specialized freezers for storage can be high. But proponents note that if properly managed, capitalization costs are spread over a greater number of schools, with lower end cost. Central operations are not without disadvantage, however, as critics point out that effectiveness may be hurt because site control is lower, and because rigidity, overstandardization, and nonresponsiveness may follow a large centralized operation. In either case, a related in-house problem is personnel because food service operations face a dilemma of low pay and high labor cost. This follows because many private-sector positions pay more for similar work, while labor costs are a major part of total overhead in food service operations.

Financial Management

Finally, no discussion of food service is complete without consideration for the complexity of budgeting. Unless the food service director is well trained, food service budgeting can be overwhelming because of the number of sites and programs. Generally, the food service manager, in cooperation with the district budget director, must establish the receipts and disbursements for each school site as part of the budget process and provide leadership in setting meal prices. This requires information and organizational skills, including the ability to analyze historic data and forecast revenues and expenditures. The complexity arises in that each school site must be evaluated as to the impact of changes in enrollments, food and labor costs, menu, meal prices, and so forth. This is difficult and precise work because food service budgeting is a cash operation—a fact that makes projection of revenue and expenditures different from other budgeting. The budgeting process must take into account a variety of factors such as historical data, demographic changes (school openings or closings), projected enrollments, effects of menu changes, changes in operating procedures, food and labor costs, meal prices, and state and federal guidelines.

The goal of financial management is accuracy of records and predictions. The process calls for budget items to be reduced to segments or subcategories and, finally, to monthly projections. Potential trouble spots can be identified in this way, and plans can be made for the entire year. As with every budget in the district, monthly projections are assembled into an annual budget wherein the revenue and expenditure sides must balance. The food service budget then becomes an integral part of the overall school district budget just like budgets for other support services. Our discussion of local choices reenters at this point, because program cost minus federal and state aid yields the cost per meal that must be charged or—alternatively—locally supplemented. For example, our district described earlier in Figure 10.3 (p. 302) served 64,000 paid elementary meals, for which it received 35.25¢ federal reimbursement and 4.5¢ state aid. The district is charging $2.00 per elementary meal (and so forth) based on its costs, which the district may subsidize if it chooses. If, when preparing a new budget, it is believed that estimated costs will go up next year, the district must decide if it will (a) raise prices, (b) shift local tax dollars to the food service fund, or (c) opt for efficiencies such as cost analysis of contracted versus in-house services. The interrelatedness and circularity of the budget process can be seen clearly in this example—in other words, we began this section by discussing cost-benefit regarding contracts versus in-house, and we have ended the same discussion by circling back to the same decision.

The budgeting side of food service is frustrating because districts have no way to reduce costs beyond the limited choices of contracting versus in-house, maximizing efficiency through choices such as central kitchens, and a few other options such as multi-district cooperative bulk purchasing or other interdistrict arrangements. Particularly troublesome is that if costs rise, the district must take money from other programs to subsidize meals or put the cost back on students. At the same time, it must be remembered that the objective of a school food service operation is to aid learning. The overall goal becomes enhancing student participation and operating as close as possible to a break-even financial ledger. Although difficult, this is mostly achievable through good management, which includes sound short- and long-range plans, an operations manager who is visible and involved, and a program supported by committed and knowledgeable boards, staffs, and other stakeholders.

WRAP-UP

The data and discussion in this chapter point to the vital contribution of auxiliary services to educational outcomes. It is common sense that equal opportunity is unavailable if children cannot get to school or if they come hungry. Although lacking in glamour, transportation and food service represent vast expenditure outlays and also represent significant liability. Transportation may consume about 4–5% of a typical district's budget, and food service is uniquely affected by its cash operation status and its atypical need to cater to client tastes and preferences. The result once again is to observe the intricately interrelated parts of a complete educational system, knowing that each piece makes a vital contribution and cannot be slighted without significant harm to children. Given the demographic data we saw earlier in this book, it appears that transportation and food service will only grow in importance, as every indication suggests that schools will become even greater caretakers and providers for children in the future.

SUGGESTED FOLLOW-UP PROJECTS

♦ Identify how transportation is funded in your state. Analyze the state funding formula to determine how many dollars are available and the relative emphasis on transportation in your state. Learn how the unaided portion is met in your local district.

♦ Discuss how transportation is structured in your district with your transportation director. Include issues related to decisions about owning versus contracting, purchasing, bid laws, maintenance and safety, driver training, and so on. Learn how routing occurs.

♦ Identify how food service is funded in your state. Analyze the mix of federal, state, and local aid to food service. Learn how meal prices are set and the philosophy that drives the local contribution to the food service fund.

♦ Meet with your district's food service director to learn how the district has structured this important operation. Include issues such as compliance with federal and state requirements and local decisions about in-house and contracted services, satelliting versus central kitchens, and so on. Discuss the qualifications of a food service director, the basis for approved menus, and other aspects of financial management.

11

LEGAL LIABILITY AND RISK MANAGEMENT

MODERN REALITIES

From the outset, this book has taken a realistic world view. We have made some blunt statements about what schools may become in the future, and we have been critical of people who devalue the contribution of schools to the economic and social lifestyle Americans enjoy. We would be remiss if we failed to take a realistic view of legal liability and risk management in schools because no one associated with education can escape the far-reaching influence of the law.

Our goals in this chapter are again framed by a set of questions. In the first half of the chapter, we approach liability and risk management from a broad perspective. We begin by asking such questions as: What does the law have to do with schools? From where do schools derive legal authority? What is the origin of liability? The last half of the chapter continues in the same vein but becomes more specific by asking: What is immunity and to what extent does it apply today? What is tort liability? What other kinds of liability arise, including exposure in important areas such as civil rights, defamation, educational malpractice, and contractual liability? And, of course, we close the chapter by asking what this means to administrators, faculty and staff, boards, and policy makers in the modern context of school funding.

The issues in this chapter are tough and unpleasant, but we live in an era of unparalleled legal jeopardy. Schools are seen as deep pockets and as the means to right all the wrongs of history—a reality that begs for wise risk management planning. As a result, this chapter is a fitting conclusion to Part II of this book by warning that liability represents a powerful limitation on what schools can achieve.

THE LAW AND SCHOOLS

To anyone even remotely associated with education, it comes as no surprise to start this chapter with the observation that the law and schools is a topic that fills entire libraries. Our work as scholars has centered on the intersection of law and school finance, requiring us to be current in both fields simultaneously. We have remarked often that most education journals are published quarterly, except school law journals, which appear at least monthly and sometimes biweekly. These small facts point to a great truth: The relationship between the law and schools is growing at a frenzied pace, allowing the discussion here to only focus on brief highlights. As noted frequently in this textbook, it is imperative for anyone associated with schools to have a working knowledge of the law for risk management purposes, but it is equally important to seek good legal counsel, as delay may be disastrous in the modern context of aggressive litigation.

WHAT DOES THE LAW HAVE TO DO WITH SCHOOLS?

The association of the law with schools is actually older than the nation. Earlier discussion in this textbook noted that the colonies passed laws requiring establishment of schools such as the Ye Old Deluder Satan Act of 1647 in the Massachusetts colony, and the nation's first compulsory education law also was passed in that same state in 1852. It is reasonable to believe such laws intended to force compliance with desired behaviors, and it further stands to reason that some people did not obey, which resulted in legal punishment of some kind. Although a grim view of what lawmaking can be about, laws are meant to apply first to lawless people, although a large number of laws are regulatory in nature.

Under these conditions, it is easy to see that schools and the law have a long relationship in this nation, and it is also easy to see that society has deemed education so useful that it seeks to censure anyone hindering the educational process. Certainly, the relationship of the law to schools today so far exceeds the first colonial laws that it is staggering. Today, schools must be concerned about the legal rights of children for equal access to educational programs, special programs for the underprivileged, fair funding, and a host of other highly specific issues relating to constitutional and statutory protections. Legal relationships extend to employment, with complex laws and legal concepts governing the rights of employees and employers so that schools are constantly embroiled in a political turmoil over who holds the biggest legal stick. As we saw earlier in Chapter 4 on accounting, fiscal affairs of schools are rigidly controlled by law because even the faintest hint of wrongdoing results in suspicion and may lead to dismissal. The concept of liability overarches all legal relationships. It is fundamental to say that school districts and everyone associated with educational policy may be liable for wrongful acts and errors of omission.

The law and schools is thus a dual relationship arising from expectations about a highly prized social commodity. One side of the relationship focuses on regulation for organizational purposes, whereas the other side focuses on liability for wrongful acts or errors. Much of this textbook relates to the regulatory aspect of the law because most of the chapter titles are deeply rooted in a governmental and public interest in education that results in a legal prescription for carrying out the educational mission—in fact, it is accurate to say that every human and organizational aspect of schools has a relationship to law and regulation. But our attention in this chapter goes to issues and costs of liability because the law and schools are close partners having profound budget implications by way of risk management.

The Derivation of School Authority

Everyone associated with education believes that schools enjoy significant authority and control over educational matters. Fewer people, however, understand that such authority is both broad in derivation and at the same time very limited. As a preface to all other issues in this chapter, it is important to lay out the sources and limits of schools' legal authority to gain a foundational sense of the relationship between schools and the law.

It is accurate to say that schools derive their legal authority from both constitutional and statutory origins. These sources are complex and interrelated. An overarching view notes that school authority originates in the federal Constitution, the United States Congress, the federal judiciary, and the constitutions of the individual states, state legislatures, state courts, and state boards of education. Each source has had a significant influence on the educational enterprise, so much so that the very existence of the local school district, its board of education, and its educational mission are derived from the combination of these powerful forces.

Federal Constitution

Involvement of the federal government in education has been both peripheral and intense. Starting with early federal interest through land grants to newly formed states to be used for educational purposes, federal involvement in education has grown to be a significant force. The federal path to involvement has been indirect because the U.S. Constitution is a document of limited powers, meaning that Congress cannot assume powers absent specific authorization in the Constitution. As we noted earlier, the Constitution is silent regarding education. In the absence of authority, Congress has had to find other ways to aid education because only a Constitutional amendment could create a direct federal role in education. In the context of this chapter, the U.S. Constitution both grants authority and creates liability for schools by endowing certain rights to citizens relating to education, while assigning actual responsibility for education to the states.

Congress

Given limited Constitutional powers, Congress has had to become the vehicle for federal involvement. Although a direct role is prohibited, Congress has found a loophole through the general welfare clause of the Constitution, which Congress has used to pass many laws affecting schools by interpreting general welfare benevolently and broadly. Under this banner, Congress has created a huge federal education bureaucracy that grants billions in aid to hundreds of programs in elementary and secondary schools and higher education. In related actions, Congress has found other ways to indirectly influence education policy by tying seemingly unrelated federal monies to education to put pressure on states to bow to federal educational policy. For example, Congress has often tied federal revenue sharing for such projects as highways to Congressional educational interests by threatening withdrawal of highway funds if states to do not support federal education goals. Likewise, passage of laws like special education and civil rights legislation powerfully affects schools. In the context of this chapter, Congress both grants authority and creates liability for schools by passing laws supporting certain educational initiatives that result in both benefit and liability.

Federal Judiciary

A significant source of authority in schools also rests in the federal courts. In a complex hierarchical legal system, federal rulings may take precedence over state courts, as in the familiar appeal to the U.S. Supreme Court as the court of last resort. In essence, federal courts have held great sway over education by applying federal Constitutional requirements to schools. Racial integration, educational deprivation, special and compensatory education, and countless other educational programs are examples of the result of federal courts' interest in educational issues. Congress's involvement at this level has been felt, too, as the members of Congress have exerted enormous control over education through the courts by virtue of their role in appointing federal judges who they hope will take a supportive view of federal interests, including federal goals for education. Similarly, Congress has been responsible for writing most of the laws tested in federal courts. The upshot is that although the federal government cannot assume a direct role in education, its influence has been disproportionate via the general welfare clause, by linking unrelated subsidies to federal educational interests, and by appointing federal judges who in turn examine Constitutional questions affecting schools. In the context of this chapter, federal courts both grant authority and create liability for schools by virtue of their politically appointed nature and by their legitimate role as guardians of the Constitution.

State Constitutions

The same authority that prohibits a federal role in education grants full power over schools to the individual states. The constitutional conventions of each state almost invariably mentioned education, writing into their earliest charters an active role for states in schools. Indeed, school finance litigation today turns first to the states' constitutional framers' intent to test whether modern state legislatures are meeting their constitutional obligations. The language of a state constitution's references to education can be a powerful influence on educational policy, granting sweeping power to the state or significantly limiting state responsibility. In essence, states have plenary power over education, subject only to higher federal protections such as Fourteenth Amendment due process. In fact, all sources of law at the state level regarding education derive from individual state constitutional authorization to its legislature. In the context of this chapter, state constitutions both grant authority and create liability for schools by requiring legislatures to create enabling educational statutes, which in turn result in both authority and liability.

State Legislatures

Short of constitutional proscription, a state legislature has authority to write any law affecting schools that it chooses. In essence, legislatures hold absolute power and are bound only by the duties and constraints interpreted by courts based on the applicable constitution. Although those duties and constraints are formidable, given federal and state education laws and constitutional requirements for educational equity, state legislatures have eminent control over education. For example, nothing in federal or state constitutions typically forbids a legislature from creating or abolishing a state department of education, consolidating or reorganizing school districts, increasing or decreasing state financial support for education, or a host of other far-reaching reforms. The source of such power and restrictions rests in each state's constitution and in its relationship to the courts, which interpret the constitutionality of state actions. In essence, states control the statutes governing education, creating and abolishing educational structures at will, limited only by the constitutionality of their actions. In the context of this chapter, state legislatures are the ultimate source of authority and liability in schools.

State Judiciary

The system of checks and balances in American government calls for separation of the executive, legislative, and judicial branches. State courts frequently have been asked to test the limits of legislative power, thereby creating one of the very few checks on legislative prerogative. State courts therefore guard the legality of state acts under the state constitution. State courts are thus a source of authority and the evaluator of liability.

State Boards of Education

Although legislatures have full power over education, most states have delegated responsibility for conducting education to a state board. State boards are arms of the state, usually created in statute and subject to legislative will. Alternatively, state boards may be constitutional creations, but are usually still under legislative control. As such, schools are legislatively based, with authority passed hierarchically to lower administrative units. In the context of this chapter, state boards both grant authority and create liability for schools by virtue of the rules and regulations they pass and administer.

Local Authority to Act

At the bottom of the hierarchy are local school boards. States, usually by legislative act, have delegated daily operations to local school districts. As such, local districts are subject to legislative control and may be organized as determined by the legislature and state board. In essence, local districts serve at the pleasure of some higher unit of government and are subject to all laws and regulations—in effect, districts are ordered to actually carry out the state's educational duties. In the context of this chapter, local boards function in a constitutionally limited context of state and federal laws under the watchful eye of a state legislature and state board of education—an environment that creates significant responsibility and liability.

WHAT IS THE ORIGIN OF LIABILITY?

The concept of liability is deeply rooted in this nation's history. Many excellent sources detail development of American jurisprudence, but all such sources begin with our inheritance from English law. Among those precepts are the key elements of sovereign immunity and tort law. Although many other aspects of law, including criminal law, at times apply to schools, issues involving torts and immunity arise most often. Both relate to liability, particularly as U.S. history has altered the original English concepts on which our system is anchored.

Sovereign Immunity

The complexity of the law makes it difficult to slice into small pieces. For example, in the previous section we saw the overlapping nature of the law and various levels of government relating to education, a relationship that has resulted in deep and significant entanglement. One consequence of that entanglement has been increased liability. For our purposes, a discussion of liability begins with sovereign immunity because the United States has nearly reversed itself on this basic tenet of law.

Sovereign immunity refers to a precept from English law that literally argued, "the king could do no wrong." The importance of this concept is immediately apparent because law is often based on following certain logic to an obvious conclusion. If, then, courts accepted that the king could do no wrong and that a king is the head of state, then the state could do no wrong. The ramification is obvious: Government is immune in its acts or omissions, a concept not greatly at odds with other sovereign views such as the divine right of kings.

Although modern Americans might look at sovereign immunity and wonder how anyone ever could have tolerated such raw power, it is the case that sovereign immunity was unquestioningly transported into U.S. law in ways that had little to do with real kings. The impact of English law and government was seen quickly in the new nation, as the 1812 Massachusetts case of *Mower*[1] held that the state could not be held liable for its acts. Although America has always scoffed at kings, sovereign immunity in this and subsequent cases was based on four distinct viewpoints that actually make good sense. One viewpoint argued that the government has limited resources so that proliferation of lawsuits stemming from a ruling, even for limited liabil-

---

1.   *Mower v. The Inhabitants of Leicester*, 9 Mass. 247 (1812).

ity, would be detrimental to public welfare. A second view held that government must be free from fear of liability to carry out its obligations because any act of law does not carry equal benefit for each citizen. A third view held that government is the people, especially in a representative democracy, such that it follows that suit against government is a suit against oneself. A fourth view also held that committing an illegal act is never within the authority of a government or its agents, so that a wrongful act exceeds any legal power. This logic was upheld as a rule of law, embedded in the view of many U.S. Supreme Court decisions, with the Court noting as early as 1869 that, "Every government has an inherent right to protect itself against suits..." and that "the principle is fundamental and applies to every sovereign power."[2] Although we again note that Americans now view such logic askance and further note that sovereign immunity is now much discredited, immunity survived nearly unquestioned in this nation until only recently. Government, including schools, could not be sued for virtually any reason. This is not to say that sovereign immunity was suddenly abandoned, but rather that gradual chipping away at the foundation of immunity has occurred. The erosion was especially aided by three separate but related concepts. The first was the incredulity of such unlimited government power, which no doubt has held some sway over lawmakers. The second was the enactment of the Federal Tort Claims Act by Congress, establishing limited liability for wrongful acts of government. The third concept was patterned after federal law, as states moved to adopt similar legislation.

The Federal Tort Claims Act was passed by Congress in 1946 using the same logic that forms our current discussion. By passing the act, Congress agreed that sovereign immunity was no longer viable in the public eye. But even yet, old concepts held sway; the act really only imposed limited liability on government by setting out the conditions for lawsuits against the federal branch. Two important observations follow. First, the act preserved immunity for intentional torts and errors of omission by employees acting within discretionary functions. Second, the act had the effect of statutorily agreeing to be sued and setting out the parameters for lawsuits. These are important observations because they illustrate that governmental liability is still limited and is effectively voluntary. Soon after passage of the Federal Tort Claims Act, states began adopting similar legislation.

Although case law is massive in tracing the assault on immunity, *Molitor*[3] provides the fundamental logic for such attacks. In this 1959 case, the state supreme court of Illinois traced the origins of immunity and its adoption into Illinois state law via two other cases styled as *Waltham*[4] and *Kinnare*.[5] Immunity had been established in Illinois for towns and counties in *Waltham* and

---

2. *Nichols v. United States*, 74 U.S. 122 (1869).
3. *Molitor v. Kaneland Comm. Unit Dist.*, 18 Ill.2d 11, 163 N.E.2d 89 (Ill. 1959).
4. *Town of Waltham v. Kemper*, 55 Ill. 346 (1870).
5. *Kinnare v. City of Chicago*, 171 Ill. 332, 49 N.E. 536 (1898).

extended to school districts in *Kinnare*, wherein it was held that a school board was not liable for the death of a laborer who fell from a rooftop, even though the district had not provided safety measures such as scaffolding. *Molitor* reversed this view in 1959, as the court held the district liable for injury to a student when a school bus hit a culvert and exploded. The court rejected the argument that permitting liability required wrongful use of public funds to settle liability claims and that depletion of the state treasury was no longer a good defense. The Illinois court quoted a New Mexico case, taking that view as its own, saying, "The whole doctrine of governmental immunity from liability for tort rests on a rotten foundation. It is almost incredible that in this modern age of comparative sociological enlightenment, and in a republic, the medieval absolutism supposed to be implicit in the maxim, 'the King can do no wrong' should exempt the various branches of government from liability for their torts...."[6] Yet although this seems to imply complete abandonment of immunity, it is true that immunity is only diminished. The effect of the Federal Tort Claims Act was to open only certain avenues, so that immunity still applies except under certain conditions. Because states have typically followed the federal lead, as a general rule government is liable only when proprietary acts, nuisances, or interstate issues are involved, although other recent liabilities (explored later in the chapter) such as constitutional infringements, have eroded immunity even further. Exceptions find government liable for preventable errors, although limited when carrying out official duties, depending on how states choose to interpret the Eleventh Amendment's guarantee of state sovereignty in interstate claims.

Proprietary Acts Exception

The unwillingness of some courts to accept absolute immunity has resulted in an exception by virtue of proprietary acts. The exception occurs as a court seeks to decide whether the activity in question was governmental or proprietary. The distinction rests in a governmental function defined as exercise of police power or constitutional, legislative, administrative, or judicial powers conferred on federal, state, or local government, in contrast to proprietary acts that are done for the benefit and advantage of citizens.

In the context of education, this distinction can be seen by separating educational activities from other school-sponsored events that are less central to the educational process. For example, athletic events outside school time or other voluntary events may raise a different liability question than when considering field trips. Rulings are not consistent, however, even within similar circumstances. For example, a spectator in *Sawaya*[7] was injured when a bleacher railing failed at a game where two districts had rented a football stadium from a third district. The state supreme court of Arizona held the third district liable, finding the event proprietary. In contrast, in an identical case of

---

6.   *Barker v. City of Santa Fe*, 47 N.M. 85, 136 P.2d at 482.
7.   *Sawaya v. Tucson High Sch. Dist.*, 78 Ariz. 389, 281 P.2d 105 (1955).

Richards,[8] the Michigan court found no liability, holding that the district did not intend to make a profit from the event and was providing an educational activity. The controlling feature seems to be how states have ruled on immunity, as illustrated by a Michigan court in *Ross*,[9] which said: "When a governmental agency engages in mandated or authorized activities, it is immune from tort liability unless the activity is proprietary in nature." In contrast, a Texas court said in *Stout*,[10] "Because a school district is purely a governmental agency...it performs no proprietary functions separate from governmental functions." Liability for proprietary acts is subject to the extent of state legislative intent in abrogating immunity and in state courts' attitude toward liability.

Nuisance Exception

A more familiar immunity exception rests in nuisances. A nuisance is acting or failing to perform a legal duty that intentionally causes or permits a condition to exist that injures or endangers public health, safety, or welfare. When a nuisance claim arises, it is nearly always in the context that the nuisance was foreseeable, and that there was no attempt or only inadequate effort to prevent an injury. Probably the most common claim relates to attractive nuisances, which require higher levels of care because the nuisance may be expected to create problems. A classic nuisance example is seen in the Michigan case of *Hendricks*,[11] where the court held that the district had not created or maintained a nuisance when it piled snow on a playground, resulting in a climbing injury to a child. The court said that to establish a claim of intentional nuisance against a governmental agency, a plaintiff must show that there is a genuine nuisance condition and that the agency intended to create a hazard. However, case law is replete with other challenges reaching opposite conclusions.

Although nuisance liability is somewhat unpredictable in that liability depends on specific laws, jurisdictions, and the unique facts of each case, the concept of nuisance represents one of the instances in which exception to sovereign immunity has been established in the modern context. Clearly, the finding of liability relies greatly on the standard of care required for the particular age of injured persons, and it is also clear that care is needed to provide safeguards against liability.

Eleventh Amendment Exception

A special situation relates to the third area in which sovereign immunity has been at least partially overturned. The Eleventh Amendment to the U.S. Constitution in 1795 provided that, "[t]he judicial power of the United States

---

8. *Richards v. School Dist. of City of Birmingham*, 348 Mich. 490, 83 N.W.2d 643 (1957).
9. *Ross v. Consumers Power Co.*, 420 Mich. 567, 363 N.W.2d 641 (1984).
10. *Stout v. Grand Prairie Sch. Dist.*, 733 S.W.2d at 296 (Tex. App. 1987).
11. *Hendricks v. Southfield Public Schools*, 178 Mich. App. 672, 444 N.W.2d 143 (1989).

shall not be construed to extend to any suit in law or equity, commenced or prosecuted against one of the United States by citizens of another State, or by citizens or subjects of any foreign state." The Eleventh Amendment was a response to two lawsuits in 1791 and 1792, in which claims against states were brought in Maryland and Georgia. In *Vanstophorst*,[12] foreign residents had brought suit against the state of Maryland for recovery of bad debts. In *Chisholm*,[13] residents of South Carolina sought a judgment against the state of Georgia. The potential for federal liability spurred passage of the Eleventh Amendment to deny recourse under applicable constitutional protections.

The Eleventh Amendment closed off an opportunity for litigants. This basis of immunity was successful for years, as the U.S. Supreme Court ruled repeatedly that the intent of the amendment was express, including barring suit against a state by citizens of another state, and prohibiting citizens from attempting to bring federal suit against their own states. Schools have enjoyed Eleventh Amendment immunity as well under the assumption that the state was implicated to such an extent that liability would extend to it.

Limits on immunity under the Eleventh Amendment, however, have been established. In some cases, states have voluntarily waived their right to Eleventh Amendment immunity. Usually, waiver is available only when the state unquestionably permits and sets forth clearly its intent to allow suit against itself as in *Edelman*.[14] Congress has purposely limited other Eleventh Amendment immunity as well, as in the Individuals with Disabilities Education Act (IDEA), where Congress intentionally denied immunity to states from federal suits for violations of IDEA. Precedent in observing specific laws has also limited immunity, as in the instance of the Supreme Court's ruling that Eleventh Amendment immunity is unavailable in claims of Fourteenth Amendment equal protection, in that Congress has granted itself power to write legislation invoking penalties for successful equal protection claims. A final limitation is important for schools, because Eleventh Amendment immunity may depend on whether courts see schools as a direct arm of the state. This distinction was made in *Mt. Healthy*,[15] when the U.S. Supreme Court held local school districts in a similar light to city and county governments, rather than in the context of traditional thinking that sees schools as an arm and extension of the state. In this case, liability was present because the Court saw schools as political subdivisions of the state due to their taxing power and autonomy.

In the total context of sovereign immunity, governments have enjoyed significant release from liability, but the exceptions and attitudes toward immunity have severely limited what was once absolute. Federal statutory limits on immunity have been an important catalyst for increased liability,

---

12. *Vanstophorst v. Maryland*, 2 U.S. (2 Dall.) 401 (1791).
13. *Chisholm v. Georgia*, 2 U.S. (2 Dall.) 419 (1792).
14. *Edelman v. Jordan*, 415 U.S. 651, 94 S. Ct. 1347 (1974).
15. *Mt. Healthy City Sch. Dist. Bd. of Educ. v. Dole*, 429 U.S. 274, 97 S. Ct. 568 (1977).

particularly in the context of the Eleventh Amendment. Enactment of state statutes likewise has severely limited immunity. Doctrinal modifications by courts regarding proprietary acts and nuisances have given further openings to claimants. The result is that neither absolute immunity nor absolute liability is the unquestioned rule, so that persons involved with schools must see liability as a daily reality demanding both care and professional advice.

Tort Liability

Loss of absolute immunity has made all units of government liable for a wide variety of acts by employees and officers. As a result, a huge body of statutes and case law has sprung up around issues of liability.

Most governmental liability arises from the law of torts. A tort is a civil wrong committed against the rights of another person. A claim for tort liability is thus broad, taking in a great many wrongs touching on every aspect of human interaction. Tortious acts may arise from contracts, defamation, civil rights, negligence, and so forth. The scope is so broad that acts of omission apply, so that negligence can be either *committing* a wrong or *failing* to act. Obviously, degrees of severity apply that may also involve the area of criminal law. Although the scope of claims is great, most torts fall into three categories: *intentional* torts, torts involving *negligence,* and *strict liability* torts. In all instances, personal liability is a concern in addition to school district liability. Intentional torts and negligence are most relevant to schools.

Intentional Torts

An intentional tort is defined as a wrong by someone who intends to do something the law has declared wrong, as contrasted with negligence in which the person fails to exercise the required degree of care in doing something otherwise permissible. Such torts involve intent or purpose and ill will, but malice may be simple indifference to the safety of others, with knowledge of the danger, or failure to use ordinary care to avoid injury. Many such instances occur daily—for example, a person lacking malice but committing an act leading to injury of another's rights, property, or person may be guilty of an intentional tort. Most such cases probably do not involve wrongful intent or malice, but there are many opportunities for claims where it is alleged that some otherwise permissible act crossed the line of negligence and was motivated by a desire to do harm when some unlawful act was accompanied by reasonable anticipation of impending harm.

One of the more common intentional tort claims in schools relates to corporal punishment. Although never universally outlawed, school personnel are often said to have crossed the intent line. Such cases usually allege assault and battery. Assault is defined as any attempt or threat to inflict injury, when coupled with a display of force that would give a victim reason to fear or expect immediate bodily harm. Battery is usually filed in such cases, as it is defined as the touching threatened by assault. Although as a general rule courts have been unwilling to completely outlaw corporal punishment, and the U.S. Supreme Court clearly said in *Ingraham*[16] that there was no violation of the Eighth Amendment's prohibition against cruel and unusual punishment, there is a vast record of intentional tort claims against school personnel over this issue. The claims should give rise to great caution on the part of personnel from both moral and legal perspectives. For example, cases have involved students who were beaten severely enough to produce medical trauma, as in *Ingraham*, which resulted in a hematoma, or as in *Mathis*,[17] which claimed posttraumatic stress disorder, and other bizarre acts such as a teacher kicking a repeatedly disobedient student.[18] Although these cases did not find schools liable, other cases have held adversely. For example, a teacher was convicted of assault and battery for having broken a student's arm by shaking and dropping him to the floor.[19] Likewise, a teacher was liable for breaking a pupil's collarbone by throwing him into a wall.[20] Liability was also found when a third-grader was held upside down by her ankles while the principal whipped her with a paddle.[21] Although all such cases seem far beyond sensible behavior, their frequent filings indicate that reasonableness does not apply to everyone in schools. Intentional torts make up a big part of case law, and much evidence suggests that schools will continue to face claims. Obviously, there is a real possibility that a claim for intentional tort may end up as a criminal claim—a concept also not altogether foreign to schools.

Negligence

A more typical tort action in schools is a claim for negligence. Negligence is defined as conduct falling below a legally established standard of care, resulting in injury to another person. As such, negligence is failure to exercise care when subjecting another to risk or danger, and which ultimately causes harm. In examining such claims, liability depends on the facts regarding breach of duty, proximate cause, and actual injury.

Duty refers to proof that the actor had a responsibility to the injured person. A duty can arise from statute, contracts, or even common sense. To be liable, the complaining party must show that a duty was breached. Inadequate supervision is probably the most common allegation for breach of duty, followed by claims for lack of proper instruction and failure to maintain a safe environment. The standard most often applied to breach of duty is the "reasonable person" test, wherein a defendant's actions are compared to

---

16. *Ingraham v. Wright*, 430 U.S. 651, 97 S. Ct. 1401 (1977).
17. *Mathis v. Berrien County Sch. Dist.*, 378 S.E.2d 505 (Ga. App. 1989).
18. *Thompson v. Iberville Parish Sch. Bd.*, 372 S0.2d 642 (La. Ct. App. 1979), *writ denied*, 374 S0.2d 650 (La. 1979).
19. *Frank v. Orleans Parish Sch. Bd.*, 195 S0.2d 451 (La. Ct. App. 1967).
20. *Sansone v. Bechtel*, 429 A.2d 820 (Conn. 1980).
21. *Garcia v. Miera*, 817 F.2d 650 (10th Circ. 1987).

the prudence and skill that would be applied by a reasonable person in the same or similar circumstances. Because our interest here relates to school-based liability, the added dimension of superior skill or knowledge is critical, so that the reasonableness test takes on the crucial characteristic of the behavior of a professional under the same or similar circumstances. Proximate cause relates to whether the action in fact caused the injury, because there is no liability if there is no unbroken chain of events leading to the defendant. Further, the negligence must be substantial—that is, negligence, although easily claimed, is not so easily proved.

The risk of liability, particularly for negligence claims, has increased greatly in the present era of eagerness to litigate almost any real or imagined offense to personal rights. Aggressive public attitudes involving freedom of speech have created a constant tension in schools, and recent events of school-based violence have caused liability fears to soar. Questions of duty continually arise regarding liability of schools and individual staff members in these difficult times, and schools are increasingly spending their scarce resources to protect against liability of all types—oddly enough, at times when violence and freedom of speech join to create great distress. A few cases illustrate the nature of claims and the need to guard against personal and financial liability.

The data on threats, intimidation, violence, and other crime in schools are disturbing. In 2001, students aged 12 to 18 were victims of approximately 2 million crimes at school. Of these crimes, about 161,000 were serious offenses including rape, sexual assault, robbery, and aggravated assault—including 24 homicides.[22] Fears of violence have been justified, as mass school shootings have occurred in various states, with Columbine-like fears abounding in nearly every state.

The issue of liability of schools and school leaders in the face of violence and other individual rights violations has been noticed by state and federal courts. In 1999, the U.S. Supreme Court spoke in *Davis*[23] to the duty of educators to address student violence and harassment under state law. The victim was a fifth-grade girl who had been sexually harassed by another student. The girl reported the events to her teachers, but the school took no action. Charges were filed, with the defendant admitting to sexual battery, whereupon the victim's mother sued the board of education and school leaders for damages under Title IX of the Education Amendments of 1972. The Court found for plaintiffs, stating that educators are on notice that they may be held liable under state law for their failure to protect students from the tortious acts of third parties. The Court further noted that state courts routinely uphold claims alleging that schools have been negligent in failing to protect students from their peers; notably, the Court cited cases from 1953, 1979, and 1982 in support for its ruling.

22. U.S. Department of Education and U.S. Department of Justice, *Indicators of School Crime and Safety 2003* (Washington, DC: Author, 2004).

23. *Davis v. Monroe County Board of Education*, 119 S. Ct. 1661 (1999).

The duty to protect students from foreseeable harm arises from the *in loco parentis* doctrine. The duty is broad, as illustrated by *Garcia*,[24] where a five-year-old boy was sexually molested when he was sent to the bathroom alone, in violation of the school's written guidelines. The court found that the assault was preventable by proper supervision, which was defined as the degree of supervision a parent of ordinary prudence would take in comparable circumstances. Although the court agreed that a school cannot foresee and take precautions against sudden spontaneous acts by other students, and that the school had no history of similar incidents, liability still inured based on the school's knowledge of danger to unattended students—knowledge implied by the school's written security policies and the principal's testimony admitting the risks to unescorted students in hallways and bathrooms.

Case law is by no means unanimous, however, in fixing liability on schools at the state level, in part because of the impact of immunity.[25] State rulings for statutory immunity have led to suits in federal court, asserting that schools have a constitutional duty to protect students from danger.[26] These causes of action, known as civil rights torts, are typically filed under 42 U.S.C. §1983, an action allowing plaintiffs to seek compensatory and punitive damages.

The liability issues at stake can be illustrated in several cases. In *Leffall*,[27] an 18-year-old student was killed by random gunfire in a school parking lot after a school dance. The issue was whether the student's constitutional rights were violated by the decision of the school district to sponsor the dance even after being asked by local police to stop sponsoring events until adequate security could be provided. Only two unarmed guards were assigned and were unable to prevent the violence. Notwithstanding prior knowledge of danger, the court noted that although students are required to attend school, they are not required to attend dances so that the state's failure to protect against private violence did not violate the Constitution. The court noted that the standard under §1983 is a "deliberate indifference" standard where the plaintiff must show that (1) an unusually serious risk of harm existed, (2) the defendant had actual knowledge, or was willfully blind to, the elevated risk, and (3) the defendant failed to take obvious steps to address the risk.[28] Similar results followed in *Rudd*[29] when a student warned his teachers that another student had brought a gun to school. Officials failed to find the weapon despite a thorough search, but later in the day the suspect pulled out the hidden gun and killed another student on his school bus. The state

24. *Garcia v. City of New York*, 646 N.Y.S. 2d 508 (App. Div. 1996).
25. For example, see *Chesshir v. Sharp*, 19 S.W.3d 502 (Tex. App. Amarillo 2000) where statutory immunity protected a teacher when a five-year-old boy splattered hot grease on his face from a hot frying pan in the classroom.
26. See, e.g., *Graham v. Independent School District No. I-89*, 22 F.3d 991 (10th Cir. 1994).
27. *Leffal v. Dallas Independent School District*, 28 F.3d 521 (5th Cir. 1994).
28. *Leffal*, 28 F.3d at 531.
29. *Rudd v. Pulaski County Special School District*, 20 S.W.3d 310 (Ark. 2000).

supreme court held that the district was not liable under the Arkansas Civil Rights Act and further enjoyed immunity from tort liability on a negligence claim.

The difficult nature of liability claims is illustrated by the fact that courts have exercised considerable caution when limiting broad constitutional freedoms in the name of safety. In 1999, the U.S. Supreme Court noted that the maintenance of discipline in schools requires that students be restrained from assaulting one another, abusing drugs and alcohol, and committing other crimes.[30] But a heavy burden is still present for school officials when deciding to aggressively infringe on constitutional rights. The controlling authority has continued to be *TLO*,[31] where the Court provided a two-part test for reasonableness in searches to prevent contraband, including weapons. The Court first held that a search must be justified at its inception and second, that it must be permissible in its scope to not excessively intrude in light of the age and sex of the student and the nature of the infraction.[32] Today, courts are considering school violence and reaching different results as these issues sometimes cross over into freedom of expression. For example, courts have examined First Amendment protections in cases of threats of violence. Although "fighting words" and threats presenting a clear and present danger historically have not enjoyed First Amendment protection, courts have taken into consideration whether such statements made in school settings are believable. For example, in *Lovell*,[33] the Court considered the suspension of a student after she threatened to shoot a counselor over a disagreement involving a class schedule change. The Court held that boundaries may be imposed on the right to free speech by prohibiting threats of physical injury; however, the Court also said that what constitutes a threat is subject to the First Amendment, so that punishable threats are limited to those statements that convey "a gravity of purpose and likelihood of execution."[34]

The cases presented here for illustration lead to the conclusion that liability is a serious issue for school personnel. The data alone are sufficient to raise anxiety and to leave school leaders without a clear road map on how to deal simultaneously with keeping schools safe and free. One line of cases leads to the view that significant restrictions may be enacted by schools to preserve safety without fear of liability, whereas another line of cases warns that courts will not automatically support ruthless trampling of constitutional freedoms. In actuality, several middle-ground perspectives provide the best course of action. First, there is a strong duty to exercise the reasonable person rule, applying it consistently and intelligently to all issues ranging from freedom of speech to search and seizure under reasonable suspicion of safety

---

30. *Davis v. Monroe County Board of Education*, 119 S. Ct. 1661 (1999).

31. *New Jersey v. TLO*, 469 U.S. 325 (1985).

32. See, e.g., *Vernonia School District 47 v. Acton*, 515 U.S. 646 (1995); see also *Smith v. McGlothlin*, 119 F.3d 766 (9th Cir. 1997).

33. *Lovell v. Poway Unified School District*, 847 F.Supp. 780 (S.D. Cal. 1994).

34. *Lovell* at 784.

concerns. Second, school leaders should not be afraid to act affirmatively, inasmuch as school personnel can be held liable for injuries resulting from failure to exercise reasonable care to protect students from harm. Third, courts generally do not hold educators liable for injuries resulting from spontaneous acts of violence if these acts are unforeseeable—as a rule, this includes injuries caused by nonstudent assailants. However, leaders are expected to be watchful because a significant duty exists when the assailant is a student. Courts will consider the student's prior conduct so that if evidence of antisocial behavior is found, the student's future violent acts may have been predictable. Fourth, there is a significant responsibility for preparedness, including risk management training. The reasoning of courts in student suicide cases may be applied to all these issues and particularly to school violence: Without adequate training, school employees may underestimate threats of violence. In essence, training in violence prevention may soon become a standard of care for educators.

Tort liability is made more serious because the concept of damages applies if liability can be established. Damages may be compensatory or punitive, according to whether they are awarded as the measure of compensation for loss or as punishment for a negligent act. Compensation may include medical bills and loss of prospective earnings, and may also be given for nonphysical injuries such as emotional distress and pain and suffering. Other awards may be given, including exemplary or punitive damages. In the latter case, the intent is to make an example of negligent behavior to reduce its likelihood of reoccurrence. For school districts and school personnel, the issue is clear: Liability represents a significant expense, either by personal vulnerability or by having to budget for liability claims.

Civil Rights

Of all the areas of liability faced by schools, in historical perspective none has received more press than civil rights liability. Stemming from the Civil Rights Act of 1875 and extending today to embrace a vast body of constitutional and statutory protections against all kinds of discrimination, civil rights has come to represent an ever-present liability concern for modern education.

Civil rights litigation has been present in the nation almost since its birth. The Civil Rights Act of 1875, however, opened a new era by seeking to prevent both lawful and unlawful discrimination against African Americans following the Civil War. Because federal law is usually controlling on states, it was reasonable to turn first to federal courts in an attempt to broadly construe liability beyond just racial discrimination. The Civil Rights Act of 1875 was the theory behind much subsequent litigation, including the famous *Brown v. Board of Education*[35] decision in 1954, which marked the end of "separate but equal" educational provisions in the United States. The basic con-

---

35. 374 U.S. 483 (1954).

cept of liability under this federal provision extended general liability to include individual and personal liability for public officials who violate the federal constitutional or statutory rights of another individual. This law, usually referred to in relevant part as §1983, denied any immunity against liability when it stated:

> Every person who, under color of any statute, ordinance, regulation, custom, or usage, of any State or Territory, subjects, or causes to be subjected, any citizen of the United States or other person within the jurisdiction thereof to the deprivation of any rights, privileges, or immunities secured by the Constitution and laws, shall be liable to the party injured in an action at law, set in equity, or other proper proceeding for redress.

The intense struggle over civil rights has never ended, nor has the liability phase ever received closure. The stakes have only intensified, as represented by the significant clarification in the *Wood*[36] decision, which examined school board members and their liability. The U.S. Supreme Court generally has held for immunity when acting in good faith, but in *Wood*, the Court noted a board member is not immune under §1983 if the board member knew or reasonably should have known that an action taken within a sphere of official responsibility would violate constitutional rights, or if an act intended a deprivation of constitutional rights. *Wood* set a new standard of "qualified good faith" immunity, wherein liability exists under three conditions. First, board members are bound to make decisions within current law. Second, ignorance of the law is no excuse. Third, immunity is lost if it is shown that the violator set out to intentionally harm someone or if actions originated in vindictiveness or spite.

A significant burden has been placed on schools by §1983 because of the vast range of possible wrongs. Civil rights legislation has abounded, and new interpretation and reinterpretation is a career for legislatures, courts, and litigants. The range is so vast that it now takes in a huge panorama of possible grievances, with governmental units, including schools, required to clearly state compliance with nondiscrimination statutes.

Yet absolute liability is not the rule either. Individual liability usually revolves around a callous indifference standard, so that if an employee acts callously toward the rights of an individual, liability may arise in individual capacity. And at the same time, §1983 liability can be very costly. The act clearly provides that compensatory damages and equitable relief may be sought. Actual damages and attorney fees are usually awarded under §1983.

The outcome of civil rights liability has created a justifiably high level of anxiety. For example, in *Kinsey*,[37] a superintendent won $250,000 for mental anguish and loss to his reputation when he was fired after vocally supporting

---

36. *Wood v. Strickland*, 420 U.S. 308 (1975).
37. *Kinsey v. Saldo Indep. Sch. Dist.*, 916 F.2d 273 (5th Cir. 1990), *reh. en banc*, 925 F.2d 118 (5th Cir. 1991).

certain candidates in a school board election. Likewise, punitive damages may be awarded, as in *Fishman*,[38] where a district fired a teacher in a dispute over First Amendment free speech claims. These awards are not among the largest, particularly in the context of recent litigation involving such issues as sexual harassment; rather, the cases cited are representative of the *less* flamboyant claims that arise under civil rights issues. The importance of liability and monetary risk of adverse judgment is only underscored by the fact that if the opposing party wins, the school district may be faced with its own attorney fees plus costs of opposing counsel, in addition to damages ranging from actual to punitive. As a result, many civil rights liability claims are settled out of court without regard to culpability because the cost of defense may be higher than the cost of settlement.

Defamation

An additional liability concern relates to defamation. In most instances affecting schools, defamation attaches to faculty and students, although claims most often relate to student records. Schools by their nature engage in much accumulation of data about staff and students, a trend that has increased greatly in relation to accountability and performance-based school reform. For example, administrators and boards must evaluate teachers and are ethically, and at times legally, required to dismiss incompetent or undesirable staff. Likewise, the whole educational process consists of gathering data on students and preserving it in perpetuity. Although these are the fundamental tasks of education, they offer ample opportunity for liability when carelessly or inaccurately carried out.

Defamation may be libel, in which case harm is done to another person in writing. Defamation also may be slander, in which case the harm is done verbally. In either case, defamation may be *per se* or *per quod*. Defamation *per se* is words requiring no proof of harm beyond their clear meaning. Defamation *per quod* requires an examination of facts. Either form is an actionable tort that may carry individual liability, and for which the only defenses are *privilege* and *good faith*. In all cases, schools are vulnerable against claims given such a record-intensive environment.

The defenses of privilege and good faith are extremely important in that they are the basis for schools to conduct their business of preparing and distributing information about pupils and teachers. Although the only defenses against defamation, they are not inconsequential in that they make student transcripts and teacher employment records possible. Great care is needed, however, because the gravity of student and staff records has resulted in a qualified privilege immunity that holds these records to a higher standard than is true in other instances. In particular, a defense of privilege in schools is more difficult than for other public officials; for example, justices and state officers have an absolute privilege as long as they act officially, and that same

---

38. *Fishman v. Clancy*, 763 F.2d 485 (1st Cir. 1985).

privilege applies to anyone involved in judicial or legislative acts such as testimony. In contrast, school personnel only have a qualified privilege in that they are protected only if carrying out duties common to such organizations and provided that they are acting in good faith. Qualified privilege is further restricted in that even truthful statements without good intent, or statements thought to be true, are actionable. Countless examples of this limit abound, as in an oft-quoted case when a teacher described a student as "ruined by tobacco and whiskey."[39] To be safe, statements must be made in good faith and may not go further than to state the facts.

Most often, schools encounter defamation problems when making statements about teachers' fitness for teaching and in written evaluations, although courts are slow to act except in clear factual instances. As noted in *Malia*,[40] qualified immunity is the common rule except when it is shown that comments were motivated by personal malice or animosity, or when the evidence against privilege and good faith is overwhelming. A similar opportunity for problems arises in permanent or anecdotal student records, particularly given records availability under the Family Rights and Privacy Act (FERPA) passed by Congress in 1974. This act stipulated in detail which records must be available to parents and students and laid out rules regarding which parts of school information are public or confidential. Under FERPA, individual student records may not be released without written consent of the parent, pupil records must be open to parents of children under 18 and to the child once age 18 is reached, a record must be kept of anyone examining school records, contents of files may be challenged, and public directory information must be identified in advance of publication.

Although different cases reach different outcomes, defamation claims are serious matters for schools, staff, and others affected by any aspect of defamation. FERPA has caused many districts to purge records and to guard their words closely. In the case of teacher defamation, districts have become more aware of individual rights and have enacted strict review policies based on sound legal advice.

Educational Malpractice

An additional area of tort concerns has been educational malpractice. Although very broad-based in its potential implications, the general issue has been the relationship between student achievement and quality of instruction—an issue likely to become more important in the future given rising accountability pressures on schools. The issue is not new, however. Since the 1970s, schools have feared that malpractice claims would eventually succeed. Although much anticipated, there have been only a few malpractice lawsuits actually filed.

---

39. *Dawkins v. Billingsley*, 172 P. 69 (1918).
40. *Malia v. Monchak*, 543 A.2d 184 (Pa. Commwlth. Ct. 1988).

Educational malpractice attempts to apply tort law to student achievement. Malpractice might be seen as an intentional tort or as a tort of negligence. These have been hard to prove, as an intentional tort would have to show clearly that the school maliciously sought to deprive a child of achievement. Claiming negligence has been more common. Early malpractice cases focused on the question of whether students have the right to a prescribed achievement level under compulsory attendance laws, whereas more recent cases have asked whether schools have been negligent in diagnosing identifiable educational needs. The seminal case to date is *Peter W.*,[41] where a student received a high school diploma under a California statute requiring graduates to be able to read at the eighth-grade level. The student's reading skill, however, was at the fifth-grade level. The student alleged negligence and argued that his parents were uninformed of his deficiencies. The lower court dismissed and was upheld on appeal. The appeals court discussed at length the duty requirement, finding no duty on which to base an action because of inability to find a workable standard of care, noting that teaching involves many different and conflicting theories of how or what a child should be taught. The primary motive for the court's logic, however, lay in public policy against allowing such suits because of the burdensome litigation that would be generated. As the court noted, to hold schools accountable for all academic functions would expose them to tort claims—real or imagined—of disaffected students and parents in countless numbers. A similar view was taken by a New York court of appeals in a case brought by a learning-disabled student who argued that he could not cope with filling out simple job applications. In dismissing the $5 million negligence suit, the appeals court in *Donohue*[42] also cited public policy, noting that solutions would require judicial monitoring of day-to-day implementation of educational policies.

Recent cases have upheld this trend, as in *Ross*,[43] when a high school basketball star was recruited to a university that promised support for academic deficiencies. The student sued for negligence and breach of contract based on malpractice and negligent admission. A federal district court dismissed, and on appeal the court stated that malpractice claims have been widely rejected, largely because of the lack of a satisfactory standard of care by which to evaluate and the potential torrent of malpractice litigation. Malpractice will continue to be an area of watchfulness, however, especially in light of accountability issues that are increasingly attracting public criticism.

Contracts

Finally, but not surprisingly, liability applies to contracts. School districts in all states are authorized to enter into contracts for hiring staff, buying sup-

41. *Peter W. v. San Francisco Unif. Sch. Dist.*, 60 C.A.3d 814, 131 Cal. Rptr. 854 (1976).
42. *Donohue v. Copiague Union Free Sch. Dist.*, 47 N.Y.2d 440, 418 N.Y.L.Q.2d 375 (1979).
43. *Ross v Creighton Univ.*, 957 F.2d 410 (7th Cir. 1992).

plies and equipment, and carrying out facility projects. As such, districts are liable for contractual performance, including breach of contract. Liability on either side usually relates to bad faith or failure to observe one or more of the basic elements of contracts. To be valid, a contract must have mutual consent including offer and acceptance, have consideration in the form of inducement to enter into the contract, be entered by competent parties and serve a lawful purpose, and conform to any other requirements of law. Most contracts in school districts do not present problems, but some special cases happen where liability may arise.

Most problems arise around the authority to enter into a contract, and such problems are defined by the state-specific nature of contract law. As a rule, only boards of education may enter into contracts for the district, although agency usually is granted to administrators to create contracts on behalf of the board. Contracts by agents still must be ratified by the board, and many of the challenges involving contracts have centered on whether a contract is valid when a board wishes to nullify an agency contract. Opposite rulings are readily found. In *Community Projects*,[44] the court held that only a board has contractual powers and that an agreement to purchase goods signed by a principal was invalid. An opposite finding came in *Hebert*,[45] when a court held that because the board had ultimate power to contract and had given power to a principal over extracurricular activities that led to a contract, it had granted an implied power to contract.

The whole of contractual authority is embodied in the concept of ministerial duties versus discretionary duties of boards as the sole contracting body in a district. Ministerial duties are those duties of a board that it may choose not to perform itself. A board may delegate ministerial duties, even though it retains responsibility for the educational process; for example, supervision of playgrounds, curriculum, and so forth. Discretionary duties are the duties the board was elected to carry out, such as evaluating the superintendent or approving the budget. Discretionary duties may not be delegated. Contracts by agents are controlled by this distinction, in that expenditure is a discretionary power that may not be delegated. However, boards often appoint an agent to deal with contracts, thus creating risk by appointing someone to enter into contracts without legal authority to actually make a valid contract. Under these conditions, a district is not legally bound if it refuses to ratify the contract; conversely, the board may choose to ratify an invalid contract. Although this seems unfair, the burden of risk falls heavily on anyone dealing with the public treasury.

For example, in *Joske*,[46] a construction company that failed to complete a job on time was barred from the site. The contractor sued for breach of contract, and the district countersued for breach. The district court's ruling

---

44. *Community Projects for Students v. Wilder*, 298 S.E.2d 434, 435 (N.C. App. 1982).
45. *Hebert v. Livingston Parish School Bd.*, 438 S0.2d 1141 (La. App. 1983).
46. *Joske Corp. v. Kirkwood School District*, 903 F.2d 1199 (8th Cir. 1990).

against the school district was reversed on appeal, holding that the district was not liable because construction and maintenance were governmental functions and immune from liability. Although the facts of each case are different and state laws on contracts vary, contract disputes finally relate to the discretionary functions of government, wherein it is settled that a board cannot contract away its governmental obligations. This cuts both ways, as in *Coalition*,[47] where a contract between a school board and a neighborhood group to create an experimental school was invalidated because under terms of the contract, the board could not close the school, which resulted in the board impermissibly contracting away a discretionary duty.

The law of contracts is highly specialized, affecting every aspect of district operations, including hiring of teachers and staff. Yet, despite the fact that it can be argued that every dollar relates to a contract for either staff or materials, the single fact remains that contracts are a board responsibility and that boards may appoint agents in most states, although no contract is valid until ratified unless allowed in statute. As a result, knowledge of individual state laws is essential to avoiding legal problems relating to the authority to contract.

Recovery Under Contracts

It is important to remember that breach of contract claims are not one-sided in the sense that either party to a contract may allege nonperformance. This raises the issue of what happens when breach occurs, given the rather complete contractual powers held by boards. Further, when a contract is alleged to have been breached, the question of recovery usually arises, either for damages or for recovery of products themselves. The likely scenario is that at least one party acted in the belief that a valid contract existed and thereby provided products or services, whereas the other party failed to pay the bill. Such scenarios are not uncommon, particularly given the discussion of agents acting on behalf of school boards.

The two issues of greatest concern in such situations are whether there is an express or implied contract, and whether it can be shown that the contract itself was invalid for any reason. An express contract is one in which the duties and rights are expressly agreed to by all parties. An implied contract is one in which the parties have acted to read a contract into the actions of the parties, even though there was no express agreement. The difference is not trivial, in that the elements of contracts are used to establish whether an express or implied contract exists. For example, accepting goods or services on behalf of a school without evidence of mutual consideration may raise questions of whether a gift was made. Under these conditions, the right of recovery is a reasonable question. In the case of an implied contract, the question must consider the value of goods or services so that a fair value can be established. If recovery is in fact permitted on an implied contract, recovery is

---

47. *Coalition v. School District of Kansas City*, 649 S.W.2d 533.

limited to the reasonable value of goods or services. In the case of an express contract, however, recovery is controlled by the value expressly agreed to without concern for whether the amount is reasonable. In the latter instance, it is particularly prudent to avoid contracts that are unreasonable because courts will generally bind both parties to an improvident contract if the contract is determined to be express.

In some instances, however, the contract itself may be invalid. The first instance of an invalid contract is one that fails to observe all the elements of contracts discussed earlier. Invalidation by absence of one or more elements would be reasonable using only common sense. For example, no contract could exist if mutual acceptance were lacking or if one party was legally incompetent, such as lack of authority to enter into contracts or when the contract is outside the law. Similarly, lack of consideration voids a contract because promises to make gifts or to perform free services do not meet the consideration test. Further, contracts may be invalid because of failure to follow a prescribed form. For example, a contract required to be in writing, but made orally, is invalid. These instances create particular problems under recovery claims in that services or products may have already been rendered or consumed before the dispute arises, making an equitable claim more difficult by asking the court to either relax the statutory requirement or to allow uncompensated benefit to one party. Although each case is unique, the general rule has been that if all other elements of a contract were observed, and if the district had authority to expressly contract, then it will be liable under implied contract so long as the form or requirements of the contract do not violate other statutory provisions. To some extent, the outcome rests in the court's attitude toward the question of whether equity or strict statutory application is more important when dealing with issues of public policy.

Case law involving contract recovery is legion. One of the areas of frequent dispute involves additional work by one party beyond the expectations of the other party. This situation most often arises in construction projects. For example, the court held for a contractor in *Flower City*,[48] where a contractor who was hired to remove asbestos from a school also cleaned up and repaired fire damage, whereupon the district refused to pay for extra services. Following denial of both parties' request for summary judgment, an appeals court found that there were genuine issues of fact. In contrast, the court ruled for the board in *Owners Realty*,[49] when a contractor performed additional work while removing asbestos. The court reasoned that no other recourse was available in that the written contract barred claims for additional compensation. As a general rule in recovery claims, courts examine three principal issues. If it is found that cause exists for a claim against a public body, the first issue is whether the goods are returnable or if they have been consumed; if the goods can be returned, courts generally permit recov-

---

48. *Flower City Insulations v. Board of Educ.*, 594 N.Y.S.2d 473 (N.Y. App. Div. 1993).
49. *Owners Realty Management v. Board of Educ. of New York*, 596 N.Y.S.2d 416 (N.Y. App. Div. 1993).

ery. The second issue is whether an implied contract will be found where it is determined that no express contract authority originally existed, as such contracts will be held outside the law. The third issue is that *caveat emptor* (buyer beware) will apply, unless fraud or abuse of discretion is found. None of these instances, however, defeats the intent of contracts by making it possible for a board to misuse its preferential position regarding raids on the public treasury.

The law of contracts is potentially confusing. Yet an overarching umbrella of common sense can be applied to permit the rule of ethics and logic in guiding behavior. First, districts do have contractual authority. Second, the elements of contracts fully apply to schools, and school boards are expected to protect the public treasury through economy and statutory compliance. Third, requirements of statutes for contracts differ among the states. Fourth, boards may appoint agents, but they may not delegate discretionary duties, and contracts and expenditure of funds are discretionary duties. Fifth, courts tend to guard the treasury at the expense of outside parties. Sixth, boards may not abuse their preferential treatment by taking advantage of the law's protectiveness toward the public treasury. Seventh, contracts are unassailable when executed in proper form and written to be specific to avoid vagueness and to bar unforeseen problems such as disputes over additional work. As a result, knowing state laws and carefully drawing contracts are the only ways for schools and school leaders to avoid serious contractual problems.

WHAT DOES ALL THIS MEAN?

The relationship of the law and schools in the United States has been in place for more than 200 years with no sign of slackening. A major aspect of that relationship has rested in legal liability. Educational policy and process are topics that stir intense public interest, and the modern desire to do battle in court has accelerated what was already an adversarial relationship defined by many groups taking interest and responsibility in the educational enterprise. It is not surprising, then, that all actions in schools including personnel matters, civil rights, interpretation and application of educational policy, and constitutional responsibility for education have been tested. Although boards, administrators, teachers and staff, policy makers, and the public can expect no slackening in the relationship, it remains that knowledge of the law and careful avoidance of legal entanglement is the path of wise leadership.

As we noted at the outset, this chapter did not intend to exhaustively review every area of law involving liability in schools. Instead, our focus turned to common concerns and issues, arguing that exposure to liability has placed everyone associated with schools in a position that demands understanding of vulnerability and understanding of the rights and responsibilities of everyone involved. Although not stated yet in these terms, this chapter has fundamentally argued that it is not necessary to be a lawyer to know the law, and that the charge is only to act as a reasonable person would act under the same conditions given the same level of skill and knowledge presumed to the position. If such care is taken, liability is lessened significantly because immunity and privilege are not dead. Inversely, absolute immunity is extraordinarily rare and should never be relied on. Judging from the facts in the vast body of case law, liability will continue to be a huge problem for schools because common sense has been glaringly absent in some instances. Liability is a deep concern for education's stakeholders because part of the budget must be diverted to insure against liability *and* because increasing lay involvement in school-based decision-making is causing liability to impact an ever larger group of persons. In sum, planning for liability is an act of budgeting—an act that calls for a plan to manage the inevitable risks every district faces.

SUGGESTED FOLLOW-UP PROJECTS

◆ Research the statutes governing schools in your state. Typically, these are codified as chapters in an annotated series and easily found in major libraries or on state government Web sites. Gather a sense of how your state legislature views education and pay particular attention to issues of local control. The various chapters might be assigned to individuals or groups who will brief your class.

◆ Conduct a search of major newspapers in your state for articles involving schools and liability. You may need to span several years. Identify the allegations and make a personal judgment on the merits of the cases as you perceive the issues.

◆ Contact the superintendent's office or the business manager in your district and inquire about whether the district has a written risk management plan. Obtain a copy and analyze it, familiarizing yourself with what the district believes is important and the measures described in it. Also inquire about a crisis plan. If no written plan exists, identify the appropriate administrator and discuss how the district approaches risk management from a philosophical and practical perspective.

◆ Talk to your school principal about what he or she does to protect against liability. Probe the scope of liability as understood by your principal and the general issues that are relevant on a daily basis in your school.

Part III

A VIEW OF
THE FUTURE

12

SITE-BASED LEADERSHIP

PULLING IT TOGETHER

Throughout this textbook, site-based leadership has been mentioned frequently. At times our discussion of this concept has been direct, but more often it has hinted at the growing role of site leadership and mostly has meant to provoke additional thought beyond our topics of the moment. The issue of site leadership should be addressed head-on, and we need to develop more fully why it is so important. Our interest is not taken from an advocacy perspective, but rather as seeing site-based leadership as a coming certainty. As a result, it makes sense to revisit the issue and to use it to pull the many parts of this book together.

The questions framing this chapter are logical, although not nearly so technical as those raised in other chapters. We begin by looking once again at the idea of site-based leadership and laying it out conceptually. We seek a framework for implementing site leadership by first asking the question, what is the strategic concept involved in site-based leadership? We follow with more questions, including, what are the roles of principals, central office, and school site councils? These questions raise other issues of membership, organization, areas of legitimate control, and data access. We then ask, what are the important site-based budget issues? General site costs, personnel, instruction, facilities, activities, accountability, and so forth—in essence, the key topics from earlier chapters in this textbook are briefly revisited under headings of basic knowledge and school site knowledge. In sum, this chapter reviews what we have explored in this book, but the discussion is now couched in the context of constituent-based leadership.

THE SITE CONCEPT

Variously named as school-based management, school-based financing, and so forth, site-based leadership has enjoyed high visibility on policy agendas in the United States for nearly two decades. Although site-based leadership has been in schools to some extent for many years, school reform and accountability efforts beginning in the 1980s resulted in a broader recognition that instructional and resource decisions should be located closer to where teaching and learning actually take place—that is, the individual school site. The fiercely competitive context in which education now finds itself also has lent a hand to popularizing the site-based concept, as emerging school choice and charter school legislation have forced states and local school districts to scrutinize their instructional and budgetary behaviors. In addition, policy makers were spurred in the 1990s to reconsider school-based leadership because court decisions on school funding in Kentucky and New Jersey profoundly affected the educational establishment. In the case of Kentucky, the *Rose*[1] decision forced redesign of the entire educational system to include strong school-based management, leading to copycat legislation in several other states as well. In the case of New Jersey, the long-embattled state education system was overturned in multiple iterations of *Abbott*,[2] requiring that the state both equalize funding between the wealthiest and poorest districts and that districts reallocate funding to individual schools in ways that make each school site accountable.

The trend, arguably first begun in modern form by *Rose*, has spread widely. In 2004, the Education Commission of the States (ECS) noted that school districts engage site-based management to some extent in virtually every state, and that five states (Colorado, Florida, Kentucky, North Carolina, and Texas) mandate site-based management in every school.[3] And the interest appears to continue, as 21 bills on the topic of school-based management were signed into law in 14 states in the period 2000–2004. The net sum is that site-based leadership, including resource control decisions at school-based levels, is firmly entrenched and is growing in popularity in the United States at the start of a new millennium.

At the root of the site-based concept is a belief that individual schools should be given real responsibility for *curriculum, staffing,* and *budget* decisions. Individual schools should be allocated a budget to carry out their educational programs, and each school must set goals and conduct performance assessments with genuine consequences for success or failure. The fundamental concept rests on a strong belief that decisions made closer to where students are located are better than decisions made at higher levels that are basically removed from daily operation of schools. The accountability aspect therefore underlies the entire idea and has been made possible in recent years through emerging accountability designs, such as production functions, data envelopment analysis, adjusted performance measures, and cost functions, which aid in selectively assessing the relationship between inputs and achievement.[4] Numerous site-based models have emerged throughout the

1. *Rose v. Council for Better Education,* 790 S.W.2d 186 (Ky. 1989).
2. *Abbott v. Burke,* 153 N.J. 480, 710 A.2d 450 (1998).
3. Education Commission of the States, *Issue: Site Based Management* (Denver, CO: Author, 2004).
4. The production function measures the maximum output obtainable from a specified quantity of inputs (e.g., test scores versus dollars); data envelopment analysis measures technical efficiency within a single data set (e.g., a more limited comparison

nation and world, and research has willingly engaged the topic.[5] Although actual practice has varied in extent of devolution in control, the vast majority of site-based designs seeks to transfer data, money, and authority to the individual school site to involve parents, teachers, and other stakeholders in genuine decision-making. As such, the concept is well conceived and represents a real opportunity to rebuild trust in public schools. Although implementation does not guarantee student performance will improve, the concept risks much on the conviction that people at the school site need genuine authority over budget, personnel, and curriculum if optimal student success is to be achieved. Obviously, the concept demands that stakeholders in schools must learn new skills because responsibility for learner outcomes is a serious matter.

FRAMEWORK FOR IMPLEMENTATION

Although site-based leadership may not lead per se to improved student outcomes, it lends considerable weight by fostering an improved school culture that may lead to better decisions affecting student achievement at the school site level. A framework for implementation necessarily demands consideration for strategic concepts, the role of various stakeholders, and newly acquired budget authority—concepts traditionally unfamiliar to individual school sites.

What Is the Strategic Concept?

Our experience in working with school districts throughout the nation to implement site-based leadership has resulted in understanding that the most difficult task is creating a basis and culture for dramatic change. Change is always threatening, and people who advocate loudest for change are sometimes the same people who resist most when the opportunity for real change is presented. It is easy to talk a good game or complain that decisions in schools are too centralized, but the literature on organizational theory clearly indicates that change must be brought on carefully and deliberately. Although it is beyond the scope of this textbook to develop strategies for change, adopting site-based leadership requires careful preparation based on planning at the district and school levels about how radical changes will be introduced and implemented. For example, an autocratic top-down imposition of site-based leadership is likely to be resented and clearly would be an irony. Likewise, a common error is to turn decisions inappropriately over to

---

group); adjusted performance measures distinguish controllable variables from uncontrolled variables (e.g., measuring achievement after adjusting for nonschool effects); and the cost function seeks to determine the cost of producing a certain outcome using price-level inputs.

5. See, e.g., Margaret E. Goertz and Allan Odden, eds., *School-Based Financing. The 20th Annual Yearbook of the American Education Finance Association 1999* (Thousand Oaks, CA: Corwin, 1999).

school site councils. People do not want to make uninteresting decisions or to be given responsibility beyond their skills, and site-based leadership does not mean simply abdicating authority to individual schools. Understanding and empathy toward the natural reactions of people to change are the first part of a useful framework for implementation and should be based on a well-designed plan that is regularly reviewed and evaluated.

Establishing site-based leadership requires understanding and participation of both the district and each individual school site. The framework for implementation requires the following three critical tasks:

- *Assessment* of history, data, and research on the individual school site
- *Developing strategies* for implementation based on the assessment
- *Creating timelines, accountability,* and *costs* for the strategies

Assessment

As we saw earlier in Chapter 7, site-based plans can be elaborate, and it is intuitive that change can lead to disastrous results if people do not have adequate understanding and training, or if they resent the goals or the process. Avoiding disaster demands careful assessment strategies on two levels. Both levels should be carried out before the transfer of decision-making responsibility begins. The first level consists of organizing the overall site plan for each individual school, understanding the historical parameters of current ways of operating, assessing the likelihood of success if site-based leadership is enacted, and making a deliberate choice at each school about whether to adopt site-based leadership. The next level consists of determining how the overall site-based plan will look at both district and individual school levels. Although all elements are essential, the most critical task comes when the site-based team that implements the plan assesses the readiness of the individual school and the district. It goes without saying that the assessment stage is no time for political posturing or dissembling, because the honesty of all stakeholders and the perceptiveness of the planning team at this juncture will either enable—or doom—how the implementation will work. In sum, assessment is the careful evaluation of the chances for success based on knowledge and readiness for fundamental and uncharted change.

Implementation

Implementation follows directly after assessing readiness for change. We have implied that implementation must be site-based if it is to succeed, which is to say that an implementation team at each individual school site must be formed that appropriately represents all stakeholders of the particular school. Generally, stakeholders should be drawn from administrators, teachers, students, and parents, as well as the community's many constituent groups such as business, industry, professionals, and older citizens. The implementation team should intentionally represent many viewpoints and must be extensively helped to focus on how site-based leadership should work at the individual school level. The eventual make-up and work of individual school site councils should be an outgrowth of planning by the implementation team. In sum, implementation is the act of building on assessment of readiness in preparation for the accountability structures that support site-based leadership.

Accountability

The implementation team and the resulting site council need to devote considerable training and energy to developing an overall plan with appropriate controls specific to each school. Parameters of each site-based plan must be determined, timelines must be set, and accountability strategies must be agreed on. The goal of these activities is not only to structure how site-based leadership and constituent-based decision-making will occur, but also to reach critical agreements on the mission, goals, and appropriate responsibility of the many participants. For example, frustrations arise when people are involved in decisions that are beyond their skills, exceed their authority, or infringe on other prerogatives or legal restrictions. Implementation plans need good counsel during development and should reflect the detailed parameters of the overall project, show specific timelines, and set procedures and accountability. In essence, the planning model for implementation at the individual school must create an accountable vision addressing the following:

- Beliefs
- Mission
- Climate
- Objectives
- Policy
- Preliminary planning document
- Collective bargaining and legal issues

Beliefs articulated by the school must be based on sound educational theory and practice. These statements should be simple and declarative, communicating a positive message of wide involvement. Belief statements should be generated by each stakeholder group and merged to consensus in a cooperative process that builds teaming. For example, the following teacher beliefs are taken from districts using site-based leadership to build positive school-based culture: *Teachers in this building* believe

- students learn basic skills as a result of their teaching.
- that expecting students to be successful in the practice of basic skills will make it happen.
- success is more important than failure.
- sharing ideas increases student performance.

- ♦ in working together to coordinate programs within teams and across grades.
- ♦ in a positive attitude toward change.
- ♦ the student is at the center of the educational process.

A similar process should be used for developing mission statements. Mission statements at the school site level should be simple and clear. Although mission statements do not guarantee success, it is important that the focus is on the direct educational experiences of every student because mission statements declare actionable intent. Examples of mission statements include the following:

- ♦ *This school will graduate* persons who will become productive, responsible citizens.
- ♦ *This school will teach* students to think as individuals and to think critically.
- ♦ *This school will empower* those individuals who accept the responsibility for student learning.

Mission statements should also be supported by goals and objectives. Goals and objectives provide greater specificity and yield measurable outcomes. Several states have enacted performance-based achievement plans that can serve as good models for implementation teams. Goals and objectives might be stated in terms of student knowledge, dispositions, and performance. For example, the following statements could be adopted by a school:

- ♦ Students will *know* where and how to access materials for conducting science investigations (*knowledge*).
- ♦ Students will show *enthusiasm* for science (*disposition*).
- ♦ Students will be able to locate resources and *apply* them to a problem (*outcome*).

Successfully implementing site-based leadership depends in part on consensus for a positive school climate. Climate is a condition that is deliberately built and requires stakeholder participation. Climate is complex and includes the following concepts:

- ♦ There is a stimulating *supportive environment.*
- ♦ There are *positive expectations* for staff.
- ♦ There is *constant feedback*—positive and negative—that is always constructive.
- ♦ There are *rewards and punishments* articulated for all levels of the educational program.
- ♦ There is a *feeling of family.*
- ♦ *Open communication* is the rule and not the exception.

- *Achievement and growth* of students and staff is the reason for the school to exist.
- There is closeness among *parents, community, and principal.*

The outcome of agreement on beliefs, mission, goals and objectives, and climate should lead to formulation of policy and the implementation phase. These concepts go a very long way toward establishing accountability for outcomes. Statements of belief and so on should be placed in policy, and implementation is the process of carrying out these aims. A guiding document should result from preparing for implementation. The document should set out everything discussed thus far, with additional admonition that it should not infringe on either collective bargaining or legal issues. The latter should be carefully checked against state statutes and have the benefit of legal counsel.

Implementation of site-based leadership is reflective of principals, site councils, staff, and parents who are charged with important, relevant, and substantive issues for which they will be held accountable. These issues comprise the real work of each site council once implementation is complete. The value is self-evident, as councils can reasonably be expected to work constructively with the following:

- Instruction
- Student achievement and growth
- Student socialization
- Critical thinking skills
- Innovation
- Attendance
- Budgets
- Completion or graduation

What Is the Role of the Principal?

Success in implementing and operating site-based leadership is in large part a function of how well assigned roles are carried out. A clear understanding of powers and limitations is essential to cooperative and productive relationships. Much research points to the critical role of principals in all school reforms simply because a lead person must provide the rallying point and a knowledge base of procedure. School principals are positioned for leadership by virtue of legal and organizational authority. As a result, site-based organizational designs cannot work unless principals understand and value shared decision-making.

Site-based leadership requires principals to take the lead by delegating decisions to appropriate levels. This is harder than it sounds, because its fundamental requirement is to give up both efficiency and control of functions previously centralized in the principal's office or at some higher level. Schools successfully engaging in site-based leadership have strong principals who are not threatened by loss of control, although these persons are in reality even stronger than in traditional schools because they must work harder and more effectively to achieve consensus where none was previously required. A key to success is that delegation of authority must be realistic. Site council members should not be asked to make inappropriate decisions or to engage in work beyond their expertise. The balance is a fine line, because much resentment arises when the work of site teams is viewed as trivial or as abdicating administrative responsibility. Principals also walk a fine line because they must support the decisions made by others if at all possible. The principal fundamentally takes the role of leader, counselor, enabler, and encourager to the site council. Within this framework, delegation is not abdication of power, and in fact the principal must become an advocate for the persons making decisions to ensure their effectiveness.

The reverse side of delegation is accountability, because site-based leadership actually raises the level of performance for each person. As we saw throughout various parts of this book, demands for accountability are increasing, and the first reason for shared decision-making is to increase school effectiveness. In fact, discussion earlier in this chapter raised the issue of measurable outcomes, and it is at the site level where this accountability is envisioned and acted on most effectively. The role of the principal is to lead and model accountability, both in personal actions and by encouraging others to create the structures that will enhance examination of all school outcomes.

In essence, site-based leadership depends first and last on strong leadership from principals. As titular and functional head of the school, it is the principal who initiates and coordinates school growth. The principal is the central link between the district, the school, and the community and is further the position-holder with the legal and (hopefully) moral authority to effectuate change. This does not lessen the contribution of other site council members, but it does point out the fact that all organizations require a key leader who can mobilize others.

What Is the Role of Central Office?

A common misperception is that decentralization reduces the role of central administration. Although relationships are changed in important ways, the central office is even more important because all site powers derive from central office decisions that enable and support site leadership. The issue of central support is critical because this level relinquishes many controls to the various school sites, including power to make budget decisions. Power is always hard to give up, and in this case even harder because central accountability to higher units of government and the community does not go away under site-based leadership.

Although the role of principals is central to site-based plans, principals are ineffective without the support of the central office and the board of education. The central office must work to educate principals and other stakeholders about decentralization, offering fiscal and other support for training and empowerment. In reality, site-based plans will not enjoy much success without active encouragement from the central office, making the role of central administration a vital one in implementing site leadership. Starting at the board level and working down through all central office ranks, organizational and financial structures must be created and supported to send a message of enthusiasm and genuineness. The central office must take the lead in transferring many decisions to the school level and must take a leadership role in training people about sources of power, authority, revenue, expenditures, curriculum—that is, the many topics explored in this book. Experience shows that when the central office moves from a position of control to a support role, site plans are significantly empowered. Conversely, districts that pay only lip service to site plans without relinquishing the necessary controls engender skepticism and resentment. Changes in central office behavior are hard to effect and, in a majority of school districts, take time to implement. Literally, an entirely new set of roles, relationships, and behaviors must be forged among the central office, principals, teachers, council members, and the community. The literature suggests the following four kinds of knowledge and skills that the central office must develop when attempting to fundamentally restructure the organization. These concepts are very familiar:

- *Interpersonal and team skills* for working together effectively
- *Technical knowledge and skills* for providing services
- *Breadth skills for engaging in multiple tasks*, especially the tasks decentralized to the site council as a result of a flattened organizational structure
- *Business knowledge and skills* for managing the financial aspects of the school site

What Is the Role of the Site Council?

The fundamental philosophical and operational shift that follows from enacting site-based leadership is significant. As we have discussed, issues of legitimate control, availability and uses of school data, and budget issues join together to form a very different way of life as site councils appropriately begin to govern the operation of schools. In short, site councils assume many tasks formerly reserved to administrative ranks—that is, site councils can have a powerful impact on the basic organizational design including site costs, personnel, activities, and so on. These concepts form the remainder of this chapter.

Organization

Although many states enacting site-based leadership have mandated key organizational and membership issues, the broad intent is that site-based councils should be organized around the goals of the individual school with consideration for overall district structure. Concern for readiness of site councils to deal with the issues under their purview is usually evident, so that many states require an information and training phase, which may last as long as one year. The driving force behind organizing should be singular: Expectations must be realistic, and the site council must have clear direction from the district. Stated simply, can the plan realistically be accomplished? At the outset, organizational questions should be raised, among which the most important are the following:

- ◆ *How* is membership on the site council determined?
- ◆ *What* matters should the site council consider?
- ◆ *Who* has formal decision-making authority?

These questions are important by setting the tone for site council relationships. Clearly, it is easiest to deal only with beliefs, vision, and policy, but site-based leadership means to go much farther. Generally, site councils are empowered to address funding, instruction, and assessment of programs at individual sites. The specificity of these roles has the potential for great benefit or misunderstanding.

Membership

Although organizational and membership structures are often mandated, experience indicates that some site council designs work better than others. Membership seems to be a key to success or failure. Groups that are too large, too small, or that do not represent the community of stakeholders have a harder time making decisions and gaining support. The success of councils has varied from school to school based on a host of issues, with data showing increased likelihood for smooth operation when the following certain structures are in place:

- ◆ *The most manageable group size* is approximately 10 to 12.
- ◆ *Composition of the council* should reflect the intent of the strategic objectives and preliminary planning goals.
- ◆ *The council should consist* of the principal, lead teachers, support staff, parents, and interested community members.
- ◆ *Members should have a broad perspective* on public schools.
- ◆ *The council must avoid* individual platforms and agendas.

Organizational design should ensure that the principal is the leader of the school site council. This requires the principal to serve as visionary, facilitator, organizer, motivator, resource for information and procedure, and risk-taker. Again, realistic expectations should follow common sense. Principals must assess their own strengths and weaknesses and help the group understand its own characteristics. A weakness in many site plans is failure to conduct good self-assessments, and a failure of districts is not providing leadership development opportunities to principals. Assessment should ask at least the following questions:

- Does the principal have the energy to work with the council?
- Is the principal willing to delegate responsibility to others?
- Does the principal manage time well?
- Is the principal receptive to new ideas?
- Is the principal confident in the role as leader?
- Does the principal work well with groups?
- Does the principal have confidence in the ability of teachers?

Along with readiness of the principal, membership on the site council means the professional staff also must be ready to engage in site-based leadership. Teachers must have skills in two special areas to make meaningful contributions. Skills are needed in both the instructional domain and the managerial domain. Teachers are usually expert in the former and quite unskilled in the latter. If staff are to contribute to site-based leadership in the true spirit of the plan, the teaching staff must be able to take on new and innovative roles. These are the areas of appropriate responsibility and the source of most frustrations. Questions to be addressed include the following:

- Do teachers see the value of site-based leadership?
- Are teacher perceptions of site-based leadership accurate?
- Are teachers ready to accept new tasks without more pay?
- Are teachers ready to share control of their classrooms?
- Are teachers ready to accept decisions of the site council?
- Are teachers ready to take direction from peers?
- Do teachers believe they should be involved in management?

Membership on the council must also include parents and community members. Although wide representation is important, all members must be able and willing to make contributions. Lay members should be actively interested in the school, and there should be a balance among parents and community stakeholders. Although all viewpoints are valued, there must be concern for ability to work in groups and for positive attitudes. Each of the questions we asked about principal and teacher readiness can be applied to laypersons as well. For example,

- Do laypersons see the value of site-based leadership?
- Are lay perceptions of site-based leadership accurate?
- Are laypersons ready to commit extensive time and energy?
- Do laypersons accept that some areas are legally off-limits?
- Do laypersons have the necessary interest in management?

Once members have been chosen on the basis of knowledge and disposition, the site council will need to meet regularly. The principal should chair the group, at least for the first year. Initial meetings should focus on reaching consensus among members on organization and process. It is important for the principal to allow everyone a voice in the decision-making process. The principal should lead the discussion concerning beliefs, vision, mission, and policies of the council. The initial process should focus on working collaboratively before trying to resolve any actual problems of the school.

Legitimate Control

Identifying boundaries of site council responsibility is crucial to proper functioning, as inappropriate duties lead to frustration and overreaching. Legal problems may arise as well if the council strays into constitutional, statutory, or other protected areas such as permissively negotiated contract items. Most likely, the school site council will concern itself with instruction and budget, at least in the early stages, and everyone must be well informed and willing to share genuine power.

Working with instruction requires deep knowledge of all participants. Members must broadly understand the instructional program at both school and district levels. The team must understand state curriculum requirements as well. The council needs access to data, although care must be taken not to violate privacy laws, including training on the implications of each decision the council makes. For example, improper access to data may lead to violations of the Family Educational Rights and Privacy Act, and the implications of a decision to track students into college and vocational programs are significant. Nonetheless, site councils need data to make guided decisions. Councils work best when they have the following types of data by grade levels and programs:

+ Enrollment data
+ Attendance data
+ Student achievement data
+ Promotion and retention data
+ Discipline counts, issues, and dispositions
+ Dropout data
+ Elementary, middle, and high school program offerings
+ Special education, vocational, and early childhood data
+ Library and resource data
+ Student demographic data such as single parent, free and reduced price meals, English for Speakers of Other Languages (ESOL), and so on
+ Other reports such as use of technology in schools, accreditation, curriculum planning, and so on

These data are designed to study issues of district and school site structure, client satisfaction, internal and external comparisons to permit benchmarking, and work environments. The data are bidirectional, in that they affect decisions about mission, goals, objectives, and programs, and at the same time they provide feedback to help make strategic adjustments. For example, data might be used to determine that the school needs to create a new objective of increasing attendance to the 95% level, or that growth in instructional costs will be no more than 2% each year. Data on achievement (when combined with budget data discussed next) might also be used in deciding to hire another primary grade teacher to reduce class size at a particular school. Conversely, the council might decide to use the money freed up from a retiring staff member to hire additional aides instead of filling the teaching vacancy. Uses of data are limited mostly by creativity and reality, whereas lack of data severely restricts the power of informed decisions.

Legitimate control in site-based leadership is an area needing very clear definition in a district and schools before site councils are empowered. Too much control is as bad as not enough. Control is bounded by the reality of all the chapters in this textbook, in that *all genuine power rests in the ability to control and direct staff and money*. Token councils spark deep resentment, and overreaching councils create equally difficult problems. Leadership at the district and school levels to appropriately empower site councils is an issue of enormous merit.

What Are the Budget Issues?

The power of site-based leadership is ultimately apparent when it is realized that budget, staffing, and curriculum are the cornerstones of educational productivity. Everything that matters in schools is wrapped up in these issues, and fully 80% to 85% of a district's budget is devoted to personnel and direct instruction—100% when support services are viewed as related to instruction! If site-based leadership is to be effective, budget issues must be laid out clearly, and the site council must be given appropriate control.

The relationship of the budget to site-based leadership is one of empowering site councils to develop a school budget for the goal of ensuring and increasing student achievement. The site council has the responsibility to create and manage the budget in such a way that promotes understanding and support by all stakeholders. The council has a further responsibility to prepare budgets that provide flexibility flowing from changes in curriculum and enrollment and that treats people and programs fairly. And clearly, it is the council's duty to provide accountability for all resources and outcomes. Competent budget knowledge among council members is therefore a critical factor. As a general rule, the budget issues relevant to site-based leadership are *overall context, general site costs, staff issues, instruction, facilities*, and *activities*, all in the context of accountability.

Basic Knowledge

The primary budget responsibility of the site council is for costs associated with the individual school site. However, a general understanding of overall budget structure is needed to avoid an information hole where people see only a small part of the picture. The site council should broadly examine overall budget issues before actively working with individual site budgets.

This textbook lays out the basic knowledge needed by school board members, administrators, teachers, and laypersons who are likely to serve on site councils. Although the knowledge in this book affects participants at different levels and is at times deeper than some people may want to go, the entire site council needs to understand money sources, the basis on which schools receive funding, and the site budget and categories of costs—that is, the issues making up this textbook! Without basic knowledge, the site council is unable to make good decisions about instruction, staffing, supplies, capital outlay, maintenance, and a host of other issues. Specifically, the council must understand the fiscal picture of district and site costs in terms of the following:

- Sources of revenue to the district and methods of taxation
- State revenue sources
- Local revenue sources
- State aid formula
- State accounting and reporting requirements

Early meetings of the council should focus on gaining basic budget knowledge. Discussions should address the previous bulleted areas and should also discuss funding of special education, transportation, and other categorical programs, all in context of the relationship between programs and revenue within the constraints of fiscal realities. The goal is to have all site council members understand the flow of money to the district and individual schools, simultaneously learning about mission, goals, and so on.

Site Knowledge

Because the council will spend its most productive time on site budget issues, it is important for members to see that some costs are beyond the control of individual schools, that is, indirect costs, whereas other costs are within control, that is, direct costs. A useful way of viewing indirect and direct costs is to see all costs that are not site-specific as indirect costs. For example, bonding for new facilities is beyond the scope of a site council, although it should help take the lead in identifying infrastructure needs. An additional concept takes in fixed costs. Fixed costs are those that do not change with fluctuations in a given level of activity. Fixed costs may be direct or indirect, but they tend to be costs that are largely overhead regardless of the educational activity that may go on within an individual school. Variable costs are the opposite of fixed costs; that is, they are expenses that vary with level of service. Finally, marginal costs are those that change if the school adds a level of service. Site councils have little control over fixed and some indirect costs, but they have greater control over direct, variable, and marginal costs, depending on how the district has organized its site-based leadership plan. The concept is important to signaling the boundaries of site councils. Examples of how various costs might be viewed include the following:

Budget Items	Cost
Teacher salaries	Direct, variable
School administration costs	Direct, variable
Capital outlay	Indirect, fixed
Social services	Direct, variable
Maintenance—custodial	Indirect, fixed
Central office salaries	Indirect, fixed
Transportation	Indirect, variable
Food services	Indirect, variable
Purchasing operation	Direct, variable
Maintenance of facility	Indirect, variable
Utility costs	Direct, variable
Learning programs	Marginal, variable
Activities	Direct, variable

The classification scheme outlined here is based on certain judgments that would change substantially if site-based leadership were conceptualized differently in the district. For example, the chart previous makes some value judgments, that is, that cost-benefit analysis showed efficiencies related to district-wide maintenance and transportation programs, and that teacher and administrative salary costs should be placed under the control of the individual site. Completely opposing values could create an entirely different design. For example, the most obvious opposite view is placing teacher and administrative costs on a district-wide basis with district right-of-assignment retained, so that the only impact of the council on personnel costs relates to decisions about hiring or replacement. Likewise, the council could be given a transportation budget (see the example of a site-based budget in Chapter 7) and retain other transportation functions at the district level. In other words, structural decisions drive everything, the cost of areas can be both direct and indirect, and structure can also affect whether a cost is fixed or variable.

The issue of control versus no control is well illustrated by utility costs because there is a basic need for heating, cooling, and lighting school buildings. One view is to place these costs at the district level as uncontrolled fixed costs. A different way is to rebate back to the school any unspent utility funds as a bonus for energy efficiency and conservation. Because site councils are concerned with all expenditures in a school, energy conservation then becomes of direct interest to the council and actually injects a measure of control where none was believed to be present. The council, with assistance from the staff, might develop an energy monitoring system. The same logic can be applied to school facilities. The site council should monitor the condition of the facility with primary concern for its instructional adequacy. In this manner, the site council can make the district aware of ongoing infrastructure needs, maintenance, and repair, and maximize efficiencies by feeding details of such plans into an overall school district capital improvement plan.

Taken together, the many topics in this textbook are all valid issues for study and development by councils under site-based leadership. Basic and site knowledge takes in a broad scope of work, and the effectiveness of site-based leadership should be judged by how well the council holds itself accountable for both knowledge and consequences. Councils should be trained to give thoughtful answers to the following questions:

- What are our schools becoming?
- What should our schools be doing?
- What are our schools capable of doing?
- What is the effect of money on schools?
- What happens when our schools get more or less money?
- How does school money get tracked?
- What is a fair aid formula, and how does our state compare?
- How should we organize for budgeting in our district?
- How is each school in our district funded?
- How do we recruit and select staff?
- How does due process affect our council?
- What are instructional budgets?
- What is the role of activities?
- What is the role of capital outlay, maintenance, and operations?
- What is accountability?
- How are districts in our state funded?
- Do we understand liability, and have we prepared a risk management plan?
- What is the budget process, generally, and in our district?
- How do we determine staffing needs?
- What are our compensation policies?
- What is instructional planning?
- How do we budget for instruction?
- What are activity funds?
- How do transportation and food service work in our district?

Revisiting a Sample District

The extended discussion earlier in Chapter 7 of school-based reform and site leadership does not bear repeating here, but from the previous list, it is clear that we believe site councils should have significant input into budget issues. It is reasonable for each school to decide how to allocate teaching and nonteaching staff to meet the school's mission, goals, and objectives. For example, one school might eliminate a vice principal in favor of an additional teacher to reduce class size, whereas another school might choose larger classes in exchange for providing aides in each classroom. A third school might trade a teaching position for a counselor to help troubled students. Similarly, the site council might choose to implement new curricula at the expense of activities, or a council might opt for new cocurricular programs that are carefully justified on the basis of contribution to learner outcomes. The possibilities are limited only by common sense and statutory authority, but it is clear that budget, personnel, and curriculum are the key assets of schools and that effective site-based leadership cannot avoid dealing with these issues in a coordinated fashion.

The sample school district in Chapter 7 was based on exactly this concept. As we set up the scenario, we raised a series of questions that now provide both review and a solid rationale for site-based leadership. At the outset, we asked the following questions that should be raised regardless of district organization. Site councils will find these particularly relevant:

- *Who has responsibility* for establishing the overall level of expenditure in a district and school building?
- *Who has responsibility* for establishing expenditures for each major program or organizational unit?
- *Who has responsibility* for selection of specific resources within the allotted dollar amounts for each program?
- *Who has responsibility* for curriculum selection?
- *Who has responsibility* for initiation of new instructional programs or elimination of current programs?
- *Who establishes* capital outlay budgets and decides how facilities and equipment are allocated?
- *Who has responsibility* for establishing salaries and benefits?
- *Who hires* personnel?
- *Who decides* which items and amounts will be cut if needed?

These are the major structural and operative issues facing site councils, going straight to the heart of how budget, staffing, and curriculum are designed. The sample district in Figure 7.6 (pp. 224–227) went directly to these issues, including a plan for assigning capital outlay and transportation discretionary funds to each site. Our sample district chose to *track* instructional budgets using detailed accounting codes to permit accumulation of data by program, *decentralize* many budget tasks, retain some central coordination at the board and director levels, *allocate* uniform amounts per pupil for instructional program purposes, *retain* transportation services centrally, *allocate* discretionary transportation budgets to schools, *decentralize* some aspects of capital outlay and equipment purchasing, and *link* expenditures to expected outcomes. Our discussion in Chapter 7 described a district that has moved to locate program and budget authority at the school level in the belief that efficiency is gained by district coordination and control of indirect costs like maintenance and construction—school sites, however, were left free to decide how programs operate, including responsibility in this particular example for about $892,000. Accountability is a central feature of our model budget, as the fund accounting structure permits program and expenditure analysis, with all expenditures justified by expected outcomes.

Although more complex than traditional ways of funding schools, site-based designs have the strong potential to do a better job of integrating district and school goals into a coherent plan tailored to meet the unique needs of each site. Our questions in Chapter 7 capture the principles and spirit of site-based leadership, in that a good site plan should have ready answers to the following queries:

◆ What is the district's overall mission?

◆ What are the district's goal statements?

◆ What is my school's overall mission?

◆ What are my school's goal statements?

◆ What were the results of the district's environmental scan?

◆ What were the results of my school's environmental scan?

◆ Does my school's educational plan reflect these needs?

◆ How can I spend my budget to address these needs?

FINAL COMMENTS

Several comments apply as we end this chapter on site-based leadership. Of paramount concern is that the chapter does not take a blind advocacy position. Site-based plans are not appropriate in all situations, although some elements are intrinsically meritorious and should be present in every school. Neither is site-based leadership a fancy scheme by which a local school board sheds its legal and financial responsibility. Nor is it a plan allowing the superintendent to avoid top responsibility. Rather, site-based leadership is a concept that can improve the efficiency of direct services to students. As a result, we believe site-based leadership has certain elements that are required of all schools in the modern context. Simply put, why should any legitimate stakeholder be denied a role in the operation of schools? And further, why should any district seek to retain power to itself when it knows that hoarding power only creates resentment among stakeholders? It is our view that these questions have only one answer, and that schools no longer have a choice except to embrace stakeholder participation. The only remaining legitimate issue is to what extent site-based leadership should be enacted.

Although questions of extent of implementation must be answered locally, all site-based leadership plans must reflect the mission, objectives, and policies of the school. Each of these has a greatly enhanced opportunity for success if they are jointly created. The site council must reach consensus on the critical issues, and the council, the principal, and the teaching staff must understand, agree, and implement the design. The ever-conscious goal must be to improve student learning within a plan to control costs. The overriding feature should be collaborative accountability regarding how to measure pupil progress, how instruction should take place, and how school resources should be allocated to programs. Site-based leadership will continue to grow in popularity, but it will succeed only by careful planning and hard work because it holds the seeds of misunderstanding, inappropriate partisanship, and inequality. On the other hand, it finally restores a long awaited parental and community involvement in schools.

SUGGESTED FOLLOW-UP PROJECTS

♦ Spend some individual time reflecting on how leadership is carried out in your district. Review the many questions posed in Chapters 7 and 12 on who holds power, answering them in light of your own experience. If your analysis identifies some significant elements of site-based leadership, spend some extra time analyzing how this is accomplished, with consideration for your own views on strengths and weaknesses in your particular school.

♦ If your state or district uses school site councils, research the reasons why councils exist. Examine statutes if relevant, and examine local board policy. Talk to your principal about the role of the site council, including its scope and authority and duties.

♦ Ask several people about their perceptions of the site council, including teachers, administrators, laypersons, and staff.

♦ Volunteer to serve on a site council. Alternatively, ask permission to attend and observe site council meetings.

13

FUTURE TRENDS IN SCHOOL FUNDING

THE BIG PICTURE

Our journey in this textbook has provided a broad contextual overview of money and schools. Funding for education is a complex topic defying simplification, even though we have tried to make it as conversational as possible. The task has been more difficult in that this book is meant to address many audiences, each with widely different expectations for depth, style, and exhaustiveness of knowledge. We introduced concepts at considerable depth, although we know that we have merely provided a foundation for the expertise that comes only from extended study and professional experience. But it is precisely this point that makes this book so relevant for our audiences: By seeing how the big picture of school money works, stakeholders are better grounded in the many necessary perspectives needed to enter the world of decision-making affecting schoolchildren.

As we close this book, there is much to be gained from reflecting on the lessons we learned and by speculating about the future. Reflection anchors our understanding of how the many pieces of school funding fit together, and an eye to the future prepares us to deal with the inevitable change that continues to make up the educational landscape. As roles shift and lines of authority, power, and influence become increasingly blurred, the future holds both promise and consequence for the choices that are presently being made. Progress and change are, after all, the tools that leaders use to create and mold the context that makes up the big picture of schooling.

WHAT ARE THE ISSUES?

A fundamental message woven throughout this textbook is that schools are facing a crisis of unequaled proportion that ranges across a complex mosaic of society at the start of a new millennium. Schools are changing dramatically, with profound implications for the future. The problem seems simple in that equal educational opportunity must be provided to every child, but the problem is vexatious because resolving it demands agreement on diverse goals and enormous amounts of money torn between starkly divergent expectations. At the very least, resolution will require increased stakeholder participation in the daily operation of schools, along with serious debate about the politics of schools and the role of equity, adequacy, efficiency, and choice. All these issues are affected by larger concerns for the economy and the nagging question of how heavily opportunity depends on money. Although we cannot resolve these issues in this book, the future is framed by these struggles. Our overriding thesis is, of course, that this is a battle to be aggressively engaged by administrators, school boards, teachers, policy makers, and laypersons if the nation is to remain strong.

Lessons from this Book

The social and economic context of education discussed in Chapter 1 laid bare a sobering lesson. We examined the condition of schools in social and economic language, finding that schools are a source of both optimism and cynicism. National reports have long predicted a dismal future as student achievement has declined. Yet Americans have historically clung to the view that education is the key to social and economic mobility, although there are data indicating that the unequal distribution of educational rewards is producing anger in an increasingly disenfranchised population at both ends of the socioeconomic spectrum. The lesson in this chapter was fourfold. First, educational opportunity has represented very different realities to people. Second, everyone wants a better life. Third, there is constant strife over the relationship between schools and socioeconomic class that threatens efforts toward national unity. Fourth, opportunity costs money, and the budget in schools is the key to better opportunities for children. We used this line of thinking to propose that schools have many stakeholders who must become involved in schools in ways that help ensure that their interests are channeled to productive ends. In fact, it was our thesis that the remaining chapters in the book would provide knowledge needed by stakeholders to enable them to become professional leaders and lay leaders in schools.

Chapter 2 built on this view of schools by moving deeper into the world of policy-making. Education is an enormous enterprise, rooted in the history and richness of American democracy in ways that have shaped our current realities. The lessons in this chapter were several. Of greatest importance was that tradition and policy never develop in a vacuum, that is, everything that exists has roots that have a rational explanation leading to present circumstances. Of equal value were the views of how and why federal, state, and local units of government have settled on their current partnership in controlling and funding education. The struggles over values in education were again apparent in this chapter, as disagreements over the worth of education and who should pay for schools have continued to play out in educational policy making.

Our basic knowledge quest led to Chapter 3 where we discussed basic funding sources for schools. We noted that taxes have been divisive throughout American history, but that massive tax systems have nonetheless developed, wherefrom schools derive vast revenues. The dilemma of funding education in the 50 states was also explored, and it was seen that, absent a significant federal role, equal educational opportunity could not be provided without the strong state-local partnership that exists in many states. We noted that states' school funding systems had their origins in a political history that has struggled to provide fair distribution of finite resources. The lessons learned from this chapter were twofold. First, although no perfect tax system can ever be built—because taxes are the product of political environments wherein insatiable needs compete for finite revenues in a context of constituent self-interest—progress has emerged from seeking a more balanced tax system. Second, real gains in equal opportunity have been made through state aid formulas, despite the sometimes ugly politics of school funding. For stakeholders, the message was clear: Work harder to improve the states' share of school funding.

Chapter 4 opened Part II of this textbook by moving from a broad policy perspective into a more detailed analysis of budgeting in schools by examining fiscal accountability. We laid out a noble view of the public trust, advocating the fiduciary role of all stakeholders and identifying how school money is structured. Admittedly a difficult topic to present in brief form, the message was that everyone needs at least a basic knowledge of the types of money received by schools, how money can be spent, and how public funds are protected against error and wrongdoing. Part of the message in this chapter was to instill respect for control of financial assets, because we are unswerving in our belief that money and staff are the key control points in schools.

Our examination of the mechanics of school money continued in Chapter 5 as we looked at the concepts and practices underlying budget planning. The first part of the chapter focused on ways to organize for budgeting, whereas the second half focused on carrying out the process of creating a budget. Implicit were three key arguments. First, we argued that without funds there are no schools. Second, we noted that the purpose of budgeting is to implement equal educational opportunity by converting dollars into programmatic priorities. Finally, we argued that money talks, making a plea to view the budget as the principal planning system by which political and legal approval is secured for providing education to children—a lesson lost when people see budgets as an accounting tool rather than as a tool for making educational decisions.

We next turned to examining the major cost determinants of budgets. The first step came in Chapter 6, as we looked at the relationship of school money to the personnel function. With some schools in financial crisis and facing prohibitive costs in a future where more teachers will be needed to cope with the problems of underprivileged children, it is especially critical for stakeholders to be knowledgeable about staffing issues because at least 80% of an average district's budget goes to personnel costs.

Chapter 7 moved to the heart of budgeting by exploring instructional costs. Much time was devoted to looking at district and school-based budgeting, including discussion of the role of site-based leadership in the future. Two key lessons emerged. First, budgeting for instruction is the most important activity in schools because it enables teaching to occur. Second, instructional budgets should reflect the needs and expertise of stakeholders. The focus of the chapter was on choosing among organizational designs to take advantage of stakeholder participation for the purpose of building support for schools and to scrutinize the relationship between spending and student learning.

Chapter 8 turned to the high price of student activities, an area far too often ignored. We set out the view that activities are integral to student learning and noted that many opportunities and pitfalls exist in funding this important dimension of the school's curriculum. The chapter focused on identifying the many activity fund accounts in a typical district and on handling money at the individual school level.

Chapter 9 moved to the topic of budgeting for school infrastructure. The focus was fourfold. First, we provided an overview of infrastructure needs and funding methods in modern schools. Second, demographic, capital program, and facility planning skills were analyzed. Third, we argued that maintenance and operation of facilities on a daily basis have far-reaching effects on community and student attitudes. And last, we couched the discussion as a continuation of our view that stakeholders must become more knowledgeable and involved in daily district and school operations. The goal, of course, was to illustrate that all parts of a school funding system must work together to provide an effective learning environment.

The vein of new knowledge and stakeholder participation was continued in Chapter 10, as we examined transportation and food services. We took the position that whereas the instructional mission of schools rightly receives great attention, it is equally true that instruction is sorely hindered when children are hungry or deprived of the means by which to travel to school. Relatedly, great liability exists for these aspects of school operations. And, obviously, neither transportation nor food service could operate without wise fiscal management. The lesson of this chapter was clear: Schools are complex fiscal organizations made up of interrelated parts that aid or obstruct the instructional mission, and stakeholders' knowledge needs to be very broad.

Our journey next moved in Chapter 11 to liability and managing risk in school settings. This chapter was based on the idea that wise stakeholders need to understand the sources of authority enjoyed by schools, the nature and limits of immunity, the problems encountered when laws and rights are violated, and the loss of discretionary revenue resulting from liability-related issues. The purpose of the chapter was to inform stakeholders of broad liability principles and to encourage careful planning for risk management. The overriding lesson, of course, was caution in all matters because the law and schools are constant companions.

Finally, Chapter 12 revisited the topic of site-based leadership, taking highlights from each previous chapter to create a unified direction. A theme of this textbook has been that old ideas about school budgets must be abandoned, and stakeholders must be invited to share in the power of money and equipped with the leadership skills to effectuate change through fiscal resource allocation. We believe the budget is the vital organ that supplies the essential nutrient (money) to an integrated and interdependent organism called schools. As such, this book is a call for wide participation and a rejection of the view that budgets are off-limits or of no interest to anyone except school administrators. To meet that goal, we developed a framework for implementing site-based leadership, examined the role of stakeholders, and laid out the areas in which administrators, school boards, teachers, and laypersons have a duty to become involved. In many ways, this chapter held the most important lesson of the book: If schools are expected to provide equal opportunity, then the budget also must be a democratic tool for equality and excellence. The modern context rejects old ways of doing business, and schools fail when public confidence erodes and budgets are indecipherable. As a result, general and specific budget knowledge appropriate to each stakeholder's level of participation is needed if the goals of public education are to enjoy widespread support.

Future Issues in School Funding

The unsettled and evolving nature of society and schools promises a full slate of issues in the foreseeable future. Major public debate is long-standing on all these issues, but the intensity is increasing as the nation's social fabric continues to experience deep stress. Fundamental change characterizes the new millennium along lines that produced wide rifts in the past. The list is familiar: the *politics* of money; the impact of the *economy* on schools; the enhancement of *equity, adequacy,* and *efficiency* in school funding; the social and economic consequences of efforts to enhance educational *choice;* and, of course, the continued devolution of *school governance.* Although we have talked extensively about these issues in the current context, a final look with an eye to the future provides appropriate closure to this book.

Politics of Money

We have often said in many venues that the way to anyone's heart is through their pocketbook. Although our view leans toward the cynical side, it expresses a worldly reality. It has always been true that people act first out of enlightened self-interest, so that charity is possible only after a hierarchy of personal economic needs is satisfied. It is also the case that economic status is the only acceptable element along which society can still stratify and segregate itself. The combined effect of self-interest and the human tendency to stratify creates a powerful force in the form of politics of money, a tendency captured long ago by Coons when he noted:

> Whatever it is that money may be thought to contribute to the education of children, that commodity is something highly prized by those who enjoy the greatest measure of it. If money is inadequate

to improve education, the residents of poor districts should at least have an equal opportunity to be disappointed by its failure.[1]

The inescapable human desire to put individual prosperity ahead of absolute equality virtually guarantees continued strife over money and schools. Politics in a representative democracy is exactly what its name implies: that is, citizens elect officials in the belief that their interests will be represented first, so that equality becomes a measure of charity after self-interest is satisfied. Money buys security and privilege, and more money buys even more security and privilege. Capitalist democracy is an odd creature, in that it is uncomfortable with the consequences of raw market forces, so that it becomes capitalism tempered by a guilty empathy that resembles charity, justified by a logic of self-help in which democracy and the opportunity for socioeconomic mobility are equated. Truly cynical people would argue that even these emotions are false, actually underlain by the secret knowledge that one of the consequences of successful capitalism is to buy the silence of a permanently dysfunctional underclass. The issue, regardless of party politics and political philosophizing, is simply that money carries weight, both practically from its power to purchase goods and privileges and from people's innate desire to gather money for their own use.

As we have implied throughout this book, the United States has long been a devotee to personal freedom and individual initiative. One of the great national achievements has been the opportunity to access socioeconomic mobility, whereby people from poor backgrounds have been able to rise to wealth, power, and freedom. The strength of often conflicting national goals has experienced ebb and flow, as social conscience has predominated at times, and as the free market has triumphed at other times. Many current social programs were born during the Great Depression in the 1930s, and many others arose from the extreme social introspection of the Great Society in the 1960s. Trickle-down economics in the Reagan years and government downsizing during the 1980s and 1990s represent the opposite side of that same coin. Many factors go into the politics of money, but it is the overriding feature that schools' financial fate relies on the conscience and charity of a public that has seen its priorities vacillate according to the times.

A realistic view of the future requires us to admit that money always dominates any decision process—in the case of schools, a process driven by money supply and public attitudes. Scarcity and lack of charity have been the rule for the last few decades in many states, beginning with tax initiatives such as Proposition 13 in California in 1978 and extending to recent efforts to eliminate many social programs in many states and to balance the federal budget. The roaring economy of the 1990s did little to offset the fierce scrutiny of government, as the overwhelming demand was to return windfalls to taxpayers rather than to invest in better or more government services. Simi-

---

1.   John Coons, William Clune, and Stephen Sugarman, *Private Wealth and Public Education* (Cambridge: Belknap Press of Harvard University, 1970), 36.

larly, the profound reforms of the No Child Left Behind Act at the start of the new millennium only spurred the demand for accountability and heightened the criticism of schools, with economic sanctions and school choice at the root of the new law. In many ways, American society has returned to its roots of independence and self-reliance, as characterized by welfare reform, get-tough criminal reform, suspicion of government, and the curtailment or elimination of many social programs. The mood of the nation has become less charitable and more inclined to embrace personal freedoms that strongly mirror the underlying politics of money. When these views combine with economic conditions and compete with other demands for equity, efficiency, and so forth, a reasonable person is likely to conclude that schools will not experience any sharp revenue increase in the near future, despite contrary claims of some retrogressive reformers.

The Economy

A continuation of the same discussion of the politics of money relates to the condition of the economy. Public economic confidence is closely watched at all levels of government on the assumption that the entire wellbeing of the nation depends on how people perceive their personal economic prospects at any moment. The old saying that "possession is nine-tenths of the law" could be restated to say that "reality is perception" when speaking of the economy because consumer attitudes create a deafening political reality.

A realistic view of the future must acknowledge that education's fate is uncomfortably tied to the economy. In fact, the overlap is quite blurred between the economy and issues like economic security and privilege, willingness to spend for social programs, continued racial and economic segregation, and so on. Despite the historic growth in school revenue over time, the impact of the economy on schools can be dramatic, as in many states taxpayer attitudes and shifting economic fortunes have led to massive tax rollbacks in recent decades. For example, the economic boom of the 1970s was followed with losses for schools during tight budgets of the 1980s, and the mindset of reductionism carried into the highly prosperous 1990s as Congress and the individual states continued to scale back many costs despite a strong economy. Similarly, economic downturn at the start of the new millennium has had consequences for schools, with economic trouble in store for some states far into the future—trouble related either to insurmountable structural deficits or to bad tax-and-spend policies such as oversized tax cuts in the boom years of the 1990s. Clearly the economy has driven attitudes about government spending over the last two decades of the twentieth century—under these conditions, schools are unlikely recipients of any economic windfall in the nearby future.

Equity, Excellence, Adequacy, and Efficiency

A close companion of self-interest and economic reality is the unending struggle for equity, excellence, adequacy, and efficiency at all levels of society. As we said earlier, these fundamentally incompatible goals are embedded in the American soul, with the result that our form of government reflects a great and perpetual vacillation between social conscience and individual freedom. The tension has been great in a nation that is still uncomfortable with its history of social inequality, trying at times to aggressively use government to remedy past injustice and at other times ignoring its unsavory past. Desegregation of schools in the 1950s, the Great Society of the 1960s, the bitter legal battles in the 1970s over school funding, the rise of racial quotas and preferences in the 1980s, and the weakening of affirmative action and revoking of many entitlements in the 1990s illustrate the nation's painful struggles with questions of equity. The same period has been characterized by cries for excellence and efficiency, as school reform has swept the country following reports of dismal achievement, and as retrenchment has sourly scrutinized every cost of government. And the legacy of such conflict was predictable, as schools and other government agencies now find themselves starved for adequate resources, appealing to a public that (at least until the next shift in national psyche) has little desire to spend more on what it sees as failing schools.

The result has been a conflicted society, often with bizarre outcomes. For example, the last 30 years has produced U.S. Supreme Court decisions barring entanglement of church and state in schools, only to see those rulings overturned or weakened in recent years. Likewise, protracted litigation upheld racial preferences in college admissions, with those decisions also assaulted with considerable success in the late 1990s. School funding litigation has followed the same uncertain path of victories and reversals, and the psychology of change and unrest has provided fertile ground for critics decrying the lack of student achievement in schools, with many states enacting stringent standards that include financial sanctions against low-achieving schools. Efficiency in government has been the motto of watchdog groups that have protested every spending increase. A new form of social strife has resulted, where brilliant political strategizing by advocacy groups has created splintering among fundamentally incompatible goals; it is not possible under the goals of such divergent groups to be equitable, excellent, adequate, and efficient at the same time because the terms are mutually exclusive. In other words, equity demands more money for the underprivileged, excellence demands that money be spent only on those groups promising the greatest cost-benefit, adequacy demands that economic starvation be ended, and efficiency always demands that less be spent.

A reasonable view of the future does not see a lessening of these demands. The terms and conditions will change, but the cries will continue and become more strident. Schools are caught in the middle and cannot fully satisfy any of these demands because, for example, satisfying equity offends efficiency. A realistic view sees only continued strife with renewed calls for choice in schooling and further devolution of government as solutions to incompatible social and economic goals.

Educational Choice

An outgrowth of the issues raised here has been demand for parental choice in schooling. Dissatisfied with the performance or safety of public schools—or for personal reasons such as economic and values segregation—many people have taken their children out of public schools in favor of more attractive environments. Still, others have left believing that choice may be the only solution to the public schools' inability to remediate social inequality. Choice in schooling has become a flashpoint in the politics of education, incorporating elements of equity, excellence, adequacy, and efficiency in a context that bears heavily on future funding for public schools—elements clearly visible in federal education policy under the No Child Left Behind Act of 2001.

It is always difficult to separate genuine beliefs from hidden agendas in the debate over school choice. Proponents present the argument that choice introduces market efficiencies into a monopolistic environment that will improve both public and private schools because only the best will survive in a consumer-driven marketplace. Proponents argue that choice makes these improvements open to everyone because it would grant public funds to nonpublic schools that can meet high standards—an argument that courts equity, efficiency, adequacy, and excellence because private schools have a record of higher achievement at lower cost and would have to be open to all applicants to qualify for public funds. Critics argue that this is a decoy by creating admissions competition, that poor people will not understand the opportunities, and that public schools will be financially and psychologically abandoned. These criticisms remain regardless of whether school choice is structured as open enrollment in all public schools in the district, as interdistrict open enrollment, or as tax credits or tax vouchers that can be transported to private schools. Critics fundamentally oppose the element of competition, arguing that it is inimical to American ideals and can only result in further economic and social separatism.

Whether the claims of advocates or detractors are sincere is interesting, but a view of the future must acknowledge that school choice is both a present and future reality. Litigation to quell tuition tax credits and vouchers has not stopped the exodus of students from public schools, and there are many signs of increased growth in school choice plans. School choice, if broadly defined to include preference in housing and open enrollment, is growing exponentially. In 2003, 15 states had open enrollment policies, 6 states had publicly funded voucher laws, 6 states had tax credit or tax deduction laws, 40 states had charter school laws, and 39 states had privately funded scholarship organizations providing tuition assistance to students. Home schooling was legal in all 50 states. These patterns continue today, and in some instances public dollars may follow students into parochial or religiously based private schools. And, of course, school choice has always existed via housing patterns for those with the economic ability to choose their residence based on attractiveness of schools—an ineradicably stubborn reality that has persisted despite failed programs like forced busing.

Again, a reasonable view of the future sees only increased demand for school choice as it is defined here. The terms and conditions of choice will always be fluid, but the demographics of public schools and continued growth of income inequality can only produce more dissatisfaction and more psychological divestiture by significant numbers of people. Schools are again caught in the middle and probably cannot fully satisfy any of the demands. A realistic view sees at best stable demand for school choice and at worst continued growth, as religious and nonsectarian private schools face new competition from entrepreneurial for-profit enterprises that see school choice as a growth industry. Although not yet universal, education has become a consumer's marketplace. Under these conditions, funding for schools faces even more uncertainty.

Devolution of Governance

Finally, all these issues come together under the aegis of devolution in governance. Our discussion of site-based leadership in earlier chapters courted this issue, as people need and want to return government, including schools, to more manageable, visible levels. Devolution has swept the nation from the highest levels down as exemplified by Congressional efforts in the 1990s to return many social programs to the states. States continue to ask difficult questions as well, and in some cases local units of government are having to assume greater responsibility for issues like welfare and other public assistance. Schools are being affected, if for no other reason than state resources are strained by new responsibilities, and schools will continue to face new competition for funding in a previously unchallenged hierarchy. Demands on schools will only increase under these circumstances, increasing even more as states seek to control student achievement outcomes through aggressive standards-based legislation and as interest grows in school-based accountability.

A realistic view of the future does not foresee a marked reversal of economic policy, opposition to growth in government, or attitudes toward social justice and school choice. The economy drives attitudes from a viewpoint of self-interest, mitigated only by a sense of basic human dignity that manifests itself in a moderate degree of social responsibility. Americans prefer personal liberty and economic competition, but they curb their innate capitalist inclinations via limited social programs. The question for the future is whether Americans will choose to expand or restrict the boundaries of social programs based on the economic and social changes predicted by economists and demographers. But in the end money drives everything, including the future of schools.

A FINAL WORD

Although this chapter might leave the impression that the future is bleak, it is only the case that we have been honest in assessing the problems facing public school funding. The United States has always been a land of enormous opportunity, and we sincerely believe it will continue on its great course and successfully meet the challenges of the future. Our hope, however, does not lead us to be blind to the fact that the nation is at a crossroad, with one path leading to renewed greatness and the other path leading to partisan demise arising from lack of national unity. Given history and the massive change drivers now propelling the nation, bleakness will come if the difficult economic and social problems we have outlined are not resolved through equal educational opportunity.

The Interstate School Leaders Licensure Consortium (ISLLC) professional standards identified in the foreword to this textbook take on new meaning when considering money and schools. Education needs great leaders who understand the relationship between money and equal educational opportunity, and the technical knowledge required to provide a bright future for children is exceeded only by the strength of character that will be needed to lead the United States to its greatest potential. *Schools need leaders who promote the success of all students by understanding, responding to, and influencing the larger political, social, economic, legal, and cultural context in which education is so deeply imbedded.* In other words, money drives everything, so that good schools depend entirely on stakeholders who understand and use money to create equal educational opportunity: administrators, boards, teachers, and laypersons joining hands to bring the United States together around our common hope—our children.

SUGGESTED FOLLOW-UP PROJECTS

♦ Identify the major issues in the nation and your state involving education. Many excellent resources exist, for example: national newspapers such as *Education Week,* magazines such as *Time* and *Newsweek,* and national organizations like The National Education Association, American Federation of Teachers, National School Boards Association, National Conference of State Legislatures, Education Commission of the States, and others. Corollaries of these organizations often exist at the state level, for example, state school board associations, state teacher union affiliates, state administrator organizations, and so forth. Most have searchable Web sites. Compare your researched list to the issues in this chapter and prioritize them in your state.

♦ Prepare a paper on the relative importance in your state of issues like the politics of money, the condition of the economy, school choice, and the demand for equity, adequacy, and excellence. The list is not limited—add other topics appropriately. Conclude with your own assessment of the future of education in your state.

INDEX